1 MONTH OF
FREE
READING

at
www.ForgottenBooks.com

By purchasing this book you are eligible for one month membership to ForgottenBooks.com, giving you unlimited access to our entire collection of over 1,000,000 titles via our web site and mobile apps.

To claim your free month visit: www.forgottenbooks.com/free236995

ISBN 978-0-267-49404-0
PIBN 10236995

CSP

LH
3
.08R4

Vol. XII.   OTTAWA, ONT., OCTOBER, 1909.   No. 1

Entered at the Post Office at Ottawa, Ont., as Second-Class Matter.

Commencement 1909.

EFORE a great attendance of students, friends, and alumni, the annual commencement exercises took place on Wednesday, June 16th, in St. Patrick's Hall. On· the platform were Rev. Dr. Murphy, Rector; Canon Sloan, and Rev. Professors Lajeunesse, Duvie, Gavary, Jasmin, Peruisset, Rheaume, Binet, ·T. P. Murphy, Fallon, S. Murphy, Collins, M. Murphy, Maguire, Stanton, Finnegan and Sherry; Hon. Charles Marcil, Judge J. J. Kehoe.· In the audience were noticed Revs. Dr. McNally, J. J. O'Gorman, J. R. O'Gorman; W. J. Teaffe, representing· the A.O.H. After the presentation of medals and conferring of degrees, His Honour Judge Kehoe delivered an eloquent address.

He recalled a former occasion, similar to the one which he now attended, when The Merchant of Venice had been presented by the students and the judge himself had taken the part ·of Portia. He referred to the loss sustained by the university in the death of the late head of the archdiocese of Ottawa. Speaking of the fields of opportunity open to young men and university graduates in particular, he stated that Canada never presented to youth such advantages as she does now. The material and physical possibilities of the country were boundless and if the young men who were now to enter, after years of preparation, into the struggle of life, would only bear in mind the lessons learned during college life he knew they would fill with credit to themselves and their university the places open for them.

Some very interesting reminiscences of early college life were contained in the address delivered by Hon. Charles Marcil, the next speaker, who also received the degree of LL.D. He told of his boyhood days in Hull. In 1875 he had crossed the ice on the Ottawa river, for there was then no Interprovincial bridge, and had become a student of the university under the direction of the late Father Tabaret, one of the pioneers of Catholic education in the city. Then St. Joseph's college, the present important seat of learning, was situted in the midst of broad fields. Parliament Hill, upon which the present governmental buildings are erected, was at one time contemplated as a site for the university, said Mr. Marcil incidentally. Like the former speakers he paid his tribute to the late Archbishop Duhamel. "The University of Ottawa is one of the greatest monuments which will remain to his memory," he said. The great work of the Oblate Fathers who had built the university was also referred to. Mr. Marcil then spoke in French in much the same vein.

Valedictory Addresses.

The valedictory addresses were delivered by Messrs. Edward Byrnes in English and A. Couillard in French. "The lessons learned in college will stand you in good stead in later life," said the first of the speakers. He referred to the feeling, almost of sorrow, with which he and his fellow graduates said good-by to their alma mater, a feeling tempered somewhat by hope for the future. He hoped that the university would continue to progress as it had and that the trophies emblematic of supremacy in athletics and debating would soon be regained. Mr. Couillard spoke to the same effect in French.

RECTOR'S ADDRESS.

We are assembled for the sixty-first annual Commencement. The first Commencement then took place just sixty years ago. An account of the exercises on that occasion has not come down to us. There were no doubt addresses in which the establishment of the colleges of Bytown, later the University of Ottawa, and the prospects of the young institution were dwelt upon.

Have the hopes and wishes expressed on the first Commencement Day been realized? Well, on that day enthusiasm may have run very high. Then. too, there have been obstacles, and hindrances and calamities that could hardly have been foreseen three score years ago.

And yet, and yet, though the results after sixty years perhaps fall short of those wished for, they do seem even better than could have been reasonably hoped for at the beginning. The tangible and material results obtained by an individual or an institution are those most readily recognized. In this order, to speak only of advantages it now offers, the College founded in Bytown in 1848 now has degree-conferring powers from church and state. It has over fifty professors, prefects and instructors. The entire time of that large number is given to the work in the five departments of the College—the Theological, Philosophical, Arts, Collegiate and Business Departments.

Much building, and much destruction by fire have been prominent features since the first Commencement Day six decades ago. As permanent net result we have two fire-proof structures ranking amongst the finest and best-equipped college buildings in Canada. Spacious athletic grounds, more than six acres, within the city limits, are a very important and useful part of the material possessions acquired during the last sixty years.

The buildings and grounds of an educational institution, and even its charter and courses of study are perhaps rather guarantees of future usefulness than proofs of past success. If the University of Ottawa has so far really fulfilled the hopes and wishes probably expressed on this occasion sixty years ago, it has been by results of the physical, intellectual and moral orders produced in the boys and young men who have been taught here. What then of the number of students and their success in life?

The attendance at first was naturally small, but it has gradually grown. The list of students was published for the first time in the University Calendar issued at the end of the academic year 1882. It shows about two hundred registered in all departments. The Calendar which will be out in a few days will show over five hundred names on the registers for the year now closing. The largest attendance so far.

In every province of the Dominion, as well as in many of the neighbouring states are found old students of the University of Ottawa, and many of them have reached foremost places in the callings of their choice. To signalize the success of just a few since last Commencement.

The list which I have here shows some old students, who during the past year (I am not out many weeks, I am sure) have reached the positions coupled with their names. The list is made out in the order of the time of appointment or election, if my memory serves me well:

Hon. F. R. Latchford, Judge of the High Court of Justice for Ontario.

His Honour Judge John J. Kehoe, Judge of the County Court of Ontario.

D'Arcy Scott, K.C., Assistant Chief Railway Commissioner of Canada.

Hon. Charles Murphy, Secretary of State for the Dominion.

Most Rev. Augustine Dontenwill, Archbishop of Vancouver, Superior General of the Oblate Fathers.

Hon. Charles Marcil, Speaker of the Dominion House of Commons.

Hon. F. A. Anglin, Judge of the Supreme Court of the Dominion.

Sir Edward Morris, Premier of Newfoundland.

To the students present this list should be rather inspiring. Almost every name on it is that of a comparatively young man who two or three decade ago, or less, was preparing for the battle of life in the old College building and on the old College grounds in Ottawa.

There are, I think, on this list just two who left College a little more than thirty years ago. Though still young, they 'are the seniors of this group, and Alma Mater in deciding to confer the degree of Doctor of Laws upon two old students this year, has with parental impartiality, as well as with parental pride, thought of them.

The Degree of Doctor of Laws may well be conferred upon His Honour Judge Kehoe in recognition of his long and successful professional career, his scholarly contributions to legal literature, and his attainment of the proud position of Judge in the courts of his country.

The Hon. Charles Marcil very fittingly receives an academic testimonial of the splendid ability and attainments which have deserved and commanded success in journalism and public speaking, and made him the first commoner of the land.

I congratulate all who are receiving medals and diplomas. A look at this year's diplomas, however, produces before all else a feeling of sorrow. On some of them there is a line unfilled. He who was to place his signature there has been summoned hence by the angel of death.

More time than is available this morning, and an eloquence not mine, would be required to express all that the University of Ottawa owes to the late Apostolic Chancellor, the Most Rev. Joseph Thomas Duhamel. As a student, he was probably present at the first Commencement sixty years ago. From that day to the day of his regretted death, less than a fortnight ago, as a model student, a devoted professor, a zealous parish priest, and during the thirty-five years that he was Bishop and Archbishop of Ottawa, he ever showed himself a loyal son and a firm friend of his Alma Mater. Long will she remember him.

Before concluding, I must say a word in acknowledgment of the gifts received during this academic year. Through the benefaction of friends and sister institutions, several hundred volumes have been added to our library. Donations of money have been received from two former students, namely:

The late Rev. Thos. J. Cronan, New Haven, Conn., $1,000.

Ven. Archdeacon Andrieux, London, Ont., $1,750.

To these benefactors, to the donors of medals, and to many others who have done us favours and acts of kindness during the year, the authorities of the institution are sincerely thankful.

Now I wish students the pleasantest of vacations. For them all, for those who are returning next year, and for those whose work here is done, I hope that the future has in store as full a measure of success as has been achieved by the best of those who have gone forth from the University during the past sixty years.

A STORM.

I HAVE witnessed several terrific storms, and I can remember one in particular that is worth describing. It occurred two summers ago while I was on my holidays up the Ottawa.

The days had been extremely hot and there seemed to be very little breeze. One generally sought the shelter of the tall shade trees where the sun's ceaseless rays could not penetrate. About two o'clock, I remember it well, I went down to the beach and got out my canoe. I paddled down the river past the old wharf for some time, wondering how the laborer could toil and sweat in such a heat. All that could be heard was the shrill, rasping noise of the sawmills in the distance.

Now and again I would look back, and gradually I saw the

sky overhead grow dark, but almost imperceptibly. Once or twice low, rumbling thunder could be heard and odd flashes of lightning darted across the lake in the distance. At once I turned and came back, for I was aware that a storm was coming up. Looking off in the west, I could see the storm approaching at a terrific rate. Then came the rain, with a very heavy wind. Whitecaps were on the lake. I managed to reach shelter in good time, and indeed I was fortunate, for the terrific wind would no doubt carry my canoe far out in the current and I could never hope to battle with such a strong wind.

It was a grand and terrible sight to see the huge billows come racing down, the mountains of water leap and plunge, dance and rush on. The black sky, which showed me clearly that a bad storm was near, was vivid with chain lightning. The thunder roared, and truly the flood-gates of Heaven were opened. It was a wonderful sight to see the sky light up now and then with huge sheets of fire that darted and raced on and then disappeared.

When the storm had spent its fury, I went up to the village to see if any damage had been done. The storm had evidently been a bad one. A regular mountain of sand was carried down from the hills, making a channel as it went along, till it reached the river. The culverts along the railway tracks were overflowing. Fences were torn down and crops were destroyed. A giant maple tree was split in two by the lightning. The spire on the village church was also struck, but the building escaped serious harm. For days after one could go down to the lower street and wade knee deep in the sand.

When evening came, the air was fragrant and sweet, a beautiful freshness pervaded the atmosphere. The western sky was all crimson and golden. Slowly the sun sank to rest. All was still. Nothing coud be heard but the silent rippling of the waters or the faint murmuring of the breezes.

J. J. B., '10·

Thomas Chatterton, the Boy Poet of Bristol.

HE intermittent discussions which for well nigh a century waged around the name of Thomas Chatterton as to the authenticity of the poems attributed by him to an imagined monk of the fifteenth century, named Thomas Rowley, left his name to the mercy of a host of critics too prejudiced to fairly judge his character or his poetical works.

It is only about fourteen years ago since the Rev. Walter W. Skeat, LL.D., Fellow of Christ's College, Cambridge, marshalled the proofs of the spuriousness of the Rowley poems and analyzed them with such convincing effect that it would be puerile-folly now to maintain their genuineness. Mr. Skeat, also, at the same time, presented in two small volumes the poetical works and letters of Chatterton to the public in a more methodical form and as much as possible, in chronological order, which has done much to redeem them from their former chaos. He has also largely modernized the spurious antique poems by supplying equivalents for old English words, thereby ridding them of their former want of interest or attractiveness to the general public. Interest is now chiefly attached to the strange life of this ill-fated poet, who died in his teens, his double acting as a pretended transcriber of ancient poetry; and writer of modern verses, his extraordinary genius and complex character.

In a small and obscure dwelling on Pile Street, Bristol, one of the chief commercial and manufacturing ports of England, Thomas Chatterton first saw the light on the 20th of November, 1752. It was but three months before this that his father, Thomas Chatterton, Sr., died. Left in his childhood dependent upon a poor widow, who, by her skilled needlework, earned for him and his little sister, her only other child, the bare necessities of subsistence, life at the very outset must have appeared to him in but sombre colors at its best. Not long after his father's death, his mother removed to a house near St. Mary Redcliff Church, "that mastery of a human hand, the pride of Bristol and the Western land," as described by Chatterton. The office of sexton of this church was held, during the poet's life, by Charles Phillips, his uncle, to whom it had come down through little less than two centuries in the Chatterton family. The young orphan, availing himself of the friendship of his uncle, the sexton, frequently resorted to the Church of St. Mary Redcliff, the church in which he had been baptized, and where his boyish mind, in wondering thought, was often absorbed by the sight of the figures of knights, ecclesiastics, eminent men, the great of bygone times, adorning its altar tombs.

In his fifth year, Chatterton was sent to the Pile Street School, the master of which was Stephen Love. Thomas Chatterton, the poet's father, who had aspired to something higher than being sexton of St. Mary Redcliff, which office he therefore declined, had been teacher of this school at the time of his death. The boy's record in Pile Street School was one of inaptitude to learn, confirming his mother's opinion of him as being extremely stupid, in fact an idiot up to about his sixth year. This opinion was shared by his sister and by Mrs. Edkin, who resided with them. But even before this age he displayed traits of character, afterwards recalled by his sister, which were not only inconsistent with his being such a weakling, but which were the first indications of his strong individuality and ambition. She says, as recorded in the excellent memoir of his life by Mr. Edward Bell, M.A., published in Mr. Keat's volume No. 1, that he would preside as master over his playmates, the latter acting the role of hired servants. She related this to instance his "thirst for pre-eminence." As an evidence of the same strong impulse in the child, she also related that a friend of the family, a manufacturer of earthenware, having promised to present Mrs. Chatterton's children with two little bowls, he was asked "what device he would like to have painted on his." His reply given with "precocious grandiloquence," was, "Paint me an angel with wings and a trumpet to trumpet my name over the world." This anecdote shows that the child was father of the man, notwithstanding the low opinion of his mental powers first held by the Chatterton family.

Between six and seven years he gave the first decisive evidence of his being fit for something better than the "gloomy abstraction" which made him a cause of annoyance and discouragement to his mother. An old music folio in the hands of his mother attracted his attention by its illuminated letters. His interest in it became a sharp contrast to his accustomed listless dreaming, and soon he was able to learn the letters which had so won upon his fancy. A large black letter Bible became his primer by which he soon learned to read. From thenceforth his precociousness was truly marvellous. At eight, when other boys of the same age were laboriously spelling their primers, he was a constant reader with an insatiable appetite for books, and at eleven he was a contributor to Felix Farley's *Bristol Journal*, when the selling of that paper on the streets of Bristol would be an occupation far more seeming for a boy of his age.

From the time Chatterton was able to read, his musings on the sculptured figures with quaint inscriptions which met his eye in St. Mary Redcliff Church acquired greater sway over his ardent imagination. They first awakened in his mind that love for a past age which afterwards became so marked a characteristic of his literary career. Later on in the muniment room of that church he found in some age-rusted chests, neglected parchments covered with the dust of centuries, which inspired his design of reviving the antiquated lore of that munificent age when William Canynge occupied Bristol's civic chair, and Henry VI. and Edward IV. successively reigned as Kings.

At the age of eight, he became a pupil of Colton Hospital, which he attended for about six years. Only the elementary branches of a common school education were taught in this charity school. To a prodigy like Chatterton, eagerly ambitious to take pre-eminence of others, it was a great disappointment to realize, as he did before long, that the education imparted in this school was so meagre, that, according to his own complaints, he could have learned more at home by self-study. He was, from the earliest, self-confident and disdainful of conditions more adapted to less gifted mortals. To the credit of Colton School, it may be stated, however, that cramming was an unknown art there and that it was not an entirely Godless school, like so many of our boasted modern institutions of learning, whose aims never rise higher than the narrow horizon of this world. That Chatterton failed to profit perseveringly to the end by the little religious instruction which he received in this school may only teach many that disregard for religion is a danger against which the English Church Catechism is an insufficient safeguard.

Colton School was also linked with historical associations, some or all of which must have left their lasting influences upon a mind so susceptible of impressions as that of Thomas Chatterton. Its site was once occupied by a monastery whose walls were wont to echo the mellow voices in prayer and psalms of the Carmelite order of Friars, when the outside world was wrapped in the silence of night. The patter of the monks' feet, once heard through its dimlit corridors, fitting counts for the hour-glass of charity and prayer, unselfish industry, heavenly patience, and heroic sacrifice, ceased when the hostile influences of the Reformation had emptied its cells and converted St. Mary Redcliff into an Anglican temple. On the site once occupied by the monastery

was built in later times, a great civic mansion, in which Queen
Elizabeth once held court in 1581. Afterwards, Edward Colton,
one of Bristol's merchant princes, acquired this mansion and converted it in 1708, into an hospital school, "the Bluecoat school of
Bristol." His new environment acted to some extent upon the
mind of Chatterton similarly with the associations which clus-
tered around St. Mary Redcliff in drawing his thoughts to the
glories of an age which he so ardently admired, for its learning,
its chivalry and romance, in contrast to the sordid age in which
he lived, as viewed by him in the commercially devoted world of
Bristol.

To Thomas Phillips, one of the teachers of Colton School, is
attributed some practical development of Chatterton's poetic
genius. Mr. Phillips was, himself, a votary of the muse, and under his direction, Chatterton and two or three others of his pupils
were induced to engage in a friendly rivalry in the art of verse
making, some of which found its way into the columns of Felix
Farley's *Bristol Journal*. That Chatterton, himself, regarded Mr.
Phillips as a true friend and greatly esteemed him can be inferred
from the feeling elegy which he composed after hearing of his
death, and which begins:

> "No more I hail the morning's golden gleam,
>   No more the wonders of the view I sing;
> Friendship requires a melancholy theme.
>   At her command the awful lyre I string."

And towards its close he sings:

> "Now rest, my Muse, but only rest to weep
>   A friend made dear by every sacred tie."

The untoward circumstances surrounding his early childhood,
not the least the lack of needed parental training, were adverse
formative influences which must always be taken into account in
reading the story of his life. Thomas Phillips' friendship was
really beneficial to him. If all the others among whom his lot was
cast, or with whom he had any relations after leaving Colton
Hospital, had been as noble and true as Phillips, it is not hard
to believe that his light would not have gone out as it did, in the
darkness of hopeless misery.

His powers as a satirst were rather indiscriminately used
against his acquaintances in Bristol, having greatly exasperated
several, among them Rev. Mr. Catcott, who really deserved bet-

ter at his hands. There is one notable example, however, of his proper use of sarcasm, as popularly regarded, which must not be omitted. An overzealous church·warden had ordered the removal of a beautiful cross from the churchyard of St. Mary Redcliff, where it had been the greatest attraction for more than three hundred years. Chatterton wrote a satire upon this act of vandalism to Felix Farley's *Journal*. It is regarded as his first contribution to that paper and was written when he was in his eighth year.

Those who have accused Chatterton of the improper use of his talents at so early an age, should not forget that he deserves much praise for the good use he had also made of them before he left his native Bristol. Besides composing several poems of a high order of merit, he had made himself remarkable for his unremitting application in the acquisition of knowledge. All his spare pocket money, while attending Colton School was spent by him in the purchase of books, such as Chaucer, Spencer, Collins and others. There is no record of any poet who, at his age, had written so much. He was an author of many poems of undoubted merit, at an age which the world's other great poets had left well behind before they had written their maiden efforts.

Before he was quite fifteen years, and after he had been nearly seven years in the school of Colton Hospital, Chatterton was apprenticed as a law clerk to John Lambert, a Bristol attorney. In the lawyer's office he continued his literary efforts, using his spare time when not engaged in the routine of clerical work, in the more congenial employment to which he had devoted himself, as a writer of prose and verse. His love of mystery and secrecy did not evidently abate on his entering upon the matter-of-fact duties of a lawyer's clerk.

It was while in Mr. Lambert's office that he palmed off on a credulous public an article written by him for Felix Farley's *Journal*, as an ancient manuscript. It was signed "Dunelmus Bristoliensis," the signature under which he sometimes masqueraded, and was written on the occasion of the opening for traffic of a new bridge over the Avon, the old one, which had been built in the reign of Henry II., having given way to a new structure. The writing purported to be a copied description of the Bristol Mayor's first passing over the old bridge. The identity of the copyist was soon afterwards discovered when he appeared personally in the office of the *Bristol Journal* and submitted another article for publication. It was about then that the rumor became current that Chatterton had transcribed ancient manuscripts found by his father in a coffer in St. Mary Redcliff, and thereby prevented their being lost to the world. This naturally led to the seemingly interminable discussion by scholars and antiquarians as to the authorship of the writings which Chatterton had attributed to a poet-priest, Thomas Rowley.

This highly imaginative young dreamer became singularly wedded in his thoughts with an age that appealed for interpretation very strongly to his genius. He was drawn gently and with insinuatingly increasing power to a past which seemed to him eloquent of the things for which he yearned, and in which his own age was sadly defective. Keats and Byron, after him, felt a like strange overmastering desire to become a living voice for the Hellenic race. It was such inspiration, which oft has rescued genius from oblivion, that moved the wizard of the North to make Scottish scenes and tales of romance so familiar to the world in song and story. The indifference of the people of Bristol to the pursuits of literature, amounting almost to scorn for poetry and romance on the part of Rev. Mr. Catcott, an enthusiast in scientific matters, only made Chatterton the more partial to the pictures of his imagination, drawn from a less materialistic age. Very different from Mr. Catcott, appeared to him William Canynge, erstwhile Mayor of Bristol, the founder, and in later years, the priest of St. Mary Redcliff, conceived by him as the patron of letters, and the dispenser of hospitality to the learned and gifted, such as the imagined monk, Rowley. In one of his best antique poems, "The Story of William Canynge," written under the inspiration of the muse which appeared to him in the form of a beauteous maid "with semblance sweet and an angel's grace," he makes Thomas Rowley say of the childhood of Canynge, Chatterton's own childhood forming the picture:

"Straight was I carried back to times of yore,
Whilst Canynge swathed yet in fleshly bed
And saw all actions which had been before,
And all the scroll of Fate unravelled;
And when the Fate-marked babe appeared to sight
I saw him eager gasping after light.
In all his sheepen gambols and child's play,
In every merry-making fair, or wake,
I kenn'd a perpled light of wisdom's ray;
He ate down learning with the wastel-cake.
As wise as any of the aldermen,
He'd wit enough to make a mayor at ten."

The boy dreamer was carried by his impetuous genius beyond

the bounds of discretion unconsciously. IIe did not realize that it was anywise wrong to attribute to another, an imagined author less alien to the scene to be commemorated, the sentiments which stirred his own being, when his main object was so praiseworthy, as he deemed the immortalizing of the storied past. By his misleading so many he abused his marvellous powers, but he might have atoned for this boyish erring, even in the short span of his life, if guided by wiser counsel, he had abandoned his deception in time instead of persisting in it until the fear of the discredit which its admission would bring upon his name was too much for his pride. •

IIis fabricating a great pedigree for the obscure Mr. Burgum of Bristol, who thoroughly believed in its genuineness and paid five shillings for it, can less easily be condoned than his spreading pretended manuscripts among his over-credulous townspeople. The ease with which he was able to gull those upon whom he had at first practised his imposition was a practical encouragement for its continuance. A desire to supply his own wants and to relieve the embarrassed circumstances in which his mother and sister, to whom he was devotedly attached, were left, may have hastened his attempt to negotiate with Dodsley and with Walpole in regard to the Rowley poems. That he rendered himself liable not only to the charge of having erréd in judgment, but of having seriously compromised his integrity was most unfortunate, but the great laxity which historical romance had reached in his age is an extenuation of his mistake, whatever motives led to its commission. It required only the dauntless, if unscrupulous, genius of a Chatterton to overleap the moral distinction between the invention of the characters of a story and its presentation by a pretended author.

If he had written the Rowley poems with the purpose of maligning any of the characters mentioned in them, or had wilfully attributed in them immoral or unbecoming sentiments to their fictitious author, he would have deserved indeed the condemnation of posterity. How many authors have more deeply sinned against truth than he and yet have escaped unscathed by public criticism? This much may be said against Chatterton, that while he manifested no guilty animus in the Rowley poems, some of their verses are not fitting language for one whom he calls "a holy monk," but not grossly so considering their context. Romance and war as treated by the genius of Chatterton have never been favorite subjects for the cloister.

A. J. McGillivray.

(To be Continued.)

CHRISTIANITY AND POLITICS.

F we consider how great an influence religion has in politics we cannot but come to the conclusion that a change in religion must needs be accompanied by a change in government. The coming of Christianity was no doubt the greatest change ever operated in religion, and therefore it must have operated a similar great change in politics. It is this which we will try to determine. Ancient society was founded on the old religion, the principal dogma of which was that each god protected his special family or city and existed for nothing else but that family or that city. From this same religion proceeded all the laws; the laws concerning men in their relations with one another, the laws of property and inheritage, in fact the laws of all proceedings, and this not according to the precepts of Justice but in view of promoting the interests of religion. Again this same creed became a government; it dictated the duties for the kings, the governors and heads of each family. All came from religion, that is, from the opinion man had formed of "Divinity." Religion, law and government were all the same thing under three different aspects.

We see that in this ancient social system religion reigned supreme in private as well as in public life. The state was a religious community, the king a pontiff, the magistrate a priest, and the law a holy maxim. There patriotism was piety, exile an excommunication, and individual liberty was unknown. Man was a slave to the state by his soul, body and riches; moreover, hatred for strangers was an obligation, the notions of law, duty, justice and affection were limited to the city, and human associations were necessarily bound within a certain circumference about the shrine of some god. Such were the conditions of Grecian and Roman laws in the earlier part of their history. Gradually, however, society bettered itself, changes were accomplished in creeds, and consequently in laws and government. Already during the five centuries preceding Christianity, religion, politics and law were becoming more and more distinct. The efforts made by the oppressed classes, and the work of philosophers and the great progress of the human mind, finally did away with the old principles of human association. The people could no longer believe in their old religion, and this fact answers the question why laws and politics became eventually detached from the creed.

This species of divorce came directly from the disappearance of the ancient religion. If law and politics were becoming more and more independent, it was because men ceased having a creed; if society was independent of religion, it was owing to religion's impotency. There came a day, however, when the religious sentiment again assumed life and vigour, when under the form of Christianity a creed again took its seat in man's soul. Shall we again see the ancient confusion of priesthood and government, of faith and law? With the advent of Christianity the religious sentiment was not only revived but it assumed a higher and less material expression. In the past the human soul and the great physical forces were all deified, now the conception of God was modified; God was essentially a stranger to the world and human nature. Divinity was at last placed outside the viible nature and above it. Again, in the past, each individual had his own god and there were as many gods as families and cities, now God was looked upon as unique, immense and universal, the Power animating the world, and the sole object of the adoration which is in man. Religion was no longer an old tradition, but a collection of dogmas and a great object of faith. It was no exterior thing; it was enthronged especially in man's reason. It was no longer matter, it became spirit, in fact Christianity changed the whole nature and form of adoration. The soul had a new relation with divinity and the fear of God was replaced by the love of God.

The Government in its own evolution came to a form identical with that which Christianity on coming would have given it, had it not evolved of itself. From these few facts we naturally conclude that Christianity not only lends itself to politics, but also that it promotes good politics as in the case of Greece and Rome, after these empires had thrown off the yoke of paganism.

J. F. SIMARD, '12·

Valedictory.

UOYED up by the tide of our existence, we find ourselves often tossed about rudely by the raging billows of adversity, and at intervals wafted gently towards our goal by a favorable breeze. First comes a storm, and then follows a calm,—a calm such as this, at the hour of graduation, and such as marks the succeeding stages of our lines,—a momentary respite that affords us leisure for a reflection of the past which to us, the members of the class '09, is our college days.

There were occasions when our strength seemed to fail us and we would fain have forsaken our task in its rude, unfinished state, but these dark times were brightened by flashes of hope, which,

> Like the gleaming taper's light,
> Adorns and cheers the way;
> And still, as darker grows the night,
> Emits a brighter ray.

One thought there was that occupied more than the ordinary the attention of our minds, and that centred around our devoted, unselfish parents. All along they have been depriving themselves of comforts and of pleasures that we might have every advantage to attain success. At present, though we can do no more than give expression to a deep sense of gratitude within, yet something tells us that this slight token of appreciation will be a welcome recompense to them.

Picture to yourselves the battle-scarred veteran as he sits by the camp-fire and opens a letter from Home! The sound of that magic word causes his strong heart, hardened to danger, to beat heavily against his bosom, and a sad longing droops his sturdy frame, or, as other thoughts-ensue, a thousand pleasant scenes, doubly dear now, come flitting back to his memory, and a thrill of delight vibrates through his high-strung nerves as he lives the old life over again. We, too, have come under its spell. It has charmed us many a time; and, to-day, the regret at leaving the old familiar college, loses much of its bitterness as it commingles with the pleasure we take in returning to the dear ones at home.

The future lies before us. Its outline is hazy and indistinct. We can form but a vague, uncertain notion of the pleasant surprises or the sad disappointments it may have in store for us. However, if we have learned to appreciate fully the value of those principles deeply inculcated into our minds during those college days, they will stand us in good stead when we are perplexed by doubt, tried by temptation, or when fortune fails us. Now, restless ambition kindles the fire within and seems to lend us strength, and cheerful hope stirs our imaginations to picture glory already won before an attempt has been made to win it. We enter with warm and sanguine interest into the cold and callous, busy and exacting world, and realize but slightly our responsibilities. However, we have principles, and these are our charts and compasses. They have been forcibly and indelibly impressed on our memories, they savor of the very atmosphere of our Alma Mater, and are all embodied in the admonition ever on the lips of those truly solicitous fathers:—"Be true to your country, to your religion, and to your God." If we cling to these principles all the mystic nature of our surroundings will vanish, the veil of doubt and perplexity be lifted, and socialism, skepticism, irreligion and the other baneful off-springs of modernism will be revealed in their naked hideousness.

We are here to say farewell,—farewell to fond companions, to the kind fathers, to dear old Alma Mater. Let us hesitate, at least for a moment; to bid good-bye,—perhaps for years, to congenial scenes and characters that day by day we were brought to prize the more,—requires an extraordinary effort.

Fellow students,—we graduates have trodden the same course you are pursuing, and would be only too glad to offer a word of encouragement to those who will fill our places. If there is encouragement needed, there is none wanting. Look into the past and you will find grounds to hope, as well as reason to swell with pride. Our Alma Mater has a name widely known, and wherever it has been heard it has elicited applause. On the gridiron old varsity has merited a lasting fame. It will live, but we would have its name crowned with still greater laurels. Ubi Concordia ibi victoria. There is our motto. It was the spirit of these words that actuated those who made our Alma Mater famous, and it is our earnest desire that you shall enter into that spirit. We trust you shall. Remember it is not always necessary to win. We could witness your defeats with very good grace, if you would fight manfully and with concerted action. We shall follow your progress, and because our fullest confidence rests in you, hope to see the trophy so recently in our proud possession brought back triumphantly to adorn the walls of Alma

Mater. Moreover, that same confidence leads us to hope that the cup emblematic of the Intercollegiate Debating championship shall soon be returned where it lately rested among our other trophies. Look out into the world to-day. There our graduates, in all walks of life, have done admirably, setting noble examples for us to emulate. In church, in state, in the professions they are among the foremost.

Fellow students, the time has come for us to shake those hands in farewell that have been so often extended in welcome or congratulation. As we do so, it is with low, faltering accents that we bid you a last lingering farewell.

College fathers! You who, in sowing the seeds of discipline, knowledge and wisdom, have labored so zealously, without reward and without cessation, the harvest season has come. The usual order is reversed. You who were the sowers are not to be the reapers We, instead, are to reap the fruits of your endeavours. It was impossible to fully appreciate the sterling value of your friendship, the incalculable amount of your self-sacrifice, until we were about to lose the pleasure of your company and the protection offered to us through the kindly word spoken in advice and the ready hand raised in admonition. To-day we realize the sad significance of our departure. We leave your tender care, but, happily, we have buried in the depths of our souls the warnings, the directions you have given us. If there has been any unfortunate occurrence in the past that recurs to your memory and throws a shadow o'er the fair prospect of our present cordiality, we would have it forgotten. If there has been any lack of due respect, any evidence of unrequited love, then we would offer our regret and promise to make the future a compensation for the past. If such thoughts should happen to arise we know full well you will cast them into oblivion and not add to our regret a still more pungent remorse. We feel that we are parting on the best of terms and trust that we may meet again to renew old acquaintances and augment our present words of gratitude by others quite as sincere.

We have been counting upon too much. Some of those same kind fathers may ere long be cold and motionless beneath the dull grey sod. The possibility chills our blood. To think that it is only too probable spreads a gloom over our countenances and brings us to reflect upon a recent very sad happening. Only a few short days ago our beloved archbishop passed away at the post of duty, with staff in hand, as he was always to be found,— the shepherd of his flock. His labours will bring their own reward. His life is a history of our university; his death marks an epoch in its progress through trials and misfortunes Always ready to proffer generous assistance, he saw it safely through a disastrous fire and lived to behold it in a state of renewed vigour.

The students of Ottawa University long ago learned to enjoy the yearly visit of their firm, but fatherly Chancellor, and they shall recall with pleasure his gentle, ennobling advice. Requiescat in pace.

Dear old Alma Mater, we reserve farewell to you until the last. We will always remember you as you are to-day—the fountain from which spring the crystal waters of knowledge.

You shall never change, though the Angel of Death may level with his destructive sword those well known and dearly cherished among us, though Father Time may erase our stately venerable edifices or remove from our minds other memories once vivid and realistic.

And as we turn to wish you a sincere and hearty farewell, it is most fitting that we should extend it to the patrons of our Alma Mater. Citizens of Ottawa, you have encouraged us on the field of sports, cheered us in defeat and victory; you have encouraged us in public speaking and taken an active interest in our debates; you have encouraged us in our studies and have attended our exercises to foster scholarship. To you we extend a farewell as we reluctantly bid·good-bye to our Alma Mater.

E. J. BYRNES, '09.

Just an "Ad."

WANTED:—A competent young man to take charge
of Corporate and Working Books. Apply
THE STAR ROLLING MILLS, LTD.

HAT very advertisement, no doubt, was the cause of
bringing to the manager's office of the above concern
not a few applicants for the vacant position.

The long oaken seat, just outside the manager's private
office, was taxed to its full capacity a few minutes after the doors
had been thrown open. Interesting enough should it be to study
the mien of those awaiting impatiently the arrival of Mr. Burns,
the president and head manager of the Company. Some were
tall and slender of form; others thick set and evidently well fed.
Two or three were attentively perusing the morning paper;
others wore a vacant look and twisted their more or less abundant upper-lip adornment with some evident signs of nervousness.
The greater number, however, were exchanging comments and
jokes that brought their hilarity into full eruption.

The manager, they had been told, would reach the office at
nine o'clock sharp. The minute hand of the large time-piece,
placed in a conspicuous position in the accounting room, was not
yet in a perpendicular position, when the last trepidations of a
handsome touring car were heard at the door. "It's the boss,"
said a janitor, lazily busy burnishing the brass fittings of the
main entrance. All hilarity ceased; all eyes were now turned towards the door. The janitor deferentially opened the door and
in came a tall, square-shouldered man of perplexing age; he was
surely fifty, yet one could have given him forty just as well.

Passing by the oaken seat, where the applicants were awaiting his arrival, Mr. Burns cast a short but searching glance upon
the long file of work-seekers. Mr. Burns had hardly sat down
at his desk when John Monroe, a junior clerk, appeared to announce that "a lot of young fellows" wanted to see him about
the "ad."

"Show them in one by one," said he, without looking at the
speaker, and smartly added, "first come first served."

The first introduced was a tidy specimen of humanity, a real Lover's Lane beau, fashionably dressed. He wore the regimental red leather low shoes, turned up trousers and a flaring necktie, knowingly tucked up into the bosom of his negligee shirt to set off to advantage a dubious bit of cut glass.

He bowed timidly and said falteringly: I came, sir...I came, hem! I came to... "To answer my advertisement," said Mr. Burns. "Yes, sir." "Well, what experience have you?" "Three years, sir, and I have testim..." "Never mind that, young man, (not allowing him time to take them out of his pocket) "I have just one question to ask you: 'What do you do when, by mistake, you make a wrong entry in your ledger'?" "I usually," replied he, "make a corresponding entry on the opposite side of the account 'by error' or 'to error' as the case might be, which would balance the erroneous entry. Technically, sir, this is what we call making 'a cross entry.'" "Well," replied Mr. Burns, "you are too technical for us, and we shall not need your services. Good morning."

The next applicant, rather slovenly dressed, but very shrewd in looks, said that he disposed of wrong entries by expert erasing, and expressed the willingness to prove that he could erase an entry so neatly that no one could detect that it had ever been made. "You are much too skillful," remarked the wide-awake manager, "we should never feel safe with our books in your hands," and the smart looking young man was shown his way out.

Applicant after applicant appeared. Each had some ingenious method, a "cute device" for adjusting wrong entries, and each was quietly dismissed with the assurance that his services were not wanted.

At last an unassuming and plainly dressed young man appeared. The manager of "The Star Rolling Mills" asked the usual question: "How do you proceed when you make a wrong entry in your ledger?" "I never make wrong entries in my ledger," quietly replied the young man. "You are the man we have been looking for," said Mr. Burns, with no little fervor in his voice; "you may consider yourself engaged," And, leaning over on the side of his revolving chair, he caught a metaphone connecting his office with the different departments of a plant covering several acres, and said laconically, "Henry! here a minute!"

In fact, a minute later, the assistant manager stood before Mr. Burns. "Henry, set this young man to work on the main books, and report to me in a week or two.'' Then turning to our young applicant, and fixing his keen eyes, searching and far-reading, upon him he said: ''Young man, I'll start you at $15.00 a week; time will tell whether you deserve less, more or nothing at all. Start your work to-day if you can, and keep good to your promise: NEVER MAKE A MISTAKE.''

A month later the same young man was called to the manager's presence and was told that his salary had been raised to $25.00 a week.

A year later he was given a substantial interest in the vast establishment, for he had kept true to his promise—he had never made a single mistake in his books.

Business students of to-day, the accountants of to-morrow, do likewise—NEVER MAKE A MISTAKE IN YOUR BOOKS!

''BUSINESS.''

THE DEBATING SOCIETY.

The annual meeting for the election of officers in the English debating society for the ensuing term was held on Friday, Oct. 1st, at which were present Rev. Fr. Fallon, the director, and the students from third form and upwards.

The meeting was addressed by Rev. Fr. Fallon, who, this year, was appointed by the administration council to direct the debating society.

He explained in a few well-chosen words the functions and significance of the society, making a comparison with the other societies of the institution, which are only secondary to the debating society. He also demonstrated the importance of the election of officers. After his remarks, the election of officers began under the chairmanship of C. O'Gorman. They resulted as follows:

President—J. T. Brennan, '10·
Vice-President—J. J. Sammon, '11·
Treasurer—M. J. Smith, '10·
Secretary—P. C. Harris, '11·
First Councillor—T. McEvoy, '13·
Second Councillor—A. Gilligan, '14·

After the elections the President occupied the chair. He thanked the students for the honorable position confided to him, assuring them that he would do all in his power to further the interests of the students and of Ottawa University.

University of Ottawa Review

PUBLISHED BY THE STUDENTS.

THE OTTAWA UNIVERSITY REVIEW is the organ of the students. Its object is to aid the students in their literary development, to chronicle their doings in and out of class, and to unite more closely to their Alma Mater the students of the past and the present

TERMS :

One dollar a year in advance.   Single copies, 15 cents.   Advertising rates on application.

Address all communications to the "UNIVERSITY OF OTTAWA REVIEW", OTTAWA, ONT.

EDITORIAL STAFF :

J. BRENNAN, '10 ;   A. FLEMING, '11 ;   M. O'GARA, '10 ;
J. BURKE, '10 ;   PH. HARRIS, '11 ;   C. D. O'GORMAN, '10 ;
                         M. SMITH, '10·

Business Managers : C. GAUTHIER '10, ;   D. BREEN, '11·

Our Students are requested to patronize our Advertisers.

Vol. XII.   OTTAWA, ONT., OCTOBER, 1909.   No. 1

FOREWORD.

Once more The Review steps forth to greet its kind and appreciative friends. Until the "Ides of June" it will keep its watchful eye ever open, like the wise old bird whose successor it is, to note and chronicle the doings of "the boys," grave or gay, in the realms of intellectual endeavour, or in the field of brawn and muscle. While feeling a certain amount of gratification at the encomiums so freely lavished on last year's issue, we are not unconscious of the fact that there is still room for improvement in many ways, and we trust that a capable and enthusiastic staff will give the matter its most serious attention. But the whole burden does not rest upon the board of editors. The students should feel it their duty to send in any contributions which they think worthy of publication, whether on literary or scientific subjects. We shall be glad also to receive from our alumni reminiscences of their old college days or phases of their present career,—these would, without doubt, prove interesting and instructive to the younger generation. Finally, since material improvement necessarily involves additional expense, we would strongly urge non-residential students to help along the good work by immediately sending in their subscription.

UBI CONCORDIA IBI VICTORIA.

At this the beginning of the new college year, there are one or two matters to which we would in all kindness direct the attention of our fellow-students. Application to one's studies, punctual attendance at class, good recitations, satisfactory examinations, though of the highest importance, are not all that is required to constitute a good collegian. He must at all times show due deference and respect towards his professors and those who in any way have authority over him, more especially if they be honoured with the sacerdotal dignity. Everywhere there are to be found ignorant, foolish fellows who are so puffed up with empty-headed vanity, that they consider themselves the equals if not the superiors of those to whom the shaping of their destinies has been entrusted. Secondly, we have our literary, scientific, dramatic and athletic associations, whose success and very existence depend on the active assistance and co-operation of the whole student body. Everyone who is eligible for membership should join these societies and do his best to advance their interests. He should feel it his duty to avoid all narrow-minded selfishness, and to stamp out with the utmost vigour every appearance of clique and sectional contention. He should cordially support and actively assist, as far as in him lies, every effort of the society officers, upon whom devolves such a large measure of responsibility and downright hard work. In a word, he must have the true college spirit of labouring for the greatest good of the greatest number, and for the honour and glory of Alma Mater. If there is complete and cordial unity, there is bound to be success.

Exchanges.

When the Exchange editor returned to his desk this autumn to take up for another year the unpleasant task of critic, he

found a bundle of "Commencement" numbers awaiting his perusal. None of the September numbers of our sister-colleges has
reached us yet, so we shall have to confine ourselves to the last
issue of last year. And, right here, let us expres the hope that
'09 will be a successful year in College journalism; that it will
mark the "*commencement*" of a new epoch in the literary work
of our educational institutions. To our brother scribes, we extend the hand of welcome. We wish them a successful year; not
only in their journalistic work, but in their studies and athletics
as well.

The D'Youville Magazine contains an interesting little sketch
on Mediaeval College life. Gee! but those fellows got it hard!
Lectures at six or seven in the morning, nothing to eat until ten,
and only truckle-beds on which to lie.

The "Valedictory" by Chas. Abbott in "St. Mary's Sentinel" is one of the most eloquent we have ever read. It is filled
with sentiments typically student-like, and with ideals truly
Catholic. We wish Mr. Abbott and his class-mates success in
their respective walks in life.

Many of us have read in the newspapers of the lecture tour
in the United States of Guglielmo Ferrero, the celebrated Italian
historian. St. Joseph's Collegian contains a review of the lectures
given up to date, and takes much ire at Ferrero's views on Caesar
compared with Napoleon. We are inclined to side with the Professor. That Napoleon was a great hypocrite no one will deny;
that Caesar was a noble type of manhood every reader of Roman
history is aware; and that he did more that is worthy of imitation than Napoleon we think all deep students of history will
admit.

The last number of the "Patrician" teems with essays on
religious topics. Among them we notice "Devotion to the Relics
of the Saints," "Christian Education," and "Persecutions under
Nero." Ther are also several very funny drawings, representing
Columbus fans.

Besides the above mentioned, we beg to acknowledge receipt
of the following: Abbey Student, Acta Victoriana, Adelphian,
Agnetian Monthly, Argosy, Allisonia, Academic Herald, Assump-
tion College Review, Amherst Literary Monthly, Bates' Student,
Bethany Student, Bethany Messenger, Columbiad, Collegian,
Comet, Central Catholic, Catholic University Bulletin, College
Mercury, Echoes from the Pines, Exponent, Educational Review,
Echoes from St. Anne's, Fordham Monthly, Geneva Cabinet,
Georgetown College Journal, Hya Yaka, Holy Cross Purple,

Laurel, Leaflets from Loretto, Leader, Martlet, Mitre, Manitoba College Journal, McMaster University Monthly, Mt. St. Mary's Record, Manhattan Quarterly, Notre Dame Scholastic, Niagara Index, Nazarene, Nazareth Chimes, Niagara Rainbow, O. A. C. Review, Ottawa Campus, Oracle, O. N. C. Monthly, Presbyterian College Journal, Pharos, Patrician, Vox Wesleyana, Vox Lycei.

Books and Reviews.

The *Contemporary Review* for September contains an article headed "Fallacies of the Doctrine of Compulsory Service." It begins by laying down emphatically the principle that to spend money upon compulsory military training of the population of the British Isles is not to follow the line of defensive policy which will provide the maximum of national security for the outlay involved. It then endeavours to show, rather vaguely, that this principle has been universally adopted by leading statesmen. Then, introducing two articles from a recent number of the Nineteenth Century Review, by prominent specialists, it goes on to quarrel with them in turn, and having quoted from them at much length and to small purpose, it finally places them to one side and concludes with the assertion, that compulsory service would be justified only to a very limited extent, which might become necessary to fill up gaps in the Territorial Army if voluntary enlistment failed. Having made this deduction, the subject is lightly dismissed, but not, however, without leaving the reader in much doubt as to the grounds upon which such a conclusion was reached. The article savours much of the pot-boiler, and one is led to believe that even this estimable review is at times pressed for material to fill its pages.

The August issue of the *Review of Reviews* has much of interest about the recent successes of aviators. These successes have brought about a conference to be held shortly in Paris. It is to discuss a code of laws governing the new method of transit. This follows naturally from the crossing of the English channel last summer. When air-ships become the vogue, frontiers will disappear and present laws governing international commerce will cease to be of value. How air-ships, with their great capabilities for speed, with their power of putting to naught all present routes of travel, and with their ability to carry both passengers and freight, are to be subjected to certain laws for their passage from one country to another, will undoubtedly be one of the important questions of the near future. The conference of Paris will be of interest as marking a new epoch in the progress of science, and will introduce a novel element in law-making.

To one wishing to get a clear and concise knowledge of the Catholic school system in the United States, with its past history, the principle upon which it is carried on, its origin and establishment, the *Catholic School System in the United States*, published by Benziger, is to be recommended. Its impartiality may be judged from the criticism of the Educational Review: "The book is characterized by fairness and candor."

Another recent book of much interest to Catholics is W. H. Bennett's *Catholic Footsteps in Old New York*. It reviews a period from 1524 to 1808. Treating as it does of the trials of the early missionaries, of the martyrdom of Father Jogues, of Bishop Carroll's efforts, of the struggle of the early colonists, it is vastly interesting, contains much valuable information, and reads like a romance.

Priorum Temporum Flores.

On Monday, Sept. 20th, the graduating class of '06 had a happy re-union in the Science Hall of the University. The following members were present: W. H. Cavanagh, W. P. Durham, R. O. Filiatreault, J. N. George, G. W. O'Toole, C. A. Seguin, T. J. Sloan and T. J. Tobin.

Messrs. M. Doyle, '08; A. Stanton, '09; J. Connaghan, '09, and C. J. Jones, '07, on their way to Montreal Seminary, which opened on Sept. 21st, stopped off and paid Alma Mater a flying visit.

Messrs. F. Higgerty, '09, and J. Connaghan, '09, two members of last year's graduation class, have commenced their theological studies at the Grand Seminary, Montreal.

Mr. A. Reynolds, who has entered Ste. Thérèse Seminary, Quebec, to continue his studies in theology, favored Alma Mater with a visit a few weeks ago.

Mr. E. Byrnes, '09, and Mr. V. K. O'Gorman, '09, have both decided to take a year's rest.

Rev. J. J. O'Gorman, '03; Rev. J. R. O'Gorman, '01, and Rev. J. Warnock, '01, are leaving early next month for Rome where they intend to spend two years in the study of Canon Law.

Mr. A. Couillard, '09, and Mr. M. Lachaine, '09, visited the University within the last two weeks. The former has entered Osgoode Hall, Toronto, in order to take up a course in law; the latter is attending the School of Pedagogy in Toronto.

Mr. I. Derosiers, '09, is at McGill University, where he is taking up architecture.

Mr. J. Corkery, '09, will attend Osgoode Hall this year. He is taking up the Law course. Incidentally he is starring on the half-back division of the Argonauts.

Mr. W. P. Breen, '12, left for Buffalo a few days ago where he has accepted a position as professor on D'Youville College. Mr. Breen will continue his studies in Buffalo.

Mr. T. J. Tobin, '06, after successfully completing a course in several European Colleges, has entered the Seminary of Ottawa.

Rev. J. J. McDonnell, '02, of Cornwall, favored Alma Mater with a visit this week. We are pleased to notice that the reverend gentleman seems to have regained in a large measure his former good health. He left behind him his best wishes for the success of the team with which he was once so prominently connected.

REV. G. I. NOLAN, O.M.I.

It was with a great deal of pleasurable pride that the Faculty and students of Ottawa University learned of the appointment of Rev. Father Nolan to the Pastorate of the Immaculate Conception church, Lowell, Mass.

A graduate of the class of '03, Father Nolan entered the Oblate Novitiate in the fall of '04, and after completing with great distinction his theological studies, he was ordained in Boston, Mass., June 15, '01. He was at once placed on the missionary staff of the Oblates, and won an enviable reputation for himself on account of his oratorical powers, and the earnestness and zeal that he displayed in his work.

His recent appointment to this important post is but another mark of the confidence and esteem in which he is held by his superiors.

His many friends here will follow his career with great interest and best wishes.

Obituary.

HUBERT ARTHUR O'MEARA.

It is with feelings of the very deepest regret that we are called upon in this the initial number of The Review to record the death, during the past summer, of one of our truest and most trusted of friends, Hubert O'Meara. Little did we think, when we dispersed last June, that before the holiday season should have passed away, Death would have claimed for his own one who for the last few years has been among the most earnest workers on behalf of our college journal. Mr. O'Meara's illness was exceedingly short, lasting but two weeks, and when the notice of his death, which occurred at the Water Street Hospital on August 18th, appeared in the daily papers, it came as a distinct shock to his many friends. The funeral was a large and representative one, and testified to the esteem in which Mr. O'Meara was held by old and young. The Knights of Columbus and the members of St. Patrick's Hall, to which societies the deceased was a member, attended the funeral in a body.

Hubert O'Meara was the son of John O'Meara, K.C., of this city, and was born in Peterboro twenty-six years ago. At an early age he came to the Capital where his family has since resided. He received his primary education in Quebec City, and later attended Rigaud College where he followed the classical course, with much distinction for five years. Here he became thoroughly acquainted with the classics and acquired a perfect knowledge of French. On leaving Rigaud he was for some years a member of the Citizen staff of Ottawa, and afterwards entered the Government Printing Bureau, where his unquestioned ability earned for him rapid promotion.

Mr. O'Meara was the possessor of many and varied attainments. He had a distinct taste for languages. Besides having a sound knowledge of Latin and Greek, he spoke and wrote French with the ease of a native, and during the last three years had made himself master of Gaelic. He was also gifted with a refined literary taste. Poems and essays from his pen have appeared frequently in The Review. His poems, especially, contained much that gave evidence of a brilliant career for their youthful author. He was deeply interested in the Gaelic Revival Movement, and was one of the most enthusiastic members of the Ottawa branch of the Gaelic League. He was likewise the first secretary-treasurer of the Gaelic Corresponding Society, which office he held at the time of his death. He had an astonishing knowledge of the details of Irish history and it was, as a rule, from these sources that he drew inspiration for his literary work. His efforts along these lines had already begun to receive recognition, for he was a contributor to the columns of the Irish national papers.

In bearing he was gentlemanly, dignified and somewhat reserved; in conversation full of original thought expressed with rare precision and rich aptitude; in his studies he was rigorously thorough; in his dealings with others he was unfailingly courteous, generous and kind; he would go to any trouble in order to accommodate a friend. He possessed all the sensitiveness of the poet, coupled with a seemingly inexhaustible capacity for hard study. This trait had much to do with his early death; for, having weakened an already delicate constitution by overwork, when sickness came, he was unable to fight against its ravages.

Thus in the flower of his youth, when Fortune seemed to be smiling most brightly, and when the future appeared to be holding out the very best promises of success, ''God's finger touched him and he slept.'' He is gone to that Heavenly Father whom throughout his short life he served so quietly and so well. In the death of Mr. O'Meara, The Review feels that it has suffered a loss that will not easily be repaired. Although never a student of the University, Mr. O'Meara possessed a deep sympathy in its aims and was ever ready to aid in any of the undertakings of the student body, for by nature he was a student, and his pleasures were found along the paths of knowledge. To the bereaved family we extend our heartfelt sympathy in their great grief, and we trust that the consciousness of Hubert's blameless life may be a consolation to them in their sorrow.

JUDGE CURRAN.

Since going to press, we have learned with deepest regret the death of His Honour Judge Curran. We hope in our next issue to give a biographical sketch of the distinguished legal luminary. Meanwhile to the family we tender our respectful sympathy.

Personals.

Rev. Father M. J. Stanton, O.P., preached the annual retreat to the English speaking boys of the University. His instructions were listened to with great interest by the students, and judging from the conduct of the latter since the closing his efforts have been crowned with success.

Rev. Father Gavary, O.M.I., whose reputation as an earnest and sincere expounder of the Gospel has long been known, conducted the retreat for the French-speaking students, and needless to say his labors were not in vain.

Rev. Fathers Murphy, Rector, and Poli, Vice-Rector, are at present attending the Plenary Council at Quebec.

Archbishop Langevin, O.M.I., of St. Boniface; Bishop Legal, O.M.I., St. Albert; Bishop Grouard, O.M.I., Athabaska; Bishop Joussard, O.M.I., Auxiliary Bishop of Athabaska; Rev. Fr. Lacasse, O.M.I., Theologian of St. Boniface Diocese; Rev. J. Ryan, Theologian of Pembroke Diocese; Rev. Fr. Bernier, O.M.I., Theologian of St. Albert Diocese; Rev. Fr. Walsh, O.M.I., Theologian of Victoria Diocese; Rev. Fr. Charlebois, O.M.I., Theologian of Athabaska Diocese; Rev. Fr. Allard, O.M.I., Vicar General, St. Boniface Diocese; Rev. Fr. Lacombe, O.M.I., Vicar General, St. Albert; Rev. Fr. Lacoste, O.M.I., Vicar General, Prince Albert; Very Rev. Fr. Magnan, O.M.I., and Grandin, O.M.I., Provincials, paid a visit to the University when passing through Ottawa on their way to the Plenary Council at Quebec.

Rev. Fr. Nilles, O.M.I., has returned from Mattawa to resume the chaplaincy of the Mother House of the Grey Nuns, Water street.

Rev. Fr. Lajeunesse, O.M.I., has become secretary of the University and chaplain to the Rideau street convent.

Rev. Fr. Fallon, O.M.I., has been appointed Prefect of Studies.

Rev. Fr. Peruisset, O.M.I., is chaplain to the Gloucester St. convent.

Rev. Fr. Browne, a native of Newfoundland, is a new member of our professorial staff.

Rev. Fr. Dewe has returned from an extended tour of Europe.

Rev. Fr. Gauvreau, O.M.I., former professor of chemistry, paid us a visit recently.

The bright and frosty autumn weather is here again, and with it comes, as regularly as the seasons, the "Grid-Iron" hero, supplanting with majestic stride and tawny mane the baseball and lacrosse player.

In the arena of manly sports at Ottawa University, Football has always held, unchallenged, the premier position in the relative importances of all branches of athletics. True it is the other games, such as baseball, lacrosse, hand-ball, and basketball, have not by any means been neglected, but when Ottawa University is mentioned, Football, as by second nature, is immediately coupled with its name. And not a mediocre brand of Football either, but the kind that wins the support and respect of the public; that makes gentlemen out of its players, and incidentally wins championships. Let us hope that the team of 1909 will have a successful season, and add another championship to the already lengthy list.

This season witnessed the withdrawal from active football duties of Rev. Father Wm. J. Stanton, O.M.I. It is with sincere regret that we chronicle this information. Rev. Father Stanton was considered the brainiest coach in the Inter-Collegiate Union, and this body suffers a distinct loss in his resignation. In 1907 the championship cup of the C.I.R.F.U. was brought to our University for the first time in its history. True, we were not champions last year, but that should not reflect discredit on the cocah or the team. The boys worked hard, likewise the coach, but the excessive weight of the opposing players told heavily against our team, and were were not successful. The team took its defeat gracefully and like gentlemen. Although not coach this year, Rev. Father Stanton is still head of athletics at the University, and directs the Association in a firm and able manner. He is also Prefect of Discipline for the term 1909-10.

The team of 1909 will be minus many familiar faces when it lines up for the initial game against McGill, Oct. 9th, at Montreal.

Frank Higgerty, our stellar inside wing, and the most consistent worker on last year's team, has gone to Montreal.

Billy Richards will be missing from the half-back line this season; Corkery, Ryan, Lalonde, Mac O'Neil, Costello, Whalen and Hart have not returned to the University.

Ed. McCarthy, manager of the teams of 1907-1908, and half-back of last year's team, has finished his studies at Ottawa. Mac's tackling and punting abilities were of great assistance to the team.

Jimmie Dean, our clever little quarter back, will not be with us this year. He will be a hard man to replace.

Nick Bawlf, the best full back of the Intercollegiate 1907-1908, and all-round athlete, whose performances and victories in the field of sport have added fame to Ottawa University's athletic achievements, will be missing from the team, and much missed at that. His terrifice speed and kicking abilities were very vital factors in winning games.

Of last year's team we have Ch. O'Neill, captain 1909 team; Jerry Harrington, manager 1909; Quilty, Mike Smith, Pete Conway, Harvey Chartrand, Fleming, Dubois and Street.

Among the candidates for places on the first team are Charlie Kinsella, Bert. Gilligan, W. Chartrand, Joe Muzanti, Jack Contway, Dan Breen, J. Brennan, J. and O. Kennedy, P. Belanger, P. Lacey, Sullivan, Geo. Whibbs, Harrington and others.

The election of Charlie O'Neill as captain, and Jerry Harrington as manager for 1909, is a most acceptable one to players and students alike. Two more popular and capable players would be difficult to find.

An Inter-Mural Football League has been formed, and captains of the respective teams elected. To such leagues as this belongs the credit of discovering many brilliant footballers.

Rev. Father Turcotte has succeeded Rev. Father Stanton as coach of the senior team. If his successful work in Small Yard can be taken as a criterion, the team should have a most satisfactory season. Good luck and success is the earnest wish of all.

Rev. Father M. Murphy is acting as coach for the second team.

The Rule Books of the Canadian Inter-Collegiate Rugby Football Union for the season 1909 have been issued by Secretary-Treasurer P. C. Harris. Players could do nothing better than acquire a perfect knowledge of the rules of the game contained in this booklet, and note carefully the changes that have been made.

As a mark of the esteem in which he is held by the Inter-Collegiate Union, Rev. Father Stanton has been elected to the high office of Hon. President of that body. This is the first time that position has been held by an Ottawan, and is a unique honor.

Mr. Winfield Hackett is the new Treasurer of the U.O.A.A., 1909-1910. Congratulations.

The complete senior Inter-Collegiate schedule is as follows:

Oct. 9—Toronto at Queen's, Ottawa at McGill.
Oct. 16—Queen's at Ottawa, McGill at Toronto.
Oct. 23—Ottawa at Toronto, Queen's at McGill.
Oct. 30—McGill at Queen's, Toronto at Ottawa.
Nov. 6—Queen's at Toronto, McGill at Ottawa.
Nov. 13—Toronto at McGill, Ottawa at Queen's.

Of Local Interest.

A stranger in our midst would surely see
Some who excite much curiosity.
As John B-ke philosophically dopes
Alone his brain with dangerous questions copes.
While G-th-r in the act of stretching, spies
A nest of spiders of enormous size.
His thoughts of those around do quickly ebb
As he doth watch the spiders spin their web.
But suddenly the sharp ring of the bell .
Undoes abruptly Charlie's little spell;
And then after much reason logical
He says, "them is a funny animal."

Notable answers given to a Lay Prof. :—
Q. What is a Lake?
A. A Lake is a piece of land with water in the middle.
Q. What water did Cartier sail through on his first expedition?
A. Eau de vie.

O'G-n: How is your arm, G-l-an?

L-f-ty says he has a base voice.

Stop that noise, McE-oy.

Levi has disposed of his lots during the vacation.

Wh-bs and Jim K. made a good go at practice one evening.
Ke-n-dy has an awful punch.

Greek Prof.: What is the meaning of *eugenes?*
O'N-1: Noble blooded beast.
Prof.: You're a follower of the ponies.

How are stocks selling, Harvey?

(Logging Chain, Jr.): Where is the gymnasium?

Pf-1: I am going down town, father.
Prefect: Oh, are you?

Professor (interrogating L-t-g): What was I saying, Ke-dy?
Ke-dy: You were asking the time.

Ga-p-n: Oh where! Oh where! is my little cat gone?

How are ponies selling, Levi?

Cr-ht-n: Rob-l-d kicked a drop last night playing in the
rain.
Br-an: A drop of what?

Prefect of Studies (illustrating the importance of making
the retreat): No person is exempt from attending the retreat except he bring me a letter from some Saint testifying as to his
sanctity; and if any of you wish to do this you may go to St.
Amour.

Some class to Ra-b-th when he could not be classified.

O'G-ra: My heavens, Wh-bs, don't break that man's n-ck.
Wh-bs: There are lots more.

H-k-t gives a good illustration of "Riding the Goat."

The M-x-can: I got shot in the thigh some time ago.
Ossie: Why did they shoot you?
J. K.: Did they think you were game?

O'G-n is going to try his Intermediate.

A drum, a drum! Mike S-th doth come.

Ke-n-dy avers that he is going in for Law. Ke-d-y is a joker.

Do you comb your hair in English or in French?

Are you a Protestant or a married man?

Which is it colder, in the summer or in the country?

How did you do in the last "test"? Nicely.

Query: Who's the Czar?

Eng. Professor: Who was this cobbler?
Brilliant Student: A famous Roman general.

"The bear shed his coat of peel!"

Who's talking now?

Junior Department

We extend a hearty welcome to all the members of the Junior Department. Now that they have passed through all the stages of that terrible malady called home-sickness, it is to be hoped that all will strive to keep up the enviable reputation of "small yard." Remember that "he who plays well studies well," and by not only keeping this maxim in mind, but also by putting it into practice, you will help in making this year's record as good as the glorious records of other years.

The Junior Department expects every member to do his duty during the term '09-'10.

Rev. M. Murphy, O.M.I., has been transferred to the Senior Department, and is replaced by Rev. W. J. Collins, O.M.I., as second prefect.

Have you seen Jim in his high diving act?

The Junior Athletic Association held its annual election of officers on Wednesday, Sept. 22. Rev. Fr. Veronneau, O.M.I., opened the meeting by giving a brief account of last year's successful work, and reminded the members that it all depended on them to make this year as successful as the one just passed.

The officers who will have the guiding of affairs in athletics this year are:

Director, Rev. J. A. Veronneau, O.M.I.; President, A. Milot; First Vice-President, E. Côté; Second Vice-President, C. Brennan; Treasurer, H. Richardson; Secretary, F. W. Harris; Councillors, R. Renaud, L. Brady and E. Nagle.

At the meeting after the election F. Poulin was chosen captain of the senior football team.

Let every one get out to the football practices. There are continual changes on every team, and though not chosen at first you never know when your turn may come. Always be ready to fill a place when called on.

Some of our junior members came back very mannish in their long trousers, but, sad to relate, they have not yet caught the senior Prefect's eye.

UNIVERSITY OF OTTAWA REVIEW

Vol. XII.   OTTAWA, ONT., NOVEMBER, 1909.   No. 2

Entered at the Post Office at Ottawa, Ont., as Second-Class Matter.

Thomas Chatterton, the Boy Poet of Bristol.

HE relations between Mr. Lambert and his apprentice were mutually unpleasant, as might be expected from the incompatibility of their ambitions and purposes. It appears the master had not the least sympathy with the literary aspirations of the servant, and that while strictly insistent on his own rights he was disposed to treat him merely as his drudge. The servant heartily despised the censorship of his overbearing master, but is credited with having faithfully performed all his duties. Pride, according to a confession made by Chatterton himself, in a moment of distraction, was nineteen-twentieths of his nature. It is not hard to conceive, therefore, that the only tie which really bound the apprentice to the office was his love of literary work, for which his clerical duties left him much leisure. He was, however, at last getting daily more impatient with the routine of office work and more ambitious to attain success by his pen. On December 21, 1768, he wrote the following letter to Dodsley, a London publisher:

"Sir,—I take this method to acquaint you, that I can so procure Copys of Several Ancient Poems; and an Interlude, perhaps the oldest dramatic. Piece extant; wrote by one Rowley, a Priest in Bristol, who lived in the Reigns of Henry 6th and Edward 4th. If these Pieces will be of any service to you, at your Command Copys shall be sent to you by

Yr most obedient servt.

D. B."

This letter remained unanswered as well as one sent by him to the same publisher two months afterwards, in which he stated his discovery of the tragedy of Ælla, for the copying of which he asked him to advance him one guinea, the amount asked by the possessor of the manuscript for the privilege of making a transcript of it.

His next scheme for introducing his so-called antique writings to the world was his attempt to gain the patronage of Horace Walpole, the author of the "Castle of Otranto," to whom he forwarded a letter and two specimen manuscripts. Walpole graciously replied, asking with model suavity where the Rowley poems could be found, and adding that he should not be sorry to print them, or at least a specimen of them. Chatterton rushed into what seems almost like a net cunningly prepared for him. On receiving Walpole's letter he at once sent him other manuscripts, but these being submitted to his friends, Gray and Mason, they unhesitatingly declared them to be unauthentic, and Walpole's next letter was as frigid and overbearing as his first was courteous and condescending. This was certainly a severe disappointment to Chatterton, who had founded great expectations upon the first encouraging letter received from Walpole. Whether the latter did right in afterwards completely ignoring him will likely remain an open question, however probable it may appear that if Walpole had extended to him the desired patronage, he would have realized his dreams of greatness instead of sadly yielding so soon to his hapless fate.

In April, 1770, Chatterton's apprenticeship abruptly came to a close, through what may be considered a strategy on his part, it being conceded that the paper writing, which was the cause of his dismissal, was purposely left by him on his desk in order that it would fall into the hands of Mr. Lambert. It was Chatterton's last will and testament, written partly in verse and towards the end in prose, stating that he would die the next day, and making amusing bequests to some of his Bristol acquaintances. During the few days preceding his writing this serio-comic document he had acted with strange caprice among Mr. Lambert's servants and this conduct, though not new to him, together with the discovery of the will, made Mr. Lambert cancel the articles of apprenticeship. Chatterton long before this had decided to try his fortune as a writer in London—that Mecca towards which so many men of genius hasten. Articles from his pen had already appeared in the Town and Country Magazine, a London periodical of the first rank, and the state of political feeling in the great metropolis suggested to one so ambitious and self-confident opportunities for the exercise of his talents as a writer.

His friends raised enough money for the expenses of his travel and immediate requirements, and in about a week after the termination of his apprenticeship he left for London with bright hopes and high aspirations which a few months of hard experience dispelled as mocking illusions. At the two places where he lodged in London, first at Walmsley's, a plaster of Shoreditch, and next at Mrs. Angel's, dressmaker on Brooke Street, Holborn, he applied himself with almost incredulous industry to writing various compositions intended for publication. As a rival of Junius he was a contributor to the Middlesex Journal, for which he wrote under the signature of "Decimus," and also a correspondent of the Town and Country Magazine and of the Freeholders' Magazine. The fair measure of encouragement with which he first met, stimulated him to such efforts that his prolific pen soon produced abundant matter for the press, which was readily accepted. In a happy vein he wrote letters to his mother and sister, promising presents, mentioning china, silver fans and fine silk. But his second month in London suddenly arrested his brief but hard-earned success, and rudely awakened him from his happy dreams. His "Excellente Balade of Charity," one of his pseudo-antique productions which he had sent to the Town and Country Magazine, was refused publication. His political articles, which pandered to the popular passions, had at last to be discounted for fear of the party in power, so that he was usually paid only a shilling for each article, and eighteen pence for one of his songs. Some of his contributions were also held in reserve and remained unpaid. His financial embarrassment seems to have stung his sensitive soul and rendered him utterly despondent in the presence of want and starvation. Was he too proud, even then, in his suffering and humiliation, to yield to the discipline of the cross and seek the refreshment promised the weary and heavy-laden? Or did he feel any of the inspiration wihch made Charles McKay write:

"Hope on, hope ever, though to-day be dark.
The sweet sunburst may smile on thee to-morrow;
Tho' thou art lonely, there's an eye will mark
Thy loneliness and guerdon all thy sorrow!
Tho' thou must toil 'mong cold and sordid men,
With none to echo back thy thought or love thee,

Cheer up, poor heart! thou dost not beat in vain,
For God is over all, and Heaven above thee—
Hope on, hope ever.''

The belief that he was sustained in the extremity of his troubles
by such Christian hopes and sentiments is discouraged by some
of his writings, particularly his poem on ''Happiness'' which
savors so much of infidelity, a likely consequence of his pride,
as well as by the rash act that terminated forever his eager ''gasping after light.'' According to a footnote by Dr. Gregory, published in Mr. Bell's memoir, he wrote, although perhaps merely
from youthful petulance, to Mr. Catcott that he was not a Christian, some time after leaving Bristol.

An undated manuscript in his handwriting and signed by
his name, preserved in the British Museum, gives his belief as
follows:

''That God being incomprehensible it is not required of us
to know the mystery of the Trinity, etc.

''That it matters not whether a man is a Pagan, Turk, Jew,
or Christian, if he acts according to the religion he professes.

''That if a man leads a good moral life he is a Christian

''That the stage is the best school of morality, and that the
Church of Rome, some tricks of Priestcraft excepted, is certainly
the true church.''

His poem, ''The Resignation,'' evidently written in suffering,
presents him in a better light. It does not appear when it was
written, but it seems so appropriate in connection with his suffering days in London, that to omit it would leave a blank which
no other of his poems could fill as well.

THE RESIGNATION.

''God, whose thunder shakes the sky,
Whose eye this atom globe surveys,
To thee, my only rock, I fly,
Thy mercy in thy justice praise.

The mystic mazes of thy will,
The shadows of celestial light,
Are past the power of human skill,—
But what the Eternal acts is right.

O teach me in the trying hour,
When anguish swells the dewy tear,

To still my sorrows, own thy power,
Thy goodness love, Thy justice fear.''

"If in this bosom aught but Thee
Encroaching sought a boundless sway,
Omniscience could the danger see,
And Mercy look the cause away.

Then why, my soul, dost thou complain?
Why, drooping, seek the dark recess?
Shake off the melancholy chain,
For God created all to bless.

But ah! my breast is human still;
The rising sigh, the falling tear,
My languid vitals feeble will,
The sickness of my soul declare.

But yet with fortitude resigned,
I'll thank the inflictor of the blow;
Forbid the sigh, compose my mind,
Nor let the gush of misery flow.

The gloomy mantle of the night,
Which on my sinking spirit steals,
Will vanish at the morning light
Which God, my East, my Sun, reveals.''

These beautiful lines revealed the deeper undercurrent of the poet's thoughts, his better silk, in marked contrast to the erratic but uncertain aspects of his character. Our judgment on such a complex being should, after all, be given in a sigh or written in sand. The critics, who have been at pains to pick faults in his work and condemn him for his vices, real or imagined, have been compared by some to owls "mangling a poor dead nightingale." They seem certainly to have forgotten that but for his one irreparable act, a heinous crime if committed in his senses, one so young and gifted might have lived to redeem all the faults of which they have accused him.

When his pen had failed him, he wrote his Bristol acquaintances, Dr. Barrett and Mr. Burgum, for the influence in obtaining a place as an assistant surgeon on board an African trader, and when he had waited in vain for an answer, it seems that his mind became unhinged by nervous prostration ending in settled despair. Disdaining all labors unsuited to his self-esteem he would not ask for alms nor even accept hospitality. Locking himself in his bedroom, he committed suicide on the 24th of August, 1770, by taking arsenic. From the stifling chamber of suffering and disgrace on Brooke Street, Holborn, to a pauper's grave on Shoe Lane, where all that was mortal of poor Chatterton was laid, seemed not a wide transition. Between the divine afflatus of the poet and the despairing thoughts of a suicide was an immeasurable chasm.

Chatterton has been referred to by some of his acquaintances as "the mad genius of Bristol." That was but one of the penalties, perhaps, of his being a born genius. Does it not seem one of the dispensations of Providence that youth is not equipped with the powers of the great which it would be so apt to abuse?

Between ten and eleven, this strange boy with the flashing grey eyes and prepossessing face, very reserved, willful, undisciplined, but affectionate, began to write poetry, and while some of his first efforts are of the common order, not a few of them are of surprising merit. Of his acknowledged poems, his "Elegy on the death of Thomas Phillips," "Heccar and Gaira," "Resignation," a political satire; "The Death of Nicon," and "The Resignation," possess undoubted strength and originality. Others acknowledged are much inferior, and some of them reflect upon his morals, one such being partly suppressed on that account, in Keat's edition. A few others might better have gone into the limbo of oblivion also.

The unacknowledged poems writen by him, but attributed to the fictitious monk, Rowley, contrary to the amenities of literature, are regarded as superior to his acknowledged poems, in strength, harmony and sustained power. The first of these composed by him, "Elinour and Juga," was written when he was but twelve years old. His "Ælla," a dramatic poem; "The Storie of William Canynge," "The Unknown Knight," "The Tournament," and "Goddyn," a dramatic poem, possess rare merit. But if he had been more patient, wisely restraining for greater achievements his ceaseless energy, he might have far excelled the best he has produced. Nearly all the world's great poets have "made haste slowly" to reach the heights. Although he has not communed so closely with Nature in all her scenes of loveliness and splendor, as some great poets of riper years, the sweet sound of his lyre was often invoked by her with more than happy effect.

The following stanzas from "Ælla," the one an imagery of Morning, the other of Spring, illustrate a lavish power of description:

> "Bright sun had in his ruddy robes been dight,
> From the red East he flitted with his train;
> The Houris drew away the gate of Night;
> Her sable tapestry was rent in twain;
> The dancing streaks bedecked Heaven's plain,
> And on the dew did smile with skimmering eye
> Like gouts of blood which do black armour stain,
> Shining upon the bourn which standeth by;
> The souldier stood upon the hillis side.
> Like young enleaved trees which in a forest bide.

> The budding floweret blushes at the light,
> The meads besprinkled with the yellow hue,
> In daisied mantles is the mountain dight,
> The fresh young cowslip bondeth with the dew;
> The trees enleafed, into heaven straight,
> When gentle winds do blow, to whistling din is brought.

> The evening comes, and brings the dews along,
> The ruddy welkin shineth to the eyne,
> Around the ale-stake minstrels sing the song,
> Young ivy round the door post doth entwine;
> I lay me on the grass, yet to my will
> Albeit all is fair, there lacketh something still."

Redcliff churchyard now contains his mortal remains, it is believed, there being a tradition that they have been transferred to that place at the desire of his uncle, Charles Phillips. A monument to his name is there erected, with an inscription whose words were written by the poet's own tireless hand, being contained in that strange last Will and Testament which he wrote on the 14th of April, 1770. If his sweet and harmonious lyre had not been so early silenced by the malign influences of fate, his body might have found a resting place in the Poet's Corner, Westminster Abbey.

The most fitting ending to this story of a great but misguided genius is the inscription on his monument, which reads:

"To the memory of Thomas Chatterton. Reader! Judge not. If thou art a Christian, believe that he shall be judged by a superior Power. To that Power alone is he now answerable."

A. J. McGILLIVRAY.

"A STORM."

HE storm was increasing in violence. Every now and then the little boat, which seemed like a speck far out on the lake, appeared on the top of a wave. The small crowd on the beach watched that white speck, whenever it appeared, with more mingled hope and despair than they would have felt for everything else in the world combined. Nor is it any wonder, since the lives of those nearest and dearest to some of the party were in great danger. Most of the women on shore were weeping, with no attempt at concealing the fact, while a few followed a safer and more sensible course, and prayed to God to intermit the storm. But what is very often according to His way, the storm seemed to grow fiercer almost immediately.

The tiny white sail tossed more frequently and more terribly. The dark waters were rolling in great long columns capped with white, frothy foam. The sky was growing darker, and black ridges of clouds, fringed on their lower edge with white curtains, were following close on the waves, as though there were a sea overhead as well as underneath. Either the sky or the lake might have been a reflection of the other, so troubled and fretted was the appearance of each. And now, oh, horror of horrors! a terrible wave had seemed suddenly to rise far out on the lake, like a huge snow-capped mountain, and the tiny sail had seemed to dip towards the water, and then it was gone!

Seven men had gone down to a boathouse, near the little village as soon as the news had spread around that three citizens of the place were out in the storm. They secured a large boat, and, jumping into it immediately, shot out on to the broad waters of Lake Ontario. Just at the moment that the big wave had appeared towards the horizon, these stalwart fellows waved their hands to the party on the beach, saluted a large Union Jack flying on the town hall, and then they were off. They struggled on for half a mile against the wind and waves, determined to rescue their friends, so long as there remained any hope that these might still be living. At this juncture they were obliged to lean on their oars with all their might, as an enormous mass of water, on its way to the shore, struck them. Their boat came near being capsized, and they were drenched with water. But, what a sight that instant met their eyes! The little boat, still upright, came into view for a moment after the big wave passed, and it was much closer than when they had last seen it.

A wild cheer from the shore went up behind them, which, in the awful roar of winds and waters, even the rescuers heard. They leaned on their oars with renewed vigor, and advanced a considerable distance in a very short time. The three men in the skiff were coming rapidly before the wind, although they had been obliged to lower their sail. But the rescuers experienced still greater difficulty in rowing against the ever-increasing gale. A deep curtain of darkness drew down over them before they came close to each other,—so much so, that the sudden change almost forced people to rub their eyes in order to see distinctly. Ominous-looking clouds hurried overhead with startling rapidity. Sea-gulls and swallows flew here and there, as if thoroughly alarmed and restless. Finally they had to give up before the gale and went off to some place of safety, known only to themselves. Gray, misty-looking clouds rushed in a direction opposite to the one in which the storm was going, probably carrying rain to the storm centre. The darkness grew more intense, and the water all around took on a like appearance. The waves dashed and slapped continually against the sides of the boats, causing them to rock and plunge fearfully. The spray was always splashing on the faces of the hardy crew.

The two boats came closer and closer. The skiff was in great danger of being upset every moment. Now they were side by side, and were held together by eager hands. One of the distressed crew stepped from his vessel into the boat of the rescuers. But just as he did so, a terrible wave came upon them with a rush. A flash of lightning darted from the clouds, and reflected wickedly on the waves. The boats were separated, and a wave washed over the skiff and capsized it, throwing the two remaining occupants into the waters. Try as they would, the men in the boat could not pick up the others. But these hung on to their own overturned skiff with a will, and were driven gradually towards shore. The waves covered them, the rain pelted them, and the lightning blinded them; but still they clung to the sails for their very lives, and, when close to shore, which was the time of greatest need, they were pulled into a larger boat by their friends. A mighty cry of joy arose from the shore, and many prayers went up to God in thanksgiving. The whole party landed at the dock with some difficulty, and the two half-drowned men were carried home. The long, swashing sound of the sea could still be heard far on the even shore, together with the occasional rolling and rumbling of distant thunder, and the dribbling rain, which characterized the passing storm.

J. SAMMON, '11·

Thomas Burke on "Obedience to Instructions"

HE subject of perhaps the ablest speech ever made by Burke was the one above named. Gibbon, the well-known historian, then a member of Parliament, and a staunch Tory, writes as follows: "Never can I forget the delight with which that diffusive and ingenious orator, Mr. Burke, was heard, and even by those whose existence he proscribed." According to Hudson, the mighty speech, taken on the whole, may be safely pronounced the finest piece of parliamentary eloquence in the language, or perhaps in the world.

Which Interest Paramount?

Burke says that, when a man is chosen to represent a constituency, he should aim, with perseverance and tolerance, to live in the strictest union, the closest correspondence, and the most unlimited communication with his constituents. Their wishes, their opinions, their business, should have the first and last call on his time, his energies, his pleasures and his abilities. In a word, he should always be ready to sacrifice his own personal interests for those of his constituents.

Members should sacrifice personal interests for those of their people; but never should they, though the loss to them be irreparable, submit their unbiased opinions, their seasoned judgments, their dictates of conscience, to be sacrificed to the people. A member who will betray his own conscientious power of judgment to the rash mandates of an enraged populace, is no man to be trusted, and sooner or later he will betray his people. One betrayal leads to another, and it is the people who are generally the losers in the end. The public blindly imagine that a member should go to Parliament, literally bound hand and foot, to do, to speak, and to vote as their authoritative mandate orders him. No self-reliant or conscientous man will accept office as a member, with such conditions of restraint, with such machine-like instructions; and, as a result, honest, reliable and capable men shun politics. What naturally follows? Their places are quickly filled by irresponsible men, in an irresponsible manner. These men do not hesitate to make multitudinous election promises, and are never over-scrupulous about the fulfillment of them. As a consequence, the peevish and exacting constituency never receives even its just demands from any government, and their sitting member, as a rule, retains his seat for one session only.

At the finish of the session he cannot receive the re-nomination, for the reason of his not making good his numerous promises. Give a member freedom to exercise his own judgment, conscience and will-power, and, if he is sincere in his desire to do his duty, his constituents will not suffer.

The common opinion to-day, even amongst educated people, is that Parliament is but a congress of ambassadors from different and hostile interests, which interests must be maintained regardless of the cost or injury or injustice to the other agents or advocates present from other constituencies. On the contrary, it is an assembly where diverse interests hold no important part. Rather it is a deliberative body in which union of interests, of nations, of creeds, holds first and lasting consideration. No local purposes, no local prejudices, should rule the minds of its members; but the general good should always be the prime object of its deliberations.

Burke says to be a good member of Parliament is no easy task. This is especially true, when we look at the conditions of England at the time of Burke's service. He represented the thriving commercial city of Bristol during very troublesome times. The United States were on the verge of a rebellion. The commercial interests of Bristol were centred chiefly on American trade. Contrary to instructions from Bristol, Burke voted that liberal concessions be made to America, and that her trade be less restricted. If these concessions were granted, Bristol would suffer greatly industrially. Burke listened, not to the impassioned demands of his hot-blooded constituents, but rather to his cool sense of justice for the oppressed. This conscientious and honest act of his cost Burke his re-election as a member, but that did not deter him from acting always for the greater good of the majority of people in America, in opposition to the lesser number in Bristol who would have profited had he acted otherwise. Taking, as an example, this action of Burke's, it is evident that a good member must put aside his own feelings, his local interests, and always keep before his mind that he is a member for a great nation, whose wide-spread interests must ever be considered, must be compared, must be reconciled when at all possible. Above all, he should not forget that he is a member of a Monarchy, whose rights, and those of the King, must be preserved diligently. "A constitution," says Burke, "made up of balanced powers must ever be a critical thing. As such I mean to touch that part of it which comes within my reach." So should it be with all representatives in Parliament.

P. C. HARRIS, '11.

BEYOND THE CITY.

ITH talking of subjects that were of mutual interest, and gazing contentedly at the lazy old Chelsea hills bedecked in delicate, stately beauty, the hours flew by until it was time to leave the song of the rapids, the wide, pleasant river, the russet and golden forest, and turn homeward. There on the crest .of the little overhanging promontory peaking through the branches came beams of subdued light. And going quickly forward we caught here and there glimpses of the sparkling orb. Then in the east we stood facing the crimson disk. It was a scene of sublime beauty, this October sunset. And perhaps it is unjust, even cruel, to attempt to describe in words what the senses alone interpreted: a little broken cliff dropping below us to the beach, a sweeping bay to the left, a long narrow neck in the distance studded with sparse elms, whose tinted leaves fluttered timidly to earth like the first ventures forth of the robin's downy brood; another such peninsula but tinier; and, far over, just beyond the reach of the two eager arms, an island nestled in the luminary's path, strangely characteristic with its tall, frowning evergreens indignant to condemnation at the fickleness of their companions. Falling draperies and filmy curtains dimming the western hills gave to the far-reaching, picturesque slopes and the hazy horizon rather the semblance of a sweet dream of the unwritten past, than perchance the result of the fairies' mystic art on the vast autumnal woods.

The sun dipped slowly but joyfully down beneath a little mirthful cloud, and soon, too soon, his golden, mellowing arc had vanished behind the hills. The pretty shades faded from the canopy over head, the water's surface lost the portrayal of the gentle hues, the forest clothed itself in stern composure, a hallowed light settled on the trees and yellow sward; everywhere grave, silent spirits seemed to sit wrapt in their concave chests, each unmindful of his fellow, and all lost in deep meditation.

Amid the excessive grandeur of such surroundings we little mortals felt foolishly out of keeping, and strolled away from the solitude of the river and the forest toward the sounds of the noisesome town.

W. GRACE, '11.

The Drink Question.

(CLASS DEBATE.)

HE question to be discussed presently is that it would be better for the common good to have the manufacture, importation and sale of intoxicating liquors carried on exclusively by the Government instead of by licensed houses. To grasp this liquor problem with all its importance and vitality, yes and with all its mortality it might be well that we take a glimpse at the sad past and a good look at the still sadder present.

We have heard it said that pride is the root of all evil, that money is the ruin of young men; but the root of all evil and the ruin of young men is the tyrannous and lasting reign of whiskey. This infamous and diabolical agent in human life is not of recent origin or appearance. Its advent was almost simultaneous with the advent of man; and it seems that its departure will be with the extinction of rational life. During pre-historic times it curled like an adder in the cradle of the human race, and from it men sucked the venomous milk that brought destruction and eternal ruin into their lives. After the many thousands of years which have elapsed, its viperous form is still at large; it has followed man to the ends of the earth, its embrace is as frequent, as deadly, as ever. Take whiskey and its depraving influences away and man compares favorably with an angel; he is then indeed "the noblest work of God," but make him a creature of this evil habit and the poor inebriate is not only deprived of all that gives superiority over the brute, but accursed with characteristics which make him resemble the most hideous of infernal beings. Every generation has offered in sacrifice the mortal and immortal lives of thousands on this altar of intemperance. Every year enrolls great numbers who are to live wretched lives in subjection to whiskey and its train of vices. Every day is the anniversary of the bitter end of some drunken, sinful, disgraceful, and worse than useless life.

It is not necessary, however, to enlarge very extensively on the universal and most serious injury which is being done by drink, and the bane which it is on the whole world. It is equally unnecessary to urge the importance of every possible means that the human mind is capable of divising being brought into play to stay the mortal ravage of drunkenness. But it is necessary that the drink problem, like other important questions, be studied in all its different phases. The nature of this traffic and more particularly the nature of those who are addicted to liquor have to be thoroughly understood.

One undisputed fact is that an individual in any business let alone in the liquor business cannot be relied upon to do what is right by others. Even within the precincts of the law the proprietors of hotels have made and are making most outrageous moral and social sacrifices to further their own selfish ends. And with regard to the whiskey business, not only the proprietors but their patrons also have to be watched and guarded by the civic authorities, else a larger percentage of them would be ruined.

The principal means employed for the limitation of intemperance have been: first, Prohibition; second, the restriction of the manufacture and sale of intoxicating drinks to licensed houses; third, exclusive control by the government.

Now experience with prohibitionary legislation has brought into clear relief the fact that it is very doubtful whether it suppresses to any extent the consumption of whiskey. Especially where it is not supported by public opinion, Prohibition is totally impotent and establishes a condition of affairs much worse than does any other system. Private houses instead of public apartments are in many cases converted into bar-rooms. The clubroom is made a rendezvous for those who wish to indulge in revelry and debauchery. Illicit selling is developed; the law is evaded in every possible way; and often under these restrictions men will drink to excess which they would not do if they had more liberty. Consequently, the real and effective prohibition resolves itself into a choice of licensed houses or government control.

When one considers the first method and knows the evil of which it is the direct cause, if God has given him even in the smallest measure the faculty of judging; if he has eyes to see and ears to hear of the atrocities perpetrated under the influence or as a consequence of whiskey; if he values to any extent domestic happiness, decent living, respectable character, physical, mental and moral health; if the faintest rays of civilization and christianity have penetrated and become part of his being; if he be not leagued with Satan in the spread of immorality, impurity and the damnation of souls, surely he will condemn in the most express and unrestricting terms the existence of licensed whiskey houses.

Let us examine this system and see what it does for the cause of temperance. Its first act is to confer on a certain few the prerogative of selling whiskey; and those who are chosen to be thus favored in many instances are not the most deserving. In any case those who hold licenses to sell spirtuous liquors are not in that business merely because they want to be in business and make a livelihood; but because they know it to be extremely lucrative. They are there to make money, and to that end the majority of them will violate every specific and instructive law. They will sell liquor to men already intoxicated, to habitual drunkards, and to minors. They will adulterate their whiskey, sell after prohibited hours, make a mockery of the Sabbath. and practice every dishonesty to amass a little wealth which is nothing but blood money drawn principally from the poorer classes. In many cases the walls are bedecked with filthy and obscene paintings, alluring musicians draw the wretched frequenters of these places from one degrading vice to another; in adjoining rooms gambling is permitted, and other more appalling sensualities tolerated. It does not take many nights of this debauchery to change a virtuous young man to one in whom the passions have undisputed sway, and finally leave totally subjected to whiskey and its concomitant vices. This is what constitutes the greater part of the evil and makes of this system one without a single redeeming feature.

If the proprietor would permit only moderate drinking in his bar, there would be less cases of paralysis, consumption and insanity in our hospitals and asylums; there would be less domestic ruin, less neglect of social duties, less disgust for work, less misery, theft and crime. But the avaricious hotel keeper is selfish in the extreme. He knows the evil results of his malicious traffic, but money is his God, and the pauperism and wretchedness which he spreads broadcast are but insignificant considerations.

It does not require very much demonstration to conclude that any system does more for the common good than the license system, and that therefore government control does. But while supporting this system in preference to others we do not mean to present it as a panacea for all the evils consequent on drink, only as a preventative for a small fraction of them. Nevertheless the elimination of this small fraction would be an immense im provement on morals, health and society at large. Its superiority may be shown by enumerating a few of its advantages.

In the first place, the very large revenues of hotel proprietors would go into the government coffers. Liquors would not be adulterated as they are under the license system, for the simple reason that brewers and brewing companies would not have the controlling interest in any, let alone the majority of the hotels. Proper officials being placed in charge, bar-rooms would be places for drinking only and not for other abominations. Liquor would not be sold to persons already intoxicated or to minors, and the law would be kept to the very letter.

It is not assuming too much to assure ourselves that these advantages would be realized under government control of the liquor traffic because the officials would be responsible to the people and a proper government would do all in its power to minimize the drink evils.

J. T. BRENNAN, '10·

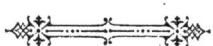

Constitutional Aspect of the School Question

Editor Review,—As so much has been written and spoken upon the school clauses of the Autonomy bill, I beg you to publish my views of the important matter, which I hope may throw some light on it and in the interest of a better understanding. The question should be discussed in a non-political spirit. Those who have discussed the school clauses are gentlemen who would disdain to avoid their obligations as private individuals, and I believe they would not urge the Imperial or Canadian governments or parliaments to avoid their obligations; hence, I will endeavor to point out the obligations and guarantees which I consider exist in favor of the Roman Catholics of the Dominions, east of the Rocky Mountains, to maintain their schools, as it seems best to themselves.

Prior to the treaty of Utrecht, 1713, France was possessed of the Hudson Bay country, which was occupied by its subjects, and by Article 10 of the treaty that country was restored to Great Britain, and under Article 14 those of the subjects of France who were willing to remain there and to be subject to the kingdom of Great Britain were to enjoy the free exercise of their religion according to the usage of the church of Rome, etc.

The articles of the capitulation of Quebec, 1759, contain similar provisions, and the articles of the capitulation of Montreal, 1760, contain more extended provisions and reservations in that respect, and among other things specially include all their communities, which include the schools and teachers thereof respectively.

The Treaty of Paris, 1763, called the Definitive Treaty, recites the Treaty of Utrecht and incorporates it with other treaties named in it and declares that the guarantees of Great Britain shall serve as a basis and foundation to the peace and to the present treaty, and for that purpose they are all renewed and confirmed in the best form, so that they are to be exactly observed for the future in their whole tenor and religiously executed on all sides, and the said parties declare that they will not suffer any privileges, favors or indulgences to subsist, contrary to the treaties above confirmed, and by Article 4 the King of France cedes and guarantees to His Britannic Majesty in full right Canada with all its dependencies, and His Britannic Majesty on his side agrees to grant the liberty of the Catholic religion to the inhabitants of Canada, and that he would consequently give the most precise and most effectual orders that his new Roman Catholic subjects might profess the worship of their religion according to the rites of the Romish church, as far as the laws of Great Britain permit.

In order to apply the terms of these treaties reference should be made to the articles of capitulation of Quebec and Montreal in which the provisions and reservations as accorded at the time are fully set forth, for the free exercise of the Roman Catholic religion, and to the end that the bishops, chapters, priests, cures, missionaries, nuns and all their communties should be free to exercise all the jurisdiction they exercised under the French Dominion.

Then follows the Quebec Act, 1774, an Imperial enactment, which after reciting the definitive treaty, confirms it and authorizes and constitutes a council for the government of the affairs of the province with power and authority to make ordinances for its peace, welfare and good government, and Sections 5 and 6 enact that His Majesty's subjects professing the religion of the church of Rome and their clergy should enjoy the rights and privileges safeguarded by the said treaty, and Section 15 provides

that no ordinance touching religion, shall be of any force or effect. until the same shall have received His Majesty's approbation.

The Constitutional Act, 1791, also an Imperial enactment,
not only does not affect the sections of the Quebec Act above
referred to but establishes a legislative council and assembly in
each province with power to make laws for the peace, welfare and
good government thereof, and Section 42 after reciting the Quebec Act provides that the legislatures shall not vary or repeal
any act or acts which relate to or affect any religious form or
mode of worship, or which shall in any manner relate to or affect
the payment, among others, of teachers, until every such act shall
previous to any declaration or significance of the King's assent
thereto be laid before both houses of parliament in Great Britain.

· The Union Act, 1840, also an Imperial enactment, authorized
the reunion of the provinces with one legislative council and assembly, authorized to make laws for the peace, welfare and good
government of the province of Canada, such laws not being re-
pugnant to that act or to such parts of the Constitutional Act
as are not thereby repealed or to any act made or to be made
and not thereby repealed, and Section 42 contains provisions
identical with those contained in Section 42 of the act of 1791.

Thus stood our constitution at the time of the passing of the
Confederation Act. The Imperial parliament had authorized the
parliament of Canada to legislate subjects to the reservations
and restrictions above referred to, and those powers have in no
way been enlarged in the direction mentioned by the British
North America Act which authorized the federal union with
a constitution similar in principle to that of the United Kingdom.
If this should be claimed as a transfer of the reserved power,
which I do not admit, then our parliament would assume the
powers and would necessarily have to follow the action of the
Imperial parliament which never legislates to alter, vary or pre-
judicially affect treaties. In the distribution of legislative powers Section 93 provides that the legislatures may   exclusively
make laws in relation to education, subject, however, to the provisions and restrictions in its sub-sections contained. The Confederation Amendment Act, 1871, confers power on the parliament of Canada to establish new provinces and make provision
for their constitution and administration and for the passing
of laws for the peace, welfare and good government of such
provinces. Section 5 declares that the Manitoba Act, 1870; shall
.be deemed valid and effectual, and Section 22 of the Manitoba

Act contains identical provisions with Section 93 and its sub-sections, except that in sub-section 1 the words "or practice" are added, which emphasizes the intended restrictions.

The question therefore apparently resolves itself into one of constitutional power. The Dominion parliament ought to follow the power delegated to it on the subject. If it cannot for political or other reasons arrive at a satisfactory conclusion, the matter should be referred either to the Imperial parliament or to the privy council. I apprehend, however, if our parliament will apply itself to the question in a non-political spirit, that it will readily reach the conclusion applicable to the subject and within the competence of its power.

Section 146 of the B. N. A. Act authorizes the admission of Rupert's Land and the North Western territory into the union on terms subject to the provisions of that act. This section manifests the intention of the Imperial parliament in respect of the terms upon which new provinces were to enter the union thereafter.

Lord Mansfield in delivering the unanimous judgment of the court in Campbell vs. Hall states that articles of capitulation upon which the country is surrendered, and treaties of peace by which it is ceded, are sacred and inviolate according to their true intent and meaning.

Sir John Bourinot (lecture Jan., 1901) says: "It is now an admitted principle that the Dominion is practically supreme in the exercise of all legislative rights and privileges set forth in the B. N. A. Act, 1867, so long as her legislative action does not conflict with the treaty obligations of the parent state."

Bourinot (Procedure, p. 5): "Canada became a possession of Great Britain by the terms of capitulation on 8th September, 1760. By these terms Great Britain bound herself to allow the French-Canadians the free exercise of their religion and certain specified fraternities and all communities of religieuses were guaranteed the possession of their goods, constitution and privileges. These terms were included in the Treaty of Paris. In 1774 parliament (Imperial) intervened in Canadian affairs and a system of government was granted to Canada by the Quebec Act (p. 10). Opposition was raised principally in the change from English law to the laws and usages of Canada. The Imperial parliament, however, was influenced by desire to adjust the government of the province and to conciliate the majority."

Garneau No. 2, page 233, also refers to the subject, and both cite the remarks of the King, who in assenting to the bills signalled the Quebec Act for special commendation "as being founded in the plainest principles of justice and humanity and that he doubted not it would have the best effects by calming the inquietudes and promoting the well being of our Canadian subjects."

Todd, No. 1, page 610: "The constitutional power appertaining to parliament in respect of treaties is limited. It has no power to change or modify in any way a treaty itself (p. 27). The mother country has never parted with the claim of ultimate supreme authority (pp. 34-35). Powers reserved relate to all questions which involve the relations of British dependencies, formation of treaties, etc."

In the argument of the Brophy case it was contended that the decision in the Barrett case was conclusive, that no rights or privileges existing by law or practice at the union had been affected or infringed, but the privy council declared, "that the main issues were not in any way concluded, either by the decision in Barrett's case or by any principle involved in that decision, and that subsection 1 of Section 22 imposes a limitation on the legislative powers, and that any enactment contravening its provisions is beyond the competency of the provincial-legislature, and therefore null and void."

In the same case in referring to the scope of the decision in the Barrett case, the lord chancellor observes "that it seems to have given rise to some misapprehension" and he declared that the appeal was well founded; "that all legitimate ground of complaint would be removed if the system (referring to schools) were supplemented by provisions which would remove the grievance upon which the appeal was founded and were modified so far as might be necessary to give effect to these provisions." The lord chancellor further declared that it must be remembered that the provincial legislature is not in all respects supreme within the province. "Its legislative power is strictly limited. In relation to subjects specified in Sections 91 and 92 the exclusive power of the legislature may be said to be absolute, but this is not so as regards education."

It would seem, therefore, unquestionable that Manitoba is contumacious by its refusal to comply with the clear direction contained in the judgment of the privy council.

His Lordship Bishop Worrell's strong plea for toleration, as well as that of many other Protestants are very commendable and perhaps it will fortify them to know or to be reminded that the origin of separate schools is due to the demands of the Protestants of Upper Canada, which led to the first legislation on that subject, and, secondly, that which gave separate schools for colored children, and that separate schools were first provided for the Protestants of Lower Canada by the Confederation Act.

Hence the right of Roman Catholics to have schools, conducted by themselves, whatever may be the opinions of those in opposition to the subject, are rights reserved and guaranteed to them under the constitution of our country and in the language of the lord chancellor: ''There can be no doubt that the Roman Catholics regarded it as essential that the education of their children should be in accordance with the teaching of their church in schools conducted under the influence and guidance of the authorities of their church.''

I therefore venture the opinion in the light of the foregoing and much that could be added that the only proper school clauses of the autonomy bills ought to be those provided by the Confederation Act; any more or any less would be beyond the competence of our parliament, and according to the observation of the lord chancellor in the Brophy case, in which he declared that the legislature had not exclusive power as regards education, the same declaration applies to the Dominion parliament. I trust therefore that this important matter may be speedily adjusted in accordance with the true spirit of our constitution and forever set at rest.

S. WHITE, K.C.

LITERARY NOTES.

Annual Meeting of the I.U.D.L.

On Saturday, October 16, 1909, at the Undergraduates' Union in Toronto University, the annual meeting of the Inter-University Debating League was held. The business of the meeting was the election of officers, arrangement of schedule for the incoming term. The following gentlemen were elected:—

Honorary President—Rev. J. P. Fallon, O.M.I.

First Vice-President—Dr. S. P. Leacock, McGill.

Second Vice-President—J. F. MacDonald, Queen's.

Third Vice-President—Prof. Kylie, Toronto.

President—P. C. Harris, Ottawa.

First Vice-President—J. T. McNeill, McGill.

Second Vice-President—A. D. Cornett, Queens.

Secy.-Treasurer—F. M. Scott, Toronto.

The preliminary debates will take place Friday, Dec. 3rd, 1909:

Queens at Toronto.

Ottawa at McGill.

Final debates January 21, 1910:

If Ottawa and Queens win, final at Ottawa.

If Ottawa and Toronto win, final at Ottawa.

If Queens and McGill win, final at Queens.

If Toronto and McGill win, final at McGill.

The much-regretted incident which following the losing of the debate at Queens Dec. 4, 1908, was discussed quite exhaustively by the delegates present. Several drastic motions were put by the Queen's representative, but owing to there being no seconder, President Harris ruled the motion out of order. The McGill representative suggested the following motion, which was seconded by the Toronto officer, and duly carried: "Resolved, that the I.U.D.L. Executive puts itself on record as being satisfied with the decision of the judges given at Queen's University in the Queen's-Ottawa debate Dec. 4th, 1908."

"That we regret the charges made against those concerned in that decision, and that we further suggest that the Ottawa University Debating Society make a satisfactory public explanation."

After the regular routine business of financial levies, etc., the meeting adjourned.

University of Ottawa Review

PUBLISHED BY THE STUDENTS.

THE OTTAWA UNIVERSITY REVIEW is the organ of the students. Its object
s to aid the students in their literary development, to chronicle their doings in and out of
class, and to unite more closely to their Alma Mater the students of the past and the present

TERMS:

One dollar a year in advance.   Single copies, 15 cents.   Advertising rates on application.
Address all communications to the "UNIVERSITY OF OTTAWA REVIEW", OTTAWA, ONT.

EDITORIAL STAFF :

J. BRENNAN, '10 ;   A. FLEMING, '11 ;   M. O'GARA, '10 ;
J. BURKE, '10 ;   PH. HARRIS, '11 ;   C. D. O'GORMAN, '10 ;
                         M. SMITH, '10.

Business Managers : C. GAUTHIER '10, ;   D. BREEN, '11.

Our Students are requested to patronize our Advertisers.

| Vol. XII. | OTTAWA, ONT., NOVEMBER, 1909. | No. 2 |

FERRER "THE MARTYR."

How the secular press loves to rant about the seething discontent of Spain, the ignorance and superstition of its people,
the half-idiotic face of its King, and the awful crime committed
against humanity in the martyrdom of Francisco Ferrer.   The
reason is not far to seek—Spain is an eminently Catholic country.
But why should the young King's personal appearance be of such
great interest to our learned scribes?   A young man who can
converse fluently in four or five languages, and who has maintained the full dignity of his high position in the councils of the
nation, to say nothing of his extraordinary proficiency in almost
every branch of manly sport, is surely not much of an idiot
after all, and his features would perhaps compare favourably
with the gin-befuddled faces of some of his self-appointed critics.
As for the ignorance and superstition of the Spanish nation, one
might ask if it exceeds that of any other agricultural and pastoral people; we can at least say this much that so far they have

steered clear of the "Christian Science" and "Spiritism," to whom some of the more enlightened (?) nations are so devoted. The "seething discontent" resolves itself into the hereditary animosity of the Catalonian province towards the rest of Spain. Barcelona, which witnessed the burning of 42 beautiful churches, the destruction of masterpieces by Velasquez and Murillo, and other priceless works of art, and indescribable scenes of violence and barbarity, is notorious as the refuge for all the anarchists of Europe. Ferrer was the leader of this awful bloodshed and destruction, and he led it as an anarchist and atheist. He tried to start riots simultaneously in three cities, Barcelona, Madrid and Valencia, but was successful only in Barcelona. To indicate his character it is sufficient to say that among his effects was found the cheque given to Morales, who afterward committed suicide, for his attempt to kill the King and Queen by throwing a bomb on the day of the coronation. By his execution justice was no more than satisfied. He was given every right in the matter of his defence, and the law was scrupulously observed. It is quite evident that he had been condemned by the consciences of the majority of Spaniards, including those who now profess to be horror-stricken, long before he faced the firing platoon in the fortress of Barcelona. His "martyrdom" is but another fiction of the canting and hypocritical yellow press.

Exchanges.

Among the contributors to the various September exchanges we notice the absence of many familiar names, whom we daresay will be greatly missed by their respective colleges. We have read with pleasure the contributions of these gentlemen in the past, and hope the same success will attend their literary efforts in the future.

We notice for the first time on our table the "Civilian," a fortnightly journal devoted to the interests of the Civil Service of Canada. We congratulate the editorial staff of the "Civilian" on the neat appearance of their journal. Most of the articles of course, have to do with questions re the service; comparisons are made between the Canadian and foreign staffs, and changes suggested. We promise to take an interest in the "Civilian." Many of the graduates of Ottawa College have situations in the local Government offices, and our students will find "Personals" in the "Civilian" is a pleasant supplement to "Priorum Temporum Flores" in the Review.

St. Mary's Sentinel, among other things, contains the life-story of the late Bishop McCloskey of Louisville. St. Mary's College has lost a sincere friend, Kentucky a worthy citizen, and the American Hierarchy a shining light, in the death of this learned and saintly prelate. We append the following:

Bishop McCloskey was a man whose endowments were of such gigantic proportions as to baffle any feeble pen, and to pretend a modest description of his kaleidoscopic activity and influence would be but the merest mockery.

Have you joined the Arctic Circle?

Yes! and they gave me quite a cold reception.—Ex.

We wish space would permit us to insert the whole of an article which appears in the Notre Dame Scholastic, under the title "The Perfect Service.". We have never read anything containing better advice for young students. Every phase of college life is touched upon, every question involved is dealt with. "The trained body," The developed mind," "Health," "Athletics," and "Sowing Wild Oats" are some of the topics discussed.

Besides the above mentioned, we beg to acknowledge receipt of the following: "The Patrician," "The Columbiad," "Trinity University Review," "The Martlet," "Holy Cross Purple," "St. Mary's Sentinel," "Assumption College Review," "The Collegian," "Echoes from the Pines," "Hya Yaka," "O.A.C. Review," "Laurel," "Acta Victoriana," "Abbey Student," "Mitre," "St. Mary's Chimes," "Queen's University Journal," "Villa Shield," "Niagara Rainbow," "Xavier," "Vox Weslayana."

Books and Reviews.

The *Nineteenth Century* for October contains an article of much interest to Canadians, by Professor G. M. Wrong, of Toronto University, regarding Canada's attitude towards Great Britain. He prefaces his remarks by commenting upon the rapid growth during recent years of Canadian news in the London dailies. Englishmen are beginning to realize, somewhat reluctantly perhaps, that the well-being of their country is to a large extent bound up in the prosperity of Canada. They are coming to see, in view of what Holland was once able to do, and in view of Germany's naval aggression, that they are no longer secure in their insular isolation, and that it behòoves them to look towards the colonies for assistance. Canadians, on their part, have no immediate fears for the future. They are fully aware of the power of their southern neighbor, but, then, they have had to face this danger so long that it has ceased to cause them anxiety. Moreover, they know that in the event of European interference they would be backed up by the United States. He then goes on to comment upon the narrow lines upon which the Canadian press is conducted and the absence of matter of world-wide interest. He dwells upon the social views of the Englishman and the Canadian, showing that in the former case they are definitely fixed, while in the latter they are in a state of formation. The Englishman looks on the Canadian as raw and crude, though his crudeness be that of strength, while the Canadian possessing respect for the nobility yet is in heart a republican. According to Prof. Wrong, Canada is not becoming Americanized, but is growing more confident of herself, and is quickly losing all thought of political union. This separation is marked by the views in both countries on the administration of justice, by the difference in the tone of the press and by different political ideals. Thus it is inconceivable to a Canadian that the head of a government should be at variance with his legislature, as was the case at one time with Roosevelt. The growth in English politics during the past fifty years has been assimilated by Canada and has helped to bring the two countries together. Again, as it would be next to impossible for the United States and Canada to be united under one government, owing to the great extent of territory, so would it be impossible to unite Great Britain and Canada; besides, in countries so widely separated there is no common opinion to which to appeal. Though not politically united, yet the burdens of government might be more equally divided. Thus there should be a levelling down in England and a levelling up in Canada. Finally, should Canada refuse to share part of the burden in some matters, might not the parent state claim the same privilege? The writer then concludes that the problems of empire are wellnigh insoluble and he urges that we dwell not so much upon the blunders made by England in her treatment of us, but rather upon the sacrifices made on our behalf.

The October number of the *Contemporary Review* has a timely article on the recent troubles in Catalonia. It points out that the revolutionary movement developed suddenly from an anti-war demonstration, and at first had the universal sympathy of all classes, even to the point of armed resistance; but the anarchistic tendencies of the mob, which resulted in such deplorable excesses, alienated the better elements. They withdrew and the movement collapsed. It then goes on to say that the revolution will be a blessing to Barcelona and to Spain in general, for separation, never more than an impracticable dream, has disappeared for the present. Carlism is a lost cause, and is only kept alive for the sake of personal political ends and as a wholesome Damoclean sword to induce the present government to behave itself. If there is to be a conflict in Spain it will be between the monarchy and republic with the ballot-box and newspapers as weapons.

Where the Fishers Go, or *The Story of Labrador*, by Rev. P. W. Browne, published by Cochrane Company, New York.

This interesting book, which has just been published, will receive a warm welcome from the best reading public in Canada and elsewhere, but especially ought it to be gladly received among the friends of the author in Ottawa University, where he is a professor. Father Browne has succeeded in telling the story of "the fishers' land" in a manner well adapted to catch the interests of the reader in the very first page and of holding it to the very end. One does not read many pages before experiencing some of the fascination for this wild and desolate country which prompted the author "to sail away to the land of myriad charms." A pleasing feature of the book lies in the fact that while it contains a vast quantity of information, it is so presented that the reader is not overwhelmed by it, but absorbs it gradually in the course of the narrative. The work is copiously illustrated throughout with beautiful photographs taken from first hand sources. These succeed in bringing the descriptions home to the reader more clearly than any other form of illustration could possibly do.

The Making of Mortlake, by J. E. Copus, S.J., published by Benziger Bros.

This is a good wholesome story for boys, well told, and containing much of interest to the college boy. It gives a good characterization of the American Catholic boy in all his phases. The interest centres in the attempt made by kind prefects and interested boy friends to reform a young delinquent named Mortlake. How successful their efforts were and why must be discovered by the reader, for to enlarge upon them would be to tell the whole story.

Among the Magazines.

The word Almanac originally designated a permanent table, showing the apparent movement of celestial bodies. The first was published by Purbach in 1457. Soon almanacs were published by magicians, who preyed upon the innocent and superstitious. King Henry III. of France placed certain restrictions upon such publications, while Charles IX required the approval of the diocesan bishop.

Much valuable information is found in almanacs of later date. Among the recent and much improved is the Catholic Home Annual for 1910. Besides the calendar for the year, anniversaries of saints, astronomical calculations, feast and fast days, it contains a wealth of valuable data which will be useful to all in their daily intercourse with others.

The pages of the Catholic Home Annual are filled with novelettes and stories of more than ordinary interest. The names of the best Catholic authors are a sufficient guaranty of their worth. Among these are Mary T. Waggaman, Marion Ames Taggart, Maud Regan, Jerome Harte, Magdalen Rock, Richard Aumerle, Cahir Healy, and others.

A well edited and assorted review of the year's events completes what will prove to be the most popular annual of the year. It should be welcomed and find a place in every Catholic home. (New York, Benziger Brothers, 25 cents.)

In an article entitled "Early Session at Ottawa," in the current number of the "America," we notice that it says that the opening of the next session of the Canadian Parliament will take place on November 11. This is the earliest date since 1896, when the present government got into power. The reason is the introduction of a bill for the erection of a Canadian navy, and the participation of Canada in Imperial defence. One great difficulty will be to determine whether the estimated expenditure of twnety million dollars will be met by a loan or by taxation. Besides this an effort will be made to change the rules of debate so as to expedite parliamentary work.

The "America" also quotes La Civilta Cattolica under the heading, "Depopulation in Civilized Countries." The wave has affected France particularly, then England, and the Eastern States. The principles of Anti-Christian "laicism" as most fully adopted in France are given as the cause.

Notre Dame Scholastic describes the true College spirit as being more fidelity to the institution, acquaintance with her traditions, sympathy with her purposes, and obedience to her regulations, than lustiness of throat at the football game.

The Educational Review in "How to Make Progress" declares the mark of excellent tutorship is to teach more, and to limit greatly the time given to test work. The best plan in new work is to teach the same subject twice, and thereby save time and trouble later.

Under the head of "The Coming Battle," the Extension introduces us to the struggle of the future, Science versus Faith. But Faith alone is armed. Science replies to the question, "Is there a God?"—"I do not know"; "Is there a Heaven?"—I do not know"; "Do you exist?"—"I do not know." Doubting everything, the enemy of Christianity has nothing firm upon which to stand.

Priorum Temporum Flores.

Mr. J. Lajoie, matriculant of '07, figured prominently on the Toronto Varsity team in the College-Varsity game played here on Saturday, Oct. 30th. "Jerry," while a student at Ottawa University, was well known in baseball and football circles, and while in the Capital did not fail to pay us a visit. On Sunday he returned to Toronto, where he is pursuing a medical course at Varsity.

Mr. V. K. O'Gorman, '09, has commenced a medical course at Toronto Varsity.

Among those who witnessed the recent College-Varsity game at Toronto was Mr. W. P. Breen, who as we chronicled before, is continuing his studies in Buffalo at Canisius College. Mr. Breen praises highly the Buffalo institution, but is still of the opinion that there is no place like home.

Mr. Jean Courtois, '09, accompanied the McGill students and witnessed their game against College on Nov. 6th. While here "Jean" did not forget his Alma Mater. He remained in the city for a few days.

Rev. J. J. Quilty, '97, of Douglas, paid a flying visit to the University a few weeks ago.

Rev. W. H. Dooner, '05, of Renfrew, and Rev. J. Harrington, '05, of Eganville, were in the city a few weeks ago. While here they seized the opportunity of seeing the first game of the season between Ottawa City and Hamilton Tigers.

After an absence of three years, Mr. C. O'Halloran, a former student of Ottawa University, has returned to complete. his course.

Mr. M. O'Neil is continuing his theological course in Ottawa Seminary.

Mr. E. II. McCarthy, '09, has entered Rochester Seminary, N. Y.

Mr. M. F. Deahy, '09, is at present a student at Ann Arbor, Michigan.

Mr. J. Connaghan, '09, passed through the city last week on his way to Osgoode Hall, where he contemplates taking up a course in law.

Mr. B. Oliver, '10, has recently returned from Toronto where he purchased a fine high-powered automobile. He treated some of the faculty to a very speedy ride on the Richmond road the other day.

J. Goodwin, '06, is taking up a law course in Montreal.

Dr. Leacy, '96, and Mr. R. Byrnes, '05' have lately joined the Benedicts. Congratulations!

We lately received word of the ordination of Rev. George D. Boucher, '04, which took place in Cincinnati last June. Ad multos annos!

Obituary.

JUDGE J. J. CURRAN, '58.

It was with feelings of the deepest regret that the news concerning the death of Judge J. J. Curran reached us last month. Despite the fact that his death was a great blow to his many friends in Ottawa, nevertheless, they had the sweet consolation of knowing that his life was one of example; and being strengthened by all the graces that the Catholic Church could bestow, his end was a fit termination to a career of the highest merit and public utility.

Hon. John Joseph Curran was born in Montreal in the year 1842. He received his primary education at St. Mary's College in that city, afterwards entering the University of Ottawa, and last by McGill University, where he obtained his degree of B. C. L. in 1862. The following year he was admitted to the Bar, and practised in his own city. He was afterwards made a Q.C. of the City of Quebec, and of the Dominion a few years later. In 1892, when a Law Faculty was organized in connection with Ottawa University, he was made Vice-Dean and appointed to one of the chairs, and, moreover, he was amongst the first upon whom the degree of LL.D. was conferred by that institution. He was finally elevated to the Bench as Puisne Judge of the Superior Court in 1895, which title he retained until his death.

As a former student he was known to have been the possessor of remarkable talent and undaunted energy, bringing upon him the esteem and respect of his comrades. The late Judge was always among the warmest admirers and sympathizers of Alma Mater, never missing an opportunity of assisting at her more important gatherings. The last time we had the honour of having the late Honourable gentleman in our midst was on the memorable occasion of the laying of the corner-stone of our New Arts Building in which he took a prominent part.

His kindly sympathy and breadth of mind were well known to all with whom he came in contact. He was a distinguished orator and a great lecturer, and did a great deal in furthering the interests of the Catholic religion. It was his oratorical powers that won for him the various high positions he held in life, and that secured for him such renown, not only in political, but also social circles.

Much sympathy is felt for the friends of the deceased in their sad bereavement.

Personals.

The Rev. Fathers Murphy and Poli have returned from the plenary council, but needless to say have no information for us regarding the work of that body.

Very Rev. Fathers Walsh and Bunoz, O.M.I., spent a day in Ottawa on their way to Toronto and Buffalo.

Canon Corkery of Pakenham paid us a visit during the past week.

The whole student body will be glad to know that Dr. Chabot the genial College physician, is rapidly recovering from a serious operation performed in Montreal.

Father Devine, S.J., the well known author and able editor of the Messenger of the Sacred Heart, paid us a visit during the past week, while attending the funeral of his mother. To the Rev. gentleman and Sister Loyola we extend sympathy.

Alderman T. Church of Toronto gave the boys a good time while in the Queen City, in spite of the fact that it was "simply awful."

The members of the Second team, accompanied by Rev. Fathers S. and M. Murphy, journeyed to Arnprior Monday and there played a friendly game of football with the team of that town, which resulted in the home team, captained by J. Sullivan, and managed by J. MacDonald, two old students, being defeated.

The III. team, the pride of the College, in the genial company of Rev. Fathers P. J. Hammersley and D. Finnegan, travelled ti the town of Renfrew for their Thanksgiving Day turkey, and incidentally to play a game of football with the Collegiate squad of that town. Our boys were victorious.

Athletics.

FORE NOTE.

In last month's issue of The Review, the "Sporting Editor" did not lose himself in optimistic prognostications concerning the prospects for a winning team, consequently he is saved the humiliating task of "swallowing" what he wrote. It would afford the keenest pleasure to be in a position to report six victories, but, unfortunately, five of the games played found "our team's" score very much on the short side. To attempt to explain away the defeats through the time-worn adage, "Hard Luck," would be directly at variance with truth. To attempt to point out the weak spots on the team might be taken as a personal "knock," so the writer will not burden you by adding his humble opinion to the numberless ones already expressed on all sides. The players themselves perhaps have their own opinions, the professors of the University surely have theirs, and the general public, too, has one carefully thought out. What it is, perhaps it is better for us not to know, for we may get an answer that would surprise us.

GAME NUMBER ONE.

McGill (20) — Ottawa College (3).

October 9th, 1909.

The first game of the Intercollegiate season 1909 was played at McGill Grounds on Saturday, October 9th, and resulted in the above score. Ottawa's three points were scored with a beautiful drop goal kicked by Capt. Charles Arthur O'Neill. The game throughout was clean, open, entertaining and fairly fast, not one penalty was handed out. Unfortunately for the team, Gilligan and Conway were knocked out and had to be carried from the field. Our team was a lot lighter than McGill, but played together well and played hard all the time. The first half ended 7-0 for McGill. In the second half McGill piled up the score to 20, while our team got but three (3). The heavy McGill line were mainly responsible for the defeat, though the back division played a very steady game.

Peter Conway and Bert Gilligan were knocked out in this game and were forced to retire. A defeat on McGill grounds is nothing novel. Ottawa College has not won a game there since it entered the Intercollegiate Union in 1905. Nor has McGill team been able to pull out a victory at Varsity Oval in years, so the teams break even on home and home games.

The team was:—Full back, Gilligan; halves, O'Neill (Capt.), Contway, Chartrand, W.; quarter, Muzanti; scrimmagers, Whibbs, Chartrand, II., Fleming,; wings, Sullivan, Kinsella, Smith, Conway, Quilty, Belanger.

GAME NUMBER TWO.

Ottawa College (11) — Queen's (6).

October 16th, 1906.

The team signalized the opening of the Intercollegiate Football season in Ottawa by winning a gruelling game from Queen's at Varsity Oval on the above date, the final score being 11 to 6 with the "garnet and grey" standard bearers in the lead. Queen's had the score 4 to 0 when the teams crossed over for the second half, but the "boys" by a wholesome finish wiped out the plurality in short order, finishing winners by a comfortable margin. About fifteen hundred Ottawans and several hundred Kingstonians witnessed the game.

Queen's total of tallies was made by rouges, while College

scored a converted try, a goal from the field, and two rouges.

Several sensational plays were pulled off on the slippery sod, "Mike" Smith tearing off a number of pretty dashes for useful gains. He scored the only touchdown College got, by intercepting a pass. W. Chartrand was responsible for the drop-goal, putting the "pigskin" over the bar for three points from the twenty-five yard line. "Pete" Conway received painful injuries by being "twisted" around the goal post. His back was severely wrenched, and he was conveyed to the hospital in the "official ambulance."

Queen's Club sent to the Intercollegiate secretary, P. C. Harris, an official protest against the rulings of Referee Harvey Pulford, Umpire W. Foran, and Touch Line Judge Jos. Fahey. They claimed they were "robbed" of a touchdown by a decision of the lineman. The protest will be dealt with by the executive of the Union at its first meeting.

The line-up of our team was as follows:—Full back, P. Conway; half-backs, W. Chartrand, J. Contway, H. Chartrand; quarter, J. Muzanti; scrimmagers, Fleming, Loftus, Dubois; wings, Sullivan, Whibbs, Quilty, Smith, **Belanger, Gilligan.

*Replaced by Phol.

**Replaced by Kinsella.

GAME NUMBER THREE.

Toronto Varsity (63) — Ottawa Varsity (2).

At Toronto, Oct. 23, 1909.

Ottawa Varsity football team travelled to Ald. T. L. Church's town, by name Toronto, to play a scheduled game against the team representing Toronto University. That they did not make much of an impression on the opposing fourteen is quite apparent by the diversity in the indicated scores. Our team was almost smothered under an avalanche of points. The huge total was made by Toronto crossing our goal-line for eleven touchdowns and diverse other things, such as rouges, converted trys, and dead ball line kicks. Ottawa's handsome total was secured by a rouge in each half.

Misses of the back division, consisting of fumbles, poor kicking, and careless passing, were directly responsible for the defeat. The team displayed poor tackling powers, and this perhaps was partly accountable for Varsity's repeated long runs of 60, 70, 80 and 90 yards for touchdowns.

The press is unanimous in its praise of Capt. O'Neil's, Bert

Gilligan's and Sylvester Quilty's all round good playing. Quilty unfortunately for the team, was severely injured early in the game. O'Neill, though suffering from a severely sprained ankle, gamely "stayed in the game" to the finish. Gilligan received a bad shaking up from his numerous tackles of the "Big Moose" Lawson, but lasted out the full game. Smith, Kinsella, Loftus and Sullivan played steady games in their respective positions.

For Toronto, Gall, Lawson and Newton were the stars, in fact the whole team was a "star" aggregation, playing a faultless brand of ball all afternoon.

The following players participated in the slaughter: Gilligan, Contway, Capt. O'Neill, Muzanti, Dubois, Loftus, Chartrand, Kinsella, Quilty, Belanger, Smith, Whibbs, Sullivan, J. Brennan.

Rev. W. J. Stanton, Hon. Pres. of the Intercollegiate Union; Rev. Father Turcotte, coach, and Winfield Hackett, treasurer, accompanied the team on the memorable trip.

GAME NUMBER FOUR.

Ottawa City (17) — Ottawa Varsity (12).

At Ottawa, Oct. 25, 1909.

The annual football game between the above mentioned teams took place on Thanksgiving Day before a small but enthusiastic crowd of 1,500 people. Neither team was at full strength. Ottawa scored first, getting a rouge on a long kick soon after the start of the play, this being the only score in the first quarter.

College swung into the game hard and fast in the second quarter, Kinsella skirting the end for a brilliant touchdown, Chartrand converting it. Then a touch in goal and the half was ended with College leading, 7 to 1.

Ottawas had the better of the third quarter, scoring two tries, unconverted, and one rouge for 11 points while College was blanked. This made the score 12 to 7, and each team got a try in the last period, putting the city team in the lead, 17 to 12. Ottawa's last touchdown was a very questionable one, but Referee Hobart said it was so, and we'll let it go at that.

Although the Interprovincial leaders took us into camp, they had to "go some" to do it. College were the equals of their opponents on the line, but in the comparison of the back-lines College loses. By this win Ottawa captures the "Carling Trophy," individual cups, and the championship of the city. The team was as follows:—Gilligan, W. Chartrand, H. Chartrand,

Contway, Muzanti, Dubois, Fleming, Loftus, Whibbs, Sullivan, Quilty, Smith, Kinsella, Belanger, Phol.

Referee, Sid. Hobart; umpire, Fred Chittick; line judges, Dr. S. M. Nagle, P. C. Harris.

M. J. Smith, Sylvester Quilty, Bert Gilligan, Sullivan, Kinsella and Muzanti were the players who performed in a stellar manner. The sure catching of O'Neill was much missed by his inability to play, not having recovered from the injuries received in Toronto.

GAME NUMBER FIVE.

Toronto Varsity (46) — Ottawa Varsity (4).

At Ottawa, Oct. 30th, 1909.

As was to be expected, the team, in the return match with Toronto, met with another defeat. Many were the comments after the game, but the truth is we were beaten by a heavier and headier team, though one not quite so strong as the wearers of the Blue and White in 1908.

The story of the game is best followed by glancing at the score summary. It will give a fair idea of how much chance we ever had of pulling out a victory. The scoring:—

1st quarters—Varsity, touch (Lawson) and convert (6); Varsity, goal from field (Gall) 3; Varsity, touch (Gall) and convert (6).

2nd quarter—Varsity, rouge 1; Varsity, touch (Lawson) and convert (6); Varsity, touch (Lawson) and convert ,6); Varsity, touch (Muir) aid convert (6).

3rd quarter—College, touch in goal (1); Varsity, rouge (1); College, forced rouge (2); College, rouge (1).

4th quarters—Varsity, touch (Lawson), 5; Varsity, rouge (1); Varsity, touch, (Thompson) 5.

Our team were most unfortunate in the work of the back division, for a lot of "muffing" was done there, and a number of good chances consequently lost. H. Chartrand, who replaced O'Neill at centre half, made a lot of costly fumbles, while the other half-backs were not up to the standard, Gilligan, on a low plunge through Varsity's line, received a painful injury to his knee and shoulder, and had to be carried off the field. "Mike"

Smith, while playing his usual dashing game, received a nasty accidental kick on the head, and was forced to retire. H. Chartrand's legs went back on him, and a sprained ankle forced him to quit the game. Breen, Phol and Kennedy replaced the injured players. Capt. O'Neil and Kinsella, on account of injuries, did not line up with the team. On the line the plunging gains of Quilty were very spectacular. The following men were in the line-up:—Gilligan, Contway, H. Chartrand, W. Chartrand, Muzanti, Loftus, Dubois, Fleming, Whibbs, Sullivan, Quilty, Smith, Belanger, Brennan.

Referee, Dr. A. H. Wright. Umpire, Dr. Patterson.

GAME NUMBER SIX.

McGill (15) — Ottawa Varsity (2).

Varsity Oval, Nov. 6, 1909.

The last game of the season in Ottawa in the Intercollegiate Union resulted in a decisive win for old McGill. This is the first time in College football that the red and white has lowered the colors of Varsity on the Oval.

At all stages of the contest, McGill seemed to have the game well in hand. Their back division protected by the usual beefy line played a good sure game, but not a brilliant one. Yet Ottawa never seemed to get going. Brainless passing and absurd back-running materially helped to hand the game to McGill. The line played its usual steady game, but this was discounted by the lack of heady playing of the half-back line.

The first half ended 11-0 for McGill. The last half was more evenly contested, but McGill scored four more points, while Ottawa could only gain two. Capt. Dan. Gillmore scored one touch, and Forbes the other. Vaughn, Black and Goodeve played star games. For Ottawa Varsity the most effective players were Gilligan, Quilty, Contway and Smith. The line-up was:— Full, Conway; halves Quilty, Contway, W. Chartrand; quarter, Muzanti; scrimmage, Fleming, Dubois, Loftus; wings, Whibbs, Brennan, Gilligan, Breen, Smith, Belanger.

Timer, W. J. McCaffrey; referee, Dr. Patterson; umpire, T. Savidge; touch linemen, J. Chrysler, P. C. Harris.

STANDING OF THE UNION.

	Won.	Lost.	To Play.
Toronto	5	0	1
Queen's	2	3	1
McGill	2	3	1
Ottawa	1	4	1

LEAGUE AFFAIRS.

An important meeting of the Executive of the Intercollegiate Union was held in Montreal Nov. 1st, at the Windsor Hotel, 8 p.m. The following were present:—

President—V. E. Black, McGill.

1st Vice-Pres.—J. F. McDonald, Queen's.

2nd Vice-Pres.—Robert Y. Cory, Toronto.

Secy.-Treas.—Phil C. Harris, Ottawa.

Committeeman—H. P. Holt (Cadet) R. M. C.

The Queen's protest against the decision in their Ottawa College game was dealt with at length by the representatives of the interested clubs. Aftr several hours' discussion, a vote was taken, and it stood 3 to 1 in favor of Secy. Harris' motion "to disallow the protest," because it could not be shown by the Queen's officer how any of his protested points affected the final score. The Union was liable to become disagreeably noted for its number of protested games if things kept on going like this, so for the sake of good sport it was strongly urged by the Ottawa representative to discourage protests as much as possible by throwing them out. Another important point was brought out, namely, that "officials must be supported if the Union desires affairs to go on smoothly." Toronto and McGill officers strongly seconded the sentiments expressed.

The protest of McGill against the final score of their game in Montreal was allowed, because Referee Smaill of the game in question wrote to, and also telephoned to the Secy.-Treas., acknowledging that he had made two errors of judgment, and asked the league to rectify matters.

PUNTS AND DRIBBLES.

The Ottawa College list of injured bids fair to equal if not outnumber the famous "hospital corps" of the champion 1907 team. Happly, the injuries this year are not of a serious nature, and so far no bones have been broken.

The Intercollegiate Union keeps up its record for protested games. Secy.-Treas. P. C. Harris has already received two. Queen's have protested the game played against our team on Oct. 16th. The referee, Harvey Pulford, the umpire, Wm. Foran, and the touch line judge, "Joe" Fahey, all come in for their "meed" of criticism.

"Ch." O'Neill, our valiant captain, kicked a beautiful drop-goal in the Ottawa-McGill game. It saved the team from receiving a humiliating coat of kalsomine. And on our old friend McGill's grounds, too. Horrors!!!

Into the valley of death rode the noble fourteen. Killed and wounded, 63 to 2.

Haven't we heard of a bigger score than that? Oh yes. St. Pat's. (3), Montreal (72). That's going some.

J. Lajoie, of 1906 team, is one of Varsity's mainstays on the line. He plays middle wing.

"Jack" McDonald can't shake off the hoodoo. At Ottawa College he sustained serious injuries "on the good-won." Last year at Varsity he developed "water on the knee." This year after one game with Toronto he fractured a "bone in his left arm." Hard luck, Jack.

P. Conway heads the list for injuries this year. Played two games and laid out in both of them. And yet they say it's a parlor sofa game.

M. Smith is starring at his old position on the wing line.

"Bert" Gilligan is now recognized as the most versatile and useful player on the team. Full-back, half-back, first wing are some of the positions he has played. Yes, and "made good" in each position. The press is loud in its praises of his effective tackling, speedy running and sure catching. Though knocked out thrice, he is still "game" and very much in the game.

S. Quilty is playing the most brilliant game of his career. His line plunging and tackling evoke rounds of applause from the spectators.

Even in defeat, Ottawa College football team use up-to-the-minute methods. They took the "airship route" in both games against Toronto Varsity.

Smirle Lawson, Varsity half-back, is playing an even more effective game than he did last season.

Newton, Dixon, Gall and Lawson comprise a unique combination of backs, each of whom is a "king" in his own position.

As seen in the press, Eddie Gleeson and Hal. McGiverin assist in coaching the Ottawas. How times have changed.

Oh, you brawny Scot and flying wing Brennan!

There will probably be snow on the ground for the final game of the Dominion championship. Sorry it won't take place at the Oval.

Toronto Varsity has a great team, and as it will meet the Interprovincial champs. in Toronto, it is a good guess Toronto will have one chance this year to drown the yells of those rude mountaineers who so often made us wish that Hamilton would remain off the map for the fall as well as during the rest of the year.

A captain of an American college team was ruled out of the game and his team penalized 35 yds. for his jumping with his knees on an opposing player who was lying on the ground. The victim was knocked cold, and if the affair was intentional the guilty captain got his just deserts.

An aggressive steady wing line, and a fumbling half-back division is a poor combination.

A correct imitation of the "Wright Brothers at Rheims" was witnessed at the Oval on Saturday, Oct. 30, by a few thousand interested spectators. The novelty was attractive.

Hugh Ritchie, the stellar side scrimmager of Varsity, picks his team for the Dominion honors. Ottawa College sincerely hopes his "pick" is the lucky one.

The Queen's team without "Ken." Williams is a weak aggregation.

The Intercollegiate this year again has a playing president, Vaughn Black holds down a wing line position on McGill team. Last year Ed. McCarthy filled the presidency and also played on Ottawa College team. Both positions were admirably taken care of.

Father Stanton's "little trick team," the College thirds, have won two hard-earned victories from Renfrew High School. 12-5 and 8-7 were the scores.

Kenneth Overend is playing centre scrimmage for Queens.

No, we have not ordered an extra sized score board for 1910.

The College Seconds journeyed to Arnprior to play a game of football on Nov. 1st. The score at the conclusion of the game stood 27-10 in favor of "us." Trick-plays, fast following up, on-side kicks and "senior brand" tackling were a few of the reasons for the victory. Father Stanton coached the Seconds for this trip. The following took in the journey, which was much enjoyed: Rev. Fathers Stephen and M. Murphy, Pres. O'Gara, Vice-Pres. Gauthier, D. Breen, L. Kelly, H. Robillard, E. Letang, J.

Petite, J. O'Brien, J. Brennan, M. Brennan, P. Lacey, Ph. Harrington, P. Lacey, O. Kennedy, H. Filion, D. Sheehy.

It was a grand game, and with such celebrated players as Kennedy, Brennan, O'Gara, and Sheehy, frisking around on the grassy gridiron, we little blame the spectators from mistaking them for the "real thing." Our old friend Sullivan was a team in himself, a pony team, while the way Jim MacDonald humped around the ends for gains couldn't be duplicated in senior company. The team were quartered at the McPhee House, and after the game Jim showed them the sights of the town, not forgetting the "town pump" and the "street car" line. Mr. O'Gara acted as manager and treasurer, and reports a huge balance from his share of the gate receipts after the heavy expenses were liquidated.

The Inter-Mural Football League is booming, and many exciting games have been played. The league is certainly doing great work in deevloping the young blood, besides affording good healthy amusement for the participants. Rev. Father Stanton is the official refere, and makes the boys play straight football all the time. The following is the standing of the league :—

	Won.	Lost.	To Play.
"A"—Capt. R. Guindon ...	4	0	2
"B"—Capt. W. Hackett	1	3	2
"C"—Capt. H. Robillard ...	2	1	3
"D"—Capt. C. Coupal	1	4	1

Why wasn't Bert Gilligan played at first wing all season? His showing in the McGill game was certainly brilliant.

The first victory for McGill on Varsity Oval in the history of the Intercollegiate Union.

Ottawa has yet to win at McGill campus.

©f Local Interest

"Some class" to Ballard, and to that can-can that he does before hitting the line.

Stronach, Simpson and Ballard have done fine work for the Seconds under the able coaching of Dr. Wright.

Prof. of Eng.: Women do not reason; they imagine.

Student: "How long have we for this competition, Father?
Prof.: It all depends on when you begin.

Student in Philosophy: "Funny if there ain't more prime matter in D-b-o-s than in me."

Where's G-u-th-r now?

Du-b-s (at Wun Lung's): You may take that back; look at the dirt in it.
Wun Lung: You have to eatee a bushhel of dirtee befole you cloakee, anyway.
Well, I'm not going to eat the whole bushel with this meal.

K-e-n-dy is some sprinter. Take care, Goerge, or you'll be arrested for exceeding the speed limit.

Dummy on the Arnprior team was pushed fifteen yards for a forced rouge. The poor fellow couldn't say "held."

> G is for G-th-r,
> "Gee Whitticker" too.
> C is for C-té,
> Surpassed by but few.

> D is for D-b-s,
> The small man of our class.
> B is for B-k-e,
> To him raise the glass.

S is for S-th,
"A drum—he doth come."
B is for B-n-n,
His par we have none.

O's for O'G-a,
The philosophical wonder.
O's for O'G-r-n,
He does like to ponder.

Lo-f-s: Lunch for mine!

Tell me, little people, where is Ga-t-i-er now?

Inquisitive student in Physics: "If blue and white and garnet and grey be placed together, what would be the result?" Bright youth: "A large score."

That 'funny little animal' is still alive.

Hello, Ma-t-in: How are St-r-ch's knees?

That was an unfortunate hit, M-k-e.

Oh, you tea roses and giant oaks!

Why was O'G-'s last English essay a disappointment?

And who was this John Brown?

JUNIOR DEPARTMENT.

All hail! King Con.

Reggie would like to know if B-ph hurts his head when he butts in.

Mr. M-hy of the curly locks may be a star scrimmager, but O! those football stockings.

During the past month the first XIV have proven their superiority over the husky Juniorate XIV by defeating them twice and playing a draw in the other game of the series.

The first XIV are at the head of the Junior City League. Their latest victory was won on Oct. 30, when they defeated the fast Buena Vista team by a score of 3-0. Keep up the good work.

In the Inter-Mural Leagues several good games have been played, the games in the Midget League especially furnishing much amusement for the spectators.

Tommy, the man from the mountain, bids fair, in time, to rival his heroes from "up the creek."

No, M-t-n is not. "King of the Kids."

J. D.'s excuse after a recent football game: "Aw, what's de use of playin' against men."

The boy with the continuous laugh, McK-y.

Vol. XII.   OTTAWA, ONT., DECEMBER, 1909.   No. 3

Entered at the Post Office at Ottawa, Ont., as Second-Class Matter.

A Christmas Letter.

"What are you writing?" asked Margaret Regan, as she surprised little Frances Moran with pencil and note paper.

"I am writing a letter," a long, long letter," replied the scholar of seven summers with old fashioned ways, reflecting the manners of grown up persons.

Margaret was Frances' school teacher. The meeting between the two at the latter's home was but an incident in a long standing intimacy between the Moran and Regan families,--an intimacy so much the more appreciated by Margaret as she was without near relatives and without other friends in whom she could confide. As often as she wished to come, their house was as free to her as her own home. Hence we will not be surprised to learn that Margaret was Frances' best friend, always excepting, of course, papa and mamma, and her brother Fred, who used to make things so pleasant when he came from college to spend his holidays.

"Writing to Santa Claus, and Christmas still ten days away?"

And Margaret smiled on the winsome face upturned to hers, but the smile soon died away in spite of herself at the memories that thought of Christmas awakened in her mind. Could Christmas ever be pleasant for her again? Alas! happiness in this world was past and gone as far as she was concerned. Too many tears had been shed to think of the approaching festival with anything but regret for what might have been. All unconscious of Frances' presence, Margaret gazed out the window at the ice-covered street and falling snowflakes; and she involuntarily shivered at the consciousness that all her hopes were chilled and dead like the flowers on her mother's grave.

"Are you crying, Margaret?" said the little one, as her own bright face darkened in sympathy.

"No, Frances, dear, it is the tears in your own eyes that make you think so."

With an effort Margaret kept back further memories by interesting herself in the letter. Frances held up the page, so awk-wardly written with pencil and so often marred by the marks of the eraser that neither she nor Margaret could make out the words. But the letter must be written. Who could help her to do it but her teacher and best friend? It is by dint of such mutual aid and confidence that most people in the world get along. The letter ran thus:

Dear Fred,—I write for you to come home at Christmas. Papa and mamma want you here, and so do I. I am praying night and morning to the Child Jesus for this, and I will hang up two long stockings besides my own, one for you and one for Margaret. From your sister, Frances.

The tears were now flowing from Margaret's eyes in earnest, and to conceal her bursting heart from the child she bent down and pressed her pale cheek against the warm and rosy one of her little friend, telling her what a dear child she was and that she hoped Fred would come indeed in answer to her letter and her prayer to the Child Jesus.

"Come now and ask mamma to let you go with me to see the nice Christmas tree that we are putting up for you at school. And on the way we will stop at the church to say one more prayer to obtain your wish."

By this time Margaret had regained her self-possession. Fred Moran's absence was another of her sorrows. It was fully a year now that he had been away. People told her she had no business liking him, since his folks were comparatively poor and Fred's earnings were but small. Never had he given hope of soon coming back. Hence with her expiring teaching certificate and her wages spent in covering the debts incident to her mother's last illness, her prospects for the coming year were dark indeed.

But Frances' letter sped on its way. In due time Fred read over the childish lines. They did not, however, change his mind.

He had not the slightest intention of going home. How could he bear the expense and loss of time entailed in such a long voyage? His Christmas must be passed where he had spent the year —in the surveyor's camp.

And so Frances' letter lay in his pocket neglectd,—year, and forgotten,—till one evening two days before Christmas. Again he perused the awkwardly written lines in amusement, but now they awakened different feelings. His parents, Margaret, his sister's prayer to the Divine Child, soon to be born into the world, —all these things were contrasted with his hard life of exploring and surveying unsettled lands. A strange longing entered his heart to be back again with those he loved, to re-visit his old home and taste once more its Christmas joys.

Thus it happened that two days after, late on Christmas Eve, the train coming into Ottawa brought Fred to his native city. It was shortly before midnight when he reached the parish church. For Fred was a good boy and a practical Catholic before all else. He considered a careful regard for his religious duties a primary requisite in meriting God's blessing upon his life. In spite of some few slight drawbacks, he felt how many favors he had need to be thankful for. And the readiness of his service on this occasion had its own reward. Holy mass and communion at the unusual hour, the message of God's minister, the peaceful faces of fervent worshippers, everything in fact to the very lights and the singing had the effect of awakening in his mind the true spirit that should reign on this festival—the spirit of thankfulness that Christ the Saviour was born into the world, that the Son of God, by making His own, our joys as well as our sorrow, sanctified all that is connected with the Christian home and family life.

The singing had ceased, the crowds had departed, darkness again pervaded the sacred edifice except where the lamps glimmered about the crib of the Divine Child, when Fred left church and strolled down the street. His old home was still lighted up. The inmates had just returned from midnight mass. He was tempted to ring,—but no, he would avoid seeing them till morning that both they and he might have some rest.

Next day preparations in the Moran home were well under way for the Christmas dinner, to which Margaret was invited at the wish of Frances.

"I have received no word from Fred," said Mr. Moran, as he took some letters from his pocket. "All the others have written, although none of them can come this year. We would have a lonely Christmas indeed, if Frances and Miss Rowan were not here.

"The letter may have been delayed," returned Mrs. Moran, as she spread the cloth and took down the dishes from the sideboard. "Fred was always careful of his letter writing. Perhaps Margaret has received news from him?"

Just the faintest tinge of color overspread Margaret's face as she replied that no news had reached her. The mutual liking between Margaret and Fred was no secret in the household, and it was only the mother's confidence in the girl and her anxiety for news from Fred had led to ask a seemingly delicate question.

In fact both parents, in their unassuming way, were interested in everything connected with the welfare of their children. Happily all of them were settled except Fred and Frances. They had even kept Fred at college for some years, but finally, with reluctance, were compelled to withdraw from him any further assistance toward this end.

"However," said Mr. Moran, "the lesson of hardship may make a better man of him. I know that all his spare moments are employed in continuing his studies privately and in preparing for the government examinations. A letter for him arrived at my office only yesterday which perhaps may contain good news.

Frances here came running in, all flushed and out of breath, to announce Fred's coming as the latter entered the door. Frances had been on the way to visit the crib and the Babe of Bethlehem, along with some other children. As luck would have it, she ran into the arms of her brother; and, mind you, he went along with them to pray beside the crib and gave each of them a copper to place in the box for the poor little ones of Christ.

The greetings in the household were warm and hearty on all sides, as much so in fact that the Christmas dinner, the roast goose and pudding were forgotten for the time being. But these were in this account the better enjoyed when everyone finally sat down. Thre was much laughing after the meal when Frances brought down to Fred and Margaret the things which Santa Claus had left in their stockings. And there was great rejoicing, too, when Mr. Moran handed Fred the letter he had received, and which was found to contain news of his success in the government examinations and his promotion to a position home in Ottawa with a fair income.

"And to think Frances," said Fred, as his sister's large blue eyes feasted on his looks, "to think your letter is the cause of it all! Are you not glad that I won't leave you any more?"

"I am more glad that you won't leave Margaret, and she

won't cry any more,'' replied Frances, breaking away from her brother and running to Miss Rowan, as the company smiled at Margaret's confusion.

But Margaret gathered up Frances in her arms and buried her face in the head of curls. This time it was not to hide her tears. Her heart was singing a song of joy and thanksgiving on this Christmas Day as Frances whispered in her ear:

"It was not the letter, it was the Child Jesus that did it all."

MONA.

The Stage of To-day and Yesterday

OT long ago an aged friend, a representative of that class who lived largely in the mystic past, expressed his regret that our stage had deteriorated so much that it was no longer an inspiration or a source of pleasure to him. "Oh," he continued, "think of the days when Edwin Forrest, Charlotte, and McCullough, the great American actors, made the stage an education for the theatre-goers. Whom have we now, and what is there to be seen?" I listened attentively and retreated, under the impression that such criticisms with slight variation are continually heard; nor is it altogether surprising. The human mind is prone to magnify the glories of the past. As the poet says, "Distance lends enchantment to the view," and all literature bears testimony that there were giants in those days. Even old Homer scored the pygmies of his time. In speaking of one of the heroes around the walls of Troy he says:

"Not ten strong men th' enormous weight could raise,
Such men as live in these degenerate days."

And so it is to-day. The giants lived in the past, the small weaklings in the present.

We know that the enthusiasm for classical plays has somewhat died out. The vaudeville has in a great many cases taken its place. Still this does not prove the statement that there are no star actors in our days. I mean classical interpreters.

We are prone to account as heroic little occurrences of the past which would not be considered in the present. This peculiarity of the human mind in part explains the criticism of the modern stage. It is only just, however, to observe that during the last sixty years there were many interpreters of the greatest classic roles, who were in the truest sense of the term masters of their art; and yet taken as a whole the general standard of excellence in the interpretation of the roles other than that assumed by the star, is incomparably better than it was even twenty years ago.

Now to-day with a large number of almost uniformly artists, it is true that the really great work of the star actors does not impress the average theatre-goer so much as it would were the star surrounded by less brilliant actors who are also looking to gain a reputation. The audience would lose the satisfaction now enjoyed of a well-grounded art work which is instructive to the auditor.

Our stage of to-day boasts of a great number of young men and women who are destined to rank with the foremost actors of days gone by. Of visitors to Canada, to whom may we listen with more pleasure than to the Ben Greet company; and very few can outclass Murphy as an Irish actor.

We have heard much of the great actors of the past, and therefore one feels warranted in comparing the wor kof the past with that of the present; and while nothing is farther from my purpose than seeking to minimize the splendid achievements of the great actors of the last century, I feel that not only does the stage to-day represent a higher degree of general excellence than ever before, not only are there more true artists and more performances that are works of art, but the standard of manhood and womanhood, the general ideals of the dramatic profession are higher than at any former period in the history of Canada.

Imagine the theatre-goers of another generation will be saying, "if you could have witnessed the Ben Greet company or Forbes-Robertson, or Irving, or Mantell, you would have seen something you could never forget."

I doubt not that many of those whose works we thoroughly enjoy to-day. but whom we are not in the habit of associating with the heroes of yesterday, will hold a high place in the pantheon of art when seen through the twilight of vanished years.

FRANK CORKERY, '11·

The Missionary Spirit.

ANADA'S future greatness has come to be a very popular topic of discussion among us. The leading dailies of our Dominion seldom let a week go by without some editorial comment upon our growing importance. All are agreed that a glorious destiny is ours, some even predict that this fair young land of the maple leaf will yet surpass in wealth and commercial importance our big republican brother to the South. Canadian statesmen paint in glowing colors the advantages which our country offers to students and workers in every department of human endeavor. "The twentieth century belongs to Canada" has become our slogan. Foreign nations are taking up the cry, and to-day the eyes of the world are centred upon Canada, the premier colony of the British Empire, as well as her acknowledged granary. If, fifty years ago, the United States held the attention of European nations as a model of material and commercial progress, we are the centre of that attention to-day, and our lot it appears to be, to relieve the congestion of population of those older European countries, whose poor especially gaze with longing eyes towards our far-off shores, knowing that here there is space to live and breathe, here there is work for willing hands, here the great boon of British-Canadian citizenship is extended to all alike. Canadians themselves realize their happy position, hence it is not surprising that statesmen and journalists, in fact all classes of people, should be inclined to discuss the future. However, if to-day we are happy and prosperous, with bright prospects of even greater things to come, we owe it to a beneficent Providence rather than to any great merits of our own. If the soil is surpassing fertile, the timber and mineral lands rich beyond comparison, then it is little thanks to us if we but turn to our own advantage the wealth so generously heaped upon us. Realizing our immense possibilities, then gratitude, not pride, should fill our hearts, and the thought uppermost in our minds should be : let us as a nation do something for the glory of God, who has done so much for us. In our mad rush after dollars and cents we are in danger of losing sight of the main factor in nation-building,—the fact that a people who fear and love God is to be preferred to a nation of millionaires. We have the experience of ages to work upon, and heavy is our responsibility. The rocks upon which other ships of state have

been shattered are "naked and open" to our eyes and should be sedulously shunned by us. The mistakes of other nations should be our gains, and on account of our similarity to the American republic in so many important points we should study especially her successes and failures and endeavor to avoid the errors she has made. If we be sincere we will not deny that the rock of destruction which to-day threatens nations and is a grave menace to ourselves, is immorality—disregard for God-given natural law; contempt for the sacred bond of marriage, and consequently the destruction of the home, which is the bulwark of society and the cradle of nations.

It is not necessary to enter into a lengthy explanation of the above statement that immorality when it becomes rampant weakens society and the state. It has been proven long ago in the case of the Roman Empire, and without making too sweeping an assertion it appears that it is being only too well proven in the case of France to-day. Granting then that we admit immorality and irreligion as an enemy to national strength, is not he who sets to work to combat our internal foes a truer patriot than he who, arrayed in the glittering accoutrements of military ostentation, prepares for imaginary or even real foes from without? We may need, it is true, military and naval defence in future, but at present we most certainly sorely need patriotic Catholic men and women to counteract the effects of the pernicious doctrines that are being sown broadcast among us. The nations of the earth are at our doors. Already there are about 150,000 Catholic immigrants in the West, and worst of all they have come to Canada almost destitute of priests. We need money, schools, churches and teachers, but most of all we need priests. Priests with the missionary's spirit. Catholic laymen should recognize that they can do a great deal to assist Catholic emigrants coming to our shores, but the great and crying need is for priests, men endowed with both teaching and pastoral offices. Without teachers of morals, no morality. Without morality, we cannot have stability and national life. If the hordes of immigrants coming to our shores are allowed to grow up without religion what must be the result? In fifty years we shall have a great unchristian and irreligious throng, a menace to good order, and an element of degeneracy.

Surely then the case is grave enough to arouse our latent sensibilities. Thus far we have considered the question only from the standpoint of patriotism; but apart from the immense benefits to accrue to our beloved Canada, if Catholic immigrants after arriving here are retained within the fold, we must consider the question from the standpoint of Faith, reflecting upon the glory that we are in duty bound to render Almighty God by preaching the gospel to the poor. There is a cry borne to us across the smiling Western plains. It is caught up by the fresh westerly breeze and wafted to us across the great lakes. It can be heard in the city mansion and in the humble country farmhouse. Its weird notes resound through our college halls and play-grounds. We can hear it if we but listen. It is the cry of souls. Poor, lone souls, out in this great lone land, wandering hopelessly without shepherds. In the words of Holy Scripture we can truly say, ''The harvest indeed is great, but the workers are few.''

How are we going to cultivate the missionary spirit? I cannot answer the question myself. I only hope the question will cause a little reflection and then at a later date that some one more competent will answer it. Let us, for the sake of Holy Religion, make this need of missionaries a factor in deciding our life's vocation. Even from a worldly point of view it is a noble thing to plant the cross on a new hilltop, and we Catholics of Canada should not be slow to recognize the nobility of such an act. But human gain or glory must not influence us. Let us rely for our reward upon Him who nineteen centuries ago sent forth twelve humble men with the words, ''Go ye therefore and teach all nations.'' These words have not lost their force. They are for us of to-day and they should rouse us to new life, knowing that if we hearken to them our reward will be great in Heaven. Let us gird ourselves for the work and with resolute hearts make at least a bold attempt to win this young land to Mother Church and God. Earthly rewards will pass away, but the canticle of a soul redeemed will be sweet music to our ears throughout the endless ages of eternity.

Let us pray for the growth of the missionary spirit among us.

A. REYNOLDS, '09.

TO MELANCHOLY.

Not in the haunts of men, O Melancholy!
..Thy presence hath been sweet;
For there thou art a vanity, a folly,
    Which we would fain secrete,
'Mid hollow smiles that hide the cares below,
As sunlight glints above the winter snow,
Or Autumn, tinting earth with colours gay,
Hides 'neath his artist touch the progress of decay.

But in the old and melancholy woods,
    When shadows flit around
Like guardian spirits of the solitudes
    And the mysterious sound
Of distant cataracts through the gray trunks heard,
Throbs down the lonely dells with echoes weird,
I love to wander with thee, and to draw
From thy calm lips high themes that elevate and awe.

Mirth singeth like the summer grasshopper
    That dies with summertide;
But thou, more constant, patiently dost bear
    The winter winds that chide
The leaves and flowers away inclemently
From the lean meadow and the shivering tree,
While the round, ruddy berries of the holly
Shine 'mid their dark green leaves—thy wreath, O Melan-
    choly!

Is it thine eyes that smile on me at even,
    Through purple twilight air,
Shining afar in the mysterious heavens
    Like tender thoughts we bear,
Deep in the silent shadows of the breast,
Of one whose love our lonely life has blest?
Or the faint lustre of the evening star,
Whose beams like lilies fall on earth from heaven afar?

FRANK WATERS.

The Founder of the Order of Our Lady of Charity and Refuge (Good Shepherd).

HE Beatification of the Venerable John Eudes, which took place in Rome on the 25th of April, Good Shepherd Sunday, will be celebrated at the Convent of the Good Shepherd, Ottawa, by a Solemn Triduum which will begin on the 13th of December next and end on the 15th.

Blessed John Eudes, the father and founder of the Order of Our Lady of Charity, whose members are known throughout the world as the Sisters of the Good Shepherd, was born on November 14th, 1601, at Ri, in the Diocese of Seez, near Argentan, Normandy. The early life of our hero was distinguished for his piety and meekness, traits of character that lived with him until his death. He had a most intense devotion to Our Lady. So intense was it, that he chose her for his spouse, placing a ring on a finger of one of her statues and signing this marriage contract with his blood.

When he had reached the age of fourteen, he was placed under the care of those great educators of youth—the Jesuits—at their College, Royal du Mont, in Caen. Here his native ability and talent, allied to application and industry, won for him a premier place of honor. The years sped on, and it came to John Eudes to choose his state of life. Already in his heart the choice had been made. He would be a priest, he would dedicate himself to the service of God. He was ordained to the priesthood in Paris on the 20th of December, 1625. Now began in truth his Christlike mission. Never, his biographer tells us, since the days of St. Vincent Ferrer, did any Missioner attract such vast crowds. At one place 40,000 people gathered to hear him, and his words were clearly understood by all. He possessed in a marked degree all the qualifications which go to the making of the true Apostle of Christ. His learning was profound; his knowledge of the Scriptures far-reaching; his zeal indefatigable; his courage indomitable; his way winning, and his heart tender and compassionate to the faults of others. How like to the Master he was in his apostolate!

When the terrible plague scourged the towns of Argentan and Caen, John Eudes braved the danger of contagion, separated himself from his brethren that he might shed the Gospel light of truth and pardon through the pestilential shadows of ignorance and disease enfolding the stricken sufferers. Huddled in a cask to rest his weak and worn form he could say: "The birds of the air have their nests, the foxes their dens, but I have not whereon to lay my head."

In 1643 Blessed John Eudes founded a Congregation of Missionaries called Eudistes; its object is to form pious, learned and zealous priests, by means of seminaries and retreats and perpetuate the missionary spirit of their holy Founder. The new Congregation was consecrated to the Sacred Hearts of Jesus and Mary, and thus the Eudistes were the first to preach the glories of the Sacred Heart of Jesus and the most pure Heart of Mary. For this reason it is said in the Decree of the Beatification, to consider Bd. John Eudes as the father, the doctor and the apostle of this sweet devotion of the most Sacred Heart of Jesus and Mary.

In 1641 Bd. Father Eudes instituted the Order of Our Lady of Charity called also Good Shepherd. There were sheep in the days of our hero who had wandered from the right path. Poor children of circumstances, betrayed, despised, rejected. He saw in them the souls for whom out of an intense love, the Good Shepherd had laid down his life. He would save them. He would build for them havens of safety where the wolf of sin could find no entry. For the succor of those lost sheep he founded the Order of Our Lady of Charity approved by Pope Alexander VII, in 1666.

How many thousands of penitent souls has this Order brought to the great white throne of the Good Shepherd! All this because Blessed Father Eudes was the true follower of Christ not only in his life, but also in his death. The last years of his life were filled with suffering and persecution, but the cup of bitterness he drained gladly in memory of the Master's Chalice. Nor was he without comfort in his dereliction for there stood by his cross the one who was always with him — Mary his Mother. The coils of the flesh were loosened, and on August 19th, 1680, the spirit of John Eudes entered into its long eternal rest.

As soon as the news of his death was known, the concourse of the people was so great that it was with difficulty he could be interred. The eagerness of the crowd to render him their last duties, his praises that were heard on all sides, were enough to show, how in Heaven, God honors the creature to whom men have given so much veneration upon earth.

The Blessed John Eudes has left voluminous writings. Nothing more holy than his works, nourished with the maxims of the Gospel, based on profound theological science and the fruit of wide experience and frequent meditation. They all speak of his eminent virtue and his zeal for souls.

Benefits of the Press.

IT is an undeniable fact that man has a greater tendency towards good than evil, and now whether the press is merely a commentator upon ideals as they already exist, or whether it is to a great extent the personal work of the editor where he expresses his own views, one, no matter which way he looks at the question, will find himself confronted by either horn of this dilemma. That the press has revolutionized the world and brought science, literature and every accommodation to man's door is a fact that has been made known to all of us since the eighteenth century. To-day not only the rich man, nobleman, or clergyman, is able to know the existing state of political, literary and scientific doings in other countries but the poor man likewise, though he be not able to have a University course nor possess the necessaries to visit these foreign countries, is able to know the things which before the press was established were only granted to the higher class. To-day he knows it all through the happy and beneficial medium of the newspapers and press productions of the different countries. What would we know of the Budget on which the fate of the political party depends to-day? What would we know of Germany's progress in trying to outmaster England on the sea? What would we know of any country? or how would we get any information if it were not for the press? Learning in itself is small, we come to the knowledge of things by comparison, and where is there a better means of comparing things than in the result of an "editor's incessant toils." If we abolish the press because many say it is a producer of greater evil than good, what other means will we adopt? Will we have recourse to gossiping which is a root of more evil than any other vice, or will we be satisfied to be entirely ignorant of the facts which surround us? Imagine the happiness and enlightenment which are brought to a lone settler in some distant part of a country by the reception of a daily or weekly paper or some press production. When newspapers were first published they simply gave out news or events of the day; but not being contented with this the people of the universe saw the good work of the press and used it as a means to assist mankind in every way. As a means of advertisement it is unsurpassed, the want column gives us every facility. A person loses an article to-day, to-morrow everyone knows about it, and this is of great assistance to the loser in the recovery of the article. We may find one in ten who will not return the article when found, but the fault lies in the individual who keeps it and not in the press which sought to recover it. So it is with the press, one in ten may be found culpable. Thus we can see from the natural tendencies of mankind that the press must naturally be good. Thousands of journals, periodicals and papers are published with a daily edition of a quarter of a million copies, to meet the demands of their constant readers. Would we not turn in disgust from such papers if they were found to be productive of more evil than good? Man being a rational animal is capable of discerning good from evil. Sensational papers and yellow journals are not long lived. To prove this—there was founded in a well-known Canadian city last year a paper which lasted six months. By an eloquent plea of His Grace the Archbishop of that city, and by the zeal of his followers, it was disregarded, and had to retire from the arena of this high vocation. Another good benefit derived from the press is the army of workers it employs, whose daily bread depends on the press. These men are employed in one of the highest callings in the land on which we all depend for our general fund of information. An editor is held in great respect, he is ranked among the first men, and frequently we find clergymen in prominent positions in press productions. Does this not show that the press must be a greater producer of good than evil? As already shown, the greater part of the world is being educated by the press, and if the press is such an evil-doer we must naturally draw our conclusion that the greater part of the world is bad, since it has been learning nothing but evil. But this assertion is easily denied for a well-known writer says: "We must not take too much stock in the opinion that there are more evil persons in the world than good." Bad men there are, and bad Christians, no doubt, but the good far outnumber the bad. Evil is so unnatural in man that his weak points are observed quicker than his good ones. Likewise in the press the evil is observed before the good and leaves the impression on our mind that "the press is a greater producer of evil than good," which is altogether incorrect.

F. BURROWS, '14·

The Referendum in Canada.

HE Referendum is an institution under which no proposal for changing the constitution of a country can become law until it has received the direct approval of the citizens. The case for and against Referendum has been fought out in lengthy debates in many parliaments during several sessions. It exists, though not under the name of the Referendum, in most of the States of the American Union.

Many people take little or no interest in our present system of government. They are not called upon to give their opinions of their sometimes worthless members. If the Referendum were introduced into Canada it would certainly have an advantageous effect. The people would take a far keener interest in politics if they knew that questions might come before them; it would engender a feeling of responsibility, promote national unity, prove a safety-valve for political agitation and conduce to the tranquility of trade and of the colonies generally. It is, moreover, the proper way of recognizing the sovereignity of the people.

The opponents of Referendum may argue as to the fitness or unfitness of the people to judge new laws coming into the country. If the people are able to choose representatives surely, they can pronounce on laws. Electors are only required to give their approval or disapproval to a matter already threshed out. Cannot any common individual do this? Besides, the people are practiced on such questions. They are accustomed to vote on Local Option, the imposition of new rates, etc. The votings on these questions are only Referendums in miniature.

Public opinion is changing in favour of this system, owing in the main to a keen perception of the evils which infect our present parliamentary system and a conviction that these evils might be mitigated by the exercise of a national vote. The chief defect of our present system of government is that the party having the majority can pass any measure they wish. In Democratic countries such as Switzerland and the United States, the articles of constitution are in a strict sense the law of the land. They cannot be altered or menaced by the small and temporary majority of a Representative Assembly. Such a majority may misrepresent the will of the people. The foundations of a country must rest on some support firmer than the transitory wishes of a majority of people. Under our modern English Constitution we cannot secure that the House of Commons shall even debate the gigantic constitutional innovations which it is prepared to enact.

Another great and most dangerous effect of our present system of government is that it stimulates instead of mitigating the influence of Party. Under the present conditions, neither the Unionist minority in Ireland nor the Home Rule minority in England exerts its rightful influence. The Referendum gets rid of this defect in our scheme of representation. For example— in the question, "should the Home Rule Bill of 1893 or a like measure pass into law?" Now if every man had a vote each would have its true weight. Both the Unionist minority in Ireland and the Home Rule minority in England would each exhibit its true strength.

Before introducing the Referendum into Canada it would be wise to return to some countries in which the Referendum has been introduced and see if it has not been a distinct success. In Switzerland the Referendum has been the form of government for a number of years. The direct results have been so many and so various that any answr, except on broad lines, would take a book instead of a paragraph. The great thing it has done has been to develop a feeling of social solidarity and brotherhood. One Swiss statesman wrote, "that every time they had a Referendum voting they had a real and vital communion or common action for the common good; and whether the measure was defeated or passed, it resulted in an accession of knowledge to the common people for future action." To-day Switzerland has more practical community of interests, with perhaps less of noisy agitation, than any country in the world. Mr. Pomeroy, President of the National Direct Legislation League, says: "There is not to-day a single public man in Switzerland openly opposed to the Referendum, and of course not a single party."

Nor is Switzerland the only country in which the Referendum exists. In France there is a Direct Legislation League, which is actively agitating, and the French cities have a large amount of municipal Direct Legislation. The same is true of Belgium and Holland, to a certain extent of Prussia and Austria, and to a limited extent of Italy. It is still more true of Great Britain where municipal matters are very frequently voted on, and parliamentary elections are to-day in reality a Referendum on one great national question—even more so than the Presidential elections of the United States. But it is in Norway that the Referendum has had its greatest growth outside of Switzerland. The liquor question is there continually voted on by the people as is also municipal taxation and appropriation of money and bonding.

If the Referendum were introduced into Canada it would greatly aid the coming of the co-operative commonwealth. I believe this because I believe the doctrine of evolution is applied to politics and reform matters as well as to other things. The theory of evolution is applied to political progress just the same as it is applied to the development of the physical side of man or any animal, or to the development of plants or any other growth—in a short step at one time, and the accustoming of the people to that step,—so that from it they can proceed to another. Every little advance gained is ground for further advance, and if Direct Legislation can be gained it can be used as the lever to gain other things; and Direct Legislation gained will be a means for practically applying a large amount of steam now dissipated in the air, which makes a great display but does no work.

Another great benefit that Direct Legislation would accomplish is that in separating the discussion of measures from that of candidates for office, it will enable us to choose better officials. For instance, I am convinced of the honesty, ability, and good intentions of a certain man. I would be proud to vote for him if we had Direct Legislation, because I would feel sure that he would honestly strive to do his duty there, and that I would have an opportunity to nullify any measure which he might advocate in the legislature, but which I felt to be wrong. Now under the present uncontrolled representative system, I must vote for a man who believes in Direct Legislation, even though his qualifications as a legislator are far inferior. De Tocqueville says that the only way to interest people in government is to make them partakers in it.

Why should not the Referendum be a success if introduced into this progressive country of ours? The majority of the people are interested in it and are making it a subject for discussion. The simplicity of this method of legislative control, the utter and immediate abolition of venality in legislative bodies, the elimination of "boodlers" from legislative halls, the bringing of the government to the theory of its founders, appeals to the average citizen, and to obtain advocates it is only necessary to obtain auditors to an explanation of what it means.

THOMAS J. O'NEILL, '11.

HIGH DISTINCTION FOR OTTAWA GRADUATE.

News has just been received from British Columbia of the appointment of Mr. Denis Murphy, B.A., '92, to the Supreme Court. This adds another to the already long list of distinctions won by O. U. graduates during the year just closed.

Mr. Denis Murphy, who is a brother of the Rev. Rector, entered Ottawa College in '87, and graduated with the degree of B.A. in '92. He won the class medal every year during his course. Upon leaving college, he took up the study of Law. Later he entered politics, and sat a number of years for West Yale in the British Columbia Legislature. Although he achieved distinction in this new field, attaining even to cabinet rank, a large and constantly increasing legal practice soon demanded his entire attention, and he consequently retired from politics. Last week he was appointed Judge of the Supreme Court.

While at college, Mr. Murphy was a member of the Owl staff, and held quite a reputation as a litterateur. In his final year he was chosen to read the valedictory, and his speech is still remembered by old students and citizens as one of the most eloquent and brilliant ever delivered at the University. To the distinguished alumnus the Review offers its heartiest congratulations.

Modern Drama and its Patrons

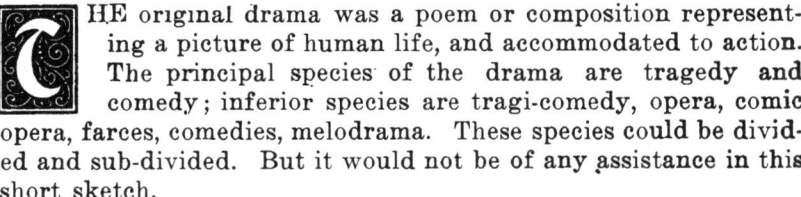HE original drama was a poem or composition representing a picture of human life, and accommodated to action. The principal species of the drama are tragedy and comedy; inferior species are tragi-comedy, opera, comic opera, farces, comedies, melodrama. These species could be divided and sub-divided. But it would not be of any assistance in this short sketch.

Let us then consider only a few of the most prominent types, and in this deliberation remark the different classes and masses that attend these dramas; the effect they have on their minds; whether they debase or uplift them; whether play-goers desire to be educated by the witnessing of these plays, or whether they simply go to the theatres to be amused and refreshed by the scenes depicted on the stage.

For examples of the various types of drama let us choose them from the hundred stages of New York City. To start with, we will take Grand Opera as given at the "Metropolitan Opera House." The audience can be divided into three general classes. These are the "swell set," the "middle class" and the "poorer people." The first set are a most necessary and vital element that goes to make for the success of the big undertaking of producing a Grand Opera. They pay enormous subscriptions for the use of boxes for the season, and go there as a rule to show their clothes and not for the love of good music. Their presence attracts a great following of "hob-nobbers" or "would-be's" or "nearly swells," who sit in the orchestra seats and ape their wealthier brethren in the boxes. This overflow of the "swell set" shows very little genuine enthusiasm for the production.

The next class, the middle or fairly well-to-do, as a rule, attend operas and plays out of sheer love of the art, and their enthusiasm is at times quite remarkable. They go away feeling that they have spent an evening most profitably.

But the acme of whole-souled ardor, unaffected, sincere pleasure and enjoyment is reached when one considers the occupants of the top galleries. There the poorer classes of people, mostly foreigners, sit night after night and drink in the sweet notes of the opera singers,—Caruso, Melba, Geraldine Farrar, Bonci, Tettrazini, Calvé, Nordica, Albani, and others. Their enthusiasm is must real and at times knows no bounds. Surely this show of feeling can have none other but a beneficial effect on their hearts and minds. It helps to cheer them up after a long day's work, and they return to their homes feeling better and cleaner-minded people.

My criticism of the swell set may be a little harsh, but for the most part it is true. They are not sincerely enthusiastic over grand opera, but merely go for vain show of clothes. By their manner of showing their pleasure at a soul-stirring rendition of a beautiful part of an opera, they simply sit and pose for those in other parts of the house, and merely tap together very lightly their gloved or bejewelled hands. Contrast this cold disinterestedness with the vivid and genuine outbursts of applause that emanate from the middle and top galleries. There is the genuine, with no semblance of sham or superficiality. Whatever the expressions of the populace are, no matter in what manner they are shown, they are thorough, open and honest.

Thus we see the influence of one division or species of drama has on the minds of the play-going public. To attempt to describe the influence of comic opera and the many other kinds of drama would take a volume. However, I will touch briefly on a few of them. The clean comic opera, with good music, is most pleasing, and the public when amused with wholesome fun will be liberal in its patronage. If the opera has a long-skirted chorus, it may not meet with the approval of some debased minds, but the verdict of the general public is for clean, bright, amusing productions. To substantiate this verdict, call to your minds the popularity of "Wang," "Dolly Varden," the "Mikado," "Les Cloches de Cornivelle," and many other wholesomely pleasing productions.

Then there is the blood-curdling, "give-me-the-child" type of cheap melodrama that appeals to the lowest classes of the poor public. This type no matter how degrading will always find audiences from the heterogeneous make-up of the world's population. "The James Boys in Missouri," "On the Bridge at Midnight," "The Fatal Wedding," "Dangers of a Shop-Girl," "Nellie the Beautiful Cloak Model," all with their maudlin love-scenes and crude immorality ,will ever find admirers in a certain element of the people.

It is much to be regretted that a "censor" of the stage is not appointed to see that none but decent plays are produced. But if the public demand indecency, then the theatrical managers give it to them. If the public shows its disapproval, the owners take the plays off and give out clean stuff. In this short form, I cannot consider any more of the types, and most necessarily conclude this brief screed, by saying that the public is the real and true censor of plays, and yet a most fickle one, as has been severely taught to many theatrical managers.   P. C. HARRIS, '11·

Poeta Nascitur, Non Fit.

HE above ancient maxim which is the title of this essay has frequently been the subject of many lively discussions, but is almost universally accepted as true. The spirit of poetry, we have been told when referring to some world-famed scribe, comes naturally, not through study or application. It has been said that one has to have some genius for, or at least inclination towards poetry, to be able to produce anything worthy of note. Many also are unshaken in the belief that all our greatest poets wrote because it was in their nature to give forth their thoughts and sentiments, not because of the appending advantages. Shakespeare has been given as an example of a poet whose knowledge was almost without limit, and some of whose works seem nothing short of inspired. He had very little education, and some have even accused him of being ignorant; but these if anything augment his greatness, for he was naturally learned. He did not need the opinions of others to help him understand Nature, but ''he looked inwards and found Her there.''

Indeed in reading some of the ancient and modern classics, we can hardly help but admit that the authors had more than ordinary tuition. There is such a subtlety of thought in every line, such perfect verification, and such a complete mastery over the subject as to place it in the extraordinary. The poetry of Horace, pervaded as it is with a mine of historical and mythological allusions, the tragedies of Shakespeare, showing the author's unlimited knowledge of Nature, are certainly greater than may be produced by men of ordinary mental powers. But even with a few examples of self-educated poets like Shakespeare, this does not prove that to be a great poet one has to discard all outside information. Rather the contrary: the poet may indeed be born, but he needs to be helped by the advice of others who have gone before him, and be guided by their experience.

No matter how much talent one has for poetry, or how lofty are his ideas, his work is sure to be wild, loose and unconnected unless restrained and refined by study. He needs to analyse his thoughts and to place them in order before he will have anything fit for production. He needs a standard, a criterion by which he may be guided, and by which consistency may be preserved throughout. We have many examples of wild, aimless poetry, carried here and there by the precarious fancy of the writer. Again his ideas need to be held in check, to be directed in a certain channel lest his very ability for writing be led to a pernicious use. Left alone, without any guidance, he would naturally be inclined towards the promulgation of false doctrines. By study one learns not only the general features of life, but especially those little peculiarities which determine a man's nature, and in which we find all our greatest poets were well versed. When Lord Tennyson first began to write poetry his works were not very well received, and many severe criticisms were passed on his initial attempts. Silent for ten years, he read, studied the old mediaeval romances, and obtained the knowledge possible. On his return he at once soared to the highest point in public esteem. "He is decidedly the first of our living poets," said Wordsworth, a commendation which he certainly merited.

It is possible even with a little talent to build up a complete system for oneself. The correct mode must be first acquired, then by slow, steady perseverance, ever correcting, ever improving, a talent for poetry may be cultivated to such a degree that after a time it comes spontaneously. We have an example of this in the person of Virgil, the greatest epic writer of his time. As a man he was gentle and amiable, but bashful and awkward in appearance. He was not original in ideas at first, nor impelled by genius in any way to write poetry. He worked slowly, carefully and laboriously with a definite object in view, patiently and incessantly polishing, and so became the model of the time for correctness and elegance of style.

It is even true that men have begun to write poetry and continued to do so with great success, without having the least inclination towards such, and even utterly devoid of genius. For an example we may take Plautus, one of Rome's most noted playwriters. He was of very humble birth, and earned a scanty living by working in mills or holding some menial position of a similar kind. To gain a better support he turned to writing, and especially towards the production of comedies, of which he made a great success. Thus a man of ordinary talent, of little or no education, by sheer mental exertion, became one of the founders of early Roman literature. Another example of this may be found in the early colonial era of the United States, where such men as George Sandys turned their hand to poetry absolutely "invita minerva," and produced works which according to many authorities are among the most poetical of the English language.

In conclusion, we may say that the old adage, "work over-comes everything" has its place here as well as everywhere else; it is a rule to be followed by everyone with a poetic ambition, and if it is strictly adhered to success will be sure to follow.

M. O'GORMAN, '11·

PAPAL DELEGATE'S VISIT.

Owing to the progress of the Plenary Council the Mass of the Holy Ghost did not take place in September as usual, but on November 18th the Profession of Faith was made by the professors of the University. The Papal Delegate, Monsignor Sbarretti, presided. At 4.30 the students filed into St. Joseph's church, where solemn Benediction of the Blessed Sacrament was given by the Papal Delegate. Rev. Fathers Hammersley and McGuire acted as deacon and sub-deacon respectively, while Rev. Father Collins was Master of Ceremonies. At the conclusion of the Benediction, addresses were presented to the distinguishd visitor, one in French by L. Côté, and the other in English by M. O'Gorman. The address in English was as follows:—

ADDRESS TO THE PAPAL DELEGATE.

Your Excellency,—

The students of Ottawa University are happy in the opportunity that is afforded them to-day of presenting their homage to the worthy Head of the Church in Canada, of giving expression to their sincere attachment to him, and of assuring him of their genuine loyalty. Your Excellency has many titles to our veneration and affection. You have been placed over us by the tender solicitude of him who is the Common Father of Christendom. Being the children of Catholic parents, and the students of a Catholic University, we take the most intense pride in displaying our love and fidelity to the Chair of Peter by our devotion to Your Excellency in your office of Apostolic Delegate. In the discharge of the duties of that high office you have proved yourself to such a marked degree thè prudent but fearless champion of the rights and interests of the Church, that you have won for yourself the deepest gratitude of the Catholics of Canada. The First Canadian Plenary Council, which under your wise guidance and presidency, was lately brought to such a happy termination, and which, we are sure, will do much for the strengthening and extension of the true faith in this young country, will pass down to history as a monument to the zeal and energy that have always characterized you in the government of that portion of Christ's vineyard that the Supreme Pontiff has entrusted to your watchful care. Among the many occasions upon which that energy and zeal have been manifested to the great profit of our holy religion, we recall one in particular wherein you fought, with determination and valor, in behalf of the noble cause to which Ottawa University is consecrated — the cause of Catholic Education. As faithful sons of our Alma Mater, we are grateful to you for the vigilance and wisdom you displayed in safeguarding religious instruction in Canada against the attacks of infidelity; and we congratulate you upon the remarkable success that has crowned your efforts in that struggle as well as in everything else that you have undertaken for the welfare of Catholicity during your residence in our midst.

We desire to thank Your Excellency most heartily for the honor of your presence here to-day. You have given another proof of your kindly interest in Ottawa University, and have strengthened the bond of affectionate loyalty that has ever united us to you.

While we rejoice exceedingly in the honor that your presence confers on us, we cannot suppress a sentiment of sadness when we think that he who, during long years, presided on occasions similar to this, and was bound to us by many strong ties, is no longer here to take his part in this day's function. As one who had received his education at Ottawa University, who followed its progress with the keenest interest, as its Apostolic Chancellor, he was familiar to many generations of students, and had well merited their love and gratitude. And so we mourn his demise, and shall long preserve his memory as that of one of our most generous benefactors, and of one of the noblest members of the Canadian episcopate.

We again renew to Your Excellency the expression of our fealty; in union with Catholic Canada we pour forth prayers of thanksgiving for the signal blessings that Heaven has granted us through your devoted rule; and we implore Providence to continue to illumine you with the light of the Holy Spirit and inflame you with His ardor, in order that, in the future as in the past, you may guide with heavenly wisdom and zeal the destinies of the Canadian Church.

His Excellency made a very happy reply, expressing the deep pleasure he felt in hearing the religious and filial sentiments expressed in the name of so imposing a body of young men. In earnest words he commented upon the importance of the recent Plenary Council at Quebec, where he said: ''The cream of Canadian Catholicity was assembled.'' His Excellency stated in strong words to his attentive hearers the necessity of preparing themselves now, in their college days, in a manner calculated to make them in after years worthy members of society and of the church.

The Profession of Faith was then made by the different professors of the University. The number of students present at the imposing ceremony far surpassed that of other years, the church being almost filled.

The following professors of the University made Profession of Faith: Rev. W. J. Murphy, Rector; Rev. Fathers Poli, Lajeunesse, Duvic, Gavary, Guertin, Peruisset, Roy, McGowan, Boyer, Sherry, Fallon, Boyon, Hammersley, Finnegan, Stanton, Jasmin, Binet, T. Murphy, S. Murphy, Pepin, Kelly, Rheaume, Normandin, McGuire, Lalonde, M. Murphy, Latulipe, Turcotte, Pelletier, Collins, Dube, Voyer, Bertrand, Veronneau, Denis, Dewe and Brown; and Messrs. Logan, O'Gorman, Dubois, Fleming, Breen and Griffin.

Around the Halls.

''Tempus fugit,'' and everything points to peace and harmony. Within the walls and within the halls of our Alma Mater we find existing a spirit that cannot be described in words, but which can be noticed by the happiness of each and every one. This concord is the result of a well organized system, and of worthy motives adopted by our prefects. They have done all in their power to make our college course one upon which we can look back with fond recollections.

The pool and billiard tables which recently have been installed are a source of much pleasure to all. In order that each member may receive his share of the sport, a schedule has been drawn up with two men on a team, and as the majority of us are not proficient in the art of holding the cue it is with envious eyes that we witness the scientific shots executed by our worthy friend "Peter," the daddy of them all.

The officers of the Reading Room Society have been elected and if you are looking for a paper or a magazine just ask George. He will furnish you with the very best reading material in the house. Under the directorship of Rev. M. Murphy, O.M.I., everything is run on a systematic basis. The following are the list of officers:

Director—Rev. M. Murphy, O.M.I.

President— M. J. Smith.

Vice-President—C. F. Gauthier.

Sec.-Treas.—A. L. Fleming.

Councillors—G. Whibbs and H. Chartrand.

Our happiness reached its climax on the evening of Dec. 3, when we learned that Ottawa University won the Intercollegiate debate with McGill. The debate was on the question of whether it was the duty of Canada to pay an unconditional cash contribution to the Imperial navy, or to undertake the creation of a separate naval force. McGill speakers upheld the cash contribution, and Ottawa the separate naval force. The McGill representatives were Messrs. L. Fitch and H. F. Angus, and those of Ottawa Messrs. A. C. Fleming and M. O'Gara. The judges were Rev. Canon Gauth, vice rector of Laval; Seargent P. Stearns, A.B.A.M., of Princeton, and Mr. B. N. Sandwell, of Toronto University. We the student body wish to tender our heroes our sincerest congratulations for the brilliant victory which they have achieved, not only because they have won laurels for themselves, but also for the institution to which they belong.

On October 18 the University Debating Society held its first weekly debate for the season of 1909-10. The subject, "Resolved that the manufacture, importation and sale of intoxicating liquors should be carried on exclusively by the government" was ably supported by Messrs. J. T. Brennan, '10, and T. F. Curry, '13. The negative was upheld by Messrs. J. J. Sammon, '11, and T. L. McEvoy, '13. Mr. M. J. Smith, '10, treasurer of the society, was in the chair. The judges, Messrs. J. J. Burke, '10; D. J. Breen, '11; E. C. Boyle, '12; M. J. Brennan, '13, and F. Ainsborough, '14, decided in favour of the negative.

October 25 saw the second debate, upon a very live issue, about that time "Resolved that trial by Judge affects the proper administration of law better than trial by jury." The affirmative,

Messrs. J. J. Burke, '10, and J. J. Kennedy, '12, were opposed by Messrs. M. J. O'Gorman, '11, and E. C. Boyle, '12. Mr. J. T. Brennan, '10, president of the society, presided. The judges were B. G. Dubois, '10, J. J. Contway, '11, P. J. Conway, '12, G. F. Coupal, '13, and T. C. Brennan, '14. They decided in favour of the negative.

On November 5 the subject was "The Abolition of Capital Punishment is in the best interests of humanity." The affirmative were Messrs. F. Corkery, '11, and E. J. Rainboth, '14; the negative, Messrs. Leo H. Tracy, '11, and J. R. Tobin, '14. The chairman was J. J. Burke, '10. On the decision of the judges, J. T. Brennan, '10, A. C. Fleming, '11, J. J. Kennedy, '12, W. Jas. Cross, '13, and T. H. Burrows, '14, the affirmative won.

The subject debated on November 16 was that "The Referendum should be adopted by the people of Canada." Affirmative, Messrs. T. J. O'Neill, '11, and J. B. Rahal, '14. Negative, Messrs. P. P. Griffin, '11, and T. C. Brennan, '14. The chair was occupied by Mr. B. G. Dubois, '10. Judges, C. F. Gauthier, '10, F. Corkery, '11, E. A. Letang, '12, T. F. Curry '13, and H. A. Chartrand, '14. The decision favored the affirmative.

November 22 saw a very interesting debate as to whether "The Press is productive of greater evil than good." The affirmative was supported by Messrs. B. G. Dubois, '10, and P. F. Loftus, '14. They were opposed by Messrs. C. F. Gauthier, '10, and F. X. Burrows, '14. Mr. C. D. O'Gorman, '10, presided. The decision in favour of the negative was reached by Messrs. M. J. Smith, '10, P. P. Griffin, '11, S. P. Quilty, '12, L. W. Kelley, '13, and J. M. Chartrand, '14.

Another interesting debate on the resolution that "The Right of Suffrage should be extended to women on the same conditions on which it is enjoyed by men," was held on November 29th. Mr. C. F. Gauthier, '10, was chairman. The affirmative, Messrs. C. D. O'Gorman, '10, and M. A. Gilligan, '14, were beaten by Messrs. M. J. Smith, '10, and H. A. Chartrand, '14. This decision was arrived at by Messrs. P. C. Harris, '11, C. F. O'Neill, '12, O. E. Kennedy, '13, J. S. Cross, '14, and A. V. Freeland, '14.

THE WASHINGTON SOCIETY.

The Washington Society held its first annual meeting on the 9th of November, at which the following officers were elected:

Rev. Fr. Finnegan—Director.

B. J. Dubois—President.

P. Loftus—Vice-President.

L. J. Pfohl—Secretary.

A. Gilligan—Treasurer.

Owing to the resignation of the Rev. Fr. Hammersley, a new Director had to be secured.

Fr. Hammersley had filled the office for several years, re-flecting great credit upon the society and upon himself.

The society was fortunate in obtaining the services of the Rev. Fr. Finnegan, who has been associated with the student body for a number of years.

To the retiring Director we desire to extend sincere thanks for his earnest effort for the betterment of the society.

To our new Director we offer good wishes and good-will.

The new officers are all energetic and earnest workers, and the prospects for the Washington Society of 1909-10 are indeed very bright.

THANKSGIVING BANQUET.

The annual Thanksgiving celebration took place on Thursday, Nov. the 25th, and proved a real success.

The members first played pool and billiards, and then partook of a most delicious turkey dinner, after which a previously arranged programme was in order, and was listened to with great attention by all.

The following members took part in the programme: Rev. Fathers Finnegan, Hammersley, Stanton, Kunz and Turcotte, and B. J. Dubois P. F. Loftus, L. J. Pfohl, A. Gilligan, H. Chartrand, P. Harris. Tracy, Gallopin, Creighton, Moore, St. Amour, Griffin, LaHaie, Martineau, Searle, Muzanti, Petit, Currie and Pelissier.

The programme ended with the familiar strains of Auld Lang Syne, sung by all.

"FOOTBALL NIGHT"

Tuesday evening, Dec. 7th, was set aside as "Football Night," and a euchre party, pool and billiard tournament, supper and an entertainment was held at the University. The fun commenced about 7.30 and much pleasure was afforded to all. The occasion will be long remembered by those who were so fortunate as to be present.

During the early part of the evening Messrs. Hackett, Quilty, and Muzanti, resplendent in brass buttons and batons, acted in the official capacity of policemen and were supposed to maintain order during the games. Needless to say those who made the most noise were the worthy officers themselves. While the several games were in progress Mr. H. Chartrand officiated at the piano in his usual capable manner. The card-sharks were afforded an excellent opportunity of displaying their knowledge of the game of euchre, and many did so during the evening. Foremost amongst the sharks was Mr. J. Harrington.

Excitment was intense during the pool and billiard tournament so much so, that both players and spectators forgot that in the next room the tables were groaning with good things to satisfy the inner cravings of the man. The tournament being over, all repaired to the refectory where ample justice was done to the good things provided. After supper the amateur performance began, which was admitted by all to be indeed a treat.

The first number on the program was some clever playing and imitations on the cornet by Mr. Germain, ably assisted by Miss Turcotte as drummer. The charms of the latter combined with her able execution of the part alloted her took the house by storm.

The next number was the decided hit of the evening. Mr. Gallopin appeared before the foot-lights in a Spanish declamation, in the rendition of which he showed extraordinary talent. Although the role was a very difficult one to assume, our Mexican friend showed that he was equal to the occasion. Later on in the evening the same gentleman excelled in the art of whistling.

Another feature of the program which elicited much applause was the Darky Ministrel Club under the able leadership of Mr. W. Hacket alias Mr. Brown. These clever artists kept the audience in roars of laughter for about half an hour. Each played his part to perfection. The troupe was composed of eight members, namely:— Messrs, Searle, Pfohl, Cusack, Griffin, Harris, Boyle, B. Chartrand, Tracy and last, but not least, Mr. Hackett, "the educated man." Mr. H. Chartrand, another of the darkies, played the accompaniments for the several songs rendered by the members. We hope to hear from the Ministrels again some time in the near future.

Sheehy and Larochelle, the magician wonders, kept their audience spell bound during their entire act, which immediately followed that of the ministrels. They even succeeded in deceiving the worthy judges in their execution of many acts of magic. The following gentlemen acted as judges to decide the degrees of perfection of the amateurs and to award the prizes:— Fathers Lajeunesse, Hammersley, Stanton, Kunz, Sherry, and Mr Walsh.

The results were as follows; 1st prize awarded to Mr. Gallopin. 2nd prize, Messrs Germain & Turcotte, 3rd prize, The Minstrel Club

Euchre—1st prize awarded to Mr. J. Harrington, 2nd prize, Mr. Rahal, consolation prize, C. Coupal.

Pool—Prize awarded to Morel and Muzanti. (Morel had highest run). Billiards—Prize awarded to Brunet and Simard. (Brunet had highest run)

The prizes having been given, all joined in the singing of "Auld Lang Syne", after which an announcement was made that we must arise at 6.30 next morning. This announcement had the effect of dispersing the crowd and each member was soon in the Land of Nod.

University of Ottawa Review

PUBLISHED BY THE STUDENTS.

THE OTTAWA UNIVERSITY REVIEW is the organ of the students. Its object
is to aid the students in their literary development, to chronicle their doings in and out of
class, and to unite more closely to their Alma Mater the students of the past and the present

TERMS :

One dollar a year in advance. Single copies, 15 cents. Advertising rates on application.
Address all communications to the "UNIVERSITY OF OTTAWA REVIEW", OTTAWA, ONT.

EDITORIAL STAFF :

J. BRENNAN, '10 ;   A. FLEMING, '11 ;   M. O'GARA, '10 ;
J. BURKE, '10 ;   PH. HARRIS, '11 ;   C. D. O'GORMAN, '10 ;
                       M. SMITH, '10.

Business Managers : C. GAUTHIER '10, ;   D. BREEN, '11.

G. GALLOPIN, Staff Artist.

Our Students are requested to patronize our Advertisers.

Vol. XII.   OTTAWA, ONT., DECEMBER, 1909.   No. 3

CHRISTMAS GREETINGS.

When this issue reaches our readers the Christmas bells will
be pealing forth their notes of peace and gladness, in unison with
the melody of angelic harps and the universal paean of "men of
good will." In the sweet effulgence of the Star of Bethlehem
everyone whose heart is true can behold his new-born dignity
as brother of Him who became the Son of man, to teach us the
glory of Christian solidarity. What heart so frigid that it beats
not quicker in the warmth of Christmas joy and generosity?
Young and old, rich and poor, feel a little better and a little
happier on this "the day which the Lord hath made." Permit
us to add our modest word of greeting amid these holy festivi-
ties, and to wish all our readers peace and plenty, a Merry Christmas and a Happy New Year.

WHY NOT DO IT NOW?

Ever since Canada was awakened last March to a realisation

that the supremacy of the power upon which her prosperity depends was seriously questioned, naval defence has occupied the foremost place in the public mind. It seems to be well-nigh unanimously admitted that Canada must, at last, do something towards helping the mother country in the matter of Imperial defence. When the subject was discussed in the House of Commons last session, the speakers were one in their opinion that Canada's contribution should take the form of a separate naval force, and a resolution was adopted to that effect. Since that time there has taken place, in some influential quarters, a reaction in favor of a direct cash contribution to the British Exchequer. There seems little likelihood, however, that this opinion will gain much headway against the conviction, so strongly rooted in the Canadian mind, and which was expressed by Lord Russel, that the colonies be given, as far as possible, the capacity of ruling themselves. We are conscious of the boundless resources of our country, of its growing population, and its extensive trade, and we feel that since Canada has taken her position among the nations of the world, she must bear the responsibilities of nationhood. We are of the opinion of the writer, who aptly said, that "Canada cannot hope limping into the arena of the world to become a commercial factor in its progress. She must march in, bearing those convincing insignia of her maturity and strength which a reasonably perfect equipment affords," and, therefore, since no one cares to deny that at some time or other it will be found necessary for Canada to have a navy for her home and coast defence, we feel that no more opportune time than the present will be found in which to begin to lay its foundation.

"ROOTER SONGS."

A great thinker once remarked that he cared not who made the laws of a country so long as he knew who was responsible for their popular songs. Had he lived in these latter days he would doubtless have applied for a position on the staff of one of those enterprising journals which provide the charms of poetical inspiration to our football enthusiasts. What in fact could be more inspiring to the poet than to wed his cadences to the lilt of a tune already popular, and thus sail in on a sea of success doubly insured by the fascination of well-chosen words set to such triumphs of musical art as "My Wife's Gone to the Country," or "Oh, You Kid"? What could be more gratifying than to hear thousands of manly voices echoing the paean of potential victory to the strains of

"Look at the score, oh—ain't they sore—
Ottawa, Hurrah!"

as they march in triumph through the streets of "Hogtown" to witness the "affray," and celebrate the joyful time by copious libations to the tune of "I'm Fu the Noo." It may, of course, occur to the thoughtful mind that Mr. John McGraw of Ottawa would perhaps be better off at home, minding the house, and keeping an eye on the School Question. But what's to be done? —the martial blast has sounded "there's something in the bottle for the (Sunday) morning," so John has to leave for Toronto and do his duty as a man and a "rooter"!

The future historian of our city will doubtless be much interested in these poetical evidences of an heroic age when the men of the "only sporting city" were accustomed to "bet coin" on their invincibility, when they "skinned" their opponents and "trimmed them to a finish." He will be duly impressed by the vigour with which they "boosted along the score" and taught the feebler folk of other places how to spell the fair name of a city "agin" which "Divil a man can say a word." He will seek to re-picture the feelings of the heroic athlete, who, gazing round at the crowd of friendly "rooters" steeled himself to do or to die to the grand old refrain,

"Hail, Hail, the gang's all here,
Hobble. Gobble, Razzle, Dazzle. etc."

And he will doubtless seek to enshrine in impassioned prose the immortal memory of the "pigskin" poet who inspired such noble sentiments.

NOTES.

The thanks of the Football Club and the whole student body are due to Rev. Father Turcotte who, this season, when the job went a-begging, consented, at no little sacrifice, to coach the team.

* * *

The impressive article of Mr. Sol. White on the Constitutional Aspect of the School Question, which appeared in our last issue. has merited the cordial approbation of the Canadian hierarchy, expressed in a number of very congratulatory letters to the author.

* * *

We were delighted to read Senator Powers' forceful letter re the Ferrer incident. Our thanks are due to both him and M. J. Gorman, K.C., who had it inserted in The Evening Journal. Would that more of our Catholic laymen took up the cudgels in defence of truth and justice.

* * *

"Catholicity first, nationality afterward"—that was the motto of the Plenary Council at Quebec, and it should be the watchword of all classes of Catholics in Canada, if we are to make any real progress. The effects of contrary sentiments are only too plainly visible in France at the present moment.

* * *

We shall be glad to receive suitable essays, poems, etc., from any of the senior students. By the way, are there no poets or short-story writers in this institution?

* * *

Query: Where do the externs get their copies of the Review? And Echo answers: "Where?"

Exchanges.

We notice among the new magazines the University Monthly, published by the University of Toronto. The editors of this review are to be congratulated on the quality of literature turned out. The articles contained in the Monthly bespeak power as well as the facility which comes from practice and experience. One of the subjects treated is entitled "A College for Women." The article throws many interesting sidelights on the much-discussed question of co-education. The motive which guides the whole seems to be the growing necessity for some more definite method of conducting lines of education for men and women in a rapidly expanding institution. Many believe that co-education is best for the students; while the opinion of as many others support the opposite view. It is true that classrooms for both sexes are usually overcrowded. Besides, under such conditions, there is generally lack of good discipline. Again, where men and women attend school together, there is always a tendency for each sex to predominate in some peculiar course, as is shown by the number of girls in High Schools who follow the teaching profession. On account of these and similar reasons, the writer favours a separate college for women, and a change of boarding house for the male students, a new one to be built for their fellow-students of the opposite sex.

This month we have received a copy of "The Echoes," a bright little journal, full of the spirit of loyalty and devotion to the institution which shelters the editors themselves. From beginning to end it exhibits that contentment and harmony which is so necessary to a community of this kind. One article in particular, which graphically describes the magic effect of "kindness" to school-mates, is worthy of everybody's notice.

Clarke College Record is among the visitors this month. The Record represents a progressive institution. The number of students is rapidly increasing. The book itself is filled with speeches from the Annual Commencement exercises.

In the November number of the Geneva Cabinet we notice an article on Culture as seen by Matthew Arnold. According to this illustrious writer, culture is a study of perfection to render an intelligent being yet more intelligent. Its greatest aim is to make the will of God prevail, to lift the raw person up to the sense of the beautiful, to bring him to sweetness, and light, to seek to do away with classes, to make the best that has been thought and known in the world prevail everywhere, to make men live in an atmosphere where they may use ideas, and use them freely.

The Notre Dame Scholastic has generally been considered as one of our best exchanges. It is replete with many classical articles and poems. To give each number its praiseworthy criticism would exhaust our store of approval, so we have to confine ourselves to the last issue which is of the same literary value as the preceding numbers. The article on "Wordsworth's Theory of Poetry" is well treated and shows deep research on the part of the writer. Looking over this article we notice the words, "there neither is nor can be any essential difference between the language of prose and metrical composition." These words have been differently interpreted, some critics holding Wordsworth's meaning, that poetry should be merely prose accommodated to metre. The reflection of the noble mind that uttered them, the index of a man who answers to our ideal of the true poet; a poet who speaks only of the beautiful, the noble and the good, and whose life is an echo of his words.

The Xaverian is also among our numbers this month. The November number contains a very interesting article entitled, "Socialism in Relation to Catholicism." The author asserts "that no Catholic can be a Socialist," but on the other hand "that a Catholic is not bound to oppose every measure put forth by the Socialists, for some of those measures cannot be opposed without opposing the Church herself."

Besides the above-mentioned, we beg to acknowledge receipt of the following: "Holy Cross Purple," "Trinity University Review," "Queen's University Journal," "St. Jerome's Schoolman," "McMaster University Monthly," "Georgetown College Journal," "The Villa Shield," "St. John's University Record," "Abbey Student," "Assumption College Review," "Hya Yaka," "The Martlet," "Laurel," "Acta Victoriana," "The Columbiad," "The Patrician," "Comet," "Agnetian Quarterly."

Books and Reviews.

The Romance of the Silver Shoon—Rev. David Bearne, S.J.; Benziger Bros. 85 cents.

Father Bearne has succeeded in again making a valuable addition to juvenile Catholic literature. It is a sweetly-told story of imaginary kings and princes of Reformation days, and is well calculated to hold youthful interest from the first to the very last page. The plot hinges upon the young Prince Olaf's boyish whim of having a pair of silver shoes. To tell how he parted with them, and how they ultimately brought about the downfall of the wayward Queen Marabout, would be to reveal the whole story. There is an atmosphere of Christmas throughout its pages, which makes it particularly acceptable at this season.

The University Magazine, for October, contains several articles of much interest. Prof. Stephen Leacock has an exhaustive treatise upon the Monroe Doctrine and its relation to Canada. C. Frederick Hamilton has a strong plea for the building of a Canadian navy. This article is being much discussed at present, owing to its accepted merit, and an account of the debate which will shortly take place upon the subject in Parliament. Lovers of the classics will derive much pleasure from the Rev. J. A. Dewe's essay on the Beauties of Cicero's Style. There are likewise several articles which would be of much interest to the philosophers.

Among the Magazines.

In the Rosary Magazine, under the heading "Temperance in Ireland," it is stated the Capuchin Fathers have been conduct-ing such a crusade against intemperance that they are quoted as predicting, "The liquor evil will soon be unknown in Ireland." This is to be the consummation which Ireland's sons in foreign lands have so long desired. And with good reason have her children wished it, since the Green Isle is the home of all the other virtues.

The Leader, of New York, proclaims the intention of the Canadian government to obtain possession of all the forts and battlefields so that Canada will have an everlasting record of the men who saved it from the enemy. Last year a commission was created to save the famous Plains of Abraham at Quebec, and not the least of Canada's possessions will be the field of Chateau-guay, where De Salaberry, with 300 French-Canadians, routed 1,500 invaders.

The Rosary Magazine for November has an article on Presi-dent Taft's liberality in matters of religion. On the occasion of the laying of a corner-stone, he said: "I am here because I be-lieve the corner-stone of modern civilization must continue to be religion and morality." "The time is coming," he said, "when all the churches are growing together." He has frequently paid tribute to the Catholic religion, and to Irish Catholics: "The hardy-hearted immigrants from Tipperary and from every part of the Emerald Isle," he is quoted as saying, "have come to the front in America as they should."

The Christmas "Extension" is to hand, and is in every re-spect a splendid number.

Priorum Temporum Flores.

Rev. Dr. H. Lacoste, O.M.I., Vicar-General of Prince Albert, paid us a visit last week, and was warmly welcomed by his many friends.

Newspapers to hand inform us that the visit of Archbishop Dontenwill, O.M.I., '80, to the Lone Star State, has been one great triumphal procession. We are eagerly looking forward to the time when his Alma Mater may receive him within her walls.

Rev. Eugene Dorgan, '86, is at present preaching a retreat at the Holy Family Church, Ottawa East.

Rev. Father McDonald, '88, of Greenfield, recently paid a visit to his Alma Mater.

Rev. W. Sloan, B.A., '06, of Vinton, will be ordained to the holy priesthood on Saturday, Dec. 18th, at the Grand Seminary, Montreal.

On Saturday, Dec. 4th, Mr. James George, B.A., '06, was ordained deacon at the Grand Seminary, Montreal, and on Saturday, Dec. 18th, his ordination to the holy priesthood will take place.

Mr. C. J. Jones, '08, of Eganville, who is a student at the Grand Seminary, Montreal, will receive sub-deaconship on the 18th inst.

Mr. J. Lajoie, matriculant of '06, figured prominently on the Varsity team in the Ottawa-Varsity game for the Dominion championship. Jerry scored the first touch-down for Toronto Varsity.

Mr. P. Marshall, '08, accompanied the College team to Kingston and witnessed their game against Queen's.

Mr. C. Hurtubise, commercial graduate of '04, was here a short time ago on his way to Duluth, where he holds a responsible position in the office of the Duluth Manufacturing Co.

Rev. J. J. Quilty, '97, visited the University a short time ago.

Mr. D. Rheaume, formerly of Ottawa College, will be ordained to the holy priesthood in St. Joseph's Church on Dec. 21st, and will celebrate his first Mass in St. Joseph's on Dec. 22nd.

Personals.

Rev. Fr. W. J. Murphy, Rector of the University, has the unique distinction of being Ottawa's representative on the Advisory Council of Education for Ontario.

Hats off to Messrs. M. J. O'Gara and A. C. Fleming, winners of the Intercollegiate Debate with McGill.

Rev. Fr. W. J. Stanton, J.T. Brennan, '10, and P. C. Harris, '11, attended the Varsity-Ottawa football game.

Dr. Hogarth, M.A., curator of the Archaemolean Library, Oxford, recently delivered a lecture in the Normal School Hall on the influence of the Hittites on early Grecian civilization, which was much enjoyed by all the students.

We are indebted to Dr. White for this rare literary treat.

Rev. Fr. Flynn, Watertown, Conn., paid us a visit while a guest of Mr. W. J. Lynch, Wilbrod street.

Mr. H. Hayes, an old pupil and Professor at Varsity, was married last week to Miss L. Brennan, a sister of the late Mr. L. Brennan, '09. The Review extends its congratulations to the young couple.

Rev. Fr. Pelletier, O.M.I., Superior of the Oblate House, Plattsburg, N.Y., recently paid us a visit.

Athletics.

Queens (32) — Ottawa (9.)

The closing game of the football season, 1909, took place at Kingston on Nov. 13, and ended with the usual result of games played in the Penitentiary Town. Neither team had a chance for the honors of the league, consequently very little interest was taken in the contest. Queen's were anxious to square the defeat at Ottawa Oct. 16, and succeeded in taking r-e-v-c-n-g-e to the tune of 32 to 9.

The first three quarters saw our team out-played in all departments, but in the final quarter they braced up wonderfully and had the ball in Queen's territory all the time. They succeeded in scoring 9 points.

Gilligan, Sullivan, Quilty, Smith and Muzanti were most conspicuous for their steady consistent playing.

The team lined up as follows:—Full back, Conway; backs, Chartrand, Quilty, Contway, Muzanti; scrimmage, Dubois, Breen; wings, Gilligan, Sullivan, Smith, Belanger, Whibbs, Kennedy, Leacy, Brennan, Kennedy.

Referee Dr. Etherington; umpire, J. Richardson; timers, Rev. W. J. Stanton, O.M.I., J. F. MacDonald; touch line judges. P. C. Harris, E. O. Slater.

A joint excursion was run by the Ottawa University and Ottawa Collegiate football teams, and was well patronized, about 200 taking in the trip. Rev. Fathers Stanton, O.M.I., and Turcotte, O.M.I., accompanied the team.

Standing of Intercollegiate Football Union, 1909.

	Won.	Lost.	Scored for.	Scored against.
Toronto	5	1	164	28
McGill...	3	3	58	70
Queen's	3	3	86	60
Ottawa...	1	5	31	180

Standing of Inter-Mural Football League, 1909.

	Won.	Lost.	
Robillard (Capt.)	5	1	(Champions)
Guindon (Capt.)	5	1	" "
Hackett (Capt.)	2	4	
Coupal (Capt.)...	2	4	

Inter-Mural Championship, 1909.

Capt. Robillard (12) — Capt. Guindon (9.)

The play-off for the championship of the Inter-Mural Football League was certainly a sensational and scientific exposition of the great Canadian autumn sport. The score, 12-9, fairly indicates the relative strengths of the two teams. Capt. Robillard's stalwarts were particularly effective on the back division. The catching, kicking, bucking and running of Lawson Sheehy, Gall Cornellier, Newton Barry, Dixon McDougall was certainly made up from senior brand football. Quarter back and Captain Robillard generalled his team like a veteran, and with the steady aggressive work of the wings, a well deserved and hard-earned victory was secured.

Thanks are due the Reverend Father Stanton for the manner in which the league was carried through to such a successful issue. The league certainly did great work in developing young players for the bigger teams next year. The four captains, R. Guindon, W. Hackett, H. Robillard and C. Coupal, are to be congratulated for the capable manner in which they handled their men, and for the prompt and punctual playing of scheduled games.

Line-up of Capt. Robillard's warriers:—Full back, F. McDougall; halves, R. Sheehy, P. Cornellier, J. Barry; quarter back, H. Robillard (Capt.); scrimmagers, Larouche, J. Ginty, Fink;

wings, Guichon, Murtagh, Pilon, Holly, Bonhomme, F. Brennan.
Referee, Rev. W. J. Stanton.
Scores:—Robillard: 2 touch-downs, 2 rouges—12; Guindon:
1 touch-down, 4 rouges—9.

The Championship Series.

Varsity! Varsity! Rah! Rah! Rah!
By the overwhelming score of 31 to 9 Toronto Varsity, winners of the Intercollegiate Rugby Union, defeated the Ottawa
Club, Interprovincial champions, at Rosedale, Saturday afternoon,
December 4, 1909, before a crowd of 10,000 people. This was the
largest gathering of football enthusiasts that ever witnessed a
game in Toronto.

A RECORD IN RECEIPTS.

Attendance (official)—9,500.
Gate receipts—$6,189.00.
This creates a new record in Canadian rugby football.
Rev. W. J. Stanton, O.M.I., Hon. Pres. C.I.R.F.U., and Secy.-
Treas. P. C. Harris, enjoyed the unique privilege of witnessing
the important championship game from the touch line. Needless
to say they enjoyed the thrilling game, more so on account of the
offices they held. The Intercollegiate has settled once and for all
that it is more than on a par with the Interprovincial League.
Ottawa University football team extends heartiest congratu-
lations to the Toronto Varsity Club, on its magnificent victory.
Three hearty cheers for the champions of the Dominion. Hurrah!
Hurrah! Hurrah!

League Matters.

The annual meeting of the Canadian Intercollegiate Rugby
Football Union will be held this year in Kingston, Saturday,
Dec. 11, 1909, at the Randolph Hotel. The business of the meeting is the election of officers for the ensuing term, drawing up
of the schedules for the senior, intermediate and junior series of
the Union. Several important changes to the playing rules are
expected to be made. The presidency of the Union this year
goes to Queen's, McGill getting the secretary-treasurership. Rev.
W. J. Stanton, O.M.I., Hon. Pres., and P. C. Harris, Secy.-Treas.,
will attend the meeting as the Ottawa University representatives.

Winter Sports.

Now that the muddy moleskins have been tucked away for the season, the students turn their attention to Canada's great winter pastimes, skating and hockey. Three fine rinks have been laid out in front of the main building of the University, and perhaps before this article is printed the students will have enjoyed their first skate. Rink number three, though smaller in size than the other two, looms largest in relative importance. On its glassy surface will the timid yet persevering amateur "cut up" to his heart's content, as long as he limits his field to the ice and not to other people's shins.

An Intermural Hockey League is in the course of formation, which bids fair to outrival the football league in thrilling and blood-tingling struggles for supremacy with stick, puck and steel. We hope that the "puck" will exclude all other brands that are not made of rubber, and that the "steels" though sharp may not be sufficient to cause us to call in the theft officer. Always use the "stick" in a legitimate manner; "stick" at nothing that is honest and gentlemanly, and finally "stick" in the game even though your side is getting badly stuck. (Choke!)

Billiards and Pool.

Welcome and greatly appreciated additions to the equipment of the Recreation Hall were made last month in the shape of a billiard table and pool table, with the usual accessories of ivory balls, cues, and cue frames.

To say that they are enjoyed is putting it mildly. Judging from the enthusiasm and vim that is shown in the billiard and pool tournaments now in full swing, this source of amusement will certainly be the popular one during the winter months. Not since the disastrous fire in Dec., 1903, have the students been fortunate enough to enjoy this scientific pastime, hence its long absence makes it doubly enjoyable. Thanks to Rev. Fathers Stanton and McGowan for their thoughtfulness in procuring the two tables.

Of Local Interest

QUOTATIONS.

C. O'G-n: "A man I am, crossed with adversity."—Shakespeare.

W-h-b-s: "Is she not passing fair?"—Shakespeare.

B-r-n-n: "Hang Sorrow! care'll kill a cat."—Ben Jonson.

Ha-r-s: "As good to be cut out of the world as out of the fashion."—Colley Cibber.

Ke-n-dy: "Beware the fury of a patient man."—Dryden.

Gi-l-g-n: "None but the brave deserves the fair."—Dryden.

P. S.: "To err is human, to forgive divine."—Pope.

K-d-y: "Lest men suspect your tale untrue,
Keep probability in view."—John Gay.

G-u-t-r: "I am always in haste, but never in a hurry."—John Wesley.

O'G-a: "Life's a short summer; man is but a flower."—Samuel Johnson.

O'N-l: "O bed! O bed! delicious bed!
That heaven upon earth to the weary head."
—Thomas Hood.

C-n-t-ay: "Youth is a blunder; manhood a struggle; old age a regret."—Disraeli.

D-u-b-s: "Laugh and be fat."—John Taylor.

O'B-l-e: "Ignorance of one's misfortunes is clear gain."—Euripides.

H-c-k-t: "Even a single hair casts its shadow."—Publius.

———

H-g-r-t-y: Lend men a dollar, Jerry, and I will be everlastingly indebted to you.

Jerry: Faith an' I know you will, and that's why I won't lend it to you.

M. Br-n-n: H-t got his feet wet the other day.

M-voy: He'll have a cold in his head about next April.

Prof. of Physics: I think there's some kind of a trust between you and O'G-n, D-b-s.

Student: A beef trust?

Prof. of Eng.: What is the meaning of ascetic?

Student: Pertaining to vinegar.

L-vi is engaged in the lumbering business now. He sends a lot of logs down the river.

I bet you'll speak the next time, C-e, and you'll buy a ticket, too, Tr-y!

Hig-r-y (pricing stoves at Esmonde's): This is a fairly good stove, is it?

Clerk: Yes; with a stove like that you'll save half your fuel.

Hig-r-y: Alright, I'll take two of them and save it all.

O that wholesale rate, H-r-s!

S. Co-up-l (explanation of counter tide): Move the moon around and then you have them.

Do you clearly see the hills and the valleys in your essay?

Your essay is very much like a big blot which becomes larger towards the end.

In Physics class: Can you feel the pain of that ans.? (Oh, you stale joker).

Br-n-an: The most adaptable man in the house.

JUNIOR DEPARTMENT.

J. D., president of the Horticultural Society, accompanied by his secretary Dominic, awarded the prizes in the recent garden competition. Fk. M-phy won the society's medal, Gordon O'R-ly being a close second.

Do not monkey with Ralph; he is up among the prize-winners in the recent Marathon.

Dan S-l-n: Tommy, where is M-l-t?
Tommy H-t: Cherchez Georgie D-z-is.

Why did Jimmie go up to the Infirmary?

"Helping the lazy ones out with a stick" during the morning rec.

Too bad, Joe, you could not catch that rest in the Infirmary.

Hockey teams wishing to play on the new rink apply to the manager, Charles F-n-er.

The billiard and pool leagues are now in full swing and great interest is being taken in the championship games. Always be on time when it is your turn to take part in a game. Remember your partner and the manager of the games expect this from you.

Congratulations to Ralph, Con, Elwood and John, our representatives in the recent Latin competition in Third Form. It is hard to put the youngsters down, eh Peter?

The generally good conduct of the boys in this department has been remarked by all. That's right, boys; "keep straight;

be manly boys.'' The Junior editor has his eye on you continually, and, by the way, he sometimes sees more than the Prefects.

The Junior Marathon was run on Nov. 24th. There were twenty-six competitors and about four fell by the way. The winners were: first, Ed. Nagle; second, Ulric McCloskey; third, Ed. Faulkner; fourth, H. Taschereau; fifth, R. Desrosiers; and R. Lahaie also won a prize.

"Oh, splash! There goes my notes."

The Junior Editor wishes all the members of this department a Happy and Joyous Christmas Vacation.

———

That two men may be real friends they must have opposite opinions, similar principles, and different loves and hatreds — (Chateaubriand.)

There are more fools than sages; and among the sages there is more folly than wisdom.—(Chamfort.)

High positions are like the summit of high, steep rocks; eagles and reptiles alone can reach them.—(Mme. Necker.)

Hypocrisy is an homage vice pays to virtue.—(La Rochefoucauld.)

It is a great misfortune not to have enough wit to speak well, or not enough judgment to keep silent.—(La Bruyère.)

Ignorance is less distant from truth than prejudice. — (Diderot.)

Vol. XII.   OTTAWA, ONT., JANUARY, 1910.   No. 4

Entered at the Post Office at Ottawa, Ont., as Second-Class Matter.

A Toast

A Toast to the land of promise,
  To the realms of the bold and free,
Where the rapids foam, as the hills they roam,
  On the way to the mighty sea.

To the land of the lofty mountain,
  Where the hidden riches sleep,
The land of the mead and fountain,
  With waters broad and deep.

To the land of summer sunshine,
  With skies of brightest blue,
The land of winter pastime,
  'Mid snows of radiant hue.

To the land of the beauteous maple,
  The Queen of the Western World,
Where all may come and make their home,
  'Neath freedom's flag unfurled.

Eiblinn

WARREN HASTINGS.

ARREN HASTINGS was born on the sixth of December, 1732. He belonged to the great family of Doylesford, and played a very important. part in the making of the greatest and most powerful empire of the world to-day—England. When Charles was King of Doylesford, it was the custom of his predecessors to mortgage all their property, and this Charles did, keeping the manor which he afterwards sold. The last Hastings of Doylesford had two sons, Howard who sought employment in the English government; and Pynaston, who, being a careless fellow, married early in life, but died a few years after his marriage, leaving one son, who turned out to be the famous Warren Hastings.

At the death of his father, Hastings was as yet very young, and, on account of a series of unfortunate events, he was forced to leave school at an early age with a very scanty education. He was now placed in the hands of his uncle, who also died. He was then given into the care of a Mr. Cheswick, who, not caring properly for the young fellow's career, secured for him a position in the office of the East India Company at Calcutta. Although Hastings might have been given a little more education before entering into this position, yet we can safely say that this step was the foundation of his great and victorious career. Failures and misfortunes are the high roads to success, and thus was the success of young Hastings obtained. While yet in the office of the East India Company, he showed his skill and valor by the way he settled the quarrels that arose between the French, the English and native tribes.

In the year 1764, Hastings returned to England, and, a few years afterwards, he went to India, where he made his abode, and where he performed the many great deeds for which his name is still so much honored even to-day. India at this time was composed of a number of savage and warlike tribes, as the Bengalese, and how he succeeded to keep the upper hand I will try to show you. When in India a short time he was appointed Governor of Bengal, Bombay, and Madras. Having gained this position, he originated a system of government which deduced order from chaos, and peace from anarchy. Few men of high rank to-day have had to form their own plan of government; and, even though they have the government planned for them before taking their positions, yet very few of them ever carry out the rules set down for them. Here we can plainly see what a distinguished man Hastings was when he formed his own system of government, followed the rules which he himself laid down, and was finally successful.

When Hastings became governor he was accompanied by two other ambitious men who were appointed to assist him. Although a man of a very strong will, yet he was persuaded by his two partners to "govern leniently and extort as much money as possible." However, being a little selfish, he wished to place all his relations from the county of Doylesford. He remained Governor of India for thirteen years, and then returned to England, where, on account of the advice and jealous plans of his two colleagues, he suffered impeachment.

It was here that the break was made in the career of that great man. Being very anxious for the progress and advancement of his people, Hastings had almost drained the treasury of money, and now, when he was to stand his trial, he had not the means to back him. Having to pay half a million dollars at the beginning of his trial, he asked a wealthy prince of one of his tribes to pay him a large tribute, and this he did. However, this amount would not suffice, and finally all his possessions were confiscated, and he was left penniless.

In 1785 Hastings received a large sum of money from the London office of the East India Company. He did not keep this long, for Burke and other such prosecutors stirred up the minds of the people, and finally led them to believe that he should be impeached. Here Hastings made one bad step by taking a general named Scott, of the Bengal army, to defend him. Although he had many troubles and difficulties, yet he was safe so long as he kept on good terms with the king. He was also aided much by the East India Company, which pleaded eagerly for his acquittal. One charge brought up against Hastings was the permission which he gave to allow English soldiers to be used in the aid of a native prince to subdue other tribes. This was brought about by the base prince, Sujah Domlah, who wished to enslave a brave people whom he, with his large armies, was afraid to attack. Still he got out of this all right, but was soon mixed up in another charge brought forth by James Fox. Fox accused him of approving the disgraceful plot which accompanied the unlawful seizure of the treasure of Cheyte Sing in the name of the country.

The trial lasted for seven long and troublesome years, during which he had such prosecutors as Burke and Sheridan. He spent the larger part of his fortune in his own defence, and had to pass the remainder of his life depending upon the company for which he sacrificed his name, and which stained a career which otherwise would have been one of the most illustrious in history. He died in 1818.

T. J. O'NEILL, '11.

Catholic Libraries for Catholic People

THE Catholics of Canada have witnessed within the past year the inauguration of a praiseworthy movement which has for its purpose Church extension. The work of the society bearing this name lies in fields hitherto untilled, or at one time abandoned. Its chief endeavour is to carry the Gospel into regions remote from the large centres of population, and to bring back sheep strayed from the fold.. In our opinion a movement of another kind might be started in the cities and towns of our country, the object of which would be to preserve the faith and morals of Catholics. The time is at hand when a decided step must be taken to remove the serious disabilities of Catholics with regard to books and libraries.

In Ottawa we have a public library. We suppose similar establishments exist in many of our cities and towns. We cannot dispute the benefits of libraries when properly conducted. But we must find fault with many of them as they exist. There are one or two things we may say without fear of contradiction: Firstly, in most of these libraries are found books which are decidedly pernicious; secondly, many of these books are given out to the public indiscriminately. We will not be guilty of exaggeration in saying that at least 10% of books in actual circulation cannot be safely read, save by the strongest, mentally and morally. We cannot be accused of mis-representation, in view of the revelations of last summer, in saying that these books are given out with little discretion to all comers. It is quite true that Voltaire will not be placed in the hands of a child; but a substitute in the form of a romance, whose characters are the personifications of the sardonic infidel's vicious principles, will be given him. Apart from the really bad works there are legions of others which are absolutely useless as means of education. The reading of them leaves no good impression. There is nothing in them which elevates the soul, or stimulates the man to exert his energy for good. Constant readers of this class of literature soon become languid, losing all ambition in life, and by this very fact showing the opposite effect to that for which the library was established.

We are not prepared to censure those who have charge of the libraries for permitting such books to circulate. They may have reasons with which we are unfamiliar for so doing. We can hardly think that it is due to carelessness. Perhaps they are governed by a desire, arising from the confusion of the ideas of liberty and license, to give to all access to all knowledge, good and evil. Beyond conjectures we cannot go. But the fact remains that Catholics and Protestants, too, if they wish to take it so, are exposed to an evil which is ever increasing. A veritable deluge of pernicious literature is rushing in through every channel and crevice, bringing with it moral ruin and desolation to thousands.

Some action must be taken by the Catholic people of Canada to offset the evil which itself is counteracting the good influence of the Separate School. We look about for a preventive. Preaching to the people on this point will not give satisfactory results. They must have books, and they will not exert themselves to a great etxent in looking for the best. It would be useless to give them an index of bad books. This would be like a drop of water in the bucket. There are tons of literature which the index could never reach. Bookstores and novel-stalls are filled with them. In some places parts of the public library have been set aside for books that can be safely read by Catholics. When this privilege can be obtained, it is an excellent solution of the difficulty.

Where it will not be conceded then it remains for Catholics to establish school and parochial libraries. We recognize that this is done in some places. But a general movement in this direction throughout the land would have more far-reaching effects than have isolated attempts. It would give to the individual endeavour a stimulus which comes from the knowledge that we are united in a good cause. We are all anxious that Catholics should have all the advantages of a sound education that can be derived from the best in fiction, history, science, etc. At the same time it is of supreme importance that the sources should be untainted. We sincerely hope that a general movement will soon be made in the proper direction. In conclusion we suggest as a slogan the title of this article: "Catholic libraries for Catholic people."

G. W. '10.

Ireland=Poland; a comparison.

(CLASS DEBATE.—Negative.)

THE occurrence of such a phenomenon in European history as the disappearance from the commonwealth of nations of a country which had existed for eight hundred years, calls for some attempt at explanation. For over a century Poland has been razed from the list of European nations.

Poland first comes under our notice during the eighth century, when she emerged from the barbarous hinterland and came into existence as an organized state. Being composed of a brave and stout-hearted people, she advanced with rapid strides until she had attained the rank of the foremost nation of Eastern Europe. She it was who bore the brunt of the Tartar invasions, and withstood the repeated onslaughts of the Mussulmen, those vast hordes of barbarians who overran the populated areas from the Great Wall of China to the gates of Imperial Rome. When Vienna was besieged by an innumerable army of Turks, the Hungarians sent word to that renowned Pole, the Great Sabieski, to come to their aid. And he, with a comparatively small army, marched to their rescue, and inflicted a crushing blow on the Turkish power. For this brave action he was justly hailed the saviour of Europe. The civilized world owes an eternal debt of gratitude to Poland for successfully preserving the Christianity and civilization of Europe against the fanatical nations of the Orient. But the world has ill repaid her debt. For Poland, once the defender of Europe, now forms but a province in the vast Empire of her ancient enemy. During the reign of Stephen Batory, 1578-1586, Poland reached her greatest size. The greatest length of the country from north to south was 713 miles, and from east to west 693 miles, comprising an area of 282,000 sq. miles. This same area in 1880 had a population of 24,000,000.

The cause of Poland's present downcast state is only too evident. Countless Russian invasions laying waste the country have placed the people in a sort of moral stupor. If Polish nationality is ever again triumphant, the triumph will come not through the efforts of the Poles, but out of the necessity and peril of their oppressors. The downfall of Poland first started in 1772, when Russia, Prussia and Austria, moved by a common desire for more territory, divided among themselves some of the choicest portions of Poland. Poland alone was too weak to successfully resist the three united nations. In 1793 occurred the total dismemberment of Poland. Russia desiring to gain more of Poland, had used her influence to place on the Polish throne Stanislaus Poniatouski, a creature of her own, who received his instructions from St. Petersburg. The people, being naturally dissatisfied with this state of affairs, desired to retrieve the fortunes of their falling land, and under the gallant Kosciusko, rose in arm against the Russians. Their success was but short lived; Kosciusko was captured and placed in a Russian prison, and Poland lay at the mercy of her traditional enemy. In 1831 occurred another insurrection against the misgovernment of Russia. Again the patriots were defeated, and the country was laid waste with fire and sword. In 1863 occurred the last insurrection. Again the patriots suffered defeat. But Russia put down this last outbreak more rigorously than any preceding one. Her persecution was so cruel and far-reaching that even to the present day the elderly Pole tells with trembling voice the horrors perpetrated by the ruthless Cossacks. 50,000 men of the best of the nation either perished on the scaffold or were sent to Siberia to languish in the most rigorous confinement. After this staggering blow the nation sank into a moral stupor, from which it has yet to recover. On the night of June 15, 1863, 2,000 patriots out of Warsaw's population of 18,000 were taken from their beds and forcibly enlisted in the Russian army. In 1793, in the streets of Warsaw, 4,000 Poles were massacred in one day by the Russian soldiers under Marshal Suwarrow. Again in 1863, 50,000 Russian soldiers camped and made order in the streets of Warsaw by firing with cannon on men and women who knelt in the snow and sang the Polish national anthem. Such an act of barbarity could be perpetrated in the last half of the 19th century only by such a nation as Russia.

The Russification process, in its two phases of mechanically crowding out Poles with Russians, and in attempting to kill the Polish language, has had some bye-products, probably not looked for by even its advocates. The legal immunity of the Russian element in Poland from abuses of governmental and social rights has brought about a complicity between police and wrong-doers of all kinds, which is almost incredible. It has, moreover, made everything in Poland which is worth while doing an evasion. Of course the Poles teach their children Polish despite the law. They study with a Russian book on top of the desk and a Polish one beneath. It is at the point of attempted forcible conversion by the Orthodox church that Russification arouses the greatest hostility of the Polish peasant. The proseletyzing activities of the Russian church are slowly but surely converting the Polish peasant into an active anti-Russian political element.

In Russia it has been and is a penal offence to teach a Polish peasant anything in Polish, and many difficulties have been put in the way of teaching him anything at all. After the insurrection of 1863, Poland lost all its old privileges. From that time all teaching both in Universities and in schools had to be given in Russian. In 1863 the Russian liberals crushed Polish liberty in the name of patriotism. It is a sign of an evil and rebellious nature in Poland if a person happens to speak a language or profess a creed different from those of the ruling caste. In Warsaw every Polish shop-keeper is obliged to keep one Russian clerk. Since its absolute incorporation with the Russian Empire in 1868, Poland is known in Russian Officialdom as the Cis-Vistula governments. In Russia, labor unions are illegal. As a result in Poland, Polish laborers are entirely at the mercy of their Russian employers. Russia has broken every promise for the betterment of Poland that she made in the treaty of Vienna in 1815.

Poland and Ireland are very similar in some respects. Both were at one time great nations. Both were conquered by a great world-power. Both suffered untold hardships, and both preserved the Catholic Faith. The people of the two countries also have many traits in common. Both are brave and generous to a fault. Both have been divided amongst themselves in critical times of their history, and the exiles of Poland, like those of Ireland, have won fame and military glory for themselves and their country under the flags of foreign lands. It has been aptly said of the Pole that he possesses the urbanity and the delightful manner of the Frenchmen and the warm-hearted ways of the Irishman. Both Irish and Polish have suffered greatly, but when we compare the relative sufferings of the two countries as impartial judges, we must necessarily concede the fact that Poland has the distinction of being the more harshly treated. Ireland has undergone great hardships, I admit, but they have suffered no great hardships late in our day, as have the Poles. When Poland was in the throes of her last revolution, Ireland was gradually emerging from her ancient sufferings. We will just compare the two countries as they stand at present. Ireland is recognized as a Kingdom, and an integral part of the British Empire. She has a national party in the British House of Commons, which watches after the welfare of Ireland with searching eyes. Great reforms have been made for the welfare of the people, curtailing the power of the landlords, and enabling the tenants to practically own their land after some years. And, finally, it is but a matter of time when the Home Rule Bill shall be passed, and Irishmen will be enabled to make their own laws.

Now let us consider Poland. Russia considers Poland not as a nation, but as an ordinary province of her Empire. She does not recognize the Polish nationality. Poland has no national party to uphold her interests at St. Petersburg. Poles cannot rise above a certain rank in the army, and religious distinctions are very finely drawn. The Polish language is forbidden to be taught in every part of Poland except Lithuania, and there the edict was only repealed in May, 1905, whereas in Ireland, England has founded a University for Catholics and the Irish language is one of the important subjects in the curriculum. Poland has no prospect at present of attaining even the present state of liberty that Ireland enjoys. There are 12,000,000 Poles in Russia, and as some writer has aptly put it, they are pinned to Russia by bayonets. Compare the state of tranquility in Ireland to that of Poland, where, in the city of Warsaw, Russia finds it necessary to keep a garrison of 200,000 troops to overawe a city of 900,000 people, and, somehow, the guns of the citadel are turned, not towards the German frontier, the only point from which a foreign enemy could be expected to come, but towards the streets and shops of the third most populous city in the Empire. Poland does not exist officially, but it is, if dead, certainly a very lively corpse.

It is a crying shame, a reproach to the powerful powers of Europe, that they should allow Poland—the land that was the most powerful bulwark of civilization against the inroads of rapacious barbarians—to remain in its present state of helplessness, officially deprived alike of its language and nationality. A land that has produced so many prominent men and women, who have occupied the first place the their respective spheres of action, in war, in literature, in painting, and on the stage, surely deserves better of its powerful neighbors than to be despised and trampled upon. Truly it is a sad fate, that such a progressive people should be thus cruelly treated in these modern days by such a great power as Russia. I will conclude with the following beautiful lines on the fall of Poland, by Thomas Campbell:

Sarmatia fell, unwept, without a crime,
Found not a generous friend, a pitying foe;
Strength in her arms, nor mercy in her woe.
Dropped from her nerveless grasp the shattered spear;
Closed her bright eye, and curbed her high career.
Hope, for a season bade the world farewell,
And freedom.shrieked as Kosciusko fell.

C. O'H., '12.

Is Modern University Training Practical ?

HIS, the great question of to-day, we may answer by stating that the majority of Universities are practical, physically and intellectually, also that we know for a fact the Catholic Universities to be practical, morally.

All Catholic Universities, wherever they may be, on this Continent, in Europe, Asia or Australia, are known by their excellent moral training, and being under the jurisdiction of the One True Faith, the morals and Christian principles which they have for their standard must be of the best calibre. As a proof of this, we find in our Catholic Universities a great many Protestant students, the reason of this is: their parents are not fanatics in religion, and on looking about them see that a large proportion of the men with real characters and principles are graduates of Catholic Universities. Again, if the moral training of our Catholic Universities were not of the best, would not the Pope, who is at the head of all Catholic interests, endeavor to introduce a better system?

Now let us turn to the physical training given in Universities of the present day: In the different walks of life, one meets with people of diverse ideas, as to the physical training given, not only in our own Universities, but also in the non-sectarian ones. Some may not approve of it, stating that it does not coincide with intellectual training, in other words a young man cannot take part in sports and follow his course of studies, without more or less distraction. On the other hand we meet men and women who insist that their children receive the proper physical training, some even make it emphatic that physical training should be attended with more importance than intellectual training; for if young people were allowed to grow up, without any physical training whatever, the National debt would be increased more by building hospitals for consumptives and other people with contagious diseases, than it will be when the G.T.P. Railway is completed.

Look around us and see the results, notice the difference between those who go in for sports and those who do not; in color, form, development, and even character; very frequently the boy who is first in sports is also first in his class, yet some people will say sport is not necessary or practical. In one sense it may not be practical, for not all University graduates are going to become prize-fighters, but if by physical training they develop the bodily element and at the same time develop the intellectual part of the bodily element by intellectual training, they will not only make strong men with healthy bodies but also men with strong and healthy intellect. An old proverb says: "All work and no play makes Jack a dull boy."

We may say that the intellectual business of a University is to set forth the right standard and to train according to it, and to help all students towards it according to their various capacities.

Now the right standard of a University is to teach all branches so that a young man when graduating will be broad, able to converse on any subject and know what he is talking about. Therefore, it is not the standard of any University to take up some particular branch, and promote this beyond the needs of the present age and leave some other branch undeveloped. For instance, let a student who is going in for engineering take up only the subjects which are absolutely necessary for his profession. Would not this man be better fitted for his profession if he knew something of geology, something about the earth's crusts, for if he knew nothing of this branch of science, he might attempt to lay the foundation of a pier in a bed of quicksand, thus losing a lot of time and a few thousand dollars in sunken material. This same man, who has followed only a course of studies which was necessary for his profession sends in a tender for a contract and is brought up before a committee and asked to explain the plans which he sent in with his tender; he has never studied literature and has not developed a means by which he can get up and explain his plans to the committee, along with his ideas on the undertaking. This man never attended the meetings of the Debating Society at the University, and he is not able to say a word in favor of his views. What kind of opinion would the committee form of this man?

It may be all right to develop one branch and it may be pleasant for a person to study only one science, because it is his or her "hobby," but we must admit that of all the branches taught in a University, practically speaking, one is of no use without another. Of what use is Geometry without Algebra, History without Geography, and in our Catholic Universities what will it profit a student to attend lectures on Philosophy if he has never taken up Latin?

This is in accordance with Cardinal Newman, who says in

his "Idea of a University": "A University should not be the birthplace of poets or of immortal authors, of founders of schools, leaders of colonies or conquerors of nations." By this he means a student should not devote all his time to Literature or History. Continuing, he says: "But a University training is the great ordinary means to a great but ordinary end, it aims at raising the intellectual tone of society, at culturing the public mind, at purifying the natural taste, at supplying true principles to popular enthusiasm and fixed aims to popular aspiration, at giving enlargement and sobriety to the ideas of the age, at facilitating the exercise of political power, and refining the intercourse of private life."

This is what we are upholding when we say that the Universities of the present day are practical intellectually, and that they are the only means by which the great but ordinary end may be attained. During the last nineteen hundred years, since the birth of Christianity, and for four thousand years before that period, University training has been built up to what it is at the present time by the most learned men of each generation, and should we now put aside the fruit, labor and experience of thousands of years? Are we to listen to a few men who pretend to be very learned and well versed in this subject, when they have had at the most only forty or fifty years to study the question, when it has required centuries to bring the University to its present state of perfection? Would you call this a practical move, to throw aside the work of hundreds and even thousands of learned men, to introduce the ideas of a few, who wish to make some financial gain by the change?

Look back over the pages of History: we find the great men University graduates: John Milton, who was one of the best of English poets, was a graduate of Christ College, Cambridge, in the year 1632. William Penn, the founder of the colony of Pennsylvania, was a graduate of Oxford in 1654. William E. Gladstone, a graduate of Oxford, was "the foremost Saxon-speaking man on the globe," according to Dr. Cryler. Let us come down to our own day, Sir Wilfrid Laurier, the biggest statesman of Canada to-day, graduated with the degree of B.A. from Assomption College. Charles Alphonse Pelletier is a graduate of Laval University. William Taft, the President of the Great Republic to the South of us, is a graduate of Yale; and the list could be continued indefinitely.

My object in numerating these University graduates is to illustrate that the education given in the Universities is sufficiently practical, for all of these men have proved to be practical enough in their private and public life. Do you not think that if these great statesmen: Sir Wilfrid Laurier, Hon. Charles Alphonse Pelletier and William Taft, along with many others, did not think the present system sufficiently practical, would not they also endeavor to introduce a more practical system?

In concluding, may I not state that the great progress of the last century in the Arts and Sciences is sufficient to prove that the present system is such that it makes practical men. Therefore, if these men are sufficiently practical, then the present system is the only ordinary means by which the great but ordinary end may be attained.

F. HACKETT, '14·

The Influence of Modern Drama.

HAT is the purpose of the drama? It is to educate and elevate the general public mind. It is to supply a standard of language and pronunciation, which may be relied on to be the best in the country. And, moreover, it is to foster the mother tongue for the purpose of promoting national unity. Thus we see that the drama, as it is meant to be, is decidedly in the direction of intellectual improvement in the nation. But, unfortunately, it is not always what it is meant to be.

One of the chief drawbacks to the success of the drama is that it utterly fails to come into close touch with the sympathies of all classes alike. No fact is more familiar to most of us than that the great majority of people regard a modern high-class drama as very tiresome indeed. And they are altogether inclined to regard the dramatic enthusiast with something closely akin to pity. Thus it is that the drama appeals only to the few. But it is also to be remembered that these few are the leaders of thought, and their sympathies are in union with authors themselves.

The ancient dramatists were superior to those of modern

times. And it is probably for this reason that their plays are still most acceptable for stage purposes. These plays delineate character with more accuracy, and contain a great deal more solid sense than is found in present-day productions. These latter have a lighter specific gravity; and instead of great masters we find numerous petty artists who, not disposed to do their best, too frequently subserviate the purpose of the drama to the end of private and heretical opinion. Owing partly to the extreme amount if freedom in these matters, the world is flooded with a host of writers of decimal calibre.

The increased number of writers in our day is a real drawback to the serious drama. The enormous spread of education has led many to take up the pen who could never have done so in the Middle Ages. Then, only true geniuses undertook to write. That is why the gems of literature of those days were not smothered in dross as at the present time. The consequence of so much overcrowdedness in poetry is a lower standard of drama, and the rendering common of an art which calls forth the highest in man.

Quite another defect of the modern drama results from the tendency of the writers to show this particular form of literature. The reason is found in the demand of the stage-owners for material which will catch the public eye. In this way many of the best writers would be deprived of a reasonable amount of profit; and hence the fruit of their genius, so far as concerns the drama, is lost.

A modern audience for the most part prefers the cheap vaudeville. Hence, it happens that modern drama, in order to compete successfully, in many cases cater merely to the basest passions of the audience. But this by no means proves that the influence of the modern drama is totally bad. For, indeed, there are still being produced mang works of high merit. Nevertheless it is true that the third-rate dramatist, in an age whose god is gold, in order to eke a livelihood finds it necessary to meet the demands of the mob, instead of dictating to them.

There is also a great tendency among our writers to make use of the drama for the purpose of spreading atheism,—and this because they rightly conclude that their doctrines will gain in weight and dignity from the very dignity of the form in which they are promulgated. In this way much that is entirely evil is sown in the minds of the unsuspecting lower classes.

The tone of the drama bespeaks the temper of the nation of the time in which the work is produced. Thus it is that we behold the true picture of society on the canvas of the drama. At a distance the surface form of the drama appears as perfect as the original masters could wish it. But upon closer inspection, the observer is often repelled by hitherto unrevealed blotches of erratic principle. False dogma, like an ugly cancer, seems to be eating the true life from the drama. Thus, from the prevalence of a certain kind of dramatic production, we are enabled to observe the state of mind of the general populace. Hence, from this we are bound to admit that the influence of the drama is productive of a large amount of evil, as for example in France, where only recently a reform has been found absolutely necessary.

To-day we see that the influence of the drama is reduced owing to the press, public libraries, etc.; in the old days the drama was the chief means of educating the people. Now that this office is performed mainly by the press, etc., the sphere of the drama is consequently just that much contracted. Hence the conclusion from all the particulars which I have enumerated is that the influence of the drama has become narrower with regard to the extension of educational good, while on the other hand it has become deeper with regard to the comprehension of evil.

J. SAMMON, '11·

Evil tendencies of the Press

(CLASS DEBATE.)

HE newspaper, as we all know, is an insistent factor of modern life. It comes pounding on our doors so regularly and so persistently that we are compelled to adopt a positive attitude towards it, and there is, I suspect, a distinct tendency among earnest and cultured people to regard it as a problem quite like intemperance or the unemployed or some other dreadful phenomenon.

It is known to all of us what great evils are produced by intemperance, and if we stop to consider the matter well there is no doubt that we shall find in the newspaper problem that we are confronted with greater evils which are more dangerous by far to the interests not only of individuals but also of the country. This is because the press, aside from giving rise to scandal and its subsequent evils, cultivates in the minds of children an interest in crime that may, and we can with great assurity predict, will lead to an increase of criminals in the near future.

The newspaper of to-day instead of giving useful information on current topics, as was the end that the press in its infancy labored to produce, is to-day, allowing scandal, romance and sensationalism to prevail instead of solid truth, which should be its first and principal object.

The object of every newspaper should be to give to the public good wholesome news. But, let us ask ourselves what is news? In answer to this query, let us go to some gathering when people are together on an evening. What do they talk about: some, indeed, may converse on ordinary affairs, but most of the conversation is concerning those things which exceed the ordinary. For instance, if Tommy spilt ink on a visitor's gown it would likely be commented on, but if he had been a well-behaved boy it would pass unnoticed. Again, if Mr. and Mrs. Brown are living happily together it may only be mentioned, but if Mrs. Brown is applying for a divorce a current of conversation will at once be opened, which, needless to say, will be discussed until, having been looked at in every conceivable way, shape and manner, the subject is dropped simply because nothing more remains to be said.

The newspaper in order to obtain news employs these very same tactics; that is, it allows all unsensational, ordinary affairs to pass, if not unnoticed, at least very sparingly referred to, and it picks out all the scandals, the murders, the robberies, the suicides, and the other sensational events which occur during the day. Does this maintain the object for which the press was first established? Decidedly not. It only means that instead of the good, wholesome news which we need in order to be versed in current events, we are given as a substitute graphic accounts of murders and robberies and other literature of the same sort.

A newspaper in order to be a successful money-making concern must be drawn up on lines which will please everybody, and in this way the feminine portion of the public becomes a part of the newspaper problem. But what do they desire from a paper? To answer this, let us go to some sewing circle on an afternoon. Women are gathered here, as they tell us, to sew, but is this what they do? No. It may have been the object for which the circle was formed, but the real result of the meeting is to give a great deal of information concerning the latest scandals and bargains

Judging by this we can easily deduce what a woman will first look for when she picks up a paper, and then everything relating to scandal that may be found.

In this way we find the editor of our daily papers in order to make his paper a financial success giving a far greater amount of advertising and scandal than is absolutely necessary. This evil, however, could be easily overcome without any financial loss, for if the press instead of giving us endless advertisements and scandals would cut them down, say to one-half, and substitute instead instructive, wholesome, carefully prepared material, the result instead of diminishing the income of the paper, would increase the circulation and thus bring in larger dividends, for the public would know that whatever they found in the papers would be true, and thus they would be able to put reliance on everything they read. If the press adopted this method, not only would the principal end for which the press was instituted be attained, that is true, honest, instructive journalism, but also the circulation would be increased by many who only then learned to appreciate it.

The question was recently asked of a prominent New York editor if he thought an honest newspaper possible. He replied that it would be possible only when an independent newspaper was organized, one which would uphold the lofty standard which the primitive press held, one which would deal less with the sensualities and passions of men, one which would have as its first and only object the enlightenment and education of man. By simply looking over the pages of our daily papers we may easily understand how far below this standard falls the press of to-day.

For an example of this, let us take the New York Herald or Journal. These papers have perhaps the greatest circulation of any two daily papers in the world, and what is their standard of news. Rank sensualism. For instance, take the trial of Harry Thaw, the self-confessed murderer of Standford White. We all remember the vivid accounts of this trial published by these leading papers. Were any good results produced? If we may believe the words of Archbishop Williams of Boston, these accounts were instrumental only in the contamination of the minds of those who read them. This example is not exceptional; we find in the daily columns accounts of jury scenes, fatal endings. of quarrels, and such matters, which equal if they do not exceed the accounts of Harry Thaw's trial.

Let us take an account of a murder or a suicide committed in a new or novel way; these are often so clearly described that we seem involuntarily to be able to picture the murder or suicide ourselves. On some weak-willed and weak-minded persons who read them, these accounts produces such a disastrous result that if we attentively follow the papers for a month or so we find a description of a murder or suicide tallying very closely with the other if it does not exactly coincide with it. The conclusion is obvious. The first account given by the paper was so sensational that the murder or suicide became so imprinted on a person's mind and on his imagination that he wilfully took his own life or deprived some one else of God's most precious gift.

Often times a reader picks up an editorial with a flashing headline and reads for perhaps fifteen minutes a detailed account of some revolutionary uprising in Mexico, but when he lays the paper down does he feel satisfied? No, he does not. He feels as though he had wasted his time over a column or two of brilliant nonsense with a news-value of about five lines.

Again the evil tendencies of the press are very noticeable in our politics. A certain paper will take such a stand for one party, and publish such slurring, slander-giving accounts of the character of the opposing party, that the readers become prejudiced and fail to see the beneficial results liable to be produced under their administration.

We have been dealing with all newspapers in general. Now let us look at those papers coming under the heading of "Yellow Journalism." These papers are of a cheaper form than the others, they consist of extremely poor news, warmed up into cheap sensational forms with the minimum of special reporting and the maximum of splash.

Noisy methods are resorted to, in so great a measure that the thing becomes one continuous shriek. Every item of news is accompanied by its own yell, with such a confusion of noises that nothing makes itself heard. The editorials are occasionally able, but without scruple or principle. They appeal to class hatred, to the anti-British sentiment of the Irish, the anti-capitalist sentiment of the laborers, to the hatred of the orderly administration of justice, always latent in the ignorant and discontented. All these methods are continually employed to fill up space, and consequently the real end for which the paper is published is entirely lost sight of. These papers usually have comic supplements made up for the most part of cartoons which, quite as unscrupulous as the rest of the paper, are often-times true.

Is this productive of beneficial results for the country at large? Decidedly not; and we have the words of a noted New York philanthropist who states that if the papers in their present form are tolerated for much longer, the state will necessarily sink under the weight of so much so-called news, the red flag of revolution will be hoisted and socialism in its most violent forms will be the result.

Archbishop Farley, who for seventeen years was pastor of St. Gabriel's, in New York, in refuting a statement made by a certain writer of an editorial in McClure's Magazine, which was a vile calumny, said in reference to the writer: "He has the traits of ignorance, superficiality, recklessness and irresistible propensity to falsity which are also the chief characteristics of the Hearst writers." These words of a man so well qualified to judge must indeed show us how careful we should be in selecting our literature; and they should encourage us to cultivate a taste in literature for only those articles which tend to enlighten, educate and instruct us.

Again we have the words of Archbishop Riordan, who in an editorial against yellow-journalism, says: The Hearst papers of New York contain some of the vilest anti-Catholic, and indeed anti-Christian leanings, that were ever published. They are not fit to go into any Catholic home, for in every edition there appear, if one is able to analyze them, editorials, which while they do not openly inculcate disbelief in the teachings of Christianity, yet so lean towards disbelief that by direction they seek direction out.

After reading these few paragraphs, I hope that you may begin to understand what great dangers we are subjected to in the newspaper problem, and that in the future you will select your newspapers only after serious reflection in order that your leisure moments spent in reading may be a source of profit to you rather than a source of evil.

P. LOFTUS, '14.

...The Suffragist...

CCORDING to the theory laid down by the Suffragist, the one thing needful for woman is the Parliamentary vote. It is held out as a universal and never-failing remedy, whereby the rough places in the world are to be made smooth and the crooked paths straight.

This faith in the efficacy of the suffrage is magnificent; but is it based on the solid foundations of reason and the public welfare. Shall women be recognized as the political equals of men? Shall they receive the higher education? Shall they support themselves by work outside the home? Shall they mark out paths in life for themselves, or shall they walk always under guidance? These and many related questions are often discussed, usually with the welfare of man, or of the home, uppermost in thought. Broadly speaking, woman has been to the social body what heredity has been to the organic body—the silent and hidden force—while man has represented environment,—the outer and apparent force. Is it desirable that this should remain true? Is it desirable, either for society, for the individual woman, or for the individual man?

Men and women are not two opposing armies seeking one another's destruction. The one sex is the complement of the other; their interests are one and indivisible. That which brings good to the man inevitably brings good to the woman, for they are indissolubly linked together. By the unalterable decree of Nature man was marked out to be the protector and guardian of the woman. He is expected to work for her, and, so far as he can, guard her from danger, though it be at the risk of his own life; and civilization insists that, where life is in peril, it is the women, and not the man, who must first be saved. The privileges of woman are neither small nor few, and she holds them by virtue of her womanhood.

The work of the world may be roughly divided into indoor work,—the work that lies around the home; and outdoor work,—the work that lies far afield and deals with matters of public and Imperial concern. Both kinds of work are equally honourable and equally necessary for the common weal, but both cannot be done effectively by the same person. The man does not attempt such a double task; he leaves the care of the home and all that belongs to the home to the woman; and the woman, since she is not a single woman, will find that if she attempts to take up the work of the man, she will fail in the due discharge of the more important work which immediately depends upon her.

Whether the woman is well equipped physically, by training and by temperament, for this larger outdoor work, even a suffragist, if candid, might admit is open to question; of her essential and irreplaceable fitness for the indoor work there can be no possible doubt. In the distribution of the world's work it is an intelligible and consistent principle that public concerns should be directed by men and domestic concerns by women, and it is a principle upon which almost all the countries of the world have invariably acted.

There is also the impenetrable tangle that besets any measure for the enfranchisement of women. The Suffragists themselves have never quite got clear of this wood, for they are disunited as to the particular kind of franchise they desire to pass. In the babel of voices some are asking for the franchise, on the same terms as men; some would include married women, others would exclude them; while there are others, again, who would oppose everything short of adult suffrage; and others, finally, who would admit women to the House of Commons, and therefore to the offices of the State.

In these various franchise schemes one wonders what is to become of the peeresses. Is the House of Lords to become a House of Ladies, too? Is the country so greatly enamoured of the aristocratic chamber as to cast its shadow over the Commons and give the wives of the peers the power, which their husbands do not possess, of voting for the representative House?

In 1892 Mr. Gladstone wrote:—

"There has never, within my knowledge, been a case in which the franchise has been extended to a large body of persons generally indifferent about receiving it. But here, in addition to a widespread indifference, there is on the part of large numbers of women who have considered the matter for themselves, the most positive objection and strong disapprobation."

Let us consider for a moment how woman has fared without this coveted vote. Have her interests been specially and markedly neglected? If we look over the field of legislation, it will be seen that as each class has been enfranchised it has brought its share of good alike to the men and women of that class.

It is frequently urged that women's wages will never be properly raised until they have the vote. But does the history of the men's efforts to raise their wages prove that the vote is such an indispensable factor in the case? It must not be forgot-

ten that the low scale of woman's wages is partly due to the
fact that many a woman—a wife or a daughter living at home—
can work and will work for a smaller wage than would be required for the maintenance of the woman who keeps herself
wholly on her own earnings. Again the man works at his trade
through all the years of his working life, the majority of women
either cease from working when they marry, or work only during such intervals as they can spare from their more pressing
home duties. Hence it is not reasonable to expect that women
would attain the skill of men, and their inferiority in physical
strength also makes them as workers less valuable. Therefore,
if women were paid at the same rate, or nearly the same rate,
as men, the tendency would be to substitute women for men.

It is very doubtful whether there will be any tangible gain
for women if they obtain the vote, and if the gain is dubious
the loss, on the other hand, is very dubious.

The woman, we say, is not to guide, nor even to think for
herself. The man is always to be the wiser; he is to be the
thinker, the ruler, the superior in knowledge and discretion, as in
power. One sex cannot be compared to the other. Each has
what the other has not; each completes the other, and is completed by the other; they are in nothing alike, and the happiness
and perfection of both depends on each asking and receiving from
the other what the other only can give.

The man's power is active, progressive, defensive. He is
eminently the doer, the creator, the discoverer, the defender.
His intellect is for speculation and invention; his energy for ad-
venture, for war, wherever war is just, wherever conquest necessary. But the woman's power is not for battle, and her intellect
is not for invention or creation. She sees the qualities of things.
Her great function is praise; she enters into no contest, but in-
fallibly adjudges the crown of contest. By her office and place
she is protected from all danger and temptation. This is the
true nature of home, and if once the anxieties of the outer life
penetrate into it, and the hostile society of the outer world is allowed by either husband or wife to cross the threshold, it ceases
to be home.

Therefore the man's duty, as a member of the commonwealth, is to assist in the maintenance, in the advance, in the
defence of the State. The woman's duty, as a member of the
commonwealth, is to assist in the comforting and in the beautiful
adornment of the State.

M. J. SMITH, '10·

MACBETH.

HE play begins with the appearance of the "Three Weird Women" on the dark moorland near Forres, which the wild weather and fire have blasted, and over which, as Macbeth and Banquo enter, a storm is passing with thunder, lightning and rain. The day has been fair before their coming, now it is foul, and in the foul weather are those who have made it to suit their wicked work.

Thus we are brought into the dark atmosphere of the play, as dark without as it is within the souls of the characters. Night and tempest pervade the play. Duncan dies in a storm. Banquo perishes in the night, in the night his ghost arises. Lady Macbeth walks with her conscience by night and dies before the dawn. Macbeth and she slay their guest in the night, and cry to the night at every dark deed they do to hide their guilt and to assist it.

Only one other element of imagination is stronger in the play — that which drenches it with blood. Every scene is crimson with it; it is like the garments in Isaiah's battle, rolled in blood. Macbeth's imagination incardadines with blood the multitudinous seas. No Arabian perfume will sweeten away from Lady Macbeth's hands the smell of Duncan's blood. Tempest and terror, blasted lightning, and everywhere the scent and sight of blood are the outward image of the inward life in the "Weird Sisters," and the murderers.

The dreadful darkness of the play, spiritual and physical, is deepened at the beginning by the supernatural prophecies which contain in them the slaughter of the King. Macbeth's soul is at one with the tempest and the blasted heath, and the supernatural cry. To Banquo the day is the ordinary Highland day, and the witches are not supernatural. He is the same when he leaves the heath as when he entered it. Macbeth is not. There is that now in his soul which drives him as hunger drives the beast of prey. He carries it with him through his interview with the King, where its urging is quickened by the King appointing his son her to the crown, where its temptation is kindled into action by Duncan's saying that he will stay the night at Inverness. The opportunity has come. He rides in front of the king with murder in his heart.

"Stars, hide your fires,
"Let not light see my black and deep desires."

Into that grey world of the supernatural which some are

said to see, Macbeth is continually carried. Terrible dreams shake
him nightly with fear. It is only he that sees the ghost of Banquo,
the very painting of his imagination dread. His courage is proof
against any mortal foe, his nerves firm against any natural horror, but not against the immortal, the supernatural. Then his
cheek is blanched by terror. As time goes on when he is no
longer young in murder the initiate fear declines; but though
the fear has gone the superstition remains. He believes the
witches. He is still the slave of their will to ruin him. The opportunities they make him see cause him now to dread, but he
listens to them as if they were true prophets. His superstition
has bred credulity, and out of his false security partly arises
the half-insane recklessness with which he presses on to meet his
fate.

These keys unlock the man. On such a temperament, naturally brave, supernaturally fearful; weak in resolve, strong in
imagination; a rude soldier with a poet's heart; honorable but
not having any moral foundation for his honor, with the conscience which is honor's guard; his honor only the custom of his
class — on such a temperament falls the heavy temptation of
ambition. He has nursed the thought of being king; he has talked it over, it is plain, with his wife. She has taken the same
infection. The witches suggest outwardly his inward ambition.
The dreadful means to reach it dawns upon him, but he has not
yet formed it into Duncan's murder. Duncan's proclamation
of his son as heir swells his thought into a kind of rage till he
is on the edge of murder. The unlooked for opportunity comes
to him. Duncan will sleep at his castle. Murder springs now
into his mind. The means, the time, are given him. His wife
hears the news. And in her also murder on the opportunity leaps
into swift life. Duncan in the minds of both is dead already.
The long cherished forces of various thoughts explode into form.

Macbeth is but the hand that does the murder. Lady Macbeth is the impelling soul of it, the incarnate slaughter. She
lifts his weakness into strength, his fears into courage, opposes
her reason to his fears, her common sense to his imaginings. It
is impossible not to admire her strength when we set aside the
evil to which she puts it. All Macbeth's hesitations go down before it. She uses all a woman's weapons. She denies her mother-
hood's tenderness, though she knows she is false to herself, as she
is when outside of the storm on which she is borne away. She
mocks him with bitter sarcasm. He is untrue to himself and a
coward, and so he is egged on to the commission of the bloody
deed, which brings such dire results.

                                        P. C. HARRIS, '11·

Inter=Collegiate Debate.

The Debating championship is here again. To the credit of Messrs. Tracy and McEvoy it is here. On Friday evening, Jan. 20, the students of the University assembled at St. Patrick's Hall to listen to the final debate of the Intercollegiate Union. "Resolved, that the importation, manufacture and sale of intoxicating liquors should be carried on exclusively by the government." In spite of the weather the attendance was good, and the proceedings rendered the evening considerable of a success. The programme opened at 8.30 p.m. with a vocal solo by Mr. P. C. Harris, following which the chairman, Mr. A. C. Fleming, in a few words, announced the subject of debate, the rules by which the judges were to be guided, and then introduced Ottawa's leader of the affirmative, Mr. Tracy.

The speeches delivered by the two supporters of the affirmative were of a very high order. Both in matter and manner of presentation, and in style, smoothness and clearness of delivery, the orations of the winners plainly savoured of victory throughout. But though our representatives upheld their side with marked ability, still they were opposed by men of no mean acquirements, and it was only after considerable reflection on the matter that the judges were able to announce their decision in favour of Ottawa College.

The approval with which the decision met among the students was vigorously testified by the avalanche of hand-clapping which followed immediately upon its announcement. The customary V-A-R was given, with perhaps a little more "ginger" added on this occasion. The programme closed with a selection from the College Glee Club, habited in the sweaters of the different courses.

This is Mr. Tracy's first appearance on our public platform, and we hope not the last. Mr. McEvoy, being a member of the lower forms, is much to be congratulated on the grammatical and literary merits of his discourse; while the executive and the members of the Debating Society wish to thank one and both of the speakers for the honor they have brought on their Alma Mater, and for the admirable manner in which they have mounted the silver trophy on top of the foundations laid by Mr. O'Gara and Mr. Fleming. Congratulations also to the Moderator, Rev. J. P. Fallon, O.M.I.

University of Ottawa Review.

PUBLISHED BY THE STUDENTS.

THE OTTAWA UNIVERSITY REVIEW is the organ of the students. Its object is to aid the students in th ir literary development, to chronicle their doings in and out of class, and to unite more closely to their Alma Mater the students of the past and the present.

TERMS :

One dollar a year in advance.   Single copies, 15 cents.   Advertising rates on application
Address all communications to the "UNIVERSITY OF OTTAWA REVIEW", OTTAWA, ONT.

EDITORIAL STAFF :

J. BRENNAN, '10 ;	A. FLEMING, '11 ;	M. O'GARA, '10 ;
J. BURKE, '10 ;	PH. HARRIS, '11 ;	C. D. O'GORMAN, '10 ;
	M. SMITH, '10	

Business Managers : C. GAUTHIER '10, ;   D. BREEN, '11

G. GALLOPIN, Staff Artist.

Our Students are requested to patronize our Advertisers.

Vol. XII.   OTTAWA, ONT., JANUARY, 1910.   No. 4

THE NEW YEAR.

Hail 1910! Another milestone has been set up on the road of History.

In reminiscent mood we peer back into the shadows that hide the year just gone. One by one arise before our mental vision the spectral forms of things that were and things that should have been—and were not; how numerous these last,—unholy progeny of sluggard's will and coward's resolutions! What gain, what progress can we boast? Perchance a little.

Perhaps as amid the pealing bells the old year breathed its last, we lifted up a corner of the curtain, and for one brief instant gazed with steadfast eyes on Life's great mirror, to see therein reflected the vastness of our ignorance, and the miscroscopic dimensions of our deeds well done.

If so, 'tis well, and we can face this new and lusty child of Father Time with braver mien, and higher hopes, and strong resolve that 1910 shall never see us flinch when Duty calls.

THE BISHOP-ELECT OF LONDON, ONTARIO.

By the elevation of Father M. F. Fallon, O.M.I.. to the See of London, Ont., the Holy Father has conferred a signal honour not only upon him, but upon the Oblate Order and the University of Ottawa. Father Fallon's work in this institution and this city is too well known to need recapitulation. Closely allied as he was with the work of the University during a number of years, he did much to enhance its fame, and we feel confident that its best interests will be in the future, as they have been in the past, an object of his solicitude.

During his sojourn in Buffalo as Pastor of Holy Angels' Church, and as Provincial of the Order in the Northern States, he has worked assiduously for the advancement of religion and Catholic education, and leaves behind him more than one monument of his indefatigable zeal. In the larger field of the Episcopate he will have more ample scope for his brilliant talents. His incisive eloquence, facile and vigorous pen, and great administrative ability will, we feel sure, when transferred to London, play no small part in the development of Catholicity, not alone in that diocese but throughout the whole of Canada. Ad multos annos!

NOTES.

We propose, in the next issue, to give a sketch of Bishop Fallon's career, which will prove interesting to his many friends, and be an incentive to higher effort on the part of the present students of his Alma Mater.

* * *

America has lost one of her greatest poetical geniuses by the recent death of John Bannister Tabb, the blind poet-priest of Baltimore. A master in the various forms of poesy, he will be remembered best of all by his inimitable puns.

* * *

Hearty congratulations to the Debating Society and its four able representatives, Messrs. O'Gara, Fleming, Tracey and McEvoy, for having brought back the championship cup of the Inter-University Debating League. Compliments also to the worthy representatives of Queen's and old McGill. Ottawa took a New Year resolution or two, but strictly on the q.t.!

* * *

Is it possible that Canadian literature is bracing up? We learn from the Register that during the past year our Canadian writers published twenty-one novels, eight volumes of essays, fifteen of travel, seven of poetry, six of biography, and twelve of history. The Canadian North-West, by the way, seems to have a special fascination for American readers, if we are to judge by the number of N. W. stories appearing in the monthly magazines.

* * *

We caught a brand-new comet on Jan. 24th! It is new inasmuch as only discovered on Jan. 17th by a South African named Berake. It is a fine, healthy-looking specimen, measuring 22 degrees, or about 35,000,000 miles, and consequently belonging to the first class. Local astronomers have named it "1910 A."

* * *

A book that will be hailed with delight by those interested in the early history of the North-West is the "History of the Catholic Church in Western Canada," by Rev. A. G. Morice, O.M.I., of Winnipeg. The author is a fascinating writer, besides being one of the most eminent ethnologists of the day.

About one hundred Christmas exchanges were received last month. They all really deserve mention, and we should like to take each one of them and pay it our little tribute. Christmas witnesses 'the greatest annual effort of the journalist. The scribe does his best to help in the spreading of peace on earth to men of good-will; and what with gaily decorated covers, and pictures reminding one of the great event, and Christmas stories breathing peace and goodness, we think he has no small share in the gospel of joy.

The Niagara Rainbow abounds in Xmas. illustrations and short stories. Among the names of the contributors we notice that of our old friend, Maurice Casey. Mr. Casey's article, entitled "The Canons of Art," is concise and well-studied. He defines art, explains the asthetic sense in man, and shows the relation between art and history.

The McGill Martlet appeared early in December, bound in a cover inscribed with the text, "Peace on Earth, etc." As usual, our McGill friend is overflowing with wit and good humour. "The Mystery of the Rainbow Socks," a detective story à la Sherlock Holmes, is the wittiest.

The University Monthly contains a number of articles of high literary merit. "The Rush-Bagot Arrangement," by W. S. Milner, shows that there is no real desire among Canadians or Americans to abrogate the Treaty. The presence of American war vessels upon the Great Lakes, he says, is due to the selfish interest of a few shipbuilders, to the activity of a few American journals, and to the problem of training recruits.

The O. A. C. Review looks decidedly Xmas-like, all decked out in holly and mistletoe. It contains a number of illustrations of farm life in Ontario. An illustrated article on "Sculpture," by D. H. Jones, B.S.A., compares the ancient and modern development of this wonderful art. It reached its greatest perfection, he says, in 500 B.C.

Besides the above-mentioned periodicals we beg to acknowledge receipt of the following: .

Abbey Student, Acta Victoriana, Adelphian, Agnetian Monthly, Argosy, Allisonia, Academic Herald, Assumption College Review, Amherst Literary Monthly, Bates' Student, Bethany Messenger, Columbiad, Collegian, Comet, Central Catholic, Exponent, Georgetown College Journal, Holy Cross Purple, Laurel, Nazarene, Nazareth Chimes, Ottawa Campus, Oracle, Patrician, Queen's University Journal, St. John's Quarterly.

Books and Reviews.

Again the leading feature of the month's reviews is the English constitutional crisis. The Budget as usual holds first place, while the other phases of the political situation are dwelt upon at length. The present outlook presents an admirable opportunity for the speculative political philosopher and economist to air their views. As the atmosphere does not appear to have been cleared to any appreciable extent by the formidable output up to date, we may expect much more upon the subject during the coming year.

THE CENTURY MAGAZINE for January has an article entitled "Personality in Football," of much interest to the lovers of this great college game. We get a brief historical sketch of its progress during the past fifty years, and an outline of the careers of its greatest exponents. The author has something to say on the subject of hero-worship, and concludes that "it is not entirely bad that there should be these stars in athletics, for most of them acquire their shining qualities through a clean life, practical self-denial, discipline, obedience, unmurmuring pluck, and a good deal of patience."

THE NINETEENTH CENTURY for December has a contribution headed "Irish Policy and the Conservatives." The writer puts forth the claim that Irishmen are beginning to look to the Conservatives rather than to the Liberals for favors. The reasons given are that: first, the Liberals have promised much but have executed little; secondly, the Conservatives, having promised nothing, are free to be more sincere and to be open to conviction. Again, he urges that the greatest benefits Ireland has received politically have been gained through the instrumentality of the Conservative party, and that the Irish mind instinctively shrinks from the Socialistic tendencies of the Liberal programme. He says that too much attention has been paid to individual points, instead of trying to grapple with the whole situation. The position of the Irish clergy is gone into at length, the writer taking the view that the hostile criticism, so often thrown at them by students of Irish affairs, is unjust and unwarranted.

SO AS BY FIRE, by Jean Connor, published by Benziger Bros., New York.

We can sum up our appreciation of this book by saying that it is a rattling good story. It holds the reader's attention from the first to the very last page. The plot is good and well worked out, and centres upon the fortunes of a young, wayward and desperate girl who impersonates the heiress of a huge fortune. To tell the outcome would be to tell the whole story. The character of Barbara, the adventurous girl, is exceptionally well drawn. The story points a strong moral, but this in no way takes from the interest of the narrative.

SEVEN LITTLE MARSHALLS—By Mary F. Nexon-Roulet, published by Benziger Bros., New York.

A sweet little tale told in the authoress' best style. We predict a good sale for this excellent book.

"ROUND THE WORLD," (Vol. VII), Benziger Bros., N.Y., $1.00.

A dainty, interesting and splendidly illustrated book, treating of a pleasing variety of subjects, e.g., German Folk Lore, American Mountain Climbing, Out-door Bird Taming, etc. A most valuable addition to the school library.

Among the Magazines.

An extremely interesting article appears in the University Monthly, just to hand. It is of a recently discussed subject, the Rush-Bagot agreement restricting naval construction on the Great Lakes. In the article which is quite lengthy, Mr. Milner endeavours to trace the origin and history of the wonderful "treaty." Arranged in April, 1817, by Secretary Rush, of the United States Department, and Sir Charles Bagot, of Canada, this famous international understanding remains a lesson for armed Europe. The agreement provided that there should be on each of the Great Lakes only one small gunboat carrying mere comparative "pop-guns." But lately, sad to recount, the United

States have under various pretexts broken their promise.   The result is a certain high tension of feeling in this country.   The writer states that it is positively certain that the vast majority of the common people of both countries is strongly in favour of the present admirable arrangement.   But he regrets very much that this is what is now evident: The signs of hostility against Canada are increasing over in the States; but it is neither the people nor the government, but the big ship-building interests that are forcing the issue.   Should Canada reply by building war-vessels on the Lakes, the destruction of peace might be at any moment precipitated, and far more important, and higher still, the noblest and most exemplary symbol of sensible harmony that the world has ever known and the sole remaining monument of twentieth century good-will would be reduced to dust beneath the awful weight of European militarism.   It is a problem that calls for the best Canadian statesmanship to work in the interests of the world of the future, so that they shall never know what it is to bear the shackles of war so long as they are people of the American continent.

The current number of America is just to hand.   This paper credits Prince Henry of Prussia with saying that the article in the London Daily Mail about Germany's preparations against England was nothing but an infamous lie.   Strange to say, Austria is fortifying and garrisoning the Tyrolese frontier opposite Italy.   This is takes as a sign of the disruption of the Triple Alliance and the effect of British diplomacy.

The last number of the Catholic Extension is on our list. This magazine is the latest exponent of Catholic religious movement, and typifies the crusade which will be carried on by the Church in the near future.   The work of salvation is aptly shown in the progressiveness of backwoods missions, by articles from the brave missionaries themselves, and by a systematic use of illustrations.   We wish the Extension success.

We welcome among others the Academic Herald, a neat little monthly which represents a community of English-speaking Germans in New York.

Priorum Temporum Flores.

On Dec. 19th, at St. Joseph's Church, Rev. D. Rheaume, '06' was ordained priest, and Rev. Mr. Prance was raised to the Deaconate.   The ceremonies were performed by Ilis Grace Archbishop

Gauthier, assisted by Rev. Fathers Poli and Duvic as deacon and sub-deacon respectively. Rev. Father Halligan was master of ceremonies. The students of the University were present in a body, and during the imposing ceremony the students' choir under the direction of Rev. Father Stanton acquitted itself creditably. The following were present on the sanctuary: Rev. W. J. Murphy, Rector; Rev. Father Poli, Vice-Rector; Rev. Fathers Gavary, Jeannotte, Sherry, Fallon, Kuntz, M. Murphy, Collins, Veronneau, J. Meagher, Corridan, Carson, Carey, Lapointe and MacMillan.

During the recent holidays Mr. W. P. Breen, who is studying philosophy at Canisius College, Buffalo, favored us with a visit. He returned to Buffalo on Dec. 5th.

Mr. M. Lachaine, '09, student at the School of Pedagogy, Queen's University, paid his Alma Mater a flying visit a few weeks ago.

Since the commencement of the new year Rev. W. H. Dooner, '04, and Rev. J. Harrington, '05 were among the visitors to the University.

Mr. A. J. Reynolds, '09, gave us a call a short time ago, being on his way to Ste. Thérèse, where he is completing his theological course.

Rev. J. George, '06, who was raised to the dignity of the priesthood on Dec. 19th, at St. James' Cathedral, Montreal, visited his Alma Mater during the Christmas vacation.

Recent callers at the University were Rev. P. S. Dowdall, Rev. J. J. Quilty, '96, and Rev. H. Letang, '04.

The other day we had the pleasure of a visit from Frs. J. Ryan, F. French, '89, and W. Dooner, '04.

Personals.

Rev. Fr. P. Hammersley spent a part of the holidays with Rev. Fr. Quilty of Douglas.

Canon Corkery, of Pakenham, paid a visit to the University during the past week.

The Very Rev. M. F. Fallon, Bishop-elect of London, paid his Alma Mater a call previous to the holidays.

Rev. Fr. Stanton, O.M.I., went up to assist Rev. Fr. P. J. Ryan during the Christmas season.

Rev. Dr. Sherry, O.M.I., spent the greater part of the holidays at Pembroke and Renfrew.

Rev. Fr. McGuire assisted Fr. Dowdall of Eganville during Christmas week.

Rev. Fr. Lajeunesse, O.M.I., paid Montreal a visit during the holidays.

Rev. S. Murphy, O.M.I., spent a few days in Cantley.

Rev. Fr. Roy, O.M.I., replaced Rev. Canon Corkery of Pakenham.

Rev. Fr. Dowdall, of Eganville, paid us a visit last week.

We chronicle with pleasure a visit from Rev. Dr. Kidd, of Toronto, while in the city with His Grace Archbishop McEvay.

The Most Rev. C. H. Gauthier, D.D., Archbishop of Kingston, was a welcome visitor to our halls previous to the holidays.

Rev. Fr. O'Connor, a native of Ireland, paid us a visit with Rev. D. A. Rheaume. The two Rev. gentlemen have been but lately ordained. The Review extends congratulations and best wishes for their future.

Rev. A. MacMillan, of Cornwall, paid us a visit recently.

The Review offers congratulations to Mr. L. Tracy and Mr. T. McEvoy, winners of the Intercollegiate Debate with Queen's University.

Mr. Martin J. O'Gara, of the Review staff, had the happy distinction of being the representative of the Arts course at the Annual Dinner given by the Faculty of Arts of Queen's University.

The following Rev. Fathers visited us while attending the Bi-lingual Congress in Ottawa: L. C. Raymond, The Brook; Cousineau, Sarsfield; Poulin, Clarence Creek; Beaudoin, Walkerville; L. H. L'Heureux, Belle Rivière.

O.U.A.A. Annual Meeting and Election of Officers, 1910.

The Annual Meeting of the Ottawa University Athletic Association was held on Saturday, December 18th, 1909, in the Lecture Room of the Science Hall. The change of date from April, as formerly, to December, was suggested by Rev. Father Stanton, O.M.I., and received the hearty endorsation of the executive and student body at large. In all colleges of any importance, elections of officers for the following season take place as soon as possible after the close of the football schedule. The early choice of officers affords ample opportunities for the different students to become thoroughly acquainted with their respective duties. Another new departure, and a most commendable one, was the holding of nominations on the previous Wednesday. Students nominated were given the privilege of either standing for election or withdrawing within twenty-four hours. In this way the director and student body were given an opportunity to consider the different candidates, and chose those best fitted to hold office. Any student whom the Director deemed undesirable was informed that he could not run for office. After the weeding-out process, resignations and withdrawals, the following were elected:—

Rev. Director—W. J. Stanton, O.M.I.
President—Alan C. Fleming, '11.
First Vice-President—Phil. C. Harris, '11·
Second Vice-President—S. Quilty, '13·
Treasurer—S. Coupal, '11·
Recording-Secretary—J. J. Kennedy, '13·
Corresponding-Secretary—J. J. Sammon, '11·
Councillors—M. O'Gorman, '11; J. Sullivan.
The various reports of the season's games, gates, expendi-

tures, etc., were read and received favorably. The treasury showed a snug balance, considering the exceptionally poor support given the team by the public. The College ''O'' was bestowed on the number of students who had ''made'' the senior teams and taken part in two games. Large photos of the football team were given to the players. After a few words of advice from the Director, the meeting adjourned with a lusty V-A-R-S-I-T-Y.

Hockey.

INTER-COURSE HOCKEY LEAGUE.

The season 1910 bids fair to become famous for pleasing innovations regarding sports at ''O.U.'' The hockey league is off to a fair start, and from present indications ought to certainly be a memorable and successful one. Instead of picking four teams from the whole student body, and playing an uninteresting schedule which was seldom finished, a real live league has been formed with the following teams: the ''Philosophers,'' the ''Arts,'' the ''Collegiates,'' and the ''Juniors.'' Each team has been fitted out in natty uniforms, with suitable crests on the sweaters. The games are played on ''Big Yard'' Arena, the scene of many a hard-fought battle. Rev. Father Stanton, O. M.I., is the official referee, and will not tolerate any semblance of rough-house work, making the students play straight hockey all the time.

LEAGUE STANDING.

	Won.	Lost.
Juniors	2	1
Philosophers	1	1
Collegiate	1	1
Arts	0	1

The following is a list of the players who have so far taken part in games:—

''Arts''—A. Kennedy, L. Kelly, F. McDougall, J. Guichon, P. Belanger, R. Guindon, J. Simard.

''Collegiate''—J. Robillard, W. Chartrand, H. Robillard, E. Nagle, M. Hogan, J. Murtagh, Shannon, Minnock.

''Philosophers''—M. J. Smith, C. F. Gauthier, Alan C. Fleming, Louis Côté, J. T. Brennan, M. K. O'Gorman, P. C. Harris.

Billiards and Pool.

A most enjoyable and profitable entertainment was witnessed by the students on Tuesday evening, January 11th, when,
through the influence of the Rev. Prefect of Discipline,
and the generosity of Mr. William O'Neill and Mr. W.
O'Hara, a scientific exhibition of the games of pool and billiards
was given by the above-named gentlemen. The pool championship of the city is held by Mr. O'Neil, while Mr. O'Hara is the
proud holder of the billiard championship of Ottawa, and at one
time Canadian champion. Needless to say, the contests were most
interesting and instructive with such experts battling for the
mastery. Each gentleman is almost invincible at his own particular game. That the students, big and small, enjoyed the playing was duly attested by the close following of the progress of
the games, the keen appreciation of brilliant shots, and the frequent outbursts of hearty applause. At the close of the pool
the score stood: Mr. O'Neil 100, Mr. O'Hara 79; the billiards:
Mr. O'Hara 100, Mr. O'Neil 54. As a slight token of appreciation, Rev. Father Stanton, in the name of the students, presented
each gentleman with a suitably engraved silver match case, for
which they expressed their hearty thanks, and promised to come
again at some future date. The students then gave a rousing
V-A-R and the evening came to a close.

Stray Shots.

Our genial friend and staunch supporter, Thomas L. Church,
has been signally honoured by the citizens of Toronto. Out of
a field of ten candidates, the "Alderman" was elected Controller
for 1910, being second highest in the voting. Hearty congratulations!

Father Bertrand's departmental store is doing grand business. Dividends will be declared next month, sure.

The "Throw-In" has been officially abolished by the C. I.
R. F. U.; hereafter the ball must be scrimmaged ten yards in from
the line.

More work for the counsellors: the football field must be
distinctly marked every ten yards. Hard luck, Mickey!

Bert Gilligan, our versatile rugbyist, has been appointed
manager of the baseball team at O. U. Success to you. Here's
hoping you bring back that Bilsky Shield for 1910!

Sylvester Quilty, our dashing wing man, has been elected by

the players to fill the position of captain of the football team for 1910. We.all hope the trick of 1907 will be repeated!

An "Indoor Baseball League" is in course of formation in the city.· The students have been promised to be allowed to put in a team, so it's up to the Matthewsons, Gibsons, Lajoies, Cobbs, etc., to limber up and let us see what sort of talent we have. The games will be played at the new Y.M.C.A. building on Metcalfe street.

Praedicamenta, Praedicabile,
Igitur, we're out to kill!!
Phi — Phi — Phi — Phil —
Philósophers play with a right good will!

Lester Patrick Brennan, Cyclone Smith, and Jack Winchester Harris showed some class as a Stanley Cup defence. Renfrew, it is expected, will try to land these stars for the Creamery Town team.

☺f Local Interest

Prof. of Geography: What would be the effect of the intense heat if one of the comets were to strike the sun?
Student: The North Pole would be *Cooked.*

Fl-m-g: What do you think of a man who marries the second time?
Hi-g-ty: He doesn't deserve to have lost his first wife.

Oh, you Grindy Forrester and Tommy Hare.

Har-s thinks that everything is a grave matter.

They say that J. Br-n-n and O. K-n-dy are drawing very large salaries from the Quyon Hockey Club.

Oh, you trainer, J. B-v-ke.

Wonder why Cu-ie never calls round at 123 now? Perhaps he thinks the number is 23!

Prof. to sleepy student: When the eyes of the body are closed, I suppose you see all the more readily with the eyes of the soul.

D-n: How is it that I didn't see you at the last debate, Fr-nk?
Fr-k: Because I wasn't there.

The earth is practically—round.

Prof. (explaining condensation of vapours): Did you ever see a snow storm in your kitchen?

Junior Department

"–But, what would Jessy say? Ay, there's the rub."

The College Junior hockey team is off to a good start in the Hurd League, having won both games played. The first game took place on Jan. 7th against the Rideaus. The Rideaus, though a great deal heavier, had to give way to the speedy Small Yard seven. By the way, we thought for a time their point player was H-k-t, our long friend in the Senior Department. The College won by a score of 3 to 2, owing in a great measure to the cool work of B. Kinsella who played goal.

The second game, on Jan. 11, was another hard-fought contest. The College opponents in this game were the Tecumsehs, who tried by every means to defeat their smaller rivals, but, thanks to the good work of Nagle and Hillman on the forward line, College was enabled to win out by a score of 2-1.

We should have won both games by larger scores. This would have happened if combination play were better developed. Remember the Small Yard expects great things of its team.

The Inter-Mural Leagues are in full swing. An account of games played will appear in the next issue. Remember, boys, you owe it to your team to always be on time when a game is to be played.

Charlie F-nier would like to know what happened at Jean-tte's table.

Why does a boy blacken his face when he is hungry?

Our new gymnasium is open. Too bad we have not snap-shots of some of the performances taking place therein. Keep faithfully to your gym work. Everything is a little hard at first, even to getting your feet out of the swinging rings.

Lonesome yet, Ralph? B-n-ot is pleased with the exchange, but wishes you had taken P-tras with you.

M-d-n, beware. See where long pants have landed Lah-e!

UNIVERSITY OF OTTAWA REVIEW

Vol. XII.   OTTAWA, ONT., FEBRUARY, 1910.   No. 5

Entered at the Post Office at Ottawa, Ont., as Second-Class Matter.

Elemental Voices.

The sound of the wind in the tree,
  Of the rain on the roof,
The voice of the surge of the sea,
  Or of thunder aloof.

What thought or remembrance is mine
  Unprobed as I bear ;
The touch of a passion divine,
  Remote and yet near.

A dream of the spirits that wrought,
  When life was unfurled,
A yearning immortal upcaught,
  From the birth of the world.

                    Archibald Lampman.

Ars Poetica

(With apologies to the shades of Horace and Boileau.)

"Our Undergrads. are all on *strike* (they are playing schedule games of indoor baseball at the "Gym") — won't you please
help us out this month?" This was the very modest request made
to me this afternoon as I emerged from a discussion of Aztec
Civilization. Being naturally obtuse, I did not see the joke? until
I had reached the quiet abode across Cumberland; then, of course,
I laughed; and I fear that some of my confreres were disturbed
by a very unseemingly exhibition of risibility. Pardon, Mes-
sieurs! I shall not again be guilty of permitting jokes with a
flavour of the *Castanea vesca* to disturb me so dreadfully. Now,
I wish to warn the genial perpetrator of this iniquity that I am
extremely sensitive in my risible organism; so please do not do it
again. But, on reflection, I would advise the genial wielder of
the "blue pencil" to think of the Solomonic dictum, in which
he utters very pertinent things about new goods and the Sun.
Is the gentle editor aware that centuries ago the "divine William"
— he of Avon had forestalled him with utterances about baseball?
He may doubt my assertion (though interrogative), so I beg to
produce the proofs:

"I will go root" — (Richard III).
"Now you strike like a blind man" — (Much Ado About
Nothing).
"Out, I say" — (Macbeth).
"Hit it, Hit it, Hit it" — (Love's Labor Lost).
"O hateful error!" — (Julius Caesar).
"A hit, a hit, a very palpable hit" — (Hamlet).
"He will steal it" — (All's Well That Ends Well).
"Whom right and wrong have chosen as umpire" — (Love's
Labor Lost).
"Let the world slide" — (Taming of the Shrew).
"He has killed a fly" — (Titus Andronicus).
"The play I remember pleased not the million" — (Hamlet).
"What an arm he has?" — (Coriolanus).
"They cannot sit at ease on the old bench" — (Romeo and
Juliet).
"Upon such sacrifices the gods themselves threw incense" —
(King Lear).

"O miserable base" — (King John).

"Let's hence to view the game" — (Othello.).

This is unquestionable evidence of the versatility of the Bard of Avon; and, perhaps, it may be a warning of the "purposes g-noble" to which our literary creations are ofttimes applied. We have budding bards amongst the "Arts" contributing contingent to the "Review," so I take the liberty of reminding these "inglorious Miltons" (the mute is eliminated) of the penalties of "Fame." Don't mind Shakespeare; there is no "infirmity" about it. William is not always orthodox from an educational standpoint; he tells ye "to fling away ambition." The Prefect of Studies is going to expurgate "Henry VIII," as this saying of the great Master of Poesy is demoralizing the classes in literature.

The following little disquisition has been just unearthed from a pile of musty manuscripts; and I take the liberty of inflicting it upon the would-be poets just to illustrate how exacting the "Art Poetic" is in its demands upon the votaries who worship at the shrine of the Muses. I may add that the writing of this little essay many years ago cured me of poetic mania.

What is Poetry? This question is as old as humanity; for Poetry like Music is co-eval with language. Rhetoricians have striven to give us a definition; but they seem to have failed egregiously, as they give us merely a *description*. They have consequently found it necessary to confine themselves to the usual concomitants of Poetry than to its essential constituent. Rhetoricians are very wonderful people. Their minds are like those watches which an iconoclastic speaks of: "None go just alike, but each one believes his own." Of course this does not apply to myself: I don't teach Rhetoric.

"Poetry," these wise people tell us, "consists in (not *of*) the harmonious arrangement of words in a sentence; and the division of a Composition into lines containing a certain succession of long and short syllables. Hence (according to this standard) whatever can be measured with a foot-rule, or employs rythm, rhyme, alliteration, or assonance, is poetry. Then it follows (according to the ordinary methods of induction) that "Limericks" should be placed in the same category as, for example, Bryant's "Thanatopsis," or Longfellows' "Psalm of Life," or possibly Tennyson's "In Memoriam." By the way, both Longfellow and Tennyson give us pictures of Grief: Tennyson, in "In Memoriam," and Longfellow, in "Resignation"; and I beg leave to ask the admirers of the former, which of the two has the truer ring, and which teaches the heart the right bearing of human sorrow?

But *à nos moutons*. The definition of Poetry as "measurable verse" is decidedly imperfect; it is not even respectably descriptive. Much of the literary stuff called Poetry, though it be "measurable verse," is very common place prose; whilst, on the contrary, a great deal of what we term Prose, is Poetry of the highest order. As an illustration of the former I submit the following (from Chapman's "Translation of Homer"): "Chapman is regarded as one who possesses true poetic instinct.—

> "Apollo's priest to the Argive fleet did bring
> Gifts for his daughter, prisoner to the king;
> For which his tendered freedom he entreats;
> But being dismissed with contumelious threats
>   (not decent rhyme!)
> At Phoebus' hands, by vengeful pray'r he seeks
> To have a plague inflicted on the Greeks."

If this is not Prose, what is it?

As an illustration of Prose which has all the requisites of Poetry, take the following (from Ruskin's description of the English fields in Spring):—

"Pastures beside the pacing brooks, soft banks and knolls of lowly hills; thymy slopes of down overlooked by the blue line of lifted sea; Crisp lawns all dim with dew, or smooth in evening warmth of barred sunshine, dinted with happy feet, and softening in their fall the sound of loving voices."

Admirable Poetry, lacking only arrangement.

Just another illustration (from a little-suspected source — Marie Corelli's "Barabbas"):—

"Set in the solemn shadows of the trees, 'twas a pale warning to the world; nevertheless, despite its frozen tragedy, it was not all despair — Remorse, repentance; and for true repentance, God hath but one reply — Pity and Pardon."

This is Poetry of the highest order; at least it seems so to us.

It is decidedly difficult to draw a strict line of demarcation between Poetry and Prose; and our canons are not necessarily the norm of others. For example:—Byron, the merciless critic of Wordsworth, (whom we regard as the Poet of Nature, without peer) says of some of the latter's poetry :—

> "He both of precept and example shows,
> That prose is verse, and verse is only prose."

Wordsworth, however, says in answer to the question: "What is a Poet?": The Poet is one who will follow wheresoever he can find an atmosphere of sensation in which to move his wings."

"Poetry," he says further, "is the first and last of all knowledge—it is as immortal as the heart of man." "Poetry," says Shelley, (not always, however, a trustworthy guide), "lifts the veil from the hidden beauty of the world, and makes familiar objects be as if they were not familiar."

Originally, Poetry and what we now call Prose were identical. "See deeply enough," says Carlyle, "and you will see musically." He might have said "poetically," and would have expressed the same thought, for Music and Poetry are twin-sisters.

In olden days when History was just being evolved, men could *see* more deeply and with less difficulty than they do now; they were untramelled by conventionality and traditional formalism. Within and without themselves they saw rythmically; not with the mathematical straight-lacedness of our modern sense of rythm, but with eyes "anoint of nature." Then it was that all nature spoke to them in the unmeasurable rythm of the wind-furrowed grain, the slow-lapsing stream, the sun-kissed ripple, and what Wordsworth calls so elegantly:—

"The soft eye-music of slow-waving boughs."

So-called "Culture" had not hampered them with a scholarship run down to pedantry; and "Form," or what the Chinese call "Face," (this has no reference to the starching of collars and cuffs in which the Celestials are such adepts!) had not stifled emotion with an overweening desire to be superior to feeling. But the inevitable came at last (possibly with the advent of Crinolines or Mother Hubbard bonnets) and critics began to discuss the newly discovered monstrosity — Prose. Hence, instead of trying to discover what Poetry means, we should ask: What is Prose?

The oldest of literary monuments — the Bible — furnishes us most interesting material in the attempt to answer this question. Looking through its venerable pages with the embarrassments of modern spectacles, we are apt to furnish its poetry with a dress of the externals of Poetry as we have it now. Had the Hebrews rythm, either accentual or quantitative? It is extremely doubtful. Had they rhyme or assonance? No; and yet without any of these external earmarks to guide us, how can we say that the Bible is poetic? Modern literary Philistines will perhaps say that it is not. But yet, the fact remains, that the Bible is the greatest poetic collection in existence. Byron regarded the "Book of Job" as the "sublimest poem ever written"; and a French critic (atheist though he was) says that the Canticles of Deborah and Barac are incomparable as Poetry.

Macaulay, in his "Essay on Milton," says of Poetry:—"It is the art of employing words in such a manner as to produce an illustration on the imagination — the art of doing by *words* what the painter does by means of *colors*. I think this expression is borrowed from Aristotle.

Shakespeare expresses the same thought when he says:—

"As imagination bodies forth
The forms of things unknown, the Poet's pen
Turns them to shape, and gives to airy nothings
A local habitation and a name."

The Poet is essentially an artist, not an artisan; he creates, but does not necessarily fashion. Mechanics, whilst desirable, is not essential. "Poeta omnis scriptor," says the author of the "Ars Poetica" — the greatest literary monument of the Augustan age. Not one or two faculties (as with the metaphysician) or several (as with the scientist) but the *whole man* is necessary to make up the poet. He is not to be measured with a foot-rule; and he cannot be categorized or labelled. "His office," says Macaulay, "is to portray, not to analyze; and he who aspires to become a great poet must first become a little child." Now, young collaborators, you will realize the difficulties that beset those who "climb Parnassus."

P. W. B.

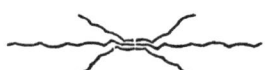

Aye, Contemplation, ev'n in earliest youth,
I woo'd thy heavenly influence! I would walk
A weary way when all my toils were done,
To lay myself at night in some lone wood,
And hear the sweet song of the nightingale.
Oh, those were times of happiness, and still
To memory doubly dear; for growing years
Had not then taught me man was made to mourn:
And a short hour of solitary pleasure,
Stolen from sleep, was ample recompense
For all the hateful bustles of the day.

—White.

THE CANADIAN NAVAL POLICY

(CLASS DEBATE.)

THE Canadian Naval Policy as laid down by the present Government is not that which is best suited to the demands of the empire.

Mr. Chairman,—Before entering upon the debate it is best to know what the Canadian Naval Policy is. It is a policy which provides for the creation of a naval force to be composed of a permanent corps, a reserve force to be a volunteer force on the same pattern, absolutely, as the present organization of the militia forces. Now this naval policy is that of the Prime Minister, who refused to send troops to South Africa until the pressure of public opinion forced him to do so. If Canada, Australia, New Zealand and the South African States had begun to build ships two and a half years ago, a certain continental power might have paused before an empire in arms in its own defense. It might have abandoned those warlike ambitions with which it is credited, and in that case the present strained situation would have arisen; but Sir Wilfrid Laurier would have none of the same preventive measures which the representatives of the other colonies desired to take. In 1899 and 1900, the Government again has given away before overwhelming public sentiment. So reluctant is Sir Wilfrid Laurier that he declines to follow the expert advice of the chief naval authority in the world. The result is that after great and unnecessary delay in the face of a probable Imperial crisis, the Dominion is to begin the nucleus of a force which, when completed, will be hopelessly inadequate to the purpose for which it is required. Instead of meeting the wishes of the people by bringing down a policy which would prove a real source of strength to the Empire, the Prime Minister is trifling with a serious national situation.

Mr. R. L. Borden says that the Government's naval proposals are either too extravagant as an experiment in the organization of a naval service, or too penurious as a contribution to Imperial defence.

The few cruisers and torpedo boats which will dawdle about our coasts can have absolutely no effect in lessening the danger of war. They will be a weakness rather than a strength to the royal navy; for, in time of war, a battleship would have to be detached from the Flying Squadron to prevent the enemy from gobbling our whole force at one gulp, and seizing the coast cities.

The Admiralty declares that a fleet unit is not complete without one big-gun cruiser of the first class; yet our Government takes the liberty to revise an expert report and tells the ancient sea-dogs of the Admiralty that they are under mistake. The Government's policy is pitifully weak and ridiculously inadequate. It will be a burning shame and a lasting disgrace to this country if this mean-spirited programme is not cast aside by Parliament as unworthy of the wealth and prospects of this premier colony, which for so many years has accepted aid in forma pauperis.

New Zealand has now decided to give a Dreadnought. She does not stipulate that it shall not be used until its Parliament decides whether or not war is just. It is assumed that if the empire is attacked there can be no question as to the justice of defending it. Therefore, the New Zealanders give a ship and attach no string to it.

Australia is now constructing a Dreadnought in England, and the auxiliaries of a fleet unit in Australia. All will be completed at once. These vessels will form a complete fleet unit such as the British Admiralty recommended for both Australia and Canada. Australia accepted this recommendation, Canada did not. Canada, which is wealthier than either Australia or New Zealand, has so far refused to provide a fleet unit, or even a Dreadnought. Australia's ships are to be under the control of the commonwealth in peace and they are to be interchangeable with the royal navy, and in time of war they will pass under the control of the British Admiralty.

Thus the Australian unit is a contribution to the Imperial navy, and to the defense of the empire. There is no string to it like there is to the proposed Canadian navy, which is not to go to war unless Parliament chooses to send it.

The fleet unit proposed by the Government would be useless because any big cruiser from an enemy's fleet could stand off out of range of our guns and blow the Canadian navy out of the water; therefore, it would have no effect in the defense of our own shores; and, as a contribution to the naval resources of the British empire it is a sorry jest. A Canadian navy without a cruiser of the improved Dreadnought class will be no navy at all.

Canada is only at the beginning of the development of its national resources. Probably for a hundred years to come we must depend largely upon the world's chief reservoir of credit for monetary backing. The occurrence of any disaster to the mother country would carry with it such a check to the material development of the Dominion as would amount to financial ruin so far as this generation is concered. Surely for this reason alone it is imperative that we contribute adequately to the effective defence of the empire. The Laurier navy will not constitute such a contribution. At least we should build a complete naval unit, including one Dreadnought and an extra cruiser of the same class as a special reinforcement to the Royal navy.

The Naval Bill of Canada ignores the necessity. A flotilla of small cruisers and destroyers will be of no value either to give or receive the hard knocks of battle.

I. RICE, '12·

NATIONAL GAMES.

HE influence of national games on public life affords a wide field for discussion. The very word national has a grave impression on our feelings. While passing by a military camp, we may hear the sweet refrains of the National Anthem. How this melodious air appeals to our senses. At once our mettle is raised on high, and everything points to peace and harmony. The same effect is caused by the result of national games.

We now ask ourselves what are the national games. In studying the question, we find that each country has its own. We first hear of national sport taking place in the ancient countries of Greece and Rome. The history of those places gives us a very vivid description of how they were put into practice. We see that the Government had practically full control over all its citizens. When a male child was a few months old, he was viewed by an inspector of the State, and if strong and robust would at the age of seven years become a student for the defence of his country. Thus, in order to develop the youth, national games were resorted to, and they have maintained their custom ever since. We have read about those famous athletes of the old world. The only reason given for their success is evidently the remembrance of the old motto: "Practice makes Perfect." Championships of all sorts were obtained, the most noticeable of which was the great Marathon race that has played such a part in the sporting history of Canada during the present age.

We now turn our minds towards other nations. Visiting England we learn that soccer football or cricket holds sway. Its appreciation and encouragement is quite evident by the vast multitudes which witness a contest between two competing teams.

Crossing the wide Atlantic to Mexico we meet with a different kind of sport, both in its essence and form. This is known as bull-fighting. To many this is cruelty to animals, and should not be practiced by rational men. Coming up the continent we enter the vast republic to the south of us. There we see that the country is in a state of intense excitement over baseball. This was quite evident last fall, when the championship series of the world was being contested by the two renowned teams of Pittsburg and Detroit. Stepping over the line into our own domain, we learn that lacrosse holds full sway. This game was first practiced by the Indians, and has continued ever since to take the hearts of the white men.

I have now shown by a few examples that each country has its own peculiar kind of sport, which may be the efficient cause of many things. It now remains to be seen what are those effects which the national game have on public life. In answer to this question, we can put forth both good and bad examples. We will first consider the case of the athlete. Take for instance a football player who has become proficient in the art. Has he received any benefit from it? This remains to be seen. In the first place, we know that the amount of strength depends on the muscles of the body; but to develop those muscles we need physical work; and as football exercises all the muscles of the body, therefore it should be practiced. Again sport is a good education for any man, because he learns to control himself on the field of battle, and to cultivate the disposition to live in peace and harmony with the many different characters which are to be found in after life. Some argue that an athlete endangers his life by practicing such games, but proper games played in the proper spirit are not dangerous. Therefore, we come to the conclusion that the national game is beneficial to the athlete.

Now, coming to the public as a whole, what are its effects? We first notice that it affords a topic of daily conversation. It is an advertisement for the place which the individual or the team represents. For many it gives time to pleasure and excitement. Therefore, the national game must be beneficial to the public.

M. J. SMITH, '10·

Religion and Science.

ELIGION implies man's union with God. The word is derived from religare, which, in its widest sense, signifies a living union of man and God. Why living? Because it is effected by vital acts of men, by his thoughts, desires and actions. It is by means of religion that we pay to our Creator the honor, the respect, the homage which is rightfully His due. Happiness can only be obtained by submission to God and by obedience to His holy will,—that is, by practicing religion.

We may consider religion as a science which far surpasses the other sciences in excellence. But there is a vast difference between the science of religion and the other sciences. The substance of the former is communicated by divine revelation of the latter by exercise of reason. The certainty of other sciences depend upon the reason of man, that of religion depends upon the wisdom and truthfulness of God. As far, then, as God excels man, so far does the science of religion excel the other sciences.

Faith is the prime requisite of religion. There are many things which our petty minds cannot grasp; but the fact that these things have been spoken and established by God Himself is sufficient proof for us to believe them. True, many things viewed in the light of reason, seem to us impossible; but, nevertheless, we believe them because we have the highest motives for our belief. Our faith in God, Who cannot err, enables us to do so.

Looking over the history of the past, and also of the present time, we find its pages debased by the opinions of many, principally men of knowledge, who laugh and scoff at the very idea of religion, who have drifted so far away from God as to hold their opinions superior to those of their Creator, who even deny the existence of God. Where such ideas exist, religion can have no place, and no honor or respect is shown to the All-powerful. Puffed up with their own erroneous opinions, they are not content to keep them to themselves, but, instead, impart them to others, giving perhaps seemingly apparent reasons, which appeal to many. The result is that many people are lead astray.

Knowledge and religion should go hand-in-hand. But, unfortunately, too often the reverse is the case. In many instances, as a man's learning increases, his virtue decreases. His faith is sacrificed; and, with his faith, his happiness. Once faith is gone, doubt and uncertainty is the result; and a man in this perplexity cannot be happy. Modern scientists have revealed many things which formerly seemed impossible. Science has revealed so many things that its study tends to encourage doubt with regard to religion, and also tends to encourage a universal belief in itself. This should not be, but it is the case.

It should be the aim of each and every one of us to increase his knowledge day by day; and it is important that he should. But it is of much more importance that we save our souls. Therefore, instead of endangering our faith, knowledge should increase it, should inspire in us more of reverence for God. Mind and soul should be in perfect unison, and should make vaster music after the acquiring of knowledge than before. It would be much better to remain ignorant but religious, than to acquire knowledge in exchange for religion.

CHAS. O'GORMAN, '10·

How beautiful this night! the balmiest sigh,
Which vernal zephyrs breathe in evening's ear,   .
Were discord to the speaking quietude
That wraps this moveless scene. Heaven's ebon vault,
Studded with stars unutterably bright,
Through which the moon's unclouded grandeur rolls,
Seems like a canopy which Love has spread
To curtain her sleeping world.

—Shelley.

A Boat Race.

EW sports are more worthy a pen than the America boat race, as seen by the runners, of whom I was one last June. I mean to show how it appeared to me, seated on the north side of the Connecticut River, or that part occupied by the Harvard followers.

At 2.30 p.m. the starter gives signal for the appearance of the crews representing Harvard and Yale Universities. There is some delay before the first crew comes from its house. Several signals are sounded before the Harvard crew shows up; but it finally appears after some seven or eight minutes of delay. The Harvard boat chooses the north side of the course, while Yale has to content itself with the south. Everything is prepared, and all eyes from either bank are turned to the starting point. All the people look down the river, but can just discern the two whitish streaks on the water, which they know represent the Harvard and Yale Universities, but which can only be seen by those nearer the starting point. A small but fast steam launch carries the referee. A great black patch occupy the space on the banks; the black patch is eleven hundred Harvard and Yale undergraduates and graduates, who evidently have collected to witness the race, but more to cheer their respective crews to victory.

Everything is very quiet, and I take another glance down the river. I notice a puff of smoke issue from a pistol. It is the signal for the crews to begin work. Two oars seem to splash into the water from each white streak; the black patch is moving, and so are the streaks. I hear the uproar from each bank of the river, and I see the streaks moving rapidly. They are working hard, and are becoming more and more visible to those at a distance. The eight oars are now four instead of two. Every head is still turned down the river. Crowds hang over the banks, and are eager to get a look at the crews. On come the splashing oars amid the cheers of the followers of the respective crews.

Harvard is ahead with her crimson jerseys; while Yale, wearing the blue, is not far behind. The oarsmen's heads and bodies are swinging forward and backward like one. The boats are now side by side, for Yale has increased its stroke, going at the rate of thirty a minute. They continue in that state for some distance, and it is difficult to distinguish which one holds the lead. On they go, with hundreds of voices vociferatng: "Keep it up, Harvard! Go it, Yale! You are gaining, Yale! Keep your lead, Harvard! Get ahead, Yale, you can beat them! Hurrah! for Yale." Both the Yale and Harvard followers break forth into songs of victory. The Harvard men are tearing away their muscles to retain the lead, while every Yale man is doing his best, and slowly but surely is cutting down the crimson lead.

The little coxswain of each crew is shouting out his lungs at the young giants, and is working to and fro with them. His yells of "stroke, stroke," are not plainly heard. He continues to urge each and every one of his eight to hold out and keep cool. The Harvard crew is only a boat's length ahead; but, just when fortune seems to favor her, her captain weakens and almost loses his grasp, which puts Harvard behind, while Yale surges to the front by a margin only. The oarsman is back to his post, and once more his crew is working well. Harvard put on a furious spurt, and gets fully even with the leading boat. A louder roar bursts from the Harvard bank. Yale fights desperately, and still leads Harvard by a few feet; and so every inch of water is hotly contested. The boats are now moving head to head, and again Harvard makes a furious effort, and slowly goes to the front. Bang! goes the pistol from the bridge, and the Harvard bank springs in one general uproar. The race is over; Harvard has won it, but Yale has fought every inch. The crews are making their way to the boat-houses, and the race of June, 1908, will be remembered as one of the most closely contested of all Harvard and Yale races.

G. B. D., '10·

There is a pleasure in the pathless woods,
There is a rapture on the lonely shore,
There is society, where none intrudes,
By the deep Sea, and music in its roar:
I love not Man the less, but Nature more.

—Byron.

Convictions are generally first impressions sealed with later prejudices.

Public Ownership of Public Utilities

UBLIC ownership aids the development of man by improving the conditions of labor, by increasing the interest of the people in public affairs, — so leading to a deeper civic patriotism, and a nobler citizenship — and most of all by changing the ideals of men. The ideal of public business is service. Every change from private to public ownership means a change of purpose from private profit to public service, from dividends for a few to service for all. It must be noted that public ownership and government ownership are not synonymous. Russia has government ownership of railroads, but there is no public ownership of railroads in Russia, because the people do not own the government. Philadelphia has not had real public ownership of her gas works, because the people do not own the council. Where legislative power is perverted to private purposes, where the spoils system prevails, and offices are treated as private property, where government is managed in the interests of a few individuals or of a class, anything that is in the control of the government is really private property, although it may be called public property.

If councils and legislatures are masters instead of the people, they are likely to use the streets and franchises for private gain, instead of the public good. If the government is a monopoly, everything in the hands of the government is a private monopoly also. If the people are to own and operate waterworks, street railways, and other industrial monopolies, they must own and operate the government. But can the people operate the government?

Looking at the question historically, there can be no doubt that industrial democracy — that is public ownership and co-operative industry — will be attained. In every department of life the trend of history has been first towards concentration, and afterwards towards diffusion. Organization, leadership, despotism, democracy, — that has been the history of religion and politics, and it will be the history of industry.

The outrageous discriminations in freight rates that have done so much to injure honest farmers, merchants, and manufacturers, and to build up most objectionable trusts, could not exist under real public ownership.

Public enterprise, whether conducted by the municipality or

committed to public service corporation, exists to render public services. Streets are public highways. They exist for the people's use. Nothing should be placed in them unless required to facilitate their use by or for the people. Only the general need of water, gas, electricity and transportation justifies the placing of pipes and wires and tracks in the streets. The public need is the sole test and measure of such occupation. To look upon the streets as a source of private gain, or even municipal revenue, except as incidents of their public use, is to disregard their public character. Adequate service at the lowest practicable rates, not gain or revenue, is the test. The question is not how much the public service corporation may gain, but what can be saved to the people by its employment.

The following are a few instances of public ownership and private ownership: In 1894, the Department of the Interior at Washington used the Bell Telephone at a cost of seventy-five dollars per 'phone; in the following year the government put in its own telephones, and it cost them only ten dollars per year.

2nd. When the French government took the telephone in 1889, rates were at once reduced to one-half, and it continued to make a prosperous gain, which in turn rates had still to be cut again. Public operation of the telegraph in England, and the public control and ownership of railroads in Switzerland, reduced rates more than seventy per cent. (70%) below cost.

3rd. In the United States the charges of private water companies are forty per cent. (40%) more per family than the charges of public plants. Nothing is more evident to thoughtful men and women than the fact that the American people are being held up and robbed by the trusts.

4th. The five cent fare in our large cities is too high, responsible municipalities having offered to operate street railways in Chicago and Detroit on a three cent fare and forty tickets for a dollar, taking the railroad from the city and paying interest on the cost of its acquirement.

5th. One of the most striking examples of the difference between public and private ownership is to be found in a comparison of the charges on the bridge in St. Louis, owned by the Goulds, and the Brooklyn bridge, owned by New York and Brooklyn. A foot passenger on the St. Louis, five cents; on the Brooklyn, free; vehicles on the St. Louis, twenty-five cents; on the Brooklyn, five cents; bicycles on the St. Louis, ten cents; on the Brooklyn, free. It is evident that the St. Louis bridge is for private gain, while the Brooklyn bridge is for public service.

6th. It happened only last winter in Boston, where one of its life's necessities is controlled by private individuals, in a high-handed, outrageous manner, perpetrated by an oath-bound coal club, that all coal dealers were forced not to sell coal to any citizen below a price agreed upon by the club; at the opening of winter the citizens of Boston found themselves completely at the mercy of a monopoly as rapacious in its instincts as is the Coal Trust, or the Standard Oil.

7th. Mayor Urquhart, of Toronto, stated: "Toronto owns her waterworks and recently cut the rates in two; Toronto owns the street railways and has leased them on terms that are pronounced by Professor Parsons and other experts to be the best yet made between a city and company; she also owns the cattle market and wharves, and is the largest owner of real estate in the city, leasing part of it in the business section of the city and along the water front at good rentals." At present there is in Toronto a movement for a municipal telephone exchange.

8th. Take another owner of local utilities — Guelph, for instance. Guelph built its fifteen mile steam road, and leased it to the Canadian Pacific under a ninety-nine year agreement. This investment cost Guelph $193,000, and it is now receiving yearly dividends amounting to about $25,000, or at the rate of 17 per cent. per annum.

Therefore, under public ownership, not only is the well-being served, and the democratic spirit preserved, but public morals are conserved, in that temptation to amass fortunes for private purses of a few is removed, while in the case of private ownership and monopolies there is waged a continual battle for special privileges that will make the people the helpless prey to corporations that become predatory bands.

Also it is safe to say that corporations and monopolies have corrupted and debauched municipal, state, and national life far more than all other agencies combined. Examine if you will the chief sources of public scandal, it matters not in which direction you look. Whether it be the whisky trust, coal, sugar, oil, or the embalmed beef scandal; whether it be the attempted debauchery of state government, the sources of all these public rprobations can be traced back to the corporations and private monopolies.

J. B. MUZANTE, '14.

A WINTER DRIVE.

HE air had a familiar feeling that December night; a familiar feeling paradoxically strange in this country where winds and clouds are well known. The streets of Ottawa as our party drove through were quiet. The sky was grey, and furry, and the weather was softly cold. The long wide avenues of shops glittered each with its great gas light swaying out behind the storm in dazzled bewilderment. The pedestrians whom we met were very differently armed. Some carried skates, other skis, while some had snowshoes.

As we rode along, the flakes of snow became unfriendly and drove into our faces. The soft shadow of a hidden street afforded us protection. Riding into this street we heard loud cheering in the distance, and pursuing on our course we arrived before a large skating arena. One of our members suggested that we should go in to see a hockey match which was being contested, and as the majority were in favour of this proposal we entered.

This was one of the greatest sights imaginable. One could not conceive how delightful it was to watch the players darting from one end of the ice to the other. Their quickness of movement almost made the spectators think that they were looking at moving pictures. The crowd cheered the players, and when the game was over we went to the nearest inn for the night.

Next afternoon we recommenced our drive, and halted about one mile outside the city, where a multitude of people were watching the ice races. We stopped a while to watch the horses trotting around the ice track, cheered on by their supporters. There were men betting on the horses which they thought would win, and as those horses came to our side of the course cheers went forth from the excited crowd.

Thinking such sport not what best pleased young people, we pursued our journey toward the Victoria slide. Here we spent the remainder of the evening in tobogganing. This we found to be a very delightful sport. Each sleigh afforded seating capacity for at least eight passengers, and when the sleigh was started at the top of the slide it flew downward with a tremendous speed until it struck the glare ice on the wide, smooth river below. Its speed here was somewhat retarded, but, nevertheless, it kept onward for almost a quarter of a mile. On both sides of the slide grew the tall mullein, a plant which is so often seen on our Canadian hills. Its tall form penetrates through the deep snow, and its ragged and torn leaves are a piteous spectacle. Of all the plants that grow, the mullein in its decay comes nearest to that most terrible form of human poverty when the victim has still, to his misfortune, vitality enough for his mere existence, yet not enough to make existence either decent or endurable.

After thus spending our evening at the slide we returned to our native village. On our return trip one of the party suggested that we should all drive to his home to spend the remainder of the Christmas eve. We were received by his parents with the kindest hospitality, and were told to sit down to supper, after which being all disposed to gaiety, an old harper was summoned from the hall. He played some very familiar airs. Then the party broke up with the kind-hearted custom of shaking hands and wishing "Merry Christmas."

F. CORKERY, '11.

THE CRUSADES.

N all countries, and in all climes, wherever the Crusades have been heard of, they have been attacked and ridiculed, as having unjust and foolish motives; and as having been carried on without sufficient reason.

But if we stop and consider why the Crusades were undertaken; what benefits occrued from them; how they were conducted, we would readily see that these attacks are indeed ridiculous, the offspring of bigoted minds.

The motives which actuated the heroes of the Crusades, which made them undergo hardships and sufferings, were as just, as honorable, as noble, as ever actuated man. The pilgrims and the Christians of the East were barbarously treated, cruelly oppressed, and, above all, put to death by the fierce Mussulmen. Such a sight filled the hearts of Christians with anger and sorrow. Humanity and religion repeatedly besought them to take up arms for their brethren and to put an end to this terrible persecution. The Greek emperor, Alexis, was harassed continually by these barbarians, and he sought the aid of the crowned heads of Europe. The chief motive, however, was to rescue the Holy Land from the infidels; to tear off the yoke from the necks of the Christians; and to give them peace and happiness.

The most powerful army ever seen was that of the Musselmen. They had flocked together from the most distant quarters, and were knocking at the portals of Europe. They had conquered and laid waste many lands, for their one desire was the desire of rapine, bloodshed and extermination.

And when their knocking had resounded, as it were, through the halls of Europe; when it became more clamorous and threatening, what were our Christian forefathers to do? Were they to ignominiously open the doors of Europe to these infidels? Were they to suffer themselves to be taken prisoners, to be sold into slavery, and probably to be tortured to death? Were they to await with fear and trembling till the vast hordes of the East broke down the doors and poured into the halls with sword and torch? Most assuredly not. The time had come to arise and go forth to fight, to drive back the infidels, and to strike a blow for themselves, for Christendom, and for God.

Pope Urban II. eloquently said in his address to the crusaders: "Warriors, the barbarous hordes of the Turks have planted their colors on the very shores of the Hellespont, whence they threaten destruction to all the states of Christendom. Unless you oppose a mighty barrier to their triumphant course, how can Europe be saved from invasion? How can the storm be averted, which has so long threatened to burst upon our countries?" We can now readily see that there were great motives, motives inspired by faith, Christian charity, and personal interests which lead the Christians to battle.

Truly, the lives of nearly two millions of men were sacrificed, but this is no ground for reproach and invective. Napoleon, in the space of twenty years, caused the death of more than seven million men, and yet he was lauded and extolled as the greatest military genius of the century, and of all times. He was reckoned as the greatest leader of all times, greater even than Alexander and Hannibal. He was the cause of the death of more men than were the Crusades, and all for glory and ambition. And yet the Crusaders are bitterly censured, while Napoleon, if not praised, is more or less excused.

If we stop and consider that all the men who were slain in the Crusades came from the many countries of Europe, and that Crusades lasted for almost two hundred years, it is apparent on the face of it that there are no grounds for these invectives and reproaches.

These heroes died that we might live, that Europe might be saved; that Christianity might live, that civilization might not be done away with. Were these, then, foolish motives?

We see that the benefits accruing from the Crusades were great and lasting. The strength of the Mussulmen was weakened, which effectually prevented them from gaining entrance to civilized Europe. Wars amongst the different European powers ceased, from the very fact that their kings and princes were off in the Holy Land fighting for their honor, their safety, and their God. Navigation also began to flourish, and this brought about great results, the most predominant of which was the discovery of the New World. Commerce was enlarged by exportations from Europe to Asia, and vice-versa, and to the frequent intercourse with Greece and Syria may be referred the revival of arts and sciences.

Many crimes and excesses happened during the Crusades, despite the wise laws made by the kings and princes. But these should not place the Crusades in a bad light, for the same things have occurred in other wars, and will always occur where a large body of men are banded together. A few bad effects cannot spoil the nobleness of any just cause. In contrast to these crimes and excesses are the nobleness, and the inspired actions of the leaders and the majority of their followers. These men were brave in danger, magnanimous and charitable in victory. These facts are universally known and cannot be disproved. The actions of the poor depraved few are certainly offset by the actions of the majority.

And I am sure that no one can think or decide that Crusades were inaugurated from a desire of plunder, and from a spirit of religious fanaticism. Deep in his heart, man should be full of love and gratitude for those Christians who sacrificed their lives and their all for Europe and their God.

P. G., '11.

High hearts are never long without hearing some new call, some distant clarion of God, even in their dreams; and soon they are observed to break up the camp of ease, and start on some fresh march of faithful service.

—Martineau.

Around the Halls.

On Feb. 6th a concert was given in the rotunda by the City orchestra. Mr. T. P. Murphy sang several rag-time pieces for the amusement of the boys, including "Dorando" and "What Has That Man Harrigan Done?" His singing was of course excellent, and hugely enjoyed. Father Lajeunesse and his "Up-the-Creekers" made a decided hit, if we may judge by the encores they received. The "Faculty Chorus" was very good, and sufficiently demonstrated that there is plenty of good material in the house. Another selection by the orchestra concluded the performance, although the boys did not seem very anxious to leave.

Father Stanton, with his usual inventive power, planned ice races for the morning of University Day, and so prevented the boys from putting in a dull forenoon. He was ably assisted by Fr. Finnegan, who acted as judge of all the events. Nearly every one was entered in some race or other, so it was interesting to all. Relays, snowshoe, sprints, egg and potato races were the features of the day. The Arts won the 1st prize on points. Most of the fellows showed a decided lack of training, except the novices. The egg and potato races were so fast that some of the eggs were scrambled and the potatoes baked.

Junior relay—Won by Arts. Kennedy, 1st; Barry, 2nd.

Novice race—Won by Commercial. Meindl, 1st; Joe Moore, 2nd.

Egg race—Tie between Arts and Philosophers. Coughlan and Contway.

Potato race—Won by Philosophers. Gauthier, 1st; Murtagh, 2nd.

Senior relay—Won by Collegiate. W. Chartrand.

1 mile—Won by Collegiate. W. Chartrand, 1st; McHugh, 2nd.

Marathon—Won by Arts. McDougall, 1st; O. Kennedy, 2nd.

Snowshoe—Won by Collegiate. Chantal.

60 yds. dash—Won by Collegiate. P. Leacy, 1st; S. Quilty, 2nd.

Arts—19 points.

Collegiate—15 points.

Commercial—12 points.

Philosophers—8 points.

The following address was read by C. F. Gauthier to Rev. D. A. Rhéaume on the occasion of his ordination. A very feeling reply was made by the young priest:

Rev. and Dear Father,—On this day so full of joy and promise, when your most cherished hopes have been realized, we, the students of Ottawa University, desire to express our gratification at seeing one of our number raised to the dignity of God's annointed.

That one of our former associates should have been found worthy to ascend the altar of God is an honor to our institution, and at the same time an incentive to high aims and noble purposes for each and every one of us.

Your distinguished career, while pursuing your studies within these walls, your studious application to tasks and your exemplary conduct, were a model for your fellow-students, and an augury of success in the chosen field of your labor.

As students of a Catholic University, we naturally honor and venerate the priesthood; we revere the priest whoever he may be. But our veneration is manifoldly increased when we behold one who has trod the paths which we are all trodding under the guidance of many of our present professors, mounted to the most elevated dignity of Christ's Disciple. We feel sure then that you will not forget we who are at present studying within these walls, and that when officiating at the altar you will implore God's blessings upon us. Rest assured, dear Father, that you will go forth to fulfill the high and honored duties of your sacred office accompanied by the most earnest prayers and sincere good-wishes of

THE STUDENTS OF THE U. OF O.

Dec. 21, 1909.

* * *

ST. PATRICK'S DAY BANQUET.

Preparations are going on apace for this great college event.

TOAST LIST AND SPEAKERS.

St. Patrick's Day—Joseph T. Brennan, '10·
The Holy Father—M. J. Smith, '10·
Canada—Chas. D. O'Gorman, '10·
Ireland's Saints and Scholars—Phil. C. Harris, '11·

Irish Party—D. J. Breen, '11; J. J. Sammon, '11·
Alma Mater—A. C. Fleming, '11·
United States—Leo H. Tracy, '11·
Soggarth Aroon—Rev. M. Murphy, O.M.I.

* * *

Toastmaster—Martin O'Gara, '10·
Director—Rev. J. P. Fallon, O.M.I.
Committee—J. J. Burke, chairman; J. J. Sammon, secretary; F. Corkery, treasurer.

Executive—L. H. Tracy, M. J. O'Gara, J. J. Contway, C. F. Gauthier.

PRIZE DEBATERS.

J. J. Sammon, M. J. O'Gorman, P. J. Loftus, C. F. O'Halloran.

Subject: Labor Unions are a detriment rather than a benefit to Society.

Chairman of Debate—P. C. Harris, '11·

Every man has his own vocation. There is one direction in which all space is open to him. He has faculties silently inviting him thither to endless exertion.

—Emerson.

Throughout his life he was a man of luck—a man of success. And why? Because he had the eye to see his opportunity, the heart to prompt to well-timed action, the nerve to consummate a perfect work.

Charlotte Bronte.

University of Ottawa Review

PUBLISHED BY THE STUDENTS.

THE OTTAWA UNIVERSITY REVIEW is the organ of the students. Its object is to aid the students in their literary development, to chronicle their doings in and out of class, and to unite more closely to their Alma Mater the students of the past and the present.

TERMS:

One dollar a year in advance.   Single copies, 15 cents.   Advertising rates on application
Address all communications to the "UNIVERSITY OF OTTAWA REVIEW", OTTAWA, ONT.

Vol. XII.   OTTAWA, ONT., FEBRUARY, 1910.   No. 5

COLLEGE MAGAZINES.

Month by month there comes to the sanctum a large number of Exchanges to remind us that the College magazine is an important and popular factor in the life of modern schools and students. There can be no doubt that the College paper, properly conducted, is of inestimable value in fostering and developing originality of thought, without which he who reads much is apt to become a plagiarist, a parasite, a bore. With a fair amount of intelligence and a good memory, one may acquire a great deal of knowledge, but unless the ideas are assimilated, a man can scarcely be called educated in the true sense of the word, — he ranks rather with the parrot and the phonograph. The College paper, by giving a more or less wide publicity to student writing, encourages not only the art of composition which involves clearness of thought and elegance of expression, but also assimilation of ideas acquired from books and lectures. The writing of even a short article on any given topic requires a considerable expenditure of mental energy on the part of the young scribe, which cannot fail to give a healthy and vigorous development to his intellectual powers. The College paper, then, even considered solely form this point of view, is of great benefit, provided that it is really the work of the students. But there is in the minds of many a shrewd suspicion that many of our College publications are the work of much more mature minds, or at least aim too high and too far for the mental calibre of their publishers. Perhaps the following extract from Collier's may sound harsh, but it certainly contains considerable truth and food for reflection:

"We have at our elbow four college papers. Nothing could be duller. They are the last place a daily newspaper would look for recruits of genius. Too much professor, too little undergraduate, that's what's wrong with them. And the undergraduate, what there is of him, tries too hard. The frog would be an ox. Nothing less than leaders for him, and policies that thunder louder than the London 'Times.' Alas, poor boy, he has not the life and experience behind him that mean real force, and the best he can do is bang sheet iron and make stage thunder. Earnestness is more than ruffling one's hair and pounding the pulpit. There is even such a thing as laughing a case out of court. Humor is the golden thread of literature, but the college paper knows naught of it and cares less. Twenty years from now your undergraduate will have grasped what a good gift humor is, and how it means perfect comprehension wedded to kind philosophy. Time was when one of these college papers was bright and gay, and full of zest and youthful mistakes, and blithe spirits went out from it to salt the journalism of a continent. May that day come again! O callow sages, grave and reverend juniors, when will you learn once more to be young and natural?"

"MENS SANA IN CORPORE SANO."

In keeping with the above true true maxim, a Physical Culture Class has been organized under the direction of the First Disciplinary Prefect, Rev. Father Stanton, O.M.I. In the college we have a great variety of sport,—Billiards, Pool, Bowling, Tobogganing, Skating and Hockey. Notwithstanding the diversity of games the great majority of the students take little or no bodily exercise, except for the 'lock-step' walks, up and down the boards, or on the cinder paths.

To undergo the strain of prolonged mental labor, we must make the body fit to cope with the conditions in which it is found. Students as a class work prodigiously with their brains, and utterly neglect all bodily exercises, and they expect to escape the consequences of this neglect. It is by reason of this principle that men who do no physical work have poor appetites. In contrast to these are those who take much physical exercise, they eat largely (no personal allusions) and are benefited by their food, because there is previous need manifested by sharp appetite. Energy comes from food only when it has been assimilated. To get energy we must give out energy. Therefore, when the time comes for Physical Culture Class, go at it with a vim; don't fool or play at it; but work and work hard; and the natural vigor of the system, much augmented by the hard regular exercise, easily forms more than enough eneregy to meet the next expenditure, and increases the blood's nutrition power.

As to the amount of work necessary on exercising days, that will depend entirely upon the strength and endurance of the subject. A safe rule is to discontinue for a few moments any exercise as soon as the muscles become too tired to perform it vigorously.

EDITORIAL NOTES.

Every week we feel more and more indebted to the "Catholic Record" and the "Catholic Register" for giving us such gems of the world's best thought and such interesting notes on current literary events as are contained in "The Reader's Corner," "The Bookworm," "On Sun-crowned Heights," and "Chats by the Fireside." They are elevating and inspiring. Would that they replaced the comic? supplements of the secular journals!

* * *

February 10th was the eleventh anniversary of the death of Archibald Lampman, perhaps Canada's sweetest poet. Incomplete indeed would be the Anthology of Canadian Poetry which did not accord him a position of honour. Since much of his choicest verse appeared originally in "The Owl," and its successor, "The Review," we take the liberty of re-printing one of his beautiful poems.

Those among the students who are interested in politico-historical questions will welcome the new book, "Psychology of Politics and History," by our own Father Dewe, of which an advertisement appears in this issue.

* * *

Camille Flammarion, he of the vivid imagination, has been giving voice to dire prognostications re Halley's Comet. It appears that about the 18th of May next, the tail of the troublesome thing will envelop the earth in cyanogen, which is the deadliest of poisons. Strange to say, the human race, though thus threatened with destruction, does not seem to be worrying about it.

* * *

Our American cousins are evidently waking up to the importance of the growing young nation north of the 49th parallel. One or two of the great New York papers have now special correspondents here in Ottawa, and considerable space is devoted to Canadian topics in American journals and magazines. In Canada on the other hand, there seems to be a greater interest in Imperial affairs; witness the close attention given to the recent British elections, and the wide-spread discussion of the Canadian Naval Bill.

* * *

There is a tendency among College papers, particularly those of the large Universities, to change from monthlies to weeklies. They have the advantage of being more up-to-date in their news. but as literary efforts they are decidedly disappointing.

Speech is the small change of silence.

Which is the coward among us? He who sneers at the failings of humanity.

The Spanish Inquisition, in The Patrician, is a well-gotten-up and scholarly article. The author treats the question from an impartial point of view, and lays the blame where it should be laid. An essay on Lorna Doone cannot but increase the reader's knowledge of Blackmore's famous story. The other articles in this month's issue of "The Patrician" are well up to the high standard of literary merit which this periodical enjoys among the Colleges.

The Fordham Monthly contains an excellent appreciation of Fenelon, the great French Bishop, and Preceptor of the Dauphin, the Duke of Burgundy. The writer accuses Fenelon of representing the world as it should be, not as it is. He pays him a graceful compliment, however, by bestowing upon him the title of "The real prophet of our present-day democracy." But Fenelon's pure principles of government pursued a course never dreamed of by their saintly author, for Rousseau took his inspiration from him ,and thus inaugurated the great Revolution.

We desire to express our hearty congratulations to the Exponent upon the establishment of a weekly edition. "The Weekly Exponent" has all the merits of "The Monthly" edition, but we fail to find in the former the columns of pungent witticisms over which we spend so many pleasant moments every time we read the latter. We trust that the fountains of mirth have not dried up completely in the editorial sanctum of our Rocky Mountain friend.

The author of "College Men in Politics" in the Trinity U. Review vindicates the practicability of young college graduates. Politics, he says, presents a magnificent field to young Collegemen. The writer then proceeds to lay down rules, which seem to have been gained from experience, by which a young politician may hope to win success.

The Niagara Index has the following to say, commenting upon the Gladstone Centenary:

"Never has England been able to turn to a subject who was more willing to do for England, to pledge his learning, oratory and sentiment more sincerely in behalf of his country, than to Gladstone. No voice was more influencing than his in national affairs."

Besides the above-mentioned, we beg to acknowledge receipt of the following:

"Abbey Student," "Acta Victoriana," "Adelphian," "Agnetian Monthly," "Argosy," "Allisonia," "Academic Herald," "Assumption College Review," "Echoes From the Pines," "Educational Review," "Geneva Cabinet," "Georgetown College Journal," "Hya Yaka," "Holy Cross Purple," "O.A.C. Review," "Ottawa Campus," "Pharos," "Rosary Magazine," "Solanian," "St. Mary's Angelos," "St. Mary's Chimes," "Villa Shield," "Vox Collegii."

Books and Reviews.

The Nineteenth Century for January has an interesting article on the present constitutional crisis in Great Britain. The following are among some of the points developed.

To abolish the House of Lords would be to leave the people to the mercy of an omnipotent House of Commons.

As the strength of a chain depends on the weakest link, so the reputation of the British Upper House depends on the character of its least reputable members.

There exists the paradox that, while the individual opinions of its leading members command respectful attention, the collective opinion of the Lords counts for little.

Examples of bi-cameral legislation: — Greece, Honduras, First Protectorate Parliament of England, Legislative Assembly in France.

The universal consent of mankind has been that there should exist two chambers.

The constitutions of the federal governments of Australia and South Africa, which were compiled only after reviewing the systems of the past, have both a second chamber.

The Review of Reviews, for February, would solve the difficulty of the Lords in a novel manner. When parliament has been dissolved the House of Lords as a body ceases to exist. It has no right to re-assemble until summoned by the King after the return of the new government. This is done by the issuing

of individual Writs of Summons to the Peers.   Since 1625 the
withholding of writs has been abandoned. But, since this power
still exists, why, ask this Review, should not the King refuse
Writs of Summons to those who have consistently refused to attend in the past; or whose attendance has not been regular?
Thus, reformation would be secured by a process of elimination.

The January number of the *Atlantic Monthly* has also a contribution on the House of Lords.   The writer claims that the
weakness of this body lies in its hereditary principle. He calls
the "gilded chamber a gilded desert."   To cure our admiraton
for it we should go and see it in session.   However, he urges
that the few who do the work of this august body are exceptionally brilliant men.   At present there are at least two hundred and fifty of its members qualified to take their places on
any governing board in the world.   When measures are introduced, however, in any way affecting the position of the
aristocracy, new forces appear in such force as to swamp the
competent element.   He points to the fact, also, that the Conservative party owing to the open sympathy existing between
it and the House of Lords plays the political game with loaded
dice, and that when it is in power there is practically but one
chamber.   The hostility of the Radicals to any reformation in
the Upper House in lieu of abolition, arises from their knowledge
that any reformation will strengthen rather than weaken it.

Round the World, Vol. VII., published by Benziger Bros.,
New York. $1.00.

The seventh volume of this interesting series is as good, if
not better, than its predecessors.   As usual, the articles treat of
history, geography, commerce, manufactures, and the history of
cities, etc.   As can be judged, they are sufficiently varied to
catch the attention of the young.   They are written with the
purpose of instructing youth, and of encouraging further reading upon the subjects treated, and we feel certain that this object will be fully attained.   The volume is illustrated with one
hundred clear, distinct and well-chosen prints.

Among the Magazines.

Says the *Scientific American*, under the heading, "Canada
and the Quebec Bridge": "Architectural and engineering
works are in no small degree an expression of the character of
the people by whom they were built.   By such standards we are

accustomed to judge the ancient peoples of Greece and Rome; and thus the Forth bridge stands as a monument of architectural triumph in the British Empire; and there is now a statue dedicated to the designer.

"But the same cause which gives fame, operates to bring disgrace upon the originator and the nation, when a great bridge of this kind falls to its destruction. The Canadian government was behind the former enterprise, and their ideal was to have an elaborate and, aesthetically speaking, a beautiful bridge. But now they propose to build a new one, which utterly fails to satisfy the requirements of the beautiful. Would it not be better for the government to call for world-wide tenders. The proposed bridge is to be built on the cantilever system. By letting out the contract to the best of New World engineers, the result would decide the comparative merits of the cantilever system with the safer and more beautiful suspension system."

The question, this paper adds, deserves the most acute attention on the part of the Dominion; because on sensible action. now depends the future fair name of not Canada alone, but of America in general.

In the *Rosary Magazine*, Marguerite Donegan pictures the sorrow of struggling Ireland. She introduces besides several songs to show how the tradition of that land is steeped in sadness. Intense lovers are capable of intense sorrow. And this truth applies most especially to the Irish. A land of unclouded joy once, for one thousand years the country has been the scene of a veritable tragedy, — so much so, that now we may truthfully assert that every sunlit hillside, every fair, sleeping valley, every bit of brown turf, every blade of green grass, is filled with Irish blood.

The current number of the *America* gives two very interesting communications, one by a Spanish astronomer, José Comas Sola, and the other by an eminent French director of astronomy, M. Deslandres. Their verdict might be read with profit by many who rush for the new modern theory concerning Mars. Says the first: "During my twenty years' observations, never have I succeeded in seeing the geometrical wonders so profusely published in every part of the world. I have ever been an enemy to these imaginations, and am convinced that they were illusions or exaggerations of the observers."

"I do not deny that there are borders that give the appearance of canals; but these borders are wide and diffuse, and rarely well defined."

M. Deslandres says: "In a letter of September, 1909, I called the attention of the editor to the fact that the Henry objective of 0.83 metre shows "no trace whatever of the geometrical network on Mars, while it distinguishes details incomparably finer than the 'supposed' canals. When the image is calm, the aspect of the planet is like that of the moon. The geometrical forms present themselves very furtively in dancing images; and appear only in small telescopes."

The Educational Review has the following from the London Teacher: "Cramming in the sense of loading the mind with a mass of words which have no clear and definite ideas to correspond with them is silly, but cramming in the sense of mastering a series of understood facts which an examiner may require is a sensible precaution."

Priorum Temporum Flores.

Rev. J. J. O'Gorman, '04, of Ottawa, gave the English ad dress at a New Year's reunion in the Canadian College, Rome, where he is making special studies.

Rev. J. Foley, of Lancaster, favored Alma Mater with a visit a few weeks ago.

Consequent on the appointment of Rev. P. J. Kelly, '05, to the parish of Wooler, Peterborough diocese, St. Mary's, Havelock, will be attended to by Rev. W. P. Meagher.

We were pleased to see Rev. Dr. McNally, of Chelsea, a visitor to the University a few days ago.

Rev. Father James Keely, '02, of Kingston diocese, who has been acting as curate to Ven. Archdeacon Casey, of Lindsay, has been recalled to his native diocese.

Wilton Lackaye, '84, the eminent actor, paid Alma Mater a visit some weeks ago. Mr. Lackaye scored a triumph at the Russell Theatre.

Rev. Father V. K. McFadden, '05, of the Cathedral staff, Peterborough, has been transferred to St. Joseph's, Douro.

While on a recent visit to the city, Rev. J. McDonald, '03, who is stationed at the Bishop's Palace, Kingston, paid the University a call.

Rev. J. J. McDonnell, '04, Rev. W. H. Dooner, '04, and Rev. J. Harrington, '04, were recent visitors to the College.

Obituary.

REV. FATHER McGOWAN.

Rev. Father McGowan, of Fort Covington, after an illness of but short duration, died at the Hotel Dieu, Kingston, on Monday morning, Jan. 31st. The deceased was a native of Ireland, being born in the County of Sligo, Oct. 28th, 1830. His preparatory studies were made at Mount Mellery, Ireland, and in the Irish College at Paris. His theological studies were completed in Ottawa University, where he was ordained to the priesthood in May, 1866. The first ten years of his mission were spent in Canada. Afterwards being adopted by the late Bishop Wadhams, he was appointed pastor at Cadyville, where he spent twenty years as a faithful and devoted priest. In 1892 he was transferred by Right Rev. H. Gabriels to Fort Covington, where he had been ever since.

It was Father McGowan's earnest wish to be buried in Pakenham, Ont., beside his cousin, the venerable Father Lavin. His Grace, Most Reverend Archbishop Gauthier, of Kingston, celebrated the Solemn Requieum funeral mass in the Cathedral, Kingston, on Tuesday morning, Feb. 1st, and with many priests from his diocese accompanied the remains to Pakenham, where all arrangements for the funeral had been made by the pastor, Very Rev. Canon Corkery.

The funeral Mass was celebrated on Wednesday morning, at which His Grace the Most Reverend Archbishop officiated. The funeral sermon was preached by Rev. B. J. McCoghlin, N.Y.

The following priests were present on the sanctuary: Rev. Canon Corkery, P. P., Pakenham; Rev. T. P. Fitzgerald, Massena, N.Y.; Rev. Father Chaine, Arnprior; Rev. Father Harkin, Almonte; Rev. James George, Arnprior; Rev. James J. McGowan, nephew of deceased; Rev. Thomas P. Murphy, O.M.I., Ottawa.

R. I. P.

Personals.

Rev. J. Bertrand and students attending our institution from Clarence Creek journeyed to that town the 17th instant, and were successful in defeating their own home team in a friendly game of hockey.

We were recently honored by a visit from His Lordship Bishop Scollard of Sault Ste. Marie diocese. His Lordship spent a couple of days with us, and delighted all who had the pleasure of listening to him by his interesting chats on conditions in his great north country.

Fr. Kuntz has recently returned from a month's holiday in Buffalo.

Miss Stella O'Brien, of Renfrew, recently visited her cousin, J. Barry, '15.

Rev. P. W. Browne of our staff gave a very interesting lecture on Saturday last before the d'Youville Circle of the Rideau Street Convent. The subject was "The Foundations of Empire."

Mr. W. Hackett lately received a visit from his sister of Stanstead, Que.

The annual banquet of the St. Joseph's Church Choir was held on the 31st ult. Rev. Fathers W. J. Murphy, T. P. Murphy and W. J. Collins were present, besides about thirty members of choir.

Rev. William Patton, O.M.I., a former Professor of Philosophy in Ottawa, is to succeed Father Kirwin as pastor of St. Patrick's Church, McCook, Neb.

Rev. Fr. Dewe is bringing out an interesting book on the "Psychology of Politics and History," of which mention is made elsewhere in this issue.

We chronicle with pleasure the appointment of Rev. Fr. Kerwin of McCook, Neb., to the pastorate of Holy Angels' Church, Buffalo, to succeed the Rt. Rev. M. F. Fallon, O.M.I., D.D., who has recently been appointed to the bishopric of London, Ont. Rev. Fr. Kerwin was lately a professor in our University, and we sincerely wish the Rev. gentleman every success in his new and onerous position.

Physical Culture Class.

The Physical Culture Class is in full swing, and is already accomplishing much good.

The following gentlemen were chosen as officers of the Class: Director, Rev. W. J. Stanton, O.M.I.; President, Leo H. Tracy, '11; Vice-Pres., T. J. O'Neill, '11; Secy.-Treas., Arthur Courtois, '11·

Indoor Baseball.

Indoor baseball, which is becoming very popular in the Capital, was given a marked impetus last week, when a City League was organized at the Y.M.C.A. Four well-balanced teams will play a schedule that extends over six weeks. Mr. Hal B. McGivern, M.P. for Ottawa, was elected honorary president of the new organization. Pres., P. J. Lee, Y.M.C.A.; 1st Vice-Pres., Allan Oliver, Pastimes; 2nd Vice-Pres., M. Chrysler, O.A.A.C.; Secy.-Treas., Phil C. Harris, Ottawa University. The schedule is as follows:—

Feb. 10—Y.M.C.A. v. O.A.A.C.
" 10—Pastimes v. College.
" 17—Pastimes v. Y.M.C.A.
" 17—College v. O.A.A.C.
" 24—Pastimes v. O.A.A.C.
" 24—College v. Y.M.C.A.
Mar. 3—College v. Pastimes.
" 3—O.A.A.C. v. Y.M.C.A.
" 10—O.A.A.C. v. College.

" 10—Y.M.C.A. v. Pastimes.
" 17—Y.M.C.A. v. College.
" 17—O.A.A.C. v. Pastimes.

STANDING OF LEAGUE.

	Won.	Lost.	To Play.
Pastimes...	1	1	4
Y.M.C.A.	2	0	4
College	1	1	4
O.A.A.C.	0	2	4

Hockey.

PHILOSOPHERS (4) — COLLEGIATE (3).

Thus read the score after an extended playing period of one hour and thirty minutes, when the hockey teams representing the "sage" Philosophers and the "rudimentary" Collegians clashed for the first time in the Inter-Course Hockey League. The game was fraught with brilliant feats, and profuse flow of gore. Everybody "nose" to whom and to what we refer. The Philosophers' coverpoint in attempting to get into the game with vim got into the visage of our fair-haired rover. The result was that he felt much "cut-up," and was forced to retire from the conflict. At full time the score read three all, and after thirty minutes of nerve-racking play, Brennan and Gauthier, on a clever piece of combination work, scored the fateful goal, midst copious and tumultuous volleys of applause from the spectators. For the Philosophers all played well, but special praise must be given the defense work of Brennan, Smith and Harris. The stars of the Collegiates were Jack and Henry Robillard and W. Chartrand.

ARTS (7) — JUNIORS (6).

The classy Arts hockey team came out on top in a game against the fast Juniors. The first half ended with Arts well in the lead with four goals to one, but in taking things too easy in the second half they just nosed out victorious. For the "Arts" course, Capt. O'Neill was the "arc-light" performer, while Leo Kelly and Marty Brennan also scintillated.

PHILOSOPHERS (8) — JUNIORS (6).

R-E-V-E-N-G-E, that sweet feeling of satisfaction, was the

lot of the students of "Sanctus Thomas," as they skated off the ice victorious over the Juniors by the score of eight goals to five. The blue shirts in the previous game caught the "P's" nappy, or sound asleep, I don't know which, and rolled up a score of 7-4. This time, however, the "Zigs" were on to the job all the time, and played with a vim that was refreshing and assuring. Half-time found the score 3-2 for Juniors. When the teams resumed play the "Phils." took a commanding lead of 5-3, but owing to a momentary "blow-up" or an attack of "brainstorm," the score was quickly tied, 5-5, when time was called. In overtime of ten minutes the score read 6-6. Once again the battle was continued, when the staying powers of the "Sapientes" proved too much for the Juniors, and they weakened, allowing their opponents to score twice, making the final tally read 8-6 for the Philosophers. To particularize the stellar players would be unfair. Every man played his position effectively, and from Harris in goal to Sauvé on the wing, no fault can be found. Undoubtedly the palm for the most brilliant player goes with the unanimous consent of all to Grindy-Patrick-Taylor Brennan, the classy coverpoint of the "Philosophers."

COLLEGIATE (7) — ARTS (4).

The under-estimated seven of the "Collegiate" course showed a marked improvement in form, and defeated with apparent ease the fast septette of the "Arts" students. It was one of the best, if not the best, hockey game played so far in the league. The play was fast, clean, and scientific, and a great game to watch. The first half saw some classy and stubbornly contested hockey, and ended 2 all. In the second period the Collegiates took a remarkable brace, and before the Arts realized it they were behind, 5-2. Still the Collegiates pressed their advantage, and despite the efforts of Capt. O'Neill's stalwarts, the score read 7-4 as the whistle blew "game over."

Collegiate, as it played against "Arts," truly deserved to win more games, and still has a fighting chance. Chartrand, Jack Robillard, T. Hillman, and Voligny played a pretty combination game, and have bunches of speed, while the defence work of Murtagh, Hennie, Robillard, and particularly Paddy Moran Munnock, was certainly superb.

"Arts" did not have on their best team. Capt. Charles F. 'Neill, Lee Kelly, and Ossie Kennedy were the best players for Arts, and with Marty Brennan on would have run "Collegiate" to the wire.

Players:—

Arts.   Collegiate:
Cornellier ... ... Goal ... ... Minnock.
Kennedy ... ... Point ... ... Murtagh.
(Capt.) O'Neil ... ...C. Point. ...H. Robillard (Capt.)
Boulanger ... ... Rover ... ... Chartrand.
McDougall ... ... Centre. ... ... T. Hillman.
Landriau ... ... Wings ... ...J. Robillard.
Letang ... ...   " ....Voligny and Shanahan.

Side Shots.

Mr. Chas. D. O'Gorman was appointed manager of the Indoor Baseball team. Joe Muzante was elected captain.

* * *

The pen sketch title "Athletics" in last month's Review was
the subject of favorable comment. Mr. Gustave Gallopin was
responsible for it. Congratulations, Gus!

* * *

There is a rumor current that quite a "wad" was dropped
by a certain Prof. on the win of Philosophers over Collegiate.
He blames Harris' phenomenal goal-keeping for the loss, but expects to get even by betting that Juniors trim the "Sapientias"
when they meet. Better keep your small change, for Mike Smith,
Joe Brennan, Gauthier, Harris & Co. have caught their winning
stride. Verbum sat sapienti!

* * *

"Ubi nunc sumus?" cried the "Sapientias" as Harris missed three easy ones. "In loco desperatissimo," groaned the goal-
tend.

* * *

Such expressions as "Bene," "Optime," "Perfecte," were
frequently heard on the sides when the "Zigliarites" pulled off
some hair-raising stunts.

* * *

Suivez! Suivez! shouted the Juniors' coach, but Louis Peach-
blow Côté and Zig Sauvé understood the parlance, so it worked
both ways.

* * *

We don't know his name, but that Junior that throws a
"feinting" or "faking" spell five times every game should be

furnished with a feather bed, so that he can die peacfully instead of expiring daily on the cold unfeeling ice, and before a hard-hearted bunch of College students.

* * *

To play hockey is human,
To score is sure fine,
To defeat the "defeaters"—
Why it's simply divine!
Juniors please take notice.

* * *

A "tie" at full time, Philosophers excited;
Two goals in the extra, Philosophers delighted.

* * *

Suggestions for the "All-Star" team of the Inter-Course Hockey League will be gladly received and published by the Editor of the Athletic Department. Address your choice to "All-Star" Hockey Team Contest, and hand it to the Prefect. They will be published next issue.

* * *

With whose coin is Fl-g buying the cigars? I wonder? Hard luck, Prof., it's like purloining bon-bons from a feeble infant!

* * *

Who's the best goal judge in the League? "Joe Simard," says Chartrand, "*not*," as he makes Joe do a "back-flap" into the heap of virgin snow. "Pas fair," dit Joe!!

* * *

Mike Smith and Capt. Gauthier are practicing the "sunny smile act" in preparation for the Philosophers' photo as champions of the League. Here's hoping!

* * *

Tommie Hare Kennedy can't see anything to it but the championship for his team. They'll never win on "store-pies" and brier pipes. McSwiggan Harrington is willing to bet any. thing from a peanut to a jacknife that "Arts" win all their coming games. Manager Sullivan of Collegiates took up the bet.

* * *

"The best hockey League in years," is the consensus of opinion among the students and professors of the "U." Great credit is due to Father Stanton for the successful carrying out of the new era of Inter-Course games.

☺f Local Interest

(Translation from an old Persian Ode, (B.C. 23).

'Faith life is just full of surprises,
    And the best we can do is to hope;
As often the people's surmises
    Don't happen to be the best dope.

Sure who'd ever think that Jim Ke-n-n-dy,
    Though for hockey he may have a care,
Should get so taken in by the malady
    That he's turned out to be Tommy Hare.

It's a marvel regarding Ph. H-r-s.
    Who in other things is pretty fair;
But this is sufficient to jar us:
    He rivals, s'il vous plait, Le Sueur.

And isn't S-th nifty around the net?
    His style is like that of Laviolette;
At centre O'N-l's the star of them all,
    Though sometimes he seems to out-Hall Joseph Hall.

"LIFE IN HOGAN'S FLATS."

Here's to the boys of Hogan's Flats,
    The greatest in the land,
Who know no sorrow, know no fear,
    And still united stand.

From early morn their tasks begin,
    And they with pleasure fill
The duties of their state in life
    At desk or window-sill.

At six o'clock that early hour
　　When chimes begin to peal,
We hear them rise from out their beds,
　　And from the flats they steal.

All morn the tumult rages high,
　　Till study does begin;
Then all must to their sanctum fly,
　　And to their books within.

At last pale Hecate holds sway,
　　And lights begin to glow,
The midnight oil in Hogan's Flats
　　Is burning, burning low.

Among the members here convened,
　　(We cannot name them all),
We have some long ones, short ones, too,
　　And some both big and small.

Our friend from out the woolly west,
　　He always wears a smile,
While Quyon Jim not quite so slim,
　　Is here to kid a while.

Let's not forget our friend Gustav,
　　Who 'splains the reason why;
With puzzled brains, his aeroplanes
　　He launches in the sky.

Who said long ones, we've a few,
　　First comes H-k-et, as good as two;
B-u-ke can't beat him, no not he,
　　Though in time he may make three.

Who wrote this you all may ask,
　　We must confess 'twas quite a task;
But if our members are not sore
　　Perhaps next month we'll add some more.

　　　　　　　　　　　　—HAPPY.

　　In Physics Class: "A preposition is a bad thing to end a sentence with."

Prof. (on election day).: ''Where is D-ly?''
Student: ''He's working at the poll.''
Prof.: ''He should be working at his own poll!''

Sm-th (in Philosophy): ''That's enough to make your hair stand on end.''
Bu-ke: ''Still, it stands to reason.''

You can't beat the drum with a drummer,
You can't do sums with a summer;
    But it's perfectly plain,
    Though I say it with pain,
You can always bum with a bummer.

J. K. went out the other day,
    Sporting a brand new Prince;
IIe placed his heel on a banana peel,
    And he hasn't *banana* where since!

G. W-bs says that during a thunderstorm he always rides with a brakeman, because the latter is a *non-conductor*, while he himself is a *sparker*, to use a *current* term!

Fl-g: ''H-t, however can you get into that small bed?''
H-t: ''Oh, I always add a couple of feet to it, when retiring.''

There's a new song entitled, ''The Dairy Lunch Duet.'' Words by Gr-f-n, music by Du-b-s.

Junior Department

Have you seen Reggie Sr. and Willie M. in their great act on the single trapeze?

What do they feed you on at Kingston? Watermelon?

Ne—ne—never mind, M-t-n, you like chicken.

Jim is of the opinion that tooth paste is a poor substitute for massage cream.

Dan S-n is not the only professional hockey player in the Small Yard. A few others can show them as well as Dan. Eh, Elwood?

See M-y and T-y in the Siamese twins act.

To mope, a verb meaning to be spiritless, sleepy or lazy. A society called the Mopesters has been formed in the Junior Department. The Junior editor regrets the formation of this society, and if the members do not disband they will receive a personal mention in next month's issue. L. B., S. G., El. and others take a friendly warning in good time.

The skating season will soon be a thing of the past, so make the most of it while it lasts. To do this you must keep the rink cleaned.

Our hockey team is still at the head of the Hurd League. They have yet to lose a game. Although the other teams are somewhat heavier they do not seem to be able to cope with the dash and combination of our representatives. Two games were played this month, the first against the Rideaus on Feb. 10, which was won by College by a score of 5 to 1. The second game was played in New Edinburgh against the Tecumsehs on Feb. 16, College again winning by a score of 2 to 1. The College defense is playing a grand game, while the combination play of the forward line has all their opponents guessing. The College team taking part in all the games is: Goal, B. Kinsella; point, A. Fournier; cover point, C. Brennan; forwards, E. Nagle, T. Hillman. D. Batterton and Faulkner.

Keep it up, boys, and we will have the Hurd Cup to place among our other trophies.

Vol. XII.   OTTAWA, ONT., MARCH, 1910.   No. 6

Entered at the Post Office at Ottawa, Ont., as Second-Class Matter.

EASTERTIDE.

ASTER ("Queen of Feasts") occupied the first place among Christian festivals; and the *motif* of its observance is found in the exultant utterance of St. Paul: "Now is Christ risen" (I Cor. XV, 20). The word Easter is found only among the Germanic peoples; for all other branches of the human family call the Feast by some modification of the Hebrew-Greek term, *pascha*. Hence the French word. *pâques*; the Italian, *pasqua*; the Spanish, *pascua*. In Spain and Italy the word is identified with a "solemnity," and is extended to other festivals, e.g., Spanish, *Pascua florida*, Palm Sunday; *Pascua de la natividad*, The Nativity. In some parts of France First Communion is called *pâques*, whatever time of the year it is administered.

Pasch is the Aramaic form of the Hebrew word, *pesach* ("the passing," or passover). This solemnity was instituted to commemorate the deliverance of the Israelites from the bondage of Egypt, and it was celebrated on the 14th of *Nisan* — the first month of the Jewish New Year. The origin of the word Easter is uncertain; but it is curious to note that it has been preserved amongst Germanic peoples rather than the Biblical term, *Pasch*. According to the "Edda" (Icelandic Saga) *Eostra* was the name of the goddess of Dawn, who opened the rosy portals of Valhalla to receive Baldur (the Sun-god), whose brow supplied man-

kind with light; and some philologists assert that this circum-
stance is suggestive of the word Easter which has the same sig-
nification as the Latin word *Resurrectio.*

Others claim that Easter is derived from the German, *ôstra*,
which signifies "a rising"; and some, amongst whom is the Venerable Bede, contend that Easter is the Saxon word, "Eostre"
(an old Saxon deity); and they tell us, further, that our April
was known as "esaternmonadth." The most acceptable deriva-
tion is seemingly the German (from "ôstra") as this also is the
parent of our word East ("where the sun rises"). At Easter the
Sun of Divine Goodness rises to enlighten mankind. The celebration of Easter dates from the earliest days of Christianity;
but it is impossible to determine accurately the exact year of its
institution. In primitive times two modes of celebrating the
Festival were in vogue; and Apostolic precedent was claimed
for both. The Western Church (Rome) celebrated Easter on the
Sunday after *14th Nisan*, i.e., the Sunday following the first full
moon after the vernal equinox; because it was on this day that
Christ rose from the dead and completed the work of the Redemption. This, it is claimed, was the practice of Sts. Peter and
Paul.

The Eastern Church (Antioch) celebrated Easter on the day
of the Jewish Passover—14th *Nisan*—regardless of the day of
the week on which it fell, and invoked the authority of St. John,
in justification of the observance. Those who observed this custom were known as "Quartodecimani" (Fourteenth Dayers).
Out of these differences arose the famous "Paschal Controver-
sies," which were acrimoniously waged until the Council of Nicea
(325) decreed that Easter should be celebrated on the Sunday
immediately following the fourteenth day of the so-called Paschal
moon, which occurs on or after the vernal equinox. This falls
invariably on March 21; so the earliest date on which Easter
can occur is March 22, the latest on April 25th.

Easter has ever been celebrated with the greatest possible
solemnity; and previous to the XIIth century, every day of Easter
week was kept as a holiday of obligation. Eastertide was pre-
ceded by a period of fasting (as it still is), and fast ended with
the cock-crow on Easter morn. The vigil (Holy Saturday) was
set apart as a special season for the baptism of catechumens;
and the Feast itself was a day of universal rejoicing. Gregory
of Nazianzen terms it "the royal day amongst days," and St.
Leo calls it "the feast of feasts."

The early Christian Emperors signalized Eastertide by setting minor criminals at liberty. All public business and public spectacles were prohibited; and by a decree of the Council of Orleans the Jews were forbidden to assemble in public thoroughfares ,or mingle with Christians, lest the festive joys of the latter should be marred. In later times St. Peter's, in Rome, was illuminated; and at mid-day on Easter Sunday the Pope, from the balcony above the vestibule, pronounced a blessing upon the world.

Easter is pre-eminently a feast of flowers, as Christmas is the feast of evergreens. In England during the "ages of faith" it was customary to strew the aisles of churches with ivy; and the special Easter flower was the lavender (*lavendula spicula*). Nowadays the Easter flower is the lily, which the Bermudas send us in ship loads. Why the lily should have supplanted the lavender is not apparent. The flowers of the latter have a highly aromatic odor and a bitterish taste; and it is suggestive of the aromatic spices which the holy women brought to the Sepulchre of our Lord on the first Easter morn. The church walls were festooned with this suggestive plant; and garlands of rose and lavender were placed on the altars and statuary. Crosses trimmed with the same trophies of the garden were distributed amongst the faithful, as symbols of the Resurrection.

Another symbol of the Resurrection, perpetuated in some of the noblest specimens of architecture, was the lion. This seems to be a puzzle to many, but the matter is very easily explained. It was formerly believed that the lioness brought forth her cubs dead, and three days later the lion, by howling, awoke them to life. Hence the adoption of the lion in ecclesiastical architecture, as a symbol of the cardinal doctrine of our faith. This also accounts for the fact that St. Mark, the Evangelist, is symbolized by the lion, as his Gospel gives us the most detailed history of the Resurrection of Christ.

Liturgical Observances.

The observances of the church at Eastertide are all symbolic. Chief amongst these is the "Paschal Candle," which is solemnly blessed on Easter Saturday. This signifies Christ — "The Light of the World" — and it is lighted during the singing of the *Exultet* — the most beautiful specimen of Gregorian hymnology in the Ritual of the Church. Whilst the authorship of this prose is not certain, it is attributed to St. Augustine; and, as he was a deacon when he composed it, it has always been sung by a deacon.

The Paschal Candle is composed of pure beeswax, and in some of the old English churches, before England became Protestant, was colossal. In 1577 the Paschal Candle made for Westminster Abbey weighed three hundred pounds. This candle is also a symbol of the Pillar of Fire which lights the Spiritual Israel through the wilderness of the world.

Closely connected with the Paschal Candle is the "Holy Fire." The lighting of fire at Eastertide is a custom which dates from the beginning of Christianity; and it was perhaps derived from pre-Christian observances which commemorated the coming of Spring. When Christianity became dominant, the Church became a depository of the sacred fire; and a lamp was kept burning to indicate its presence to the people. There are still in existence some of the old contrivances for the lighting of the sacred fire; they are known as "Cressets" and may be seen at Furness and Calder Abbeys, in England.

Social Customs.

Closely related to the liturgical functions of Eastertide are certainly expressions of popular feeling which we term social customs. Amongst these may be mentioned the blessing of lambs and the hallowing of food. The blessing of lambs took place either in the church or in the home. This custom is perpetuated in the Easter observances of some religious communities, where, on Easter Sunday, a lamb, set upon a huge platter, surmounted by a little banner (a red cross on a white field) is placed in the centre of the dining-table. Whatever remains of the hallowed food is, after the repast, cast into the fire. The most widely observed popular custom is, undoubtedly, the "Easter Egg." Some antiquaries declare this to be of Christian origin; but it is evidently older than Christianity. Eggs were eaten (after having been colored) in the remotest antiquity, in commemoration of the advent of Spring. Even at the present day the egg is a prominent feature of the Feast of Noruz (New Year) held throughout Central Asia, about the 25th of March. The custom is also recorded in the "Sagas" of the Northland. According to these old traditions, the earth was symbolized by an egg, and ancient temples, in consequence, were oval in shape. This typification is found in nearly every oriental cosmogony.

A writer on Eastern Cosmogonies (Bellew), discussing this custom, says:—In ancient Persia, long centuries before the coming of Christ, the people were all worshippers of fire. According to their belief, there was a great spirit that had existed from

eternity. From him came the first light; and from this light
came two brothers—Ormuzd and Ahrimann. Ahrimann grew
jealous of his elder brother, and was condemned by the great
spirit to pass three thousand years in utter darkness. On his
return from the lower regions, he created a number of evil spirits
to oppose the good spirits created by Ormuzd; and when the
latter made an egg containing good genii, Ahrimann made another full of demons and broke the two together, so that the
good and the evil became mixed in the new creation. In commemoration of this legend, the Persians, even at the present
day, send and receive colored eggs. Whatever we may think of
this legendary origin of the "Easter Egg," it is evident that the
egg-giving custom is a very ancient institution. The custom of
egg-giving has now become very general; but the eggs are sometimes as ancient as the custom!   }

Within recent years a new industry has had great vogue —
the manufacture of bonbons in the form of eggs. It began in
Paris, and thence spread to the other large cities in Europe; and
even in Canadian cities the bonbon egg is quite common. Russia,
where Easter is kept most religiously, inaugurated another
fashion in the egg line a few years ago — the manufacture of
Easter eggs of glass. So great is the demand for these newest
creations that nearly all the glass factories of Russia begin immediately after New Year, each season, to manufacture eggs for
the Easter trade. Most costly specimens are prepared for the
Czar and the Russian nobility.

,In mediaeval times Easter eggs were blessed by the priest;
and a special form of blessing was authorized by Pope Paul V.
The red dye used in the coloring of these eggs was supposed to
symbolize the Blood of the Redemption. Another custom of those
days was what was termed the *Ovagium*, which in reality was
the payment of tithes to the priest, by gifts of eggs.

In addition to the customs attending the Easter celebration
of former times, there were certain sports and pastimes which
were performed under the patronage of the Ecclesiastical authorities. The most singular of these was the playing of hand-ball
in church. The church dignitaries participated in these games
with the common folk. This game is said to be symbolic of the
Sun which is supposed to give three leaps on Easter morning
to make atonement for its darkening during the days of the
Lord's entombment. Hand-ball playing was the special amusement in France; in Spain there was an Easter dance, known as
the *bergeretta*, which is, so it is asserted, still in vogue among the

Andalusian peasants. In England the ball game was also a favorite Easter sport in which the City Fathers engaged with due parade and dignity.

Another very peculiar custom existed in France, even as late as the XVIth century. At Puy it was customary when, at the first psalm of matins, a canon was absent from the choir, for some of the canons and vicars, with processional cross and holy water, to visit the house of the absentee, sing the "Haec Dies," and, if he was in bed, to sprinkle him with holy water. He was then led back to the church; and, in punishment, he had to give a breakfast to all who had taken part in the procession. Similar customs existed at Nantes and Angers; but they were prohibited by Diocesan Councils in 1431 and 1448.

Eastertide closes with Low Sunday; but what is the origin of this appellation we have been unable to discover.

P. W. B.

"Insula Sanctorum et Scholarum."

("The Isle of Saints and Scholars.")

"When Erin first rose from the dark swelling flood,
"God blessed the green island, He saw it was good;
"The Emerald of Europe, it sparkled, it shone,
"In the ring of the word, the most precious stone."

From her earliest days, with the exception of the three centuries that followed the death of St. Patrick, we find Erin's sky darkened by an almost endless succession of evil-menacing clouds. While 'tis true that the darkest hour comes before the dawn, it would seem in the instance of Ireland, that each dawn ushered in a darker and a still more foreboding firmament. Fifteen hundred years ago one vast murky cloud was lifted from Ireland's sky never to return to mar the beauty of an Irish day dawn. It was the dark cloud of paganism, swept away forever by the brilliant rays of Christian sunshine, and leaving the Irish nation illumined with the light of Catholic Faith. And, gentlemen, that same light of Catholic Faith burns with just as bright effulgence and warmth to day as it did in the very freshness of its birth.

You have often read the account of the marvellous rapidity with which the Apostle Patrick converted the Isle to the Catholic

Faith. How he braved the dangers of the deep and won a blood-less victory over the forces of paganism by the sword of truth that conquers but does not sting or destroy. So well did he con-duct his Christ-like campaign that we soon find pagan temples changed into Catholic Sanctuaries, and the ceremonies of Druid-ism giving way to the Sacrifice of Calvary. He found Ireland universally pagan, he left it universally Christian; the future birth-place of Europe's most glorious martyrs; the second home of Christianity; the island of Saints and Scholars.

At the time of Patrick's death, churches and chapels, con-vents and monasteries, colleges and schools, covered the isle, and from hill and dale one grand perpetual note of thanksgiving was wafted to the throne of God.

'" 'Tis more blessed to give than to receive.'' So with her characteristic generosity, Ireland was anxious to share her divine treasures with those not so fortunate. What shall I say of Ire-land, writes Herne, who, despising the dangers of the ocean, emi-grates with her troupes of philosophers, and descends on Europe's shores. Her Christian teachers were everywhere. Her mission-aries emerged from the schools founded by Patrick, and flashed over the charred remains of European civilization the torch-light of learning. The scholarship engendered in the universities, seminaries, cloisters, training schools of Ireland refurnished Eu-rope after the hordes of Goths and Vandals had ravaged the south and had dashed to the ground the beacon light of civiliza-tion. Ireland's teachers and missionaries were found along the vine-clad hills of Germany, pushing into the interior of the coun-try, carrying the faith of Rome where Roman legions never trod, and the name of Christ was never heard. In the Eternal City they were found visiting her tombs and catacombs ,where were the shrines of martyrs. Even in the far East were they found, treading with reverential steps the places made holy by Our Lord Himself.

And we young Irish-Canadians who honor St. Patrick be-long to that same race. We are the descendants of those Irish martyrs and saints. As soldiers on the field of battle are stirred to extraordinary deeds of strength and valor by the recital of the victories of their ancestors, so should the struggles of the past, which have crowned with undying glory those who have gone before us, animate us to follow in their footsteps and retain with unfailing tenacity that gift of faith which they preserved with such unwavering fidelity.

Yes, in truth, Ireland's children are children of the Cross, and they have brought it in triumph to every land. Denied the right to live at home, they went abroad carrying with them that pearl of great price, the faith and love for the Church of Rome. And they have planted it in every land. Read the history of the English-speaking, and upon what page will you not find recorded the great zeal of Ireland's saintly missionaries? Is there a country in which her priests have not sown the seeds of Christianity nad reaped a glorious harvest? Of the sixty archbishops and bishops of the United States, forty of them are of Irish parentage, to say nothing of the large percentage in the rank and file of Holy Mother Church. The world's greatest churchmen, statesmen, generals, authors, poets, are mostly of Irish descent.

In Ireland and England witness the following famous names:—Edmund Burke, Cardinal Newman, Daniel O'Connell, Cardinal Manning, Robert Emmett, Cardinal Moran, Thomas Moore, Cardinal Wiseman, Gratton, Aubrey De Vere and John Redmond.

In the United States recall the names of John Boyle O'Reilly, Cardinal Gibbons, Matthew Carey, Archbishop Ryan, Bourke Cochrane, Archbishop Corrigan, Daniel Dougherty, Archbishop Farley, General Montgomery, Archbishop Ireland, Quigley, and many others.

In Canada we have many illustrious Irishmen, both in church and state:—Thomas D'Arcy McGee, late Archbishop O'Brien, late Sir John Thompson, and Archbishop Walsh, Archbishop Cleary, McEvay, Bishop Scollard, and the Hon. Chas. Murphy, Secretary of State for Canada.

All these names are potent proofs that Ireland is still worthy of the proud title of the Island of Saints and Scholars.

Let us turn from the higher to the lower walks of life. Find anywhere an Irish family, even in the smallest hut, in the most remote regions, and there you will surely hear mingled with the gentle murmur of the evening zephyrs, the deep-toned sounds of the Catholic Angelus. This is the precious heritage that we must guard and keep safe from all invasion. It should be more precious to us than life itself. Let us strive to be firm in the faith which St. Patrick brought to the Irish people, and after the faith, the liberation of our beloved little gem of the ocean should be our constant prayer, and like the saintly Soggarth Aroon:

"After Christ, their country's freedom,
"Do the Irish prelates preach."

PHIL. C. HARRIS, '11.

How to Enjoy Nature.

T is well to breathe the fresh air, but of little use to beat it. It is not enough to listen, to see, to catch the faint odor of flowers in the mind, but the unattainable reason of it all must be had. No matter how busy a healthy, strong-minded man may be, there comes a time when he is content to be at ease and to seek comfort and rest in any place whatsoever. No man can build a pathway through the air leading to the sky. He knows this, and does not attempt such a foolish freak. If he also knows that he can see only with his own eyes he is well equipped to enjoy Nature.

A flower is never so beautiful as to him who sees it and knows wherein its beauty lies. Let him who hears the sweet song of the bird from the lofty tree-tops be happy. Let the student forget all laws of mathematics when out of doors. Let him walk hand in hand with Nature as a child walks with his father, and let him wonder. It is as enjoyable to wonder as to know. When we look at the stars we wonder, but when we view them through a telescope they appear as suns and we begin to lose all our innocent fancies of Nature which were so dear to us. It is a wise saying, "he that increaseth knowledge, increaseth sorrow." Hence the boy's constant desire is to avoid knowledge and go a-fishing.

In order to enjoy Nature we must be continually on our guard. Wild animals con only be seen in their native haunts. They are like men. They are never happy unless they are at hime. Consequently if an animal loves the swamps we must go among the weeds and water and wade knee-deep in mud to witness the creature's peculiar methods of passing the day. An animal is no more at home in a menagerie than man is in a balloon. Fish will not live on dry land. Many animals know more concerning man's habits than the latter does of, let me say, a mink or a muskrat. I once heard an old trapper say: "There's a mink around here that gets the best of me every time. He knows a trap ,and I can't put one where he don't see it."

When we hear of animals as I heard this old trapper speak of them, we see them in an altogether new sphere of light. We are far more interested in them. We see something in them that we never saw before. They are cunning, and a man will be wide awake who catches them napping. Hereafter we must approach their haunts as one who knew all their cunning tricks and delusions.

The most nourishing feature of rational enjoyment is the appreciation of out-door life, as a whole. He who once tastes this beauty will find it very difficult to stop. Even when commenced as a means of pleasure or pastime, it becomes a task before we can end it. We are too fond of variety and cannot remain at one thing long enough to enjoy the true pleasure that it gives. Let the green fields and meadows be treasures in our eyes and let us not seek to find out if the sky meets the earth whre it appears to. Such interest is a true one because a natural one, and we need not blush if we are laughed at by some of the great scientists of the day.

To be an admirer of Nature it is not necessary to have a knowledge of natural science. It is an old and a wise saying, "experience is the best teacher." Let the student of Nature go out in the morning, refreshed by Nature's sweet restorer, and if he does not draw in a new idea with every breath, he at least oxygenates his blood.

T. J. O'NEILL, '11·

A Few Recollections of the Irish.

N the 17th of March,—Ireland's national anniversary, —the heart, the sentiment, the spirit and the patriotism of the Irish race pours forth in love and fidelity for the dear little island across the sea.

Whether in the encouraging centres of Canada, or in the busy places of industry in the United States, the sons and daughters of Ireland greet one another with a hearty cheer and with best wishes.

The memories which cling around that illustrious man, St. Patrick, have been on the tongues of the most educated men of all times. Nothing but what is upright and honourable can be said of St. Patrick. The good results of St. Patrick's works have spread everywhere. They have been instrumental in the building of nations. His bravery has won for him the admiration of men of every sect. He went about with the fear of God in his heart, but of no man on this earth. When the occasion demanded, he went among knights and princes and performed the sacred duties of his office. With the cross of Jesus crucified, he travelled among pagan tribes to instill into their hearts the pious teachings of the Catholic Church. He went fearlessly, never considering himself before the honor and glory of his Protector. His wonderful career has inspired not only Irishmen but all people to better lives and more honourable endeavours. Wherever there are sons of Ireland, honour will be paid to St. Patrick, the greatest missionary the world has ever known. He linked Ireland to the Church as it was when he died. It was a wonderful life-work for one man. This one missionary not only converted Ireland, but he made history by his life, and much of it after his life had ended. The sons of Ireland may regard his life with honor. He was a large figure in the world's history.

We must not think that Ireland's heroes ceased with the death of St. Patrick, because since then and to our present day she has produced and continues to produce some of the world's greatest men. When a cloud of destruction seemed to be hanging over Ireland, when many a dark day was undergone by the Irish people, when the sun of hope was obscure, God in His infinite mercy raised up some leader either in the Church or laity who has preserved the Irish race, their religion and country.

Upon reading history, you will find the names of Ireland's

earnest and self-sacrificing men. Ireland has a right to be proud of Davis, Mitchell, Smith O'Brien, Duffy, J. Blake, Dillon, Mc-Manus, Reilly and Meagher. Day and night they labored incessantly for Ireland. I do not intend to dwell on the life of O'Connell. He is well known to all. He took a prominent part in public questions and was acknowledged as the leader of the Irish Catholics. He was a chief figure in Irish political history, and was one of the greatest popular leaders the world ever saw.

After these men the line of heroes seems to continue. The year 1867 saw some of Ireland's grand old heroes. Of such characters are the familiar men, Allen, Larkin and O'Brien. Their whole ambition was to save Ireland and her religion. They and many more spent their lives behind the prison walls of England.

These Irishmen have given a fine example to the rising generation. Their examples are loyalty to their country and loyalty to the Roman Catholic Church. To-day we have true Irishmen among us. How remarkable it is to hear them express their love and patriotism for the dear little "Green Isle." Their devotion to Ireland lifts them so high above the criticism of petty minds as to make them the glory of their race. There are many who, if they betrayed their country could better themselves in this world, yet not a man has shown himself untrue to the cause of Irish nationality or considered himself before his country. Irishmen with such characteristics should receive the support of not only their fellow-Irishmen, but the sons of Irish parents. Such Irishmen deserve honor and praise. These Irishmen should not be misrepresented. Stand by them, maintain their rights, fight for their cause, cherish them, and by so doing you will be true descendants of that illustrious Irish race.

It is true that the history of Ireland has been a sad one. Many a wave of sorrow has visited its shores. Often discouraging trials and tribulations have swept over the land. However, her high ideals and love for liberty, her examples of manhood and womanhood, have brought encouragement to human liberty the world over.

This encouragement has spread to other shores and firmly established itself. The early Irish people that settled in the United States were among the strongest advocates for American Independence. They had been chased from their dear land, and now they desired to be free and independent of their oppressors. Trace them in American history, read their heroic deeds, their patriotism, fidelity, courage and self-sacrificing works, which are a credit to the Irish people. During the War of Independence, they were not only prominent on the land, but very conspicuous in naval fights. It was Capt. O'Brien and his crew that captured the British ship "Margaretta."

In the war of 1812 there were many brave Irishmen. It was Jackson at New Orleans, Commodore Stewart on the sea with his "Constitution," McDonough on Lake Champlain, and Perry on Lake Erie, who made their presence felt, and whose skill and ability won for them the admiration of Irishmen and Americans.

Again in the Mexican war were the Irish with that determination and assiduity that characterizes every Irishman. Kearney and Shields were great generals in this war. In appreciation for his work, Shields was elected to a seat in the United States Senate on three different occasions.

Thus we may realize how instrumental the Irish were in obtaining liberty and freedom for the United States. How many an Irishman sacrificed his life for the land of the stars and stripes! The Irish should be protected. Their rights should be respected. They should be held up as a monument if patriotism and bravery manifested in the wars of the States. As they have built the United States, they should have a strong voice in the governing of the country. We want no division of race or class, but equality of everyone, and a square deal for all.

Almost every country has a right to be proud of the Irish race. Wherever they have gone, they have shed honor and glory on the coutnry. Their religious reputation is a glorious one. Their missionaries have flocked to every shore, and spread the teachings of the true faith to the inhabitants. Consequently we may see and realize their high ideals and devotion to religion, liberty and national integrity.

J. CURRIE, '13·

St. Patrick's Day Banquet.

T. Patrick's Day has once more come and gone, and once more the Irish students of Ottawa University celebrated the day in their usual manner. The annual St. Patrick's Day Banquet was this year equal if not superior to any of its predecessors. It was held in the students' refrectory, which was gaily decorated for the occasion with streamers of red, white and green; portraits hung on every side decorated with appropriate flags, and in the centre of the hall were arranged the numerous trophies of the garnet and gray.

During the banquet music was supplied by the city orchestra, which was indeed in itself a treat. An interesting feature of the musical part of the programme was the rendition of a medley of Irish melodies upon the harp by Master G. Freeland.

The material part of the banquet having received due consideration, the toastmaster, Mr. Martin O'Gara, '10, arose, and spoke as follows:

We are gathered together to-day about this festive board to celebrate the feast of St. Patrick and the national day of Ireland.

It is, first of all, a religious festival, for it is the day specially set apart by holy Mother Church upon which she duly honours one of her favorite and most illustrious children. We are to-day counselled to draw inspiration from the life and labours of one of God's noblest servants. 'In this aspect of the day, Irishmen are not alone in paying homage to St. Patrick, but all true Christians join with them in admiration at the marvels he accomplished in his mission of peace.

But not only is this the feast day, but it is likewise the national day of Ireland; for the labours of St. Patrick were wholly centered within her shores. So great was his success and so great was the imprint made by him upon the future life of its people, that Ireland has since been unswerving in her allegiance to the doctrines which he taught, and the religion of the land became one with the national life of the people. No better proof of this truth could be given than that the feast of her patron saint should be also her national day.

So that wherever Irishmen are to be found, whether it be within the shores of Erin, or abroad in the homes of their adoption, they gather together on this day to do honor to their great Apostle, and to renew their pledges of affection and loyalty to the Emerald Isle.

I have much pleasure, therefore, in calling upon you to drink the toast to St. Patrick's Day, to which Mr. C. O'Gorman will reply.

Mr. Chas. O'Gorman, '10, responded in the following manner:

The Day We Celebrate.

Mr. Toastmaster, Your Excellency, Very Rev. and Rev. Fathers and Gentlemen,—

To-day Irishmen the world over are congregated to celebrate their great religious and national feast. To-day the sweet strains of the harp are heard and many an Irishman turns his eyes longingly towards that land of sunshine and shadow. Why is it that on this day the enthusiasm of Erin's sons and daughters knows no bounds? What has happened in the lapse of time which has set this day apart from all others? What is commemorated that should so inspire and stimulate religion and patriotism?

It is the day set aside on commemoration of St. Patrick, the evangelist of the Emerald Isle. He it was who raised Ireland from the depths of paganism and idolatry, who first preached to her people the saving doctrines of Christianity, and who left them as a legacy that great religious boon, which even from a merely temporal point of view, has been the source of all their happiness and of all their greatness. He it was who gained for Ireland that much-coveted title of "Isle of Saints and Scholars." To him also do the Irish race attribute, with unending gratitude, the constancy that characterized their unswerving adherence to the faith, during the long centuries of religious persecution to which they have been subjected.

Picture Ireland in its primeval beauty; its angry coasts and quiet fields lying inland; picture its dales, its hills, its crystal streams and mountain lakes; picture the lakes of Killarney, famed in history for their beauty; picture the mountains mirrored in their depths; and above all, picture the Irish people in this beautiful country, an intelligent, feeling, though rude and barbarous people, sunk in paganism and idolatry.

Such was the country and such the people to whom St. Patrick spoke the words of truth. Filled with holy zeal for the salvation of souls, he travelled the length and breadth of that pagan land. From north to south, from Munster to Leinster, from Meath on the east to rock-bound Galway on the west, he made one grand triumphal procession, teaching and preaching to the people as he went along.

Then followed Ireland's golden age, where her schools were the most flourishing in the world, and when her sons went forth as missionaries and teachers to all the countries of Europe; when her convents were filled with holy virgins; when peace and plenty reigned supreme and the whole land was crowned with glory. But alas! the time came when she was robbed of all her strength and the chains of slavery were placed around her graceful form. The time came when many poor souls were forced to leave the land they loved so well and seek their fortune on foreign shores. The time came when even life depended upon the rejection of eternal happiness. But the Irish race, true to the lessons taught them by St. Patrick, true to their religion and true to their oGd, could not be induced to give up their priceless heritage. Death they could endure; but apostasy, never.

The fire which St. Patrick lit on the Hill of Slane, and concerning which the Druids remarked: "If that light is not put out before morning, it will never be put out," has continued to shine with undiminished brilliancy, both in the centuries of Ireland's national prosperity, and in the era of religious persecution and political degradation, thus fulfilling the prediction of the angel to St. Patrick that the light of Divine Faith would never cease to burn in Ireland with all its original splendour. The angel having presented to the kneeling saint a glorious picture of the little green isle in its future grandeur, disappeared declaring, "such shall be the abiding splendour of Divine Truth in Ireland."

Well may we love and cherish the memory of St. Patrick. Well may we raise our voices in his praise and honor. Well may we set aside a day in commemoration of him who has done so much for mankind in general and for the Irish race in particular. May that great love which fills our hearts on this festive occasion be ever constant, and persevere until that final day on which, according to the promise made on the Mount, Patrick shall be told to count his flock upon the right hand of the Judge; for there is no name in Irish history that should command our veneration and gratitude as should that of our illustrious Apostle.

"Thus, therefore," saith the Lord, "so long as the sea girdeth this isle, so long they name shall hang in splendour o'er it like the stars of God."

The next toast was proposed in the following words:

One of the most marked characteristics of the Irish people since the coming of St. Patrick, many centuries ago, has been their unfailing allegiance to Catholicity. Irishman and Catholic are well nigh synonymous terms. It is but fitting, therefore, that on an occasion such as this, that we should do honor to the venerable head of this religion. I ask you, then, to drink to a toast to Pius X, to which Mr. Smith will respond.

Mr. M. J. Smith, '10, replied in these fitting words:

Toast to Pius X.

There is no toast to which Irishmen respond with greater pride and enthusiasm than that of our Supreme Pontif; for he is the representative of that power to which they are attached with more profound affection and reverence than they could possibly entertain for any other power, even though it should be that of the world's mightiest and most benign ruler. No question can be raised regarding the love that they bear for the land of their forefathers; none are bound more loyally than they to every form of legitimate temporal authority; but, far exceeding their patriotism, far more profound than their respectful obedience to worldly power, is the humble submission and childlike devotion that they have ever displayed towards the Chair of Peter.

Yet, whilst the Irish people have ever been remarkable for the bond of generous and loving loyalty that has held them in affectionate subjection to the Vicar of Christ since the time of St. Patrick, and whilst the principle of that bond is supernatural, uniting them to the Roman Pontif, not because of any natural traits that he might possess, but because of his sublime office, there is something in the character of Pius X, something in the nature of his government that peculiarly appeals to his Irish children. This is the rule, not of severity, but of fatherly love; he is of the common people, filled with sympathy for their legitimate aspirations; he is democratic and intensely simple. All this appeals strongly to the Irish people, and adds a new bond to that which during the past fifteen centuries has securely bound them to the Supreme Head of God's Church. They have long felt the oppressor's tyranny, and they have long prayed for the day when they would be ruled by a government in which the tyrant's oppression would be replaced by the justice and benevolence that should characterize rulers in their relations with their subjects. At home, in America, in Australia, and wherever else they may have emigrated, they have proved themselves the fervent lovers and ardent defenders of whatver is dmocratic. IInce, while they behold in Pius X, the Pope whom Christ has placed over IIis Church, and who is consequently worthy of their most sincere loyalty, they see in him likewise the incarnation of fatherly tenderness and of intense solicitude, for even the temporal welfare of the common people, and so their love goes out to him with especial fervor.

In the government of Christ's Church, though but a few years have elapsed since his election, Pius X has proved himself in zeal, in tact, in sagacity, in everything that goes to make up an ideal Pope, a worthy successor of that long line of illustrious men who have filled the sublime office of Bishop of Rome. With a courage and a wisdom truly apostolic, he attacked the forces of modernism, redoubtable though they seemed at the time, and not only vanquished them, but so completely annihilated them that, whereas a few years ago modernism was so much talked of and apparently so powerful an enemy of all Christianity, it now attracts but little attention and has scarcely more force than those irreligious movement of ages gone by that live only in the pages of history.

In the combat which the impious conduct of the French government forced upon the Church, Pius X, though no man loves peace more than he, and though none is more anxious to enjoy the good-will of all, and to encourage that condition of mutual supprt and sympathy that in an ideal community should exist between Church and State,—Pius X, the man of peace and conciliation, displayed himself the intrepid and uncompromising defender of the rights of religion. Though, unfortunately, he has not succeeded in restoring the Church in France to that condition of peace and of supreme sway that was hers in the glorious days of French Catholicity, he has infused into her a new life, and has secured for her prelates an independence in matters religious and a liberty in their relations with the Holy See that they have not enjoyed in centuries.

The Irish who pride themselves in the indomitable courage that has characterized them in the war of three long centuries that the enemies of our holy rligion have heartlessly waged against them, and who rejoice, above all else, in the fact that from the time of their conversion down to the present day they have sacrificed everything earthly in the defence of the rights of the Church, glory in this great man, the fearless and invincible champion whom God in Ilis divine providence has provided, to defend the holy citadel against the violent attacks that are being made upon it by the powers of heresy and irreligion.

In solicitude for the welfare of Catholicity, as a token of the affection that they have borne for the See of Peter, as a mark of gratitude for all that their connection with Rome means for them, they send forth a fervent prayer, on this the feast of their patron saint, for him now gloriously reigning as their Supreme Pontiff.

The Lord preserve him and give him life, and make him blessed upon the earth; and deliver him not up to the will of his enemies.

The toastmaster proposed the next toast thus:

Ireland was the land of our forefathers, Canada is our present home. Among the over-sea dominions of the Empire she occupies the first place. Iler rapid development, her rich grain-fields and mineral wealth, are commanding the attention of the world. To the land of the Maple Leaf, the land which has offered a happy home to so many of Erin's exiled sons and daughters, I ask you to drink a toast to which is coupled the name of Mr. Gauthier.

Mr. C. F. Gauthier, '10, responded to the toast to the Land of the Maple Leaf:

Canada.

It is indeed a source of great pleasure to me to be called upon to respond to the toast of my native country. Every man is possessed of a deep love for the land of his birth, and it affords him no small measure of gratification to sound her praises, to recall those events in her history that have won her renown, to extoll the bravery of her sons, to hold up to admiration the wisdom of her laws or to proclaim her extraordinary natural resource.

Canada, compared with the nations of the old world, has but a short history. She cannot to-day be numbered among the great powers. But no one would attempt to deny that the future has great things in store for her, and that the next century will behold another nation on the American continent possessed of many millions of happy subjects, and rivalling the most famous states of ancient or modern times in its mines, its manufactures, its fisheries, its fertile lands, and in everything that goes to make a country powerful and prosperous.

The history of this country from the time when that intrepid explorer, Samuel de Champlain, sailed up the St. Lawrence and took possession of the new territory in the name of the King of France, is one of successive discoveries disclosing richness of natural resources, previously unsuspected. France was blind to the greatness of the empire which lay within her grasp, and it took England two centuries to realize that the country of the fur-traders was something more than a barren and inhospitable region. The most sanguine hopes of its most ardent statesmen have been exceeded, and at present we behold a land to which people from all quarters of the globe are flocking in order to make for themselves happy homes, especially in the wheat fields of the West, whose wonderful fertility is but a recent discovery.

Among those who have come to our hospitable shores to seek their fortunes in that natural wealth with which a benign Providence has bountifully enriched our country, and to enjoy her free institutions and her just laws are numerous sons of that great saint, whose feast is to-day being observed the world over with solemn religious ceremony. They have been driven hither by a system of religious and political tyranny, which in duration and heartlessness has never been equalled. One of the most pathetic pages in our history is that which recounts the part that our country played in connection with the Irish immigrants, that famine and persecution drove from their homes in the sad years of '47 and '48. In that exodus, thousands of the Irish exiles who directed their course to Canada never caught sight of the promised land, but fell victims on shipboard to that terrible fever that claimed so many of the sons and daughters of the flying Gael.

Thousands more scarcely landed on Canadian soil when, in the depths of human misery and poverty, they, too, laid down their lives in behalf of faith and fatherland.

More hallowed bones Canadian soil does not contain than those of the poor Irish martyrs who sanctified our land in their death, and enriched it with their noble example of unswerving fidelity to their religion and their country.

No American monument stands on a more hallowed spot or is sacred to more heroic souls than that which has been recently erected over the silent graves of the nameless Irish immigrants that found their last resting-place on the lonely island of Grosse Isle. Let it be said to the eternal honor of the great Irish Catholic organizations that showed its veneration for the memory of its poor but saintly dead, in the erection of that magnificent monument and in the impressive celebration that accompanied its unveiling, that it has given an evidence of devotion to lofty ideals more glorious than which America has never witnessed. They have made a chapter in the annals of Canada which in generations to come will be an inspiration to Canadians, that will teach them that there is some thing more sublime in life than the possession of brute force or the accumulation of immense wealth.

It is not a matter of wonder, gentlemen, that the Canadian sons of a race possessed of characteristics such as are exhibited in the graves and monument of Grosse Isle, should have risen to positions of the first eminence and should have attained the most remarkable success in every walk of Canadian life.

Irishmen are indebted to Canada for the hospitality extended to them in their pitiful exile, but they have paid her back a thousandfold by their fidelity to Canadian national ideals, by the brain and brawn that they have generously expended for the development of our resources, by the prominent part that many of them have played, notably the illustrious Thos. D'Arcy McGee, in the building up of this great Dominion, and by their deep love for religion and learning that are prime traits in the sons of St. Patrick in Canada to-day, just as they were, of their forefathers in the isle of saints and scholars.

Let us hope that this condition of sympathy and aid will continue to characterize the relations between Irish-Canadians and the other elements of our population, and that it will result in the production of a people harmonious, prosperous, educated and religious.

Mr. O'Gara introduced the next speaker in this manner:

During the past six months events have occurred of tremendous importance to Ireland. The political upheaval in Great Britain has caused such a disposition of parties as to place the balance of power in the hands of the Irish leader. We feel to-day that Erin is closer the realization of her hopes than ever before; and we take this opportunity of expressing our confidence in the men who have accomplished so much in her behalf.

Mr. D. J. Breen, '11, thus eulogized the Irish Party:

The Irish Parliamentary Party.

Deep in the heart of every Irishman, besides an ardent faith in her religion, is an undying love for his fatherland. The recollection of its sufferings, past and present, cannot fail to strike a cord of sympathy in his warm and tender heart, while every redress of evil, every burden removed, is a source of joy and consolation to him. This is why we Irish, with good reason, drink a toast to the Irish Parliamentary Party, whose strength and energy have been sacrificed for Ireland's interests, and this is why we express our hearty approval of its labor, and display our gratitude for the long-sustained struggle that it has maintained in behalf of the land we all love.

Never, since the days of Parnell, has there existed such union, such a splendid party-spirit as is manifested by the Irish nationalists to-day. Under the able leadership of their illustrious chief, the members of the Irish National Party have pledged themselves to carry on the noble fight for the freedom and uplifting of the Irish race. For long years they have fought with overwhelming odds against them, urged on by patriotism's pure and unblemished flame.

The testimony of Mr. Balfour is on record as to the power, ability and tact of that party, "which," he declares, "to be the ablest and most effective for its purpose of any political agency in existence." How could it be otherwise when its councils are presided over by such experienced, sagacious and resourceful parliamentarians as John E. Redmond, T. P. O'Connor and Joseph Devlin, and when he who has so often received the testimony of the confidence and attachment of its members by re-election to its chairmanship is universally admitted to have no peer in oratory or debate in the British Parliament, or perhaps anywhere else in the world. Little wonder, then, that we should pride ourselves in having at our head men who have won the admiration and esteem of all nations, who have shown themselves worthy to be entrusted with the sacred cause of our religious rights and political liberties.

Why should we lavish our praises on the Irish Party? What has it done to merit such consideration! It has achieved many and glorious victories. Measure after measure has been wrenched from a government whose policy is to make no concession except by force. By its skill and aggressiveness, it has secured, within late years, the Land Bill, bettering the condition of the tenants; the Laborers' Act and the Town-Tenants' Act. The decrease of Irish taxation, the housing of the peasantry and other less important benefits, won through the persistent efforts of the Irish Nationalists, bid fair to the building up of a nation, which by a skilfully executed plan was doomed and well-nigh reduced to extinction. Greater and more important than all these is the boon of a National University, which was obtained but a short time ago. The establishment of this new university marks the close of a long and bitter controversy and is the beginning, let us hope, of a new chapter in Irish history.

Ireland's sons and daughters, bright, intellectual, thirsting after knowledge, were denied that precious boon of education because they were not of the right political or religious complexion. They were compelled to turn from their homes on the sunny hillsides of Ireland to bid adieu to their native country, and to seek a livelihood in alien lands. The wonder is, as a leading Irish journalist recently remarked, not that many became "hewers of wood and drawers of water," but that numbers rose to position of power and influence. Now that Ireland has a right to a National University, she will rise to the glorious standard which she had attained before the cruel hand of oppression brought desolation and ruin.

To the student of Irish history, one strange, sad fact is pre-eminent. It is that the Irish people are fettered, their progress impeded, their country misruled and the inhabitants groaning under the yoke of tyranny. For this, one and one only remedy exists; that is the granting of complete self-government in matters purely Irish. It is as necessary for the welfare of Ireland as air is for the life of man. Home Rule is bound to come; prospects never were brighter. The Irish, a freedom-loving people, will not endure to be ground down, and surely it is not in England's interests to foster a spirit of discontent, which would be a weakness in the heart of her vast empire.

To the Irish Parliamentary Party we are glad to express our appreciation of the heroic work done in the past; to assure its members of our affection, trust and support. We are proud of a party which, in spite of enemies and detractors, shows a cohesion, a tenacity of purpose, an integrity and incorruptibility unparalleled in the history of politics. And we have the utmost confidence that to the glorious achievements which it has accomplished in the past, the not-far-distant future will add others even more glorious, among them the destruction of the dominating power of the House of Lords, the hereditary foe of Irish rights and of all progressive legislation, and, finally, the winning of a complete measure of self-government for their long-suffering country.

Let us then respond with generosity to their appeal for aid, let us unite our efforts with theirs, and not many more St. Patrick's Days will pass before Irish representatives will be able to meet, not in England's capital but in Ireland's, to hail Ireland a nation once again.

The toastmaster, arising, spoke as follows:

It would be altogether unbecoming on an occasion such as this did we not bear in mind the obligations which we owe to our Alma Mater, and did we fail to express our heartiest wishes for her continued success. It is with much pleasure that I propose the toast to Alma Mater, and of calling upon Mr. Fleming to reply.

Mr. Alan C. Fleming, '11, toasted Alma Mater in these becoming words:

Alma Mater.

Gentlemen,—You have just raised your glasses to the health of old Varsity, and I have the honor to respond to your toast.

I am sure it is a source of deep sentiment to you as members and friends of a Catholic institution of learning to be assembled in honor of one who was a founder of Catholic institutions. There is no necessity for me to recall to you the glories of that era of Catholic learning which was inaugurated by St. Patrick, and which won for Ireland the fair title of "Isle of Saints and Scholars"; but it is worthy of remark that, to the lofty ideals of religion and education, implanted in their hearts by their great Apostle, the Irish have ever been faithful. During long centuries of persecution they never lost sight of these ideals, nor did they ever consent to the separation of religion from education. They have always maintained that while the intellect is being stored with human science, receiving a purely natural culture, it should likewise be stored with a knowledge of heavenly things, and be given a moral formation, far more necessary to man than training that has for its object mere temporal success.

While in many other countries, Catholic education has had to struggle for existence, because of the hostility of governments, in Ireland the people have fought under the leadership of priests and bishops for the preservation of their schools. One of the most notable victories won by them since their unjust oppression visted their land, was that of a few years ago, when they wrung from the British Parliament a law establishing a Catholic university.

Like Catholic institutions of learning in Ireland, and like similar institutions in almost every other country, Alma Mater has had many severe trials; trials which, although not persecutions, nevertheless were of a very serious nature. I do not intend to rehearse the difficulties which were encountered, or the losses which were suffered; but I am sure that in her hour of severest trial she was consoled by the knowledge that she had become a living force in Canadian life, and that her sons after having won distinction in the narrower domain of the student, had attained to fame and honor in the broader field of the world's activity. The past few years form most glorious pages in her history, for they have heaped honor on many of her former students, and demonstrated the excellence of the training which she imparts. During that time one of her sons has become an Archbishop, and the Superior General of a Great Order, another a Bishop, another a Prime Minister, a third a Judge of the Supreme Court of Canada, a fourth a Secretary of State, a fifth a Bishop, and a sixth a Speaker in the House of Commons, and a seventh a Judge of the Supreme Court of British Columbia. An enviable record, indeed, and one well calculated to bring joy to those who were responsible for the formation of these men, and who delight in their success. May the sons of Ottawa long continue to win seats among the mighty, and to bring honor and distinction to themselves and to their Alma Mater.

The present scholastic year, now well past its zenith, has brought with it a very respectable degree of success for the student body. We have met the representatives of our sister universities on several occasions and upon different fields, and while not always victorious, we have made a creditable showing. Although we did not succeed in bringing back to Ottawa the coveted emblem of the football championship to rest among the accumulated trophies of the garnet and grey, yet under the circumstances that was hardly to be expected. Let us hope, however, that greater success will attend the representatives of Alma Mater upon the gridiron, and that the many victories of the past which have made the name of Ottawa College famous, may be repeated in the future.

In the other great field of Intercollegiate competition — the Intercollegiate Debating Union — we have been singularly successful. Our students have met the students of two great Canadian universities in public debate, and have come off victorious from both encounters. As a result the Intercollegiate cup, emblematic of the championship of the Union, now rests within our walls for the second time since our entrance into the League.

Such, gentlemen, is a brief summary of the events of the year, from the student standpoint. It may not be as bright as some in the past; let the past then serve as an inspiration for the future, and let us hope that the years to come have in store the most glorious achievements for the students of Ottawa University.

We have not with us at this banquet as many of our old students as we should wish, but I am sure that wherever there

is a graduate of Ottawa College to-day he is carried back to the
bosom of his own kind mother by the memory of the St. Patrick's
day of other years, that he visits her in spirit to mingle once
again with the companions of his college days, to partake of all
the joy of a college banquet, to listen to the oft-repeated story
of Ireland's sorrows, and to wish to Alma Mater, as we all do
on this happy occasion, every mark of prosperity and every success in that great work of Catholic education to which she has
so nobly devoted herself.

Mr. O'Gara introduced the next speaker as follows:

Alma Mater claims among her children citizens of the Great
Republic to the south of us. It is a land whose growth and development have no parallels in history, and we are proud to say
that in the building up of this great nation those of Irish descent
have played a prominent part. To the United States is also due
much credit for the generous aid accorded Ireland in the times
of need. I therefore take much pleasure in requesting you to
drink the toast to the United States, and of introducing Mr.
Tracy, who will respond.

Mr. Leo H. Tracy responded thus to the toast to his native
land :

Toast to United States.

I am indeed glad to respond to the toast to my native land
on this happy festive day, which commemorates not a conquest
of men but a conquest of souls. Ireland's services to humanity,
the tragedy of her history, the unquenchable fire of her patriotism, the promise of her industrial awakening, the hope of her
political emancipation,—all these have been crystallized in the
discourse of previous speakers. I speak of America.

You all do know, it is a matter of history, she was once a
subject of Great Britain. I need not recapitulate the origin of
the struggle between Great Britain and her American colonies.
Suffice it to say that the colonies conceived the claims of the
parent country as incompatible with their freedom and happiness. But, obeying at the same time the dictates of patriotism,
and the duty of allegiance, they represented their wrongs to their
sovereign and claimed their rights.

Britain would not change her policy, and so they were forced
into war. With the outcome of that war you are all familiar.
But, apart from the fact that it established the independence
of the colonies, it immortalized some of the most unselfish patriots
and most generous benefactors of humanity that the world has
ever known. I need speak no eulogy of Washington, Franklin,

Sullivan, Barry or Patrick Henry. Though departed from this world, they live in our affections; their names are a talisman of power, the watchword of freedom, the emblem of patriotism, the shout of victory. They cast around us a halo of glory, for they continue to receive the homage of mankind for their glorious deeds. Thus will the memory of these men live on forever with increasing veneration.

If the heavens thundered and the earth rocked, yet when the storm passed, how pure was the atmosphere that it cleared; how bright the new planet which appeared in the political heavens,— that Republic which has ever since shown the world in the concrete what is meant by liberty and justice! A nation where the oppressed and downtrodden have found that peace and happiness of which they were deprived elsewhere.

I do not lose sight of the fact that there are those who see the fulfillment of Carlyle's prophesy foretelling the downfall of this Republic. I do not forget that there are those who proclaim that the same fate will overtake our country as befell Sparta and Carthage. To all such we send defiance, declaring that "this Republic was not born to die!" Our fathers who laid its foundation in their blood, whose patriotic spirits keep vigil from the ramparts of Bunker Hill, bequeathed to their blood-bought land immortality! Yes, more, the sons of these fathers, locked in the shock of a brothers' duel, ordained from the bloody field of Gettysburg, "that this home of the brave" shall ever be the "land of the free!" blazing on all the folds of the national ensign: "Liberty and Union, now and forever! one and inseparable!"

To-day the United States, like your fair Dominion of Canada, is a land of wonderful prosperity and glowing promise. Well may she boast of the success that has crowned her industry, and of her prodigious resources. But it is not in this that her principal glory lies—ideals, pure, lofty, divine,— are the soul of American civilization. Imperfect now they may be, but slowly they will develop, and with them the nation's life will broaden and deepen, realizing a greatness still more lofty, a grandeur more enduring.

Columbia has never been vanquished by any trial or been unequal to any test. Founded upon right principles, she has nothing to fear from the vicissitudes of time. Her watchwords are virtue, education and freedom. Her constitution is the product of some of the greatest minds that the world has ever produced. And so, resting upon a foundation that is built, not on the shifting sands of irreligion or tyranny, but on the immovable rocks of justice and virtue, she has triumphed over all obstacles, and is now more powerful and more majestic than ever.

To whom, gentlemen, does she owe this greatness? To all her faithful sons, who have labored unselfishly for her aggrandizement. But it is only proper that, on this day, we should pay a tribute to those sturdy sons of St. Patrick who have immigrated to our shores, than whom none are more fervent lovers, none more gallant defenders of liberty, and none more faithful citizens of the great American Republic. Irish blood has flowed on every American battlefield; Irish brains have planned and carried to a successful issue many of America's greatest material undertakings, and have done honor to American arts, sciences, and learned professions; and Irish faith has been and is to-day the backbone of American Catholicity.

By the sympathy that America has shown for suffering Ireland, by her continued moral and financial support, she has discharged a portion of her debt to the Emerald Isle for what Irishmen have done for her institutions. And when the day of Ireland's deliverance comes, no flag will be unfurled to the breeze with greater enthusiasm and rejoicing than will that of the Stars and Stripes.

Soggarth Aroon.

Soggarth Aroon was then proposed, to which Rev. M. Murphy responded in a very able manner.

Amongst those who answered to the toast to "Our Guests" were: His Excellency Mgr Sbarretti, Senator Power, Mr. E. Devlin, M.P., Rev. Father McNally, D.D., and Dr. Freeland. The remaining guests were Rev. Canon Sloan, Dr. Sherry, Frs. Fallon, McGuire, T. Murphy, S. Murphy, Collins, Stanton, Finnegan, Hammersley and McGowan.

Letters of regret were received from the following: Rev. J. N. Dozois, Provincial of the Oblates; Rev. W. J. Murphy, Rector; Rev. Father Poli, Vice-Rector; Rev. Fathers Collins, Latulippe, Browne, Kelly and Dewe; Hon. Charles Fitzpatrick, Senator Coffey, Messrs. J. Clarke, W. J. Kane, B. Slattery, E. P. Gleeson and Dr. Chabot.

The success of the banquet was largely due to the Director, Rev. J. Fallon, who was ably assisted by a committee composed of the following gentlemen: Chairman, M. J. Smith, '10; secretary, John J. Sammon, '11; treasurer, Francis Corkery, '11. Executive committee: Martin O'Gara, '10; Chas. P. Gauthier, '10; Leo H. Tracy, '11, and J. J. Contway, '11.

University of Ottawa Review.

PUBLISHED BY THE STUDENTS.

THE OTTAWA UNIVERSITY REVIEW is the organ of the students. Its object is to aid the students in their literary development, to chronicle their doings in and out of class, and to unite more closely to their Alma Mater the students of the past and the present.

TERMS :

One dollar a year in advance.   Single copies, 15 cents.   Advertising rates on application
Address all communications to the "UNIVERSITY OF OTTAWA REVIEW", OTTAWA, ONT.

EDITORIAL STAFF :

J. BRENNAN, '10 ;	A. FLEMING, '11 ;	M. O'GARA, '10 ;
J. BURKE, '10 ;	PH. HARRIS, '11 ;	C. D. O'GORMAN, '10 ;
	M. SMITH, '10.	

Business Managers : C. GAUTHIER '10, ;   D. BREEN, '11·

G. GALLOPIN, Staff Artist.

Our Students are requested to patronize our Advertisers.

Vol. XII.   OTTAWA, ONT., MARCH, 1910.   No. 6

EASTERTIDE.

Best Easter greetings to the readers of The Review. The canticle of this season is one of victory — the greatest victory the world has known. Joy to humanity, liberation from sin and from the sorrows of the tomb, the acquisition of grace and happiness — all these are placed within our reach by Him who, by His own inherent power, on Easter morn shattered the chains of death and entered into the glory of the Resurrection. Long enough had He been despised, spurned, ill-treated. The humiliations of Bethlehem, of Egypt, and of Nazareth, His prayers, fastings and privations, the tears and agony of His bitter Passion and every drop of His Precious Blood, had been weighed in the scales of divine justice, and now add to the lustre of His reward and triumph. But His victory is also ours, for it was for us that He died and rose again.

The Patrician contains a short biographical sketch of Cardinal Satolli, under the title of "The Passing of an Illustrious
Prince." Francis Satolli prepared himself for the high dignity
to which he ultimately attained by a long course of study, in
early youth, and by resource and extended effort in early manhood. Through the influence of Dr. Pecci, he fell under the eye
of Pius IX, who appointed him successively Professor in the
Perugian Seminary, Professor of Dogmatic Theology in the
Propaganda and Rector of the Greek College, Monsignor, and
finally Archbishop of Lepanto. About this time Archbishop
Satolli paid his first visit to the United States, where he endeared himself to all by the ready way in which he adapted himself to American ways and customs, and by the democracy he
evinced. In fact, so pronounced was his admiration of America,
that he was nicknamed the American Cardinal. In 1892, Pope
Leo appointed him Papal Legate to the United States. His
success in settling several mooted questions between the United
States and the Vatican led to his elevation to the Sacred College. When he died he was Prefect of the Congregation of
Studies at Rome.

Besides the above mentioned, we beg to acknowledge receipt of the following: Acta Victoriana, Agnetian Monthly, Collegian, Columbiad, Exponent, Fordham Monthly, Ilya Yaka,
Holy Cross Purple, Laurel, Leader, Allisonia, Argosy, Notre
Dame Scholastic, Martlett, Mitre, Nazarene, Nazareth Chimes,
Abbey Student, D'Youville Quarterly, Trinity University Review.

Books and Reviews.

The March issue of the *Nineteenth Century* contains the following interesting paragraph in an article headed "Alcohol in
Relation to Life.": "The question as to what constitutes mod-

eration, therefore, becomes a matter of importance. It is obvious that what may be moderation for one man may well be excess for another. Attwater's experiments were conducted with 2½ oz. of absolute alcohol per diem, but such a dose would without doubt be excessive in some people; and if it be necessary to draw an arbitary dividing line between excess and moderation, probably that of Dr. Anstie, which is to-day used by many of the largest insurance companies in America, would be more generally acceptable, but even this is considered too high by Prof. Abel, a colleague of Dr. Attwater on the committee of fifty. Anstie put moderation at 1½ oz. of absolute alcohol; this would represent about 4 oz. of whisky, two or three wineglasses of sherry or port, a pint bottle of claret or champagne, or from four to six tumblerfuls of light ale or beer.''

Students of history will find in the same review an excellent contribution, entitled ''Fresh Light on the Quebec Campaign, From the Missing Journal of Gen. Wolfe.'' The journal touches upon many points not mentioned in the young general's letters and despatches, and in two or three passages they confirm unexpugnably the theory that the landing on the Heights of Abraham was not only the design of Wolfe from the beginning, but might have succeeded at first had he received proper naval support. There are other dramatic touches which reveal more clearly the nature of Wolfe's herculean task and the shortcomings of his coadjutors.

The Empire Review for March has a timely article treating of an ''Imperial Colonization Scheme,'' in which the author strongly urges upon the British Government the necessity and advisability of emigration to alleviate some of the domestic troubles at home. Besides, he points out, that the Government by failing to take advantage of the opportunities offered in this respect by the colonies is making vain all the sacrifices of the past to acquire just such facilities.

We have much pleasure in drawing the attention of readers to the fact that the April number of the *Century Magazine* contains a strong plea against the evils of socialism.

Essays, Literary, Critical and Historical, by Thos. O'Hagan, M.A., Ph.D.; published by Wm. Briggs; $1.00. This is a neat little volume containing essays on a variety of subjects. They are written in an easy finished style, and show a considerable breadth of reading on the part of the author. They likewise do much credit to him both as a student of history and as a thinker. The one headed ''Poetry and History Teaching Falsehood'' is perhaps the most interesting and timely. It is to be regretted that more works on the same lines have not reached the publishers in the cause of truth.

Captain Ted, by Mary T. Waggaman; published by Benziger Bros.; 60c.

This is the newest addition to our juvenile library, and will, we are certain, be eagerly read by our young friends. In Captain Ted, Miss Waggaman has again succeeded in producing a book of live interest and one which is well fitted to substantiate her claim to a place among the best writers of juvenile fiction.

"Psychology of Politics and History." — By the Rev. J. A. Dewe; London, Longman's Green & Co., 1910.

Politics, in the wide and better sense of the word, have always had a healthy interest for right-minded persons, if only as one very important phase in the history and development of human society. To the Catholic especially aware, in some measure at least, of the part played by the Church in that history and development, such a psychological treatment of the various problems and principles involved should appeal with irresistible force, and should secure for Father Dewe's admirable treatise the success it so eminently deserves. For it is no small part of its merit that it makes a seemingly dry subject not only clearly intelligible, but supremely interesting as well. And this, not merely for the expert, but what is far more no less clear to those to whom the subject — and the present reviewer is certainly one of them — has seemed, hitherto, wholly beyond their comprehension.

The reviewer's chief difficulty, in such a case, and where space is necessarily limited, consists in deciding on the points to which particular reference should be made. It is, therefore, a possibly too obvious method of escape from his dilemma to refrain from any decision whatever, and to leave it to the reader to discover for himself, as he assuredly will, the many merits which the book possesses. The present reviewer, at all events, finds himself not only disposed, but, so to speak, constrained to adopt the obvious course suggested, and to content himself with conveying the very general, but very favourable impression left on his own mind by a perusal of Father Dewe's book.

It is, in fact, an able and adequate account of that "thing of supreme importance," namely, the "study of the souls of men; the laws that govern the human characters and passions''; of the principles,—religious, philosophical, and political,—that have influenced the growth, development and consciousness of

that complex entity which is the sum, and something more besides, of the countless individuals who go to make up human
society.   F. W. G.

Among the Magazines.

Says the Ave Maria, ''Many Catholics more strict than wise,
speak of the modern Lent as a feeble survival, an institution
that has outlived its usefulness. The faithful of our day are
only playing with the discipline that characterizes former ages,
and Lent has been better given up altogether, it is so little more
than a pretence.'' To these Catholics Bishop Hedley offered a
stern rebuke in a sermon which he preached recently. ''There is
little need of fasting in the modern Church; not that the sins
of men are lighter or rarer than they used to be, or that the justice of God is not as adorable and as terrible as in the past. But
the world has grown more ''spiritual.'' It may not have become
much better; but better or worse, the masses of men are less rude
and primitive; they think more, are more sensitive in feeling and
imagination, have a wider range of sympathy, and are more influenced by ideals. The effect of this on religion cannot be doubted. As the world has progressed ,interior religion has progressed.
We have more of what is called devotion or piety; and we are
more easily touched by the goodness of Almighty God. All this
has its relation to fasting as a penance. When we say that severe
fasting is not needed in these days to the same extent that it
was in the past, we are only saying that fasting is a means to
an end and that there are other means of drawing near to our
Heavenly Father, which ,in the course of Providence, are now
more easily practised. The devotional life, then, is one reason
why the penitential codes and discipline of former days have
been to so great an extent mitigated. Another reason why Lenten discipline has been partially abrogated is referable to our
system of cold storage and adulteration of food. With bad cook-
ing, good Lenten food is so hard to get, and costs so much, that
the exact observance of the mitigated discipline is mortification
enough. Had our forefathers lived as we do, it would have been
altogether impossible for them to fast as they did.

The current number of the Rosary Magazine. In this excellent periodical we notice an article entitled, ''Catholic Chapel
in State University.'' Under this heading the writer imparts
the most welcome news that in the University of Wisconsin, at

Madison, there has recently been dedicated a beautiful Catholic chapel, the cost of which is $60,000. In respect of such a spiirt of toleration, Wisconsin is far ahead of her sister States. It is to be hoped that other great Universities will follow in the footsteps of this one. But the move has this other mark of interest. Since the attendance of young men at Catholic schools seems to be an unattainable ideal, it is consoling to know that they are in a Catholic atmosphere.

The present number of the "America" speaks on the subject of "Canadian Orangemen Rampant." The Loyal Orange Lodge at St. Catharines Ontario, attacks the French-Canadians of the eastern part of that province for trying to put their language on a footing of equality with English in the public schools of Ontario. The Orangemen contend that this is the first step in a campaign which aims at driving the English-speaking electors out of the eastern counties of Ontario. They say that official permission to use French in these schools would result in English being neglected and ignored, and that the French Canadians want to accomplish in the eastern townships of Ontario what they have achieved in the eastern townships of Quebec, and that this means practically the extension of the Quebec system to Ontario and ultimately to the whole of the Dominion. The Catholic Record of London calls on the government to do as King Edward did,—not to recognize this secret society.

Queen's University Journal contains an excellent article on Heredity. After referring to such common instances as heredity of complexion, features, walk, etc., the writer passes on to heredity of intellectual and moral traits. He cites examples of families which have been famous in certain callings for generations, the Bachs in musical composition, the Arnolds in literature, the Rothschilds in finance, etc. "Although great men do not always have great children, yet on the average intellectual and moral traits run in families, just as bodily ones do.

It is with feelings of surprise that we peruse the article on St. Patrick by S. D. C. in the Manitoba College Journal. This being the month of March, most of the Exchanges contain some comment on Ireland's great national festival. Nearly all these remarks are complimentary, some of them are sympathetic, coming even from the pens of Protestant editors. S. D. C.'s article, however, seems to have sprung from no other source than a pet aversion to Catholicity. Without deigning the support of a single authority, and with as much finality as Podsnap, he settles St. Patrick's birth-place — a question over which historians have wrangled for centuries. He chooses these events from the life of the Saint, and describes the others as mere myths, "for the propagation of which he says the Church of Rome has become famous." His disdain for the historians of that denomination he expresses in the derisive appellation "Romish writers."

S. D. C.'s remarks would look more in place in the columns of the Orange Sentinel.

Priorum Temporum Flores.

Rev. Father Quilty, '97, P.P. of Douglas, paid us a call last week while in the city.

Rev. J. MacDonald, '04, and Rev. J. J. MacDonnell, '04, paid Alma Mater a visit while in the city for the Wanderer-Ottawa hockey match.

Tom Costello, a former student of the University, favoured us with a visit a few weeks ago.

Nick Bawlf, '09, the star full-back of Ottawa College, and who has been playing hockey for Haileybury, paid us a visit lately.

Rev. Father Letang, '04, was a visitor to the University a few weeks ago.

Mr. Doyon, ex-student of Ottawa College, now attending McGill University, paid us a visit a few days ago.

Rev. Father Dowd, of Cantley, favoured Alma Mater with a visit a few weeks ago.

Rev. J. Harrington, curate of Eganville, was a visitor to the University a few days ago.

Rev. Dr. McNally, P.P. of Chelsea, paid us a visit lately.

Rev. Father Fitzgerald, P.P. of Bayswater, was a recent visitor to the University.

Mr. L. Kehoe, a former student of Ottawa College, favoured Alma Mater with a visit lately.

Personals.

We were recently honored by a visit from His Lordship Bishop Grandin, O.M.I., of Athabaska. He delighted all by his interesting stories of the far west.

The consecration of the Rev. M. F. Fallon, O.M.I., Bishop-elect of London, will take place in London on April 25th. Many old friends from the Capital, and not a few from the University, will be present at this happy event.

Fr. Cavanagh, S.J., of Montreal, visited us and delivered an interesting lecture in Rideau St. Convent.

Fr. Raymond was a visitor to his Alma Mater last week.

Fr. Dowdall of Eganville, and Fr. Cousineau of Sarsfield, Rev. Dr. Sinnott and Fr. McRory, O.M.I., of Tewksbury, Mass., were among our recent visitors.

The following honored us with their presence on St. Patrick's Day: His Excellency the Apostolic Delegate Mgr Sbarretti, E. P. Santon, Esq., Senator Power, E. B. Devlin, Esq., M.P., Canon Sloan.

Athletics.

Hockey's Exit.

The last act of the hockey drama was witnessed at Rideau Rink March 9th, when after "Arts" defeated the Small Yarders, the curtain was rung down on one of the most successful hockey seasons in years at Ottawa University. The innovation of Inter-Course contests proved to be a sapient move. Excellent sport was witnessed and the best of spirit prevailed in all the contests. That we have ample material for an Intercollegiate hockey team was shown on many occasions, and it is hoped that next year will find the O. U. hockey team occupying a berth in the Intercollegiate circuit.

Baseball.

With the advent of Spring and the storing away of hockey paraphernalia, baseball, that king of scientific games, comes into prominence. It would be a little premature to prophesy what our nine will be like, but from the present outlook we can be assured of a good team. Plenty of material is in sight, and with scientific coaching of which we are certain, the students may look forward to a snappy and enjoyable baseball season. Mr. Bert. Gilligan, the manager for 1910, has already arranged games with several American college nines. He expects to make a strong bid for that "Bilsky Shield" in the City League series, which will be arranged shortly. The election of captain will be deferred till the players are seen in action. The captain's position is a most important one, and the player, besides knowing the "inside"

Champions Inter-Course Hockey League, 1909-10
"Arts" Team.—Ottawa University.

. Kelly, P. Bélanger, Chas. F. O'Neil (Capt), O, Kennedy, J. Kennedy (Mgr.), J. Guibor
McDougall, P. Cornellier, Rev. W. J. Stanton, O.M.I. (Director), M. Brennan.

game, must be able to control the men. With harmony amongst
the players, manager and coach, there seems to be "nothing to
it" but the championship pennant. The city teams will be strong,
so it's up to the College players to get out as soon as possible
and limber up. We have the "stuff" for a good game in Ch.
O'Neill, Charlie Kinsella, Tony Muzante, Ben Dubois, McGilli-
cuddy, Ginty, Joe Moore, Morel, Bert. Gilligan, Kelly, Brennan,
Guindon and others.

Indoor Baseball.

On March 17th the two final games of the Indoor Baseball

League were played on the ''Y'' floor, with Ottawa University and Pastimes returned the winners. The championship of the League goes to the Pastimes' aggregation of ball-players, who showed by the type of ball put up that they will be factors in the race for the pennant in the City Ball League later on in the season. Congratulations are extended to the winners.

Hand Ball.

The popular sport of handball is again attracting much attention. Two leagues, a junior and senior, are in process of formation, when picked teams will battle on the ''alleys'' for supremacy. To Philosophers, M. O'Gorman and Osias Sauvé, have been allotted the pleasant task of arranging the schedule of games, etc.

Inter-Class Baseball.

The scheme of Inter-Class hockey proved so successful that the same is about to be experimented with in baseball. Whether it will be as successful remains to be seen.

The Hockey Finals.

Arts (10) — Philosophers (0).

On Saturday, February 26th the final game for the championship of the I. C. Hockey League was played before a crowd of two hundred students, professors and spectators.

A glance at the score about tells the tale of the contest. Ch. O'Neill's Arts' men showed their superiority in stick-handling, shooting, checking and systematic team play. Under the effective coaching of manager Tommie Hare Kennedy, the ''Arts'' team developed a great system of attack and defense, and their tireless checking back forestalled all efforts of the Philosophers' forward line to penetrate the opposing defense. From Cornellier in goal to O'Neil at centre, no weak spot was noticeable. Belanger, Cornellier and Brennan comprised a stone-wall defence, while O'Neill, Kelly, Kennedy and Guibord completed a dangerously aggressive forward line, all good shots, skaters and checkers. In all ten goals slipped by the Philosophers' net guardian, one of which was scored by a player on his own side. Smith, Brennan, Harris, Côté, Gauthier, Fleming and Gorman worked hard to withstand the onslaught, but there was not a chance in a hundred of denying victory to the ''Arts'' team. Rev. Father Stanton acted as referee in his usual efficient manner.

"Arts" (Big Yard Champs) (9) — Small Yard (1).

When a good "little" team meets a good "big" team, the inevitable always happen. Why, of course the "big" team wins. Such was the case when a team of small calibre, but big aspirations, met the dauntless "Arts" seven to decide the championship of the University for 1910. The game took place at Rideau Rink before a large attendance of students from both departments. The rivalry was of quite as keen amongst the players as amongst the onlookers. Rev. Father Binet acted as referee, and proved a most capable official, giving the greatest satisfaction to both teams. For the first ten minutes of the play, the contest was pretty evenly fought, but after that it was a case of "how many" for the Arts' team. Their defense was adamant, and their forward line easily up to the standard of City League hockey. The zig-zag rushes of Kelly, Kennedy and O'Neill proved the undoing of "Small Yards'" defense, and Kinsella, Brennan and Fournier were continually trying to stave out fusilades of shots from the sticks of the Arts' forwards. The final score was 9-1 for Arts, and is a fair indication of the ability and superiority of the Arts over the Small Yard. Rev. Father Collins and Phil Harris acted as time-keepers for the important event. The leading score merchants were easily O'Neil and Kelly, who had their "shooting eyes" on the nets all the time. Manager Tommie Hare received many hearty congratulations on his team's victory, and is reported to have signed all his men for next season. As a manager, Kennedy is awarded the palm.

Standing of Indoor Baseball League.

	Won.	Lost.
Pastimes...	5	1
College	3	3
O.A.A.C.	2	4
Y.M.C.A.	2	4

Final Result I. C. Hockey League.

	Won.	Lost.
Arts	4	2
Philosophers	3	3
Collegiate	3	3
Juniors	2	4

Off-Sides.

The "Arts" champion team expect to be banqueted at the Russell for bringing a championship to Ottawa.

Have you seen the classy post cards of the champion "Arts" men?. The manager's pose reminds one of Weldy Bate of the Ottawa's.

Pittaway has employed an extra staff of photographers to meet the unheard-of demand for photos of Tommie Hare's pets. The one of Newsy Lalonde O'Neill is now being issued in the third edition.

Get out and limber up that whip. Get the spring kinks out of it and make the ball team. We may discover a Matthewson or Wild Bill Donovan "in embryo."

Practice hitting the ball. We were sadly deficient in that respect last year.

Victoria Day Sports.

In Ottawa people look to Ottawa University Athletic Association to provide the bill of sports and amusement for Victoria Day, so with the characteristic foresight and activity of O. U. and its officers a programme of events is being arranged.

In the morning a City League ball game is scheduled. The finish of the Ketchum Marathon for boys will take place in front of the grand stand.

In the afternoon a ball game between an American College team and Ottawa University will be the feature. A ten-mile Marathon over last year's course will be run. A matched race of 100 and 220 yards' dash between our fast sprinter, Charlie Kinsella, Bobbie Kerr, Tom Siebert, and the American champion, will complete the list of attractive events.

Bowling Championship.

After a successful and very interesting series of games, the Intermural Bowling League was brought to a whirlwind finish when the following teams captained by G. Coupal and A. Guindon, and the following students:—Senior champions — George Coupal (Captain), S. St. Amour, L. Bonhomme, C. O'Halloran, P. Cornellier, B. G. Dubois; Junior champions—Alderic Guindon (captain), J. Perron, O. Brunette, J. Cusack, E. Couture, H. Courtois, romped off with the coveted championships of the great roaring game.

To Rev. Father Bertrand, O.M.I., and the several captains

is due quite a meed of praise for the businesslike manner in which the lengthy schedule was run off.

Pool and Billiard League.

The cue artists of "O. U." after an exciting number of well-contested games closed the league last week. During the winter months a vast deal of good clever sport was witnessed by the student body. In a very short time raw recruits became quite scientific in the arts of billiards and pool, and gave some of the "professionals" quite a tussle before the supremacy was decided. The team composed of Messrs. Kennedy and Simard, Searle and Turcotte, are in the finals for the championship of the league, and the tables will be covered for the season as soon as the deciding games are played.

Tennis.

The scientific game of "forty love" or "deuce" is to be revived at "O. U." A dirt court is being laid out at the southeast corner of the College campus, and some fast work will no doubt be performed on it by the expert tennis players. To assure the successful carrying out of scheduled games, Mr. Peter F. Loftus has been appointed manager of the whitewashed and netted court.

Croquet.

The fascinating and popular game of "croquet" will now have a place in the long list of summer sports at the "O. U." A smooth court is being prepared, and soon the mallets and balls will be seen shooting around the enclosure. To see that things are run in a businesslike manner, Mr. Frank J. Corkery will act in the capacity of manager.

Of Local Interest

The merchant has his resting time,
The lawyer turns from pleas,
The parson has vacations,
And the toiler has his ease;
The clerk has time for leisure,
The doctor's hours may crawl,
But the man who is a knocker
Never rests at all.

Junior Student: What are the two most sought for goods?
Philosopher: Dry goods and wet goods.

Si-r-d: When I am asked to play the piano, I never say "I can't."
Bu-ke: No, you sit down and let the people find it out for themselves.

Fl-ing: I intend to be either a clergyman or a brakeman.
O'G-n: Why so?
Fl-ing: Well, I'm good at coupling.

Br-n-n: If butter is twenty cents per pound, what will a ton of coal come to?
H-r-s: Ashes.

Tr-cy: In what State do we find the most marriages?
Hig-ty: In the state of matrimony.

Co-g-lan: Where are you going this afternoon, B-rke?
B-rke: Why to Hull, of course.

Good-night, Con.

How is Riley, Joe?

Prefect: Peek-a-boo, I see Ginty hiding behind a tree.

Some class to Ga-th-r's French, — Vous faisez un bonne room-mate, Boyle.

Tr-cy has secured a position in the mint. Come clean, kid.

O'G-n: When will Ba-y and Gu-h-n be allowed to go down town again?

K-n-dy: On the first of April.

Jerry (after G-l-gan had handed him a burnt match): Wake up, Gil-gan, that's no good.

Gil-gan: It was alright the last time I used it.

Pretty well charged now, Charlie?

They say that in Pakenham the people at Easter time turn towards the "rising son" when he goes home.

Rum$_o$r has it that Ga-t-ier was caught trying to crawl to the top girder of the new hotel. It's not incredible, either.

Mr. B-rke, you ought to get busy and crack a few jokes for next month.

1, 2, 3, and you're out, C-rrie.

Sm-th: I haven't looked at a book for a month.

Manager Tom Hare will banquet the champion Arts' team at the Russell within the course of a week or two.

"Isaac, when his father's knife was raised to slay":
A voice (in explanation): That's where the goat butted in.

In Physics: Why are cups used?
Student: To spoon it.

O'H-: Have you got change for a dollar?
Hi-g-r-ty: Yes, have you got the dollar?

Junior Department

Prof.: "Well, P. Bel-n-ger, what rank did you have in class this month?"
Pat.: "Plural."

On March 12 the dwellers in Small Yard had a baseball game, a football game, and in the evening played the Sterlings the deciding game for the Hurd Cup in the City Junior Hockey League. A summer game, an autumn game, and a winter game all on the same day. Now what do you think of our Canadian climate?

A number of Small Yard made an excursion to the sugar

bush on March 13, and from all reports thoroughly enjoyed themselves. Special mention may be made of W. M-t-neau and W.
F-l-y.

Owing to our allotted space being taken up with the report
of the St. Patrick's Day celebration. the Junior editor will be
obliged to hold over some copy till next month.

ST. PAT'S IN SMALL YARD.

This year for the first time Small Yard held a banquet in
honor of Ireland's patron saint.

In the words of Father Dewe, we had not only a banquet
but we had also a feast, and much praise is due to those who
prepared the menu and supervised the preparation of the material part of our banquet.

After all had enjoyed the meal as well as they knew how
(and they know how) our toastmaster, Rev. Father Collins, arose
and congratulated all who by their presence made our initial
banquet a grand success. By speaking a few words on Irishmen's fidelity to the Catholic Church, he introduced the first
toast in honor of Pius X.

This toast was ably responded to by Mr. J. McNally, who
in clear terms showed that Irishmen have always loved their
faith and revered the vicar of Christ. He also dwelt upon the
special love of Pius X for Alma Mater and our country. Mr.
Harry Richardson also delivered a notable oration on Pius X in
French. This speech was answered by much applause from a
very attentive audience.

Father Collins then introduced the toast, "The day we celebrate," coupled with the name of Con Mulvihill. Mr. Mulvihill
gave us a few very eloquent words on the land of the Shamrock
and on its patron St. Patrick. Con is certainly an orator not to
be despised.

The next toast was in honor of Our Yard. This was ably
responded to by A. Milot, our president. Mr. Milot told the boys
to obey their Prefect, as it was for their own good and the will
of those who sent them here.

Prefaced by a few remarks on the glories of past College
football and lacrosse teams, the toast, "Athletics," was introduced, coupled with the names of Messrs. Martin and Renaud.
The speech made by Mr. Martin was excellent. He said a few
words about Irish athletics, but the greater part of his oration

was on College sports, especially those of Small Yard. Mr. Martin is a very eloquent speaker and a coming orator of renown. Athletics by Mr. Renaud does not mean to sit on the coils from one end of recreation time to the other. At the close of his speech Mr. Renaud was rewarded by much applause from a very interested audience.

> Breathes there a man with soul so dead,
> Who never to himself hath said
> This is my own, my native land.

With these words, Father Collins introduced the toast "Canada," coupled with the names of Messrs. Brady and Mayrand.

Mr. Brady fluently and clearly told of the Canadian people, their religion, and their love òf the land of their forefathers; he also spoke of Canada's innumerable resources and their future development. The applause given to Mr. Mayrand showed him that his eloquence was not ineffective, and that he had not failed to convince his hearers.

Mr. E. Nagle, in answer to the toast "Our Hockey Team," gave us a few pointers which we cannot fail to thank him for.

The next toast, "The Junior Editor," was responded to by J. D. O'Neill, who tried very hard to get a few explanations from the Small Yard editor of the Review, but I think he failed to scare that personage.

Father Collins then in a few words thanked those who in any way helped to make this banquet a success. He then called upon Father Dewe to give us a few words.

Father Dewe expressed his satisfaction at being called upon to speak at such a banquet. He stated that English-speaking Catholics had always been friendly and sympathized with the Irish when the tyrants of England persecuted the natives of the Emerald Isle.

Father Voyer spoke in French and established his reputation as a public speaker.

Our first Prefect, Father Veronneau, next gave us his views of an ideal man. The example he took was St. Patrick. The speaker said that a person must not only possess physical and intellectual powers to be a man, but he must also possess that moral courage so characteristic in Ireland's patron.

MOST REV. AUGUSTIN DONTENWILL, O.M.I., D.D.

SUPERIOR GENERAL

Vol. XII.   OTTAWA, ONT., APRIL, 1910.   No. 7

Entered at the Post Office at Ottawa, Ont., as Second-Class Matter.

DOMINUS CUSTODIAT.

The Lord preserve thy coming in,
The Lord preserve thy going out;
Keep watch and ward thy soul about,
And guard from all assaults of sin.

The Lord make fat thy sacrifice,
Consume it in His living fire;
Grant thee thy very heart's desire,
His richest blessings passing price.

O faithful servant! called to rule,
To teach God's family on earth
The things of true and lasting worth,
Which God hath taught thee in His school.

May this day's welcome be the prayer
That God vouchsafe thee length of days;
To see thy sons shew forth His praise,
And prove them worthy of thy care.

God's Angels guard thy homeward way;
God's Angels, at the hour of death,
Receive, in peace, thy latest breath,
And bear thee to Eternal Day.

—F. W. GREY, Litt. D.

Visit of His Grace Archbishop Dontenwill,
Superior General of the Oblates.

N Wednesday, April 6th, His Grace Archbishop Don-
tenwill, Superior General, O.M.I., arrived at the Uni-
versity, and at 10 30, in the rotunda of the college, a
reception was held in his honor by the students, at
which the faculty assisted.   As His Grace entered the hall he
was greeted with the usual Varsity yell, after which he was presented with two addresses, one in English, read by Mr. Leo H.
Tracy, '11; the other in French, by Mr. O. Sauvé, '11·

The address in English was as follows:—

To His Grace the Most Reverend Augustin Dontenwill, O.M.I.,

D.D., Superior General of the Oblates of Mary Immaculate.
Your Grace,—

Memories of the past have already betrayed to you the feelings of this gathering. It is not a land strange and unknown that
you re-visit here to-day, but the hallowed precincts that cradled
the hopes of your youthful days, when, as one of ourselves, and
in company with friends so good and true, you drank of the
sacred fount of knowledge, grieved at our student disappointments and rejoiced in our triumphs.

Time has brought many changes since then, but the olden
spirit still survives within these college walls. It survives also
in the hearts of the many loyal sons of Alma Mater, who, after
being fitted for the battle of life, have gone forth into the wide
world, and have obtained, by their unwearied devotion, the recognition of their merit and training in places of honor and
confidence amid the varied spheres of activity they have entered.

Yet, even in the midst of success, their minds often travel
back again with gratitude and regret, to the friendship and
gladness of their college days. From far and near their sympathies are united with ours on this day, in offering respectful
homage to Your Grace, and in rejoicing that Providence still
watches over the destinies of this place of learning, by choosing
one of our own to be the First Superior of the Oblates of Mary
Immaculate.

In conclusion, let us express the earnest hope and prayer

that it will ever be in your power to give effective encouragement to those who devote their lives to the success of our Alma Mater.

THE STUDENTS OF THE UNIVERSITY OF OTTAWA.

University of Ottawa, April 6th, 1910.

His Grace in fitting words thanked the student body for the hearty welcome extended to him. He recalled to mind many reminiscences of the good old days which he himself passed within the college walls, both as a student and professor, and expressed a sincere wish that Alma Mater might continue in the good work that she has been doing, both in the intellectual and the athletic fields, and that she might continue to send forth men who would be able to fill with honor the different stations in life. Before concluding his remarks, His Grace announced that in the not far distant future a holiday was in store for the students, an announcement which, of course, was not at all unwelcome to the student body. The assemblage broke up with another Varsity yell from the students.

Wednesday. April 20th, was the occasion of another event which will be long remembered by those who were present. It was that of a banquet in honor of the distinguished visitor, held in the students' refectory at the University. The walls were tastefully decorated for the occasion with bunting of various colors. Appropriate flags, artistically draped, were hung here and there, and the whole dining hall presented a gala appearance. The banquet commenced at 6.30.

The following were present:—Most Rev. A. Dontenwill, O. M.I., Sup. General; Very Rev. N. Dozois, O.M.I., Provincial; Mgr. Routhier, Very Rev. W. J. Murphy, O.M.I., D.D.; Very Rev. G. Bouillon, Very Rev. J. A. Plantin, Very Rev. P. Corkery, Very Rev. J. A. Sloan, Rev. F. Lombard, Rev. M. J. Whelan, Rev. L. Mangin, Rev. J. Chatelain, Rev. A. A. Labelle, Rev. A. Cousineau, Rev. S. Hudon, Rev. A. Guillaume, Rev. J. C. Deguire, Rev. C. Poulin, Rev. J. A. Myrand, Rev. F. X. Brunet, Rev. J. H. Touchette, Rev. V. Pilon, Rev. J. F. McNally, Rev. J. B. Bazinet, Rev. L. Raymond, Rev. W. C. Cavanagh, Rev. J. A. Laflamme, Rev. J. F. Brownrigg, Rev. T. P. Fay, Rev. G. Fitzgerald, Rev. L. Archambault, Rev. R. J. Bazin, Rev. V. Bouchard, Rev. R. Lapointe, Rev. W. F. McCauley, Rev. R. A. McDonald, Rev. P. F. Ryan, Rev. D. A. Campbell, Rev. J. J. Lacey, Rev. J. Ryan, Rev. I. A. French, Rev. T. Holland, Rev. F. G. Gray, Rev. J. J. Quilty, Rev. J. J. Meagher, Rev. J. P. Harrington, Rev. G. Nolan, Rev. J. J. Foley, Rev. J. A. Belanger, Rev. J. Lemay, Rev. G.

Prudhomme, Rev. C. Beauchamp, Rev. J.Gascon, Rev. P.W. Brown, Rev. Dewe, Rev. W. Charlebois, Rev. C. Charlebois, Rev. Du-haut, Rev. Paillier, Rev. J. E. Jeannotte, Rev. J. J. Bacon, Rev. J. Sebastian, Rev. A. Lemieux, Rev. G. Gauvreau, Rev. G. Ouel lette, Rev. R. Barrett, Rev. P. Adrian, Rev. Poli, Rev. J. Fallon, Rev. Peruisset, Rev. Guertin, Rev. Rhéaume, Rev. Binet, Rev. Boyer, Rev. Boyon, Rev. Hammersley, Rev. Finnigan, Rev. Stanton, Rev. Gavary, Rev. Jasmin, Rev. Kelly, Rev. Kunz, Rev. Lajeunesse, Rev. Lalonde, Rev. Latulippe, Rev. McGuire, Rev. M. Murphy, Rev. S. Murphy, Rev. T. Murphy, Rev. Collins, Rev. Nilles, Rev. Normandin, Rev. Pelletier, Rev. Pepin, Rev. Roy, Rev. Sherry, Rev. Turcotte, Rev. Veronneau, Rev. Voyer, Rev. Dubé, Rev. Denis, Rev. Fr. Bertrand, Rev. Gervais, Sir H. E. Taschereau, Mr. L. Kehoe, Dr. Grey, Dr. O'Brien.

Letters of regret were received from:—Bishop Lorrain, Very Rev. T. W. Smith, O.M.I., Provincial, U.S.A.; Rev. R. J. McEachen, Rev. D. R. Macdonald, Rev. R. F. Halligan, Rev. D. D. McMillan, Rev. Fr. McRory, Rev. M. E. Fogarty, Rev. D. Mc-Donald, Rev. J. F. Hanley, Rev. T. W. Albin, Rev. D. Rhéaume, Rev. P. S. Dowdall, Rev. R. A. Carey, Rev. J. B. Magnan, Rev. J. V. Meagher, Rev. G. Garand, Rev. Fr. Delaney, Rev. O. New-man, Rev. W. H. Dooner, Rev. W. A. Macdonell, Rev. J. C. Mea, Rev. E. L. Limoges, Rev. Canon Belanger, Rev. P. Bedard, Rev. L. Marquette, Rev. Fr. Lortie, Rev. D. J. Casey, Rev. T. Dussere, Hon. N. A. Belcourt, Hon. Chas. Murphy, Hon. Rodolphe Le-mieux.

About 8.30, the banquet being over, most of the guests re-paired to St. Patrick's Hall, where the English Debating Society held the Annual Prize Debate.

The first number on the programme was a chorus by the University students entitled "Dominus Custodiat." This beau-tiful ode was written specially for the occasion by Dr. F. W. Grey, the words being set to music by the gifted composer, Mr. A. Tremblay. Masters A. Jeannotte and C. Champagne in their rendition of a vocal duet, entitled "Les Enfants du Croisé," were greeted with outbursts of applause. The next number on the pro-gramme was the Prize Debate, the subject being, "Resolved that Labor Unions are more detrmental than beneficial to society." Messrs. M. J. O'Gorman, '11, and P. E. Loftus, '14, were the af-firmative speakers, while Messrs. J. J. Sammon, '11, and C. M. O'Halloran, '12, upheld the negative side of the question. Mr. D. J. Breen, '11, acted as chairman. Each debater showed no mean ability in the handling of his subject, and each deserves the highest praise for his efforts.

The judges were: Rev. Duncan A. Campbell, B.A., '90; Rev. Thomas P. Murphy, B.A., '88; Rev. Leon C. Raymond, B.A., '93. While the judges were deciding as to which side carried off the palm of victory, the French Choral Society sang a chorus entitled "La Mort de Jeanne d'Arc."

His Grace then in a short address announced that the decision of the judges had been given in favor of the affirmative, and that the medal for oratory had been awarded to Mr. M. J. O'Gorman, '11. He congratulated each speaker for his admirable showing and expressed the great pleasure which he experienced at being present on such an occasion. He laid great stress upon the fact that Catholic youth should receive the proper training in order that they might become worthy citizens, and he said that in no other place in the whole Dominion was this object better carried out than in Ottawa University. He wished every success to Alma Mater and promised that he would do all in his power to further her interests. After a short address in French by His Grace, the meeting ended with the singing of O Canada by the Choral Society.

The next day (Thursday) the promised holiday was granted to the students.

C. D. O'G., '10.

HORACE TO HIS LYRE. (ODE XXXII).

My friends have asked a song. To thee I sing
O Lyre, companion of my idle hours.
If e'er with thee beneath the shade I've tuned
Some theme that may live on for many a day,
Come now, dear Lyre, and chant a Roman ode.
Thou, first caressed by him of Lesbian fame,
Who, fierce in fight, yet 'mid the shock of arms,
Or when his storm-tossed bark was safely beached,
Sang Bacchus and the Nine and Venus, too,
With Cupid e'er close-following at her heel,
And Lycus, of dark eyes and raven locks.
O thou, Apollo's glory, charming shell,
Welcome thou art e'en at th' Olympian's feast,
Sweet comfort thou amid my daily toil,
Be kind to me whene'er I seek thine aid!

—XERES.

Rt. Rev. M. F. Fallon, D.D.,

Bishop of London, Ont.

The new Bishop was born in Kingston, Ont., May 17, 1867. His father, Dominick Fallon, was born in Leitrim, Ireland, and his mother, Bridget Egan, is a native of Limerick. Both came to Canada when very young, and have since resided in Kingston. Bishop Fallon received his early education from the Chrstian Brothers of his native city. He afterwards attended the Kingston Collegiate, from which he subsequently matriculated for Queen's University. After one year's attendance at Queen's he came to the Capital and became a student of Ottawa College. While a student in Ottawa, His Lordship showed himself to be abundantly supplied by nature with those characteristics, which mark out men to be the leaders of their fellows. He entered with zeal into all the activities of college life. He took a prominent part in the English Debating Society, and soon gave evidence of a natural gift for public-speaking. He was, likewise, one of the organizers of the first annual St. Patrick's Day Banquet, a function which is still continued by the students as one of their most hallowed traditions. It was while he was still a student at Ottawa that the Owl first made its appearance as a College journal. Bishop Fallon was on the first board of editors and had the honor of contributing an article to the first number. .

Some years ago Bishop Fallon was renowned throughout Canada as a football coach.

After five years in Ottawa College he graduated with much distinction in 1889 along with Rev. Father Wade-Smith, his successor as Provincial of the Oblate Order in the United States, and the late Rev. D. V. Phalen, editor of the Antigonish Casket.

Having thus finished a very brilliant college career, he listened to his Master's call and entered upon a course of theological study in the Ottawan Diocesan Seminary, where he remained three years. He then decided to enter the religious life and joined the Oblate Order. He was sent by his superiors to make his novitiate in Holland. While there his health became so poor as to cause them serious apprehension and by a special dispensation he was permitted to finish his novitiate in Rome. His probation being over, he again took up his studies as a student of

RIGHT REV. M. F. FALLON, D.D.
BISHOP OF LONDON, ONT.

the Gregorian University, and in 1894 was elevated to the priest-hood. Before leaving Rome he succeeded in obtaining his degree as Doctor of Divinity.

The same year the young priest left for Canada and the following autumn again became attached to his Alma Mater, in the capacities of assistant prefect of discipline and professor of English, in the latter position succeeding the late Professor Glassmacher, who had retired. He likewise became managing editor of the Owl, which office he held for a number of years. It was only natural that the students should welcome his return and should look to him to reorganize the football team which had deteriorated during his absence. Nor did they look to him in vain. With renewed vigor he took hold of it, with what success the outcome of the eventful seasons of '94, '95, '96, and lastly 99 will more than tell. He was even more successful than he had been during his student days and he became acknowledged by the Canadian press as the matchless coach. and the foremost authority on rugby in Canada. Two years after his return from abroad he was appointed vice-Rector of the University, a very singular honor for so young a man. The following year he acted as rector during the absence of the Rector, Rev. Father Mc-Guckin. In 1898 he succeeded Rev. Father Constantineau as parish priest of St. Joseph's Church of this city. He acted in the capacity for three years. While parish priest he endeared him-self to the parishioners, old and young, by the lively interest which he evinced in their behalf. It was during his pastorate that the decoration of the church was begun, and he took a particular interest in the children of the parish. He made frequent visits to the schools, inaugurated the Children's Mass and organized the Children's Choir. At this time, also, he started a Catholic paper called the Union of which he was editor.

Bishop Fallon was a charter member of the Ottawa council of the Knights of Columbus, and was for a time chaplain. He took an active interest in all Irish societies. He was for a num-ber of years county chaplain of the Hibernians and to his efforts was due the success of their first annual parade. The Ottawa Hibernians have forwarded a handsome address to the new Bishop in which flattering reference is made to the work done by their former chaplain in Ireland's cause.

The news of Father Fallon's removal to Buffalo, after his three years as parish priest of St. Joseph's Church came as a great shock to his parishioners and to his many friends in the Capital. The numbers who crowded the station the day of his departure and the feeling there shown testified, more than any words could possibly do, to the esteem in which he was held by all, irrespective of race or creed.

On leaving Ottawa, he became pastor of Holy Angels' Church, Buffalo, and also superior of Holy Angels' College. Here he continued to display the untiring activity and persevering zeal which had so characterized him while in Ottawa. In Buffalo the scope of his work was greater and he took full advantage of the fact. He again displayed his interest in children's work by building what is recognized as the best primary school in the United States at a cost of $200,000, and by organizing a body of school boys into the O. M. I. Cadets. Although superior of the college, Father Fallon entered actively into parish work and won the admiration of all those with whom he came in contact by his fascinating manner, his ready sympathy, and his intellectual attainments. Six years ago he was appointed provincial of the Oblate Order in the northern province of the United States, and this broadening of the field of his activities he readily grasped as an opportunity to do even greater work in the spreading of the truths of religion. One of the most important things he did as provincial was the purchasing of a valuable property in the vicinity of Washington University, where it is proposed to build a theological college for Oblate students. He also established a number of Oblate missionary houses in the western States of Nebraska, Wisconsin and Oregon. The new bishop took a very prominent part in the public life of Buffalo. He was prominently mentioned as successor to Bishop Quigley, and again as Archbishop Dontenwill's successor in New Westminster. Before leaving Buffalo Bishop Fallon was presented with a purse of three thousand dollars by his parishioners, and was tendered a banquet by prominent citizens of Buffalo at which were present several Protestant clergymen and a Jewish rabbi.

During the past nine years Bishop Fallon has visited Ottawa on several important occasions. It will be remembered that he accompanied Cardinal Gibbons at the time of the laying of the corner-stone of the new university, and that he introduced the Cardinal at the reception held in the Russell Theatre. He likewise delivered two lectures at the annual St. Patrick's Day concert, given by the St. Patrick's Literary Association. The subject of his first lecture was "Daniel O'Connel," and his second "Irish Catholic Education in America." Bishop Fallon has visited Rome twice recently. On both occasions he was present at the election of the Superior General of the Oblate Order.

Bishop Fallon is a preacher of rare ability. He speaks with all the ease and fluency of the natural orator.

Bishop Fallon is not only known to Canada and the United States, but his scathing denunciation of the Coronation Oath, some years ago, caused such a feeling in Canada that a resolution was introduced into the Canadian Parliament by the Hon. John Costigan to have the offensive clauses removed. The subject was then brought up in the Imperial Parliament. The London Tablet of that date had very flattering things to say of the Canadian priest who had re-opened the discussion.

On Monday morning, April 25th, Bishop Fallon was consecrated in the magnificent cathedral of St. Peter's, before the most distinguished gathering of church dignitaries, Catholic societies, and prominent Canadian laymen, in the history of London. There were present upwards of thirty archbishops and bishops; one hundred visiting priests from different parts of Canada and the United States; members of the various religious orders; seventy priests of the London diocese; representatives of the different Catholic societies, the Knights of Columbus, St. Vincent de Paul, and the C.M.B.A., besides a great number of the new Bishop's personal friends. One of the most interesting features of the ceremony, and certainly the most affecting, was the presence of the parents of the new Bishop and his six brothers. This incident is without parallel in the history of the Church in Canada. The huge church was taxed to its utmost capacity to accommodate the vast congregation that sought admission.

The ceremony of consecration was performed by Archbishop McEvoy, of Toronto, assisted by Bishop McDonald of Alexandria and Bishop Scollard of Sault Ste. Marie. Rev. Jas. P. Fallon, O.M.I., Ottawa, acted as deacon of the mass. The sermon was preached by Mgr. Shahan of Washington. At the first pontifical vespers, in the evening, Rev. Geo. Nolan, O.M.I., of Lowell, Mass., was the preacher.

Aside from the actual consecration, there were many other interesting features, including addresses and presentations. The magnificent episcopal ring of heavy gold, set with diamonds, was the gift of Mr. M. P. Davis, of Ottawa. Personal friends of the Bishop, members of the Knights of Columbus of Ottawa, presented a purse of seven hundred dollars. Rev. Father Wm. Murphy, O.M.I., on behalf of Ottawa University, presented the pontificals magnificently bound and specially made in Europe. Former parishioners of Holy Angels' Church, Buffalo, offered a purse of three thousand dollars, and the beautiful ecclesiastical robes were a personal gift. Mgr. Meunier, Windsor, for the London clergy; Senator Coffey, for the London laity; Mr. C. J. Foy, for the provincial council of the Ancient Order of Hibernians, and for the Ottawa branch of the same order, all presented congratulatory addresses. Many other addresses were received from societies in Ottawa, Windsor, Detroit, Buffalo, and other centres, where Bishop Fallon is well known.

The selection of the new Bishop of London has aroused much interest in Canada and the United States, and it has been extensively commented upon by the daily press. Catholics of Canada have indeed cause to be proud of the return to their midst of such a young and distinguished son of the Church. Bishop Fallon has already had a brilliant career, but we feel confident that his greatest work has yet to be accomplished, and that in his new field he will have occasion to thoroughly display those many talents which have been so generously conferred upon him by a bountiful Providence.

EXPERIENCE.

Behold yon rough and flinty road
 Where youth, now youth no more,
Gropes whining, seeking crumbs of loaves
 He cast away of yore.

—The Century.

"Canada during French occupation."

SLIGHT knowledge of Canadian history will inform us that the first colonists in Canada were French, and that those early pioneers marked their coming with much cost of life and suffering. It is with deep sympathy that we read of the early Indian wars and massacres; the bitter famines and relentless privations endured by the set tlers along the banks of the St. Lawrence; nor must we forget the heroism displayed by those peasants in the fair fields of Acadia, so vividly described by Longfellow in that beautiful poem, "Evangeline." Thus the thousands of English-speaking people who have come to Canada in later years are greatly indebted to the French-Canadian race for the peace and prosperity which they now enjoy, and for which the sacrifice and achievements of their forefathers have no parallel.

It is on this account that the great intellects of the day are busying themselves preaching national unity. The population of Canada is composed of two distinct nationalities, the English and the French; and if Canada ever hopes to be numbered among the great nations of the world, her subjects must form one united whole; but something is still lacking at times in cordiality or mutual appreciation between these two renowned races. In 1897 Sir Wilfrid Laurier pointed out the necessity of unity. He said, "if we are ever to make a nation of Canada, if we are ever to solve successfully any of these difficulties that may arise, we can only solve them by mutual concession and reciprocal good-will."

The early history of Canada leads us back to the time when Jacques Cartier landed on Canadian soil, in the year 1535 A.D. The accounts of this first voyage were most disastrous, and out of some seventy men only a few returned to France. One of the three vessels which formed the company of explorers had to be abandoned, and the unsuitable equipment for the severe cold, together with scurvy, which spread among the crew, played havoc with human life. In 1541 Cartier again sailed for Canada and landed at Cape Rouge, this time being equally unfortunate. The Indians became hostile, and together with starvation, constant attacks from those warlike tribes, most extreme exposure to the cold, and hardships of all kinds, he abandoned the fort and sailed for home. The next spring M. de Roberval came over, but met with ill-fate also. His men were murdered by the Indians, and an insurrection breaking out in the camp, caused him to sail for France. In the year 1549 he tried his luck for a second time, but the vessel was wrecked and all was lost. We next hear of the Marquis de la Roche landing forty victims at Sable Island, and where some twenty perished from cold and hunger. About this time began the fur trade with the Indians. The French king granted charters to different companies and a trading post was established at Tadousac, at the mouth of the Saguenay.

In 1603 Samuel Champlain explored the St. Lawrence as far as Hochelaga. We now first hear mention of Acadia, a name derived from an Indian word signifying "abundance." It is learned that the first settlement was made on an island in Passamaquoddy Bay about 1604. The hardships endured on this island were so severe that on the following year the entire settlement moved to Port Royal, now Annapolis. Here the people built homes for themselves and everybody lived in peace and harmony until the English completely destroyed the colony in the year 1613. Fugitives went to other points, and joined by their friends from France, Acadia, far famed in history, came into existence. Champlain erected other trading posts, one where the City of Quebec now stands, and another near Montreal. He joined the Algonquin and Huron tribes in an effort to free themselves from the violent attacks of their fierce enemies, th Iroquois. The year 1617 was one of extreme hardship, and Champlain had to appeal to France for aid, and made two trips across the sea for provisions. Quarrels between the French and Indians became more numerous. The winter of 1628 was one of great scarcity. War had broken out between England and France, and the companies' vessels, having been intercepted by the English under Sir David Kirke, failed to reach Quebec. The following year Champlain surrendered all the trading posts to England and returned to France. The English flag floated over the forts and buildings in Canada for three years, but in 1632, by the treaty of St. Germain-en-Laye, France again possessed Canada.

Thus we can picture to ourselves the many hardships which those early pioneers had to endure from the beginning of French occupation, up to the death of Champlain, in 1635. Even from this period onward the stations occupied by the French were for the great part held in face of fighting and endless peril from the tomahawk of the ruthless savages. Nevertheless, the

French withstood the many encounters and responded with equal force. The second century offered more advantages to all. The numbers began to increase and multiply, and the country was opened up to a very great radius, thus increasing trade, and spreading the Christian religion over the land. Nevertheless, the prosperity which seemed to prevail was often darkened by the bloody attacks of the fierce Iroquois. The best accounts that we have of those early days are handed down to posterity by the Jesuit Fathers, who endeavoured with the cost of their own lives to preach and teach the Christian religion to this war-like people.

On the other hand, the Iroquois were determined to extricate themselves from the French invaders. In the spring of 1660 a massacre was planned for along the St. Lawrence, but this cruel act was not put into execution. The Hurons and the French endeavoured to drive back their bitter enemies, and as a result of this the treatment received by Dollard and his companions from the Iroquois is a well known incident in Canadian history.

Finally the English were accused by the French king of encouraging the Iroquois in their destructive work, and this led to the declaring of war in 1690. The New England colonists made many fruitless attacks upon French territory. Such was the state of affairs for over half a century, until peace was signed, after the battle of the Plains of Abraham, in 1759. All was lost and won. The French handed over all Canada to the English except a few islands in the Gulf of St. Lawrence, and from that time onward we have fought for the English flag.

From the above sketch we see how much the present population of Canada owe to the French pioneers. We see the many effects of the long and tedious wars; and the hardship and drawbacks which all had to encounter, all on account of the absence of the one essential point, "unity." Then may we voice the sentiments of our great statesmen, in declaring that good understanding between these two races is essential for the welfare of our country. For the old maxim is, "united we stand; divided we fall."

M. J. SMITH, '10·

National Types of Wit and Humor

O even suggest that our readers do not know what is humorous, would be a rather dangerous proceeding for the writer, but we will crave your indulgence while we define with the aid of various authorities what is Humor, Wit and Laughter.

That quality of the imagination which gives to ideas a wild or fantastic turn, and tends to excite laughter or mirth by ludicrous images or representations, is called Humor. It is less poignant and brilliant than Wit, hence it is always agreeable. Wit directed against folly often offends by its severity; humor makes a man ashamed of his follies, without exciting his resentment. Humor may be employed solely to raise mirth and render conversation pleasant, or it may contain a nice kind of satire.

Wit is the faculty of associating ideas in a new and unexpected manner. Pope aptly defines Wit as "What oft was thought but n'er so well expressed." Wit consists in assembling and putting together with quickness, ideas in which can be found resemblance and congruity, by which to make up pleasant pictures and agreeable visions to the fancy.

Laughter or convulsive merriment is an expression of mirth peculiar to man, consisting in a queer noise and configuration of features with a shaking of the sides, and successive expulsions of breath. Types of laughter are a true index of mental calibre. Who is not familiar with the loud "guffaw" of the shallow-pated rustic; the meaningless "titter" of the society dame; the brainless "tee-hee" of the silly young school girl?

The prosperity of the jest lies chiefly in the ear of him who hears, as does beauty in the eye of him who sees. Beyond that, it lies in the personality of the narrator. To analyse further is not of much avail. A request to define beauty once brought the apt reply: "That is the question of a blind man." So of humor: the only one requiring a definition of humor is he who has no sense of it, and all the definitions in the world would never make him understand what it was.

It is equally difficult to draw any exact line of division between Wit and Humor, though many have tried to do so. I have defined above, With and Humor, I leave it to the reader to make the precise division. They are in truth different sides of the same thing. Humor is nature, we know; Wit is art. Humor has its sources in the emotions; Wit in the intellect. From Humor comes laughter, but Wit may fail to negotiate even a sickly smile.

Of one thing we are sure — a sudden contrast between the expected and the actual, will provoke laughter, unless a more serious emotion intervenes. Any departure from the line of expression or deportment sanctioned by common usage has everywhere and always been a fruitful source of laughter, of caricature, and of satire.

The classic Greeks are responsible for the following jokes. They told of the simpleton who resolved never to enter the water until he had learned to swim; of the curious person who stood before the mirror with his eyes shut in order to see how he looked when asleep. The ship-wrecked mariner, who clung to the anchor to keep from sinking, and the case of a man who demanded of an acquaintance whether it was he or his brother who had recently been buried, are also examples of ancient Greek humor.

The best characteristic of German jesting is its excellence. It was Heine who wrote to an author from whom he had received a book, "I shall lose no time in reading it." Often French wit is of the merely absurd type. Thus it was a French courtier who said of a man famous for obesity that he found him sitting all around a table by himself. That is really better than our now ancient American jest on the approaching fat man. "Here comes a whole crowd."

Dutch wit and humor are not of a sort to appeal to us often. It is ponderous and rarely sarcastic. A controversy is said to have taken place between Zealand and Holland, the thrilling question was: "Does the cod take the hook, or does the hook take the cod?" Let this illustration suffice.

As to the English, they are not dull, as we sometimes contend; they are merely different. To say that it is necessary to have "raised letters, a diagram and a club" before an Englishman can see a joke is far too severe a condemnation. As a rule, Humor rather than Wit is the British characteristic. The fun is bound in absurd situations that have no suggestion of malice towards anyone. Dickens tells of two men who were about to be hanged, and were together on a scaffold erected in a public place. All about them, below, an immense concourse waited. Suddenly a bull, which was being taken to market, ran amuck in the crowd, and began goring persons right and left. Bill, on the scaffold, turned to his companion, and said: "I say, Jim, it's good thing we're not in that crowd."

There is no occasion to study separately the Humor and Wit

of the Scotch and the Irish.   It is a vile calumny that it requires
a surgical operation to get a joke into a Scotchman's skull. Some
of the brightest Wits have been Irishmen.   Most of the jests
anent the Scotch have to do with their penuriousness, while those
about the Irish are in the form of bulls.   A well-meaning Irishman said to a distinguished man on whom he hoped to make a
good impression: "Sir, if you ever come within a mile of my
house, I hope you will stop there."   Again, an Irishman remarked to another, referring to a third, "You are thin, and I am thin,
but he's as thin as the two of us put together."

PHIL C. HARRIS, '11·

Post-Victorian Poetry.

"Addition and subtraction, multiplication and division,
such is the task of the critic." Even if the calculation is cor-
rectly made, and even if the balances of one age are neatly and
satisfactorily closed, who can insure us, in the following age,
against the veering of opinion, which shifts like an ever-chang-
ing sail on the sea of criticism? What is the blessing of one
man is the bane of another. Thus the critics of poetry are
guided by no absolutely infallible standard; whereof results the
difficulty of censuring Kipling for his want of idealism, or Keats
for his dearth of realism.

The critics of poetry must remember the conditions attach-
ing themselves to the poet's heritage. The man of science has
a notable advantage over the poet. His inheritance, though of
recent date, is an edifice on which the many have laboured per-
sistently and willingly. The poet, on the other hand, really
has not the alternative of falling back upon the vast world's
store of meter. He must perforce be an individual builder, —
an originality itself. Unlike his brother of the sciences who
merely adds another stone to the pile of knowledge, the poet,
in an altogether different sphere, must grow him up a fresh
and tender twig at the roots of the tree of knowledge, deriving
sustenance thereof, it is true, but developing only as a separate
shoot from the bosom itself of the Earth whence he receives his
poetical nature.

But while poetry labours under a disadvantage, its history
is far from being at an end. The past lives on in the minds of

our modern poets and a "hidden stream of imaginative energy flows down the ages."

A truly great poet possesses a splendid poise of intellectual powers. Underneath the harmony and imaginativeness of his works there lie the rigid threads of severe poetical logic that give the whole coherence. His capacity is guaged by his ability to assimilate a vast amount of outside influences. The measure of his originality is his ability to react on those influences in such a way as to stamp his own personality through them upon the succeeding ages. In Tennyson, for example, we fail to find an absolute balance of parts. Though he takes up life just as it is, and deals with it in the concrete, still his powers of assimilation were developed to excess. And in this last respect, he represents the Victorian age. His poetry, always beautiful indeed, expresses rather much of current opinion in the philosophy, politics and religion of his own time. His works, while immortal in many respects, do not approach to "the organ tones of Milton, the piercing sweetness of Shelley, the grave simplicity of Wordsworth, and the concentrated richness of phrase of Keats.

To the mild realism of Tennyson may be compared with effect the strong materialism of Kipling. The poetry of the latter rests not so much upon literary influence as upon the primitive, hunting, slaying instinct in our blood. In his verse, we seem to hear the whir of the machinery that moves the world. In these respects he is resembled by our Canadian poets, —to such a degree in fact, and of such a nature in this country, that "a sponge might be wiped over the surface of Canada, and intellectually the world would be hardly the poorer." However this may be, it is no more correct to say that Canadians have not poetry in potential than it is to say that Kipling across the seas is wholly destitute of the harmony and imagination of Keats.

Keats, Wordsworth and Yeats represent the absolute idealists. Yeats represents the Celtic element in our poetry. The influence of Celtic legends and myths has always been felt through the medium of the Welsh and Breton traditions. The Scotch and Irish civilization, however, through political isolation have not been able to occupy their just sphere in European literature. Now, however, there dawns the first faint gleam of hope through the renewal of intellectual life in Ireland. And in this hope, be it remembered, are centred the highest of our Celtic desires. The Gaelic League succeeds Parnellism, and its immediate purpose at least is to create an Irish literary awakening. Already there shows great promise for the future, and much depends upon the representative Irish poet, Yeats. His poetry always has that singing quality which haunts the sense long after its experience is past:

The Poet Wishes for the Cloths of Heaven—

"Had I the heaven's embroidered cloths,
Enwrought with golden and silver light,
The blue and the dim and the dark cloths
Of night and light and the half light.

....

I would spread the cloths under your feet,
But I, being poor, have only my dreams.
I have spread my dreams under your feet,
Tread softly because you tread on my dreams."

....

"Modern poetry," says Yeats, grows weary of using over and over again the personages and stories and metaphors that have come to us through Greece and Rome, or from Wales and Britanny through the Middle Ages, and has found new life in the Norse and German legends." The Irish legends," he continues, "in popular tradition and in old Gaelic literature, are more numerous and as beautiful, and alone among great European legends have the beauty and wonder of altogether new things. May one not say, then, without saying anything improbable, that they will have a predominant influence in the coming century, and that their influence will pass through many countries?

What limits may we set to the scope of influence of Celtic legendary history and hidden lore? Though emigrated Irish are become truly sophisticated, is there not assurance that they will take kindly once again to the imaginative wonder of their race?

In conclusion, may we not say that the formative minds of Europe are already wearing a new thread of mysticism which will become the leading-string of our new-born poetry of the twentieth century? The nineteenth century reacted against the eighteenth, and in turn this new philosophy of wonder will react against the nineteenth. Modern poetry tends to withdraw itself from temporal interests, and to vest itself more and more in the bodiless, shapeless reality which haunts the under-currents of this life and earth, and which flits about allowing only the hem of its garment to be touched as it vanishes over the world.

                                        J. SAMMON, '11·

Napoleon in Rome

THE year 1787 saw the beginning of the French Revolution, in which the scum and rabble of the country deluged fair France with the blood of her best citizens. Everything gave place to the worship of the goddess "Reason." They even tried to put down the Catholic Church from the exalted position it had held in France for ages by forcing the clergy to take what was called the Constitutional oath which had been condemned by the Pope. For this the mob in their blind fury wished for revenge on the Church as a whole and on the Pope in particular.

About 1793 an excuse which would be accepted by European nations was found in the murder of Banville. This was brought about by the man himself as he drove about Rome displaying tricolored bannerets against the papal protest. Popular feeling was aroused and a mob followed him to, and murdered him in, the house of a French banker, La Montte.

It was not, however, until 1796 that this matter was taken up by the French authorities who were too busy at home to bother with external affairs. They then planned to send an army into Italy, and thus draw off some of the Austrian forces from the Rhine, where a desultory war had been carried on for some time. There was another motive, however, and that was to crush the Pope, as was shown by the original plan which was to convey the French forces to Civita Vecchia, the principal port of the Papal States.

Napoleon was then a young Republican general, 26 years of age, and comparatively unknown. He found the plan of conveyance impracticable, so, like another Hannibal, he marched across the Alps. After routing the Austrians, he prepared to march against the Pope, but Pius VI, knowing the inferiority of his troops and unwilling to shed blood unless compelled to do so, sent Azara, the Spanish minister, and others, to treat with Napoleon. The latter eagerly accepted any suspension of hostilities for he knew that he would need all his forces against the Austrians who were concentrating their forces in the north. By this treaty the Pope was compelled to give up Ferrara and Bologna, pay a large indemnity and give up 100 of the best pictures, statues and other works of art in Rome. The last were to be selected by French commissioners.

Not having to watch the south, Napoleon turned all his attention to the north, and soon drove the Austrians back into

Tyrol. He then formed the Transpodane Republic, which he virtually gave to France.

Meanwhile, the delegates of the Pope and the French government were discussing terms of peace, but could come to no agreement because the conditions put forth by the Directory were exorbitant and touched both the spiritual and temporal power of the Pope. Napoleon was displeased with the result as he wished to conciliate the Pope, thus restoring the character of France in the eyes of the world.

The hastily raised army of the Pope was no match for the veteran one of Napoleon, who sent 8,000 men under Gen. Victor to attack the eastern side of the Papal Territories in 1797. He defeated the papal troops near Imola and later formed a junction with another army of the French. Napoleon, however, was not yet ready to drive the Pope from Rome, so he entered into a treaty containing 26 articles, some of them demanding exorbitant indemnities.

The French Directory, displeased because the Pope had been left with any power whatever, secretly encouraged a revolutionary party in Rome, one of whom, Dupont, a party of papal soldiers shot during a fracas before the palace of the French Ambassador. The death of this man gave the Directory the excuse they wanted. Gen. Berthier was sent to take possession of Rome, which he did in Dec., 1797.

Then came the climax of their cruelties. The Pope, a man 80 years old, was forced to leave his home despite his entreaties to be allowed to die in Rome. He was treated with great and unnecessary cruelty and all his property confiscated. From Siena, where he was first taken, he was sent to Florence; later to Valence, in which city he died, worn out with age, grief and suffering. The reorganized government by the titles of its offices was made to resemble ancient Rome in its palmiest days, except that no religion was recognized.

After the overthrow of the Franco-Roman Republic, which lasted less than two years, the Neopolitans occupied Rome, while the Austrians had driven the French from the peninsula. Napoleon on his return from Egypt, overthrew the Directory and established the Consulate, he himself being first Consul. As soon as possible he turned his attention to Italy, but this time as a friend to the Pope. His first work was the signal defeat of the Austrians. Then he made a Concordat with Pius VII., but in publishing this agreement he added what were called the Organic Articles, despite the protests of the Pope. These articles curtailed the freedom of the Catholic faith, which had been re-established in France by the Concordat.

The Pope gave the new Emperor everything possible to avoid trouble. The end was reached, however, when Napoleon asked the Pope to annul the marriage of his brother and a Protestant lady, for in a matter of conscience like this the Pope could not be moved. The Emperor again resolved to use force, marched southward, and into Rome, holding the occupant of St. Peter's chair a prisoner in his own palace.

All the Cardinals and other clergy not native born subjects of the Pope were driven out, but Pius VII was more powerful as a prisoner than he had been free. Every edict he issued was respected by his people, and as they forbade all complicity and intercourse with the French, little could be accomplished. Once more force was resorted to, and on July 5th, 1809, the soldiers forced their way into the Quirinal palace and carried the Pope to Savona, from which place he sent forth his edicts, but it was with great difficulty.

In 1810 the Consulta, which had been appointed to organize a government, was dissolved, as Rome was considered a fully organized French department. A temporary governor was appointed, who set about refurnishing the Quirinal palace, as Napoleon had at last announced his intention of visiting Rome.

This state of affairs continued up to 1812. Meanwhile many works of benefit to Rome were being carried on by the French, such as the draining of the Pontine marshes, the transformation of the Pincian hill into a public garden, excavations in the Forum, and the great cemetery of Campo Verrano was also begun by them.

The latter part of the year 1812 brought ominous rumors that Napoleon's power was on the wane. The Roman people hailed it with joy, as it would bring back their beloved Pope, Pius VII. Soon after Murat seized Rome and drove out the French, so Rome was once more in the hands of the Neapolitans. Napoleon, being hard pressed in France, had Pius VII. removed from Fontainebleau to be carried to Savona if he was successful, and to Rome if he was not, as he did not wish to be forced to restore the Pope to his possessions. His reverses continued, so on the 10th of March he issued an edict setting Pius VII. at liberty. And so it was that the Pope entered Rome, welcomed home by a tumultuous greeting from the people, and took up his residence in the palace so magnificently prepared for the reception of Napoleon — now a prisoner on the lonely island of Elba.

A. GILLIGAN, '14.

PSYCHOLOGY OF SLEEP.

IT was with pleasure that the faculty and students of the Arts' course listened to a very instructive and pleasing lecture by a former graduate, in the person of Dr. Daniel Phelan, the well-known alienist and criminologist, on the Psychology of Sleep and Some of its Circumstances.

"Many of the delusions of the insane are really dreams, which they have not been able to separate from their waking experience." This statement, interesting as it is, was only one of many made by the Doctor during the evening's discourse.

The periodicity of sleep was first referred to by the lecturer. The human brain as an organic structure followed the laws of periodicity, a pronounced characteristic of all nature. It gave way to sleep as a result of a condition of weariness which was all humanity's daily experience, and was caused by the fatigue of the nerves and muscles of the body, the organs of movement, comprehension, and the higher intellectual faculties, a fatigue which was equally applicable to the organs of digestion, respiration and circulation. The conditions which attend sleep were next developed by Dr. Phelan. Consciousness was the last of the mental powers to succumb, while among the sense faculties, hearing kept watch the longest. The most interesting and fascinating phenomena in connection with sleep were dreams. Formerly considered to be actions of the gods, they were now recognized to be the residue of the activity of a slumbering brain. There was an absence of self-consciousness and judgment in dreams which accounted for their fantastic and disconnected course. It was a well known fact that dreams had been reproduced in reality, those which foretold sickness particularly. For instance, certain bodily ailments made themselves felt to a healthy man in a dream, when they were too slight to do so among the various interests of the day. Dreams were only of the duration of a few seconds or at most of minutes, though to the sleeper they often seemed very much longer.

Speaking of sleeplessness the Doctor said it implied a condition of ill-health in some shape or form. He then brought his lecture to an end after a lengthy analogy on the natural phenomena of dreams and the manifestations of insanity.

His lecture was a real treat to his audience, and the students will eagerly await a return lecture of the learned Doctor on any other phase of the interesting subject of which he has made a specialty.

University of Ottawa Review

PUBLISHED BY THE STUDENTS.

THE OTTAWA UNIVERSITY REVIEW is the organ of the students. Its object is to aid the students in their literary development, to chronicle their doings in and out of class, and to unite more closely to their Alma Mater the students of the past and the present.

TERMS:

One dollar a year in advance. Single copies, 15 cents. Advertising rates on application Address all communications to the "UNIVERSITY OF OTTAWA REVIEW", OTTAWA, ONT.

EDITORIAL STAFF :

J. BRENNAN, '10 ;	A. FLEMING, '11 ;	M. O'GARA, '10 ;
J. BURKE, '10 ;	PH. HARRIS, '11 ;	C. D. O'GORMAN, '10 ;
	M. SMITH, '10·	

Business Managers : C. GAUTHIER '10, ; D. BREEN, '11·

G. GALLOPIN, Staff Artist.

Our Students are requested to patronize our Advertisers.

Vol. XII.   OTTAWA, ONT., APRIL, 1910.   No. 7

BENEDICTUS QUI VENIT IN NOMINE DOMINI!

At last the hopes and wishes of the past few months have been realized, and we rejoice in the visit of Ottawa's distinguished alumnus, His Grace Archbishop Dontenwill, O.M.I., Superior General. Twenty-seven years ago he was graduated M.A. in the old College building, and from that time his advancement has been as rapid as it was brilliant. First as professor at Ottawa, then as Director of St. Louis College, afterwards as Bishop of New Westminster, Archbishop of Vancouver, and finally Superior General of the Oblates, Divine Providence has crowned him with great honours and great responsibilities. During all these years he has ever manifested the kindliest interest in the welfare of Alma Mater, and his visits, though necessarily short, have always been delightful. On this occasion, he comes vested with power and authority over her, second only to that of the Pope himself, and she will enjoy, for several weeks, the benefits and pleasure of his gracious presence. Knowing as he does the grand work she is accomplishing, knowing also her trials and difficulties, he will foster and increase her power, that she may ever go steadfastly forward, taking greater advantage of the admirable opportunities which her scope and position afford, till she stands unrivalled at the very pinnacle of Catholic education in Canada. The visit of the beloved Archbishop cannot fail to be for the faculty a source of strength and consolation in their devoted labors, and for the students one of inspiration to greater effort and higher ideals. Ottawa has been singularly honored in the past two or three years by the dignities and attainments of her graduates; to Archbishop Dontenwill, who has cast the greatest halo of glory round her, she bids respectful and loving welcome.

AD MULTOS ANNOS!

The University of Ottawa has again been honored by the elevation of one of its distinguished Alumni to the sublime dignity of the Episcopate. To readers of the "Review," and its predecessor, the "Owl," Rt. Rev. M. F. Fallon, Bishop of London, needs no introduction. He was one of the founders as well as one of the most brilliant editors of our college magazine, and his memory in that connection will ever serve as an inspiration to the youthful scribes who may for the moment guide its destinies. Only a few years have elapsed since Bishop Fallon left these halls to continue his masterly career as pastor, missionary and Provincial of the Oblate Order in the neighboring republic; and now in the flower of his manhood and the full strength of his magnificent qualities of mind and heart, he returns as Bishop to Ontario, at the behest of the Vicar of Christ. And though the spirit of Catholicity knows neither race nor tongue, nor frontier, we feel sure that he experiences a particular joy in being thus called to labor once more, and in a larger sphere, for the good of souls in his native province. Need we say that his joy has its counterpart in the hearts of the Catholics of Ontario, and especially of the students of Ottawa University. We are confident that Alma Mater will always claim his kindliest wishes, and we trust that she may, in the near future, be able to extend fond welcome and due honor to her former student, professor and Vice-Rector. Meanwhile she joins her voice to that of Catholic Canada in congratulating the new Bishop, and wishing him a hearty "Ad multos annos."

As the Greeks rejoice in commemorating the memory of Demosthenes, and the Romans in recording the eloquence of the immortal Cicero, so do Americans pride in extolling the talented Webster. With these words the "Laurel" opens a well-written little sketch of the great American lawyer, statesman and patriot. The writer chooses with remarkable good judgment several little events and anecdotes which throw light upon the great statesman's character. Webster was remarkable for his wit, love of nature, and affection. While at Dartmouth, he was noted for application, being the hardest working boy in his class. He mantained throughout life a sincere and warm love for his Alma Mater, and his first appearance before the Supreme Court was to plead her cause. His speeches before the American Senate are of course the brightest gems in America's eloquence. But we think the Laurel is rather extravagant in its claims when it describes "Liberty and Union" to be the greatest since Demosthenes.

"Man comes into this world without his consent, and leaves it against his will. During his stay on earth his time is spent in one continuous round of contraries and misunderstandngs by the balance of our species. In his infancy he is an angel; in his boyhood he is a demon; in his manhood he is everything from a lizard up; in his duties he is a fool; if he raises a small check he is a thief; and then the law raises the devil with him; if he is a poor man he is a poor manager and has no sense; if he is rich he is dishonest, but considered smart; if he is in politics he is a grafter and a crook; if he is out of politics you can't place him as he is an undesirable citizen; if he goes to church he is a hypocrite; if he stays away from church he is a sinner and damned; if he donates to foreign missions he does it for show; if he doesn't he is stingy and a tight wad. When he first comes into the world, everybody wants to kiss him; before he goes out everybody wants to kick him; if he dies young there was a great future before him; if he lives to a ripe old age he is simply in the way and living to save funeral expenses. Life is a funny road but we all like to travel it just the same."—Hya Yaka.

The March issues of nearly all the Catholic College magazines contain accounts of how St. Patrick's day was spent in our s.ster colleges. Some of them like ourselves celebrated with feasting and speech-making; others gave special concerts, and still others, particularly the Catholic colleges, held athletic contests. All the Catholic periodicals, and even some of the non- sectarian ones contain references to Ireland and to Ireland's heroes. The Patrician has a neat little sketch on Daniel O'Connel, "Reminiscences of Killarney," a poem, and "St. Patrick in Ireland," a prose sketch, are the best articles in the March Angelos.

We beg gratefully to acknowledge receipt of the following: Abbey Student, Acta Victoriana, Agnetian Monthly, Argosy, Allisonia, Academic Herald, Central Catholic, Columbiad, Echoes from the Pines, Exponent, Fordham Monthly, Geneva Cabinet, Georgetown College Journal, Hya Yaka, Laurel, Leader, Martlet, Pharos, Patrician, Queen's University Journal, Trinity U. Review, Vox Colegii, Villa Shield, Xaverian, Xavier, Vox Wesleyana.

Books and Reviews.

The University Magazine, for April, among other excellent contributions, has a well written and carefully thought out article entitled "The Lords, the Land and the People," by Dr. Francis W. Grey, of Ottawa. The author having a very intimate knowledge of English life and conditions, was particular happy in the choice of his subject. It is particularly refreshing, especially at the present time when so much is being printed upon this question, to hear from one who is writing from knowledge gained from personal experience.

"Canada vs. Australia?" is an article in the current issue of the *Empire Review,* in which the writer treats of the emigration problem and reviews the advantages offered to the prospective emigrant by Canada and Australia. Such subjects as climate, productiveness of the soil, education, character of the people, future possibilities are dealt with. The article is of much interest to the general reader as presenting a contrast between the two great rival colonies.

Essays, Literary, Critical and Historical, by Thos. O'Hagan, M.A., Ph.D.; published by Wm. Briggs; $1.00.

Owing to the limited space at our disposal and also to the fact that a rather lengthy review was given to Rev. Father Dewe's new book, we were unable to give, in our last number, as extended a notice as we would have liked to this excellent book. The essays comprise a variety of subjects ranging from a sketch of the "Princess" to the Italian Renaissance and the Popes of Avignon." They are written in the easy fluent style of one who is thoroughly master of his subject. There is a particular charm about the volume, springing from the originality of the views and the fearlessness with which they are put forth. As we stated

THOS. O'HAGAN, M.A., Ph.D.

last month the essay deserving particular mention is the one entitled "Poetry and History Teaching Falsehood." The author is to be congratulated upon his able efforts in the cause of truth.

Dr. Thos. O'Hagan is a graduate of Ottawa University, and a post-graduate of Cornell. For a number of years he has taken a most active part in the advancement of Catholic education in Ontario. He has been a voluminous contributor to current magazines, periodicals, and newspapers. At present Dr. O'Hagan conducts a department in the Toronto Catholic Register, and contributes monthly to the Rosary Magazine. He has recently travelled extensively in Europe, studying history and languages at the leading universities on the continent. His present volume bears the distinct stamp of these studies. Dr. O'Hagan likewise engages a reputation as a brilliant platform speaker, having lectured with much success in Canada and the United States. His previous literary works have always been very favorably received, and we feel confident that the present volume will gain new laurels for their highly gifted author.

The Young Man's Guide, by Rev. F. X. Lasance; published by Benziger Bros. Price 75c.

Says a zealous priest: "The Young Man's Guide is indeed a safe and sane guide. Common sense is stamped upon every page of the book. Manliness and Christian refinement and gentleness are strenuously inculcated. Flattery and human respect are mercilessly condemned. Catholic doctrine is set forth and expounded in a concise, forcible, interesting and convincing manner. The temptations and dangers that surround our Catholic youth in the world to-day are clearly pointed out, and the weapons to combat them are well indicated. The publication of this work is very timely, and doubtless every pastor who has at heart the temporal and eternal interests of the young men of his parish will hail its appearance with joy and use use every means in his power to gain for it the widest possible circulation among those for whom it is intended — in particular among the young men of our populous city parishes." There is no doubt about it that the crying evil of modern teaching and preaching is the almost total absence of getting into touch with the young man at the time when he most needs help. Hence it is that this admirable little book of Fr. Lasance's, which contains enough of practical information, and just enough of philosophical and mystic discussion to resolve the doubts of the young man who is so prone to such things, is a manual the most adapted to the requirements of our age of any which we have seen.

Among the Magazines.

In the Catholic Review, *"America,"* we notice an article on Canadian Tariff Agreement. It reads as follows:—"The negotiations between President Taft and the Canadian Minister of Finance, the Hon. W. S. Fielding, which were begun at Albany on March 20, were concluded at Washington on March 26. Until the official announcement is made, full details of the agreement cannot be given. But the fact that a definite agree-

ment, which removes all the points of difference between the
two countries, has been reached, is made clear. The Secretary
of State, Mr. Knox, has issued a statement to the effect that
intermediate rates have been accorded to a sufficient number of
American imports to remove the imputation of undue discrim-
ination and that the American minimum rates will be granted
to Canadian imports after March 31.

The *Rosary Magazine* contains many recent incidents which
may be of interest to many people. An article entitled ''Cardinal praises the President,'' shows the high esteem in which
President Taft is held by Cardinal Gibbons. He says the President is not only a man of strong Christian character, but a man
of kind and gentle disposition. Another article entitled, ''Redmond on the Irish Question,'' may be of importance to loyal
Irishmen. The Irish Parliamentary chief says: ''Though we
are surrounded by uncertainties and grave anxieties, still I feel
that we Irishmen have reason to be proud of the position into
whch our cause has emerged from all the disappointments and
defeats and sacrifices and sufferings of the past; and even if
the worst should happen, and we have to enter upon a new
period of acute conflict with the present Liberal party, I have
no fear whatever for the future. The very stars in their courses
are working for Home Rule for Ireland, and it is now merely
a question of time.

The ''*Leader*'' contains a short summary of ''St. Patrick's
Day in Ireland.'' The writer, James O'Leary, tells us very
briefly but concisely how the Irish spend St. Patrick's day. He
says, ''Early morning breaks. In fields here and there can be
seen eager groups of children and grown-up people gathering
shamrock, then off to early mass. In the afternoon some attend the procession and enjoy themselves in various other ways,
and finally can be heard the praises of the shamrock.''

''It grows through the bogs, the brake, and the mireland,
  The dear little, sweet little Shamrock of Ireland.''

The *Canadian Messenger*, as usual, contains many little items
of interest to Catholics. According to it, the signs of a great
quickening of the Faith in France are almost certain to come
true. The Lenten course in the Cathedral of Notre Dame, in
Paris, was followed by large congregations, larger in fact than
for many years. The same consoling news is given from other
parts of that unhappy nation. The Messenger also states that
Father Conrady, the well known missionary to the lepers, who
passed through Canada a couple of years ago, has contracted
the disease and is dying in the leper colony near Canton, China.

The many friends of Rev. T. Wade Smith, O.M.I. ('89) will be pleased to hear that he has been promoted to the Provincialship of the Northern Province, U.S.A., recently vacated by Bishop Fallon. Father Smith is an old Ottawa boy, and took the full course of classical studies at Varsity. He was afterwards professor and prefect in the institution. He has always taken a kindly interest in Alma Mater, and during the last few years has paid her several very welcome visits.

Rev. W. J. Kerwin, O.M.I., ('98), has been recently appointed Pastor of Holy Angels' Church, Buffalo, a post of special honor and importance. Father Kerwin will be remembered by the later alumni for his geniality as Prefect of Discipline.

Rev. Fr. McRory, O.M.I., a former professor, and now Master of Novices at Tewkesbury, Mass., spent a couple of days with us on his return from the episcopal consecration at London, Ont.

Another welcome alumnus was Fr. T. Curran ('88), of Prince Edward Island, a member of the famous football team of '88, champions of Canada.

Fr. G. Nolan, O.M.I. ('03), Pastor of Immaculate Conception Church, Lowell, Mass., preached the evening sermon at the consecration of Bishop Fallon, and did full justice to the occasion.

On Tuesday evening, April 18th, His Grace Archbishop Dontenwill, O.M.I., was tendered a reception by the local Council of the Knights of Columbus, of which Order he is a member. The Superior General delivered a very interesting address on Catholic Higher Education.

Very Rev. W. J. Murphy, O.M.I., and Rev. Jas. Fallon, O.M.I., brother of the newly-consecrated Bishop of London, went up to represent the University at the august ceremony.

The Review extends hearty congratulations to the Ottawa alumnus, Dr. Thos. O'Hagan, ('78), on his promotion to the Editorship of the Chicago New World, left vacant by the death of the talented Charles O'Malley.

VICTORIA DAY, 1910.

Joint Track and Field Day Sports.

The Ottawa Amateur Athletic Association and the Ottawa University Athletic Association will hold a joint Track Meet on May 24th at Varsity Oval. It is a new departure, but will doubtless prove a most successful undertaking. The move was proposed by Rev. W. J. Stanton, O.M.I., and met with the unanimous approval of the O.A.A.C. Mr. Weldy Bate, the Wizard of Hockey, has been chosen as chairman of the meet, which should be proof positive that a fine afternoon's outing will be given to Ottawa's sport-loving populace. No efforts will be spared to make the day a memorable one in Track and Field Day Annals in Ottawa. The following flyers will likely be seen in action: Bobbie Kerr, Bobbie Cloughen, Frank Lukeman, Charlie Kinsella, Kilt, Nutting, Williams, Bonhag, Goulding, Pauls, and many local athletes. The following committee has been elected: Chairman, Mr. Weldy Bate; Geo. S. May, Geo. Duncan, R. Gaisford, G. Marsden, Wm. Foran for O.A.A.C., Rev. W. J. Stanton. O.M.I., and Phil C. Harris for O.U.A.A.

CHAS. P. KINSELLA.

Ottawa University's Crack Sprinter and
All-Round Athlete. Touted as Bobbie
Kerr's successor. Champion of Canada.

When Charlie Kinsella com-
peted under the O. U. colors
at Hamilton May 15, 1909, at
the Bobbie Kerr meet, the
Toronto and Hamilton sport
writers were unanimous in
their praise of his excellent
clean-cut sprinting. He romped off with the 100 yards dash
heats and final, before thousands of Hamiltonians, who
gave him a great ovation.

"Watch that fellow, Kin-
sella," was the familiar slogan, and rightly so, as his
record will show. The O. U.
are proud of Kinsella's work
and expect some sensational
sprinting from him at the Victoria Day meet, May 24, 1910,
at Varsity Oval.

A GRAND RECORD.

1906—Won 100 yds. dash at
    O t t a w a Collegiate
    Sports. Time: 11
    secs.
1907—Won All-Round Cham-
    pionship at O. C. I.
    Sports.
    Won 100 yds. dash.
    Time: 10 3/5 secs.
    Won 220 yds. dash.
    Time 22 4/5 secs.
    2nd 400 yds. dash.
    3rd half mile.
    Won shot put.
1908—Won 100 yds. dash at
    Trenton, Ont.
    2nd to Bobbie Kerr at
    Labor Day Sports,
    100 yds.
    2nd 220 yds.

1909—Won 100 yds. dash at Bobbie Kerr Meet at Hamilton, May
.15. Time: 10 2/5.

2nd 100 yds. dash, time 10 secs., at C.A.A.U. Championship
Meet, Ottawa, May 24th.

2nd 220 yards. Time: 22 2/5 secs.

Won 100 yds. dash, Bayswater, July 1st.

Won 100 yds. dash, Aug. 12th, Ottawa.

Won 220 yds. dash, Aug. 12th, Ottawa.

3rd 100 yds. at Toronto Exhibition, Sept. 12th.

Won 100 yds. and 220 yds. championships at O.A.A.C.
Sports, Ottawa Exhibition, Sept. 18th. Time for 220
yds.: 22 secs. flat.

Won 100 yds. dash at O.C.I. Sports for ex-pupils.

Baseball.

O. U. (3) — Columbias (6).

The "Columbia Blues" opened up the baseball season Saturday, April 23, with an easy victory over the "O. U." ball
tossers. Perhaps it was the great crowd that caused the students
to perform erratically, and make some glaring miscues; however,
the damage was done in the first few innings when Tony Muzanti
was banged for a single, double and triple, which gave Columbias two runs. A dismal procession of moist errors, after two
were down, gave the Blues three more ,and it was good-bye to
the game for O. U. The students succeeded in annexing scores
in the first, third and seventh innings, tallying 3 in all against
Columbias' 6. For the "O. U." Capt. Mac O'Neill, Killian, Lamoureux and Ch. O'Neill played the steadiest and most effective
ball. Mr. A. M. Payne umpired.

Of Local Interest.

Stop gazing into pure extension, Tr-c-y.

Prof.: Loqui Latine.
Student: I can't.
A Voice: Then make signs.

You naughty, bumptious ones!

Hig-r-ty (going up town): Talk about the sun's rays, but
look at our Rea's.

HINTS.

Sapolio is good for cleaning desks.

Don't forget to include your glossaries as usual in your philosophy essays.

Keep one eye on the comet and the other on the Prof.

Some class to O'R-l-ey's twirling!

"Natura non facit saltus."

One nag's transl.—Nature does not make salt.

(Better consider it privately.)

Example of absolute right—To be born with a silver spoon in one's mouth.

Watch Mr. Br-n-an's classy puns since he has joined the Study Hall Knights.

Prof. of Physics: In the vibrating spiral how would the swimmer be?

Ha-r-s: He would be crooked.

Fourth Form hits are all copyrighted and are not for sale.

A LA TENNYSON.

The student hath a merry life.
"'Twas better to have loved and lost."
He says when they pull out the knife
"Even at a little cost."

Q-l-ty: It looks like rain.
W-h-bs: I guess I'll get my tent up.

Bu-ke: What is admittance?
Hi-g-ty: Twenty-five cents.

Ha-k-t must have a high temperature.

Junior Department

Baseball is booming in Small Yard this year, the First Team being in the Junior City League with Collegiate, Sandy Hills, Strathconas, St. Patrick's II and Pastimes II, whereas the Second Team is in the Hurd League for players under 18 yrs. of age. The Third and Fourth teams also promise by their showing of late that they will win all the exhibition games they play. The players who have participated in the First team games so far are:—Milot, Deschamps, McClosky, Renaud, Brady, Tobin, Harris, Richardson, Nagle, Poulin, Batterton, Doran. The following are the teams whom Small Yard have played:

Diamonds vs. Small Yard, 6 to 12—Won.

Diamonds vs. Small Yard, 7 to 20—Won.

(Big Yard) Nationals vs. Small Yard, 2 to 8—Won.

Juniorates vs. Small Yard, 11 to 1—Lost.

Collegiates vs. Small Yard, 4 to 8—Won.

Fourth Form vs. Small Yard, 2 to 8—Won.

Thus it is seen that Small Yarders have won 5 and lost 1 game.

But we must not forget the Third or Fourth teams. The Third team defeated Juniorates 13 to 11, and were defeated by the same club, 14 to 11. They expected to play Kent School, but the latter failed to appear on the scene. The following are Third team's players:—Sullivan, Lamonde, Madden, Dozois, Quain, Marier, Braithwate, Belliveau, Guertin, Richardson.

The Fourth team, alias The Midgets, defeated the Juniorates, 10 to 8.

Bank St., about 3 p.m. of a recent afternoon: "Hurry up, M-" "Ah, we're too late."

Will T-n-y catch first team?

An echo of the Prize Debate: "Look out for the janitor."

McK-y is always in a hurry for fear he might miss his place near the Prefect's table in the refectory.

Say, M-l-t, who swiped the butter?

Reminds us of an old story, "Hunted Down" on some of our Junior's faces.

Why is it that on a rainy holiday a number of the members of the department come down all togged out for a pleasant afternoon? Ask M-l-t.

A little more playing about the yard might make ball-players of some of our *stars*.

"I can hit any old pitcher." Eh, B-y, and a few others.

Tag, you're it.

SUMMER RESORTS

Experience, the testimony of thousands and the popularity of the several fishing, hunting and tourist districts located on the lines of the Grand Trunk Raiyway System, is conclusive proof that they are the Elysium of the sportsman, and the Mecca par excellence of the tourist.

The "Highlands of Ontario" is a land dotted with Lakes and Rivers, rivers that have their source in the northern forests and flow until they join the vast inland seas, Superior, Huron, Erie or Ontario, whose waters are in turn, borne by the broad St. Lawrence to the Atlantic Ocean. This great Tourist Railway reaches all the principal resorts in this vast territory, including Lakes Orillia and Couchiching, the Muskoka Lakes, a popular resort 1,000 feet above sea level, where thousands of people annually make their summer homes for rest and recuperation. The Lake of Bays district, where some of the finest hotels in Canada are to be found, and a locality replete with natural beauty and loveliness, with splendid fishing - Maganetawan River, the very heart and centre for sport, for rod and gun: Lake Nipissing and the French River, where wild and rugged scenery is to be found, and the atmosphere filled with health-giving properties: the Temagami region, a forest reserve containing 3,750,000 acres of lakes, rivers and wilderness, the scenic grandeur of which is incomparable. Magnificent fishing and hunting in season - The 30,000 Islands of the Georgian Bay is another most delightful and beautiful territory, where the most interesting trips may be taken. The steady increase of travellers to this locality is alone proof that it is becoming the most popular resort on the inland lakes. The Algonquin National Park of Ontario, a comparatively new and attractive region, little known to the lover of Rod and Gun and the tourist, has all the summer attractions that appeal to the denizen of the city. This territory has been set aside by the Provincial Government of Ontario solely for the delectation of mankind The gamiest of black bass, speckled trout and salmon trout are found here in goodly numbers. Hunting is not allowed. The Algonquin Park covers an area of 2,000,000 acres, there being no less than 1,200 lakes and rivers within its boundaries.

Good hotel accomodation is found in all the districts mentioned, and a postal card addressed to the General Advertising Department, Grand Trunk Railway System, Montreal, will receive prompt attention, and illustrated publications of any of the districts will be quickly sent to all inquirers.

The Kawartha Lakes.

When Samuel de Champlain was leading the Hurons through the beautifu Kawartha Lakes he fancied the butternuts and other low trees were orchards set out by the hand of man, so picturesque and charming were the shore-trees laced and laden with running grapevines. And to this day, though the farmer has made his home in the "Highlands" and the picturesque war canoe cf the Indian is gone from these waters, the shadowy shores of Kawartha Lakes are still beautiful to behold.

Owing to the high altitude of these lakes, nearly 1,000 feet above the sea level, the air is pure, and laden with health-giving and soothing balsamic odors from the pine and spruce-clad hill—it renews physical vigor, restores the nervous system, invigorates the mental faculties, and gives a new lease of life. To those who suffer from hay fever, the Kawartha Lakes are a haven of heaven given relief and security.

Easy of access (three hours from Toronto by the Grand Trunk Railway) pro-use in its gifts, and diverse in its attractions, having its fashionable resorts, and its delightful facilities for "roughing it." Why not throw business to the janitor for a month, cast care to the dogs? and when you return from the "Bright Waters and Happy Lands" (the English rendering of the Indian word "Kawartha") you will be a new creature, fortified for another year's trials.

UNIVERSITY OF OTTAWA REVIEW

Vol. XII.   OTTAWA, ONT., MAI, 1910.   No. 8

Entered at the Post Office at Ottawa, Ont., as Second-Class Matter.

WORTHINESS.

Whatever lacks purpose is evil; a pool without pebbles breeds slime;
Not any one step hath Chance fashioned on the infinite stairway of
  time;
Nor ever came good without labor, in toil, or in science or art,
It must be wrought out thr' the muscles — born out of the soul
  and the heart.

Why plow in the stubble with plowshares? Why winnow the chaff
  from the grain?
Ah, since all of His gifts must be toiled for, since truth is not born
  without pain!
He giveth not to the unworthy, the weak, or the foolish in deeds;
Who soweth but chaff at the seedtime shall reap but a harvest of
  weeds.

As the pyramid builded of vapor is blown by His Whirlwinds to
  naught,
So the song without truth is forgotten; His poem to Man is man's
  thought,
Whatever is strong with a purpose in humbleness wrought and
  soul-pure,
Is known to the Master of Singers, He toucheth it saying, "Endure."

                                        —Charles J. O'Malley.

Reception to Bishop Fallon

HE 17th of May was the occasion of a visit from His Lordship Bishop Fallon to our city. The students of his Alma Mater took advantage of the opportunity to give him a very warm reception. In the morning His Lordship administered First Communion and Confirmation to a large number of children in St. Joseph's Church, of which church he was formerly the pastor.

Accompanied by the Rector, the Very Rev. Wm. Murphy, O. M.I., he arrived at the University, where assembled in the rotunda were His Grace Archbishop Dontenwill, Very Rev. L. N. Dozois, O.M.I., Provincial, the faculty, and several hundred of the students.

The students gave him a welcome as might be expected from young men going to college to one who was near and dear to them. An English address was then read to His Lordship by Mr. Leo Tracy, while Mr. Julien did the honors for the French element. The English address was as follows:

To His Lordship
    The Right Reverend Michael F. Fallon, O.M.I., D.D.,
        Bishop of London, Ont.

Your Lordship,—

The destinies of men and things are ruled by the Providence of God; and we deem it no small mark of the divine favour that the students of the University of Ottawa should have this occasion to tender you a public welcome after your return to participate once more in the life and honours of your native land. Hence this reception we give you is fraught with deep and earnest feeling, for is it not a great happiness for Alma Mater that, in one of the sons she reared in love and loyalty, the Sovereign Pontiff has recognized those sterling qualities of heart and mind which fit him for a seat amongst the successors of the Apostles? It is a crown upon her work as well as an acknowledgment of your personal merit and services to Catholicity.

Many years have passed away since Your Lordship occupied a place in our ranks. It is long even since, as member of our teaching staff and Vice-Rector of the University, you devoted your energies to fostering among us the undaunted spirit of Catholic activity.

You have been employed in other fields, but, in the face of success or difficulty, your mind no doubt has often wandered back to the scenes and times when your chief triumphs and sorrows were those of the students of the University of Ottawa.

This present moment is a return to the cherished days of yore. You are with us again as one of ourselves. The old college spirit you loved so well—a spirit of enthusiasm, sympathy and loyalty —still throbs in the hearts of all. We feel that your success and triumph is likewise ours, for, in your elevation to the ranks of the episcopate of this province, we obtain one more proof that the University of Ottawa is no mean factor in promoting the material and religious welfare of our land. The number of our alumni who have been recently called to occupy positions of responsibility in Church and State is surely a matter for congratulation. While we are justly proud of the many public men who success reflects credit on their Alma Mater, our eyes are turned with special interest and esteem on those who have been advanced in spiritual jurisdiction, because they exercise a more potent influence on Catholic life, activity and education.

In wishing Your Lordship every success, in begging Almighty God to bring your labours to a happy fruition, we know that you will join with us in a further prayer for the future progress and prosperity of our common Alma Mater.

His Lordship's reply, which contained an eloquent appreciation of the kind words just spoken, was enjoyed most heartily by all. His Lordship replied thus:

Rev. Fathers and my dear students,—You can just look at me, and can easily tell what may happen to any of you. At the same time, I tell you, from the experience of one who stood there at one time, and stands here now, that there is more fun in that semicircle than there is in this. As I listened to all those wonderful things you said, I was anxious to have my old professor get out of this rotunda, because he might open up some closed books, and spoil the poetry of that address. I never hear a eulogy of that kind without thinking of a little story of a man who dropped dead, let us say in New York, and anybody who goes to New York, if he does not have to, deserves to drop dead. However, he dropped dead, and was picked up, and reported by the coroner as unknown. A lady came in to view the body, and claimed it as the body of her husband, and said "Give him the best possible burial, everything of the best." They got the most expensive undertaker in the city, got a costly casket and shroud, and he was being prepared for burial, when suddenly his jaw dropped. The supposed widow happened to see him, and said, "That is not my husband, take him away, I will not pay for the funeral." They had to take away the costly casket and rich clothing, and he was buried as a pauper in a $5 box. As the corporation undertaker came along, he said, "If you had kept your mouth shut you would have got a decent funeral." (Laughter). Now when I hear those eulogies, I say to myself it is better for you to go to a quiet corner; if you open your mouth, you will get the $5 box. At the same time, I am very glad to be here. I cannot help feeling, of course, though almost a quarter of a century has rolled by since I first entered the Ottawa College as a student, that not a single thing has changed in me with regard to the student body. I have been one of the boys from the beginning, and I dare say will be one of the boys to the end. (Cheers). There is nothing that I ever regretted more than having to leave the class room. Of course, the reverend professors may say that is nonsense, but I tell them it is true. There is nothing I regretted more than to be obliged to leave the class room. I loved the work, and I got along fairly well with the students, and I think perhaps the work done for them was not altogether to their disadvantage. However, it has pleased God to so fix my place that I am what you see here to-day. I do not like to be the subject of these demonstrations — I really do not. It is embarassing. When I am as old as some of the older Bishops of the country I might put up with it as they do, and are expected to do, but at present it is only embarassing. I want, however, to express my gratitude to the rector and the faculty of the University, and to you its students, for your kind reception. I am not going to make any promises. I do not think a graduate of an institution ought to be expected to make promises. I think he has no backbone if he has to make promises. Unfortunately, it is true of this institution, as it is true of all the Catholic colleges of Canada and the United States, that their graduates do not support them as they should. Their graduates do not give them either the moral or the material assistance that they could easily render and, as a consequence, I know of no work that is more disheartening than the work of the professors of the faculties, who are endeavouring against criticism, against coldness, against a spirit of hostility where it should not exist — who are endeavouring by day and by night, for no salary, for the bit they eat and the rag they wear — who are endeavouring to keep up the cause of Catholic education, and that is the greatest cause in the world. I should like to have you young men meditate sometimes upon the sacrifices that are made for you. I should like to have you think sometimes of what it means for the religious congrega-

tions that are engaged in teaching, of what it means for priests
and bishops much more than it means for the Catholic people, to
support this network of institutions; and I should like you to be
charitable to their shortcomings, if they have any. This institution
had its shortcomings when I was here. The food might have been.
better (Laughter), but it was sufficient, and I do not notice that I.
have fallen away to a twenty pound skeleton yet. There is a good
deal of nonsense talked on that subject, and no one knows it better
than I, because I did some of it when I was here. I have no doubt
if we could have in this institution the unlimited resources of the
State there would be laboratories, perhaps, and libraries. There
would be chairs of physiology, of biology, of paleontology, of
assyriology, and all the other ologies, but the fundamentals are here,
and are to be found in every other Catholic institution, notwithstanding the sacrifices, notwithstanding opposition, notwithstanding
the hostility, and notwithstanding the criticism. I am not going
to make any promises. I am, and I always have been, as far as
I would be allowed to be, and I always will be, as far as I am:
permitted, what every graduate of Ottawa University should be —
its friend in season and out of season, its friend in sunshine, but
particularly its friend in storm. I do not know what I shall ever
be able to do for the institution. I know I owe to it all I have.
Whatever there has been of success, whatever there has been of
straightness, whatever there has been of manliness, whatever there
has been of a desire to try and help others along the hard road
of life in my career, I got that here in this institution from the
Oblates of Mary Immaculate. (Cheers.) And the very least I can
do is to offer to them to-day the tribute of my affectionate gratitude, and to say to them — and it was true in the days when
I was associated with this institution — that no sacrifice was asked
of me that l was not proud to attempt, no work was asked of me
that I ever refused. There is no line on record — and it is not
much praise either — but there is no line on record, or off the record, that will indicate that at any time during the years I was in
this institution as a professor, any work that was given to me, or
any work that was offered, met anything but a willing response,
and was done to the best of my ability. I want to say now that
no request that this institution can make of me, no kind of assistance that is within my power, will be denied it. It is my alma
mater, my dear kind mother in the intellectual order, and I should
just as soon be faithless to the mother who bore me in the natural
order as to be faithless to the mother who bore me in the intellectual order. (Applause.) I say here I am a graduate of this Uni-

versity; I have returned to the province in which this University finds its chief work; and if the rector of this University or its faculty can use me; if my services in any sense will tend to help and develop the work that is being done here, then I offer those services, and that work, and I can say this: that nobody can say that Dr. Fallon ever stepped forward and offered himself to accomplish anything, and retired without making god his offer. I have been perhaps too active in stepping forward; I have been so long in the forward line, so long in the scrimmage, (applause and laughter) that at all events I can say that it may be difficult for me to sit back in the dignified position which a bishop is popularly supposed to assume, but which I do not pretend to assume. I do not feel one single bit different, except in thankfulness to God, but from a natural point of view I am no better, and I hope I am no worse than I was five or six months ago. I cannot take this thing as seriously as others do. It is no use; I never was serious, (laughter). You know I never was serious; my fellow students know I never was serious, but I think my fellow students know that with all my faults I tried to be fair and straightforward, and to do the right thing whether in the class room or on the athletic field, or in the other spheres of student life. (Cheers.)

A banquet followed the reception, served in the dining halls of the University, His Lordship being the guest of honor. The other guests were: His Grace Archbishop Dontenwill, Very Rev. L. N. Dozois, Very Rev. L. N. Campeau, J. A. Sloan, G. Bouillon, T. W. Smith, O.M.I., Prov. U.S.; W. J. Murphy, O.M.I., Rector; the Revs. J. A. Myrand, G. Charlebois, O.M.I., F. X. Brunet, M. J. Whelan, G. Filiaudeau, C.M., G. Fitzgerald, J. Sebastian, O.M.C., J. T. McNally, D.D., A. Duhaut, O.M.I., A. Newman, J. Bacon, O.P., A. Pallier, O.M.I., J. J. Quilty, J. A. French, J. Jodoin, O.M.I., J. M. Guilbault, A. A. Labelle, J. E. Jeannotte, O.M.I., F. Pintal, C.O.F., S.S.R., J. A. Dewe, P. W. Browne, W. Gray, and Sir E. Taschereau.

The following members of the faculty were present: Rev. W. J. Murphy, Rev. J. A. Poli, Rev. J. P. Fallon, Rev. J. A. Lajeunesse, Rev. W. J. Stanton, Rev. A. D. McGowan, Rev. J. H. Sherry, Rev. J. Bertrand, Rev. L. Binet, Rev. J. B. Boyer, Rev. F. Boyon, W. J. Collins, J. F. Denis, Rev. E. Dubé, Rev. D. Finnegan, Rev. J. A. Gavary, Rev. P. Hammersley, Rev. A. Jasmin, Rev. W. Kelly, Rev. A. H. Kunz, Rev. A. Lalonde, Rev. E. A Latulipe, Rev. L. LeJeune, Rev. P. J. McGuire, Rev. M. Murphy, Rev. S. Murphy, Rev. A. Normandin, Rev. A. Paquet, Rev. A. Pelletier, Rev. E. Pepin, Rev. L. Peruisset, Rev. L.

Rheaume, Rev. A. B. Roy, Rev. E. Turcotte, Rev. A. Veronneau, and Rev. O. Voyer.

In the evening His Lordship delivered a very beautiful sermon in St. Joseph's Church.

BOY INVENTORS OF AMERICA.

Wireless telegraphy and the conquest of the air have taken a firm hold on the youths of America, and hundreds of lads of tender years but advanced ideas are devoting their talents to the invention or construction of machines in both these lines.

One of the most remarkable inventions made by a boy is a device for signaling on elevated roads. It is in use on part of the Brooklyn "L" system, and is the work of Morris Schaeffer, 15 years old, a school boy. Morris was offered $18,000 for this patent, but on the advice of friends refused it. The boy expects to be able to get $50,000 for the idea from the railroad company.

Of quite a different character is the machine invented by Donald H. Miller, a student of Columbia University. This, by the mere touching of keys, similar to those on a typewriter, translates Chinese into English. It can also be used to translate any other language. The contrivance resembles an adding machine.

From darkest India comes the record of the achievement of Claude Moore, the son of a poor coal miner. Young Moore, who is 20 years old, was reduced to the sum of 2 cents when he received word from the patent office that it had issued him a patent on a corn husker. Thereupon, Claude, who is a thrifty youth, sold this patent to the harvester trust for considerable real money.

A most ambitious piece of work has just been successfully finished by Francis Lee Herreshoff, the young nephew of the famous yacht designer. This is the construction of a high-power racing automobile with which has been developed the tremendous speed of 80 miles an hour.

Herreshoff has also patented a device for subduing the glare of acetylene lamps. The mechanism does away with the necessity of extinguishing the lamps, for it softens the glare, making it hardly more noticeable than an oil lamp.

"THE MOTHER OF PARLIAMENTS."

HE future historian will set down the year 1910 as one of the momentous epochs in the annals of the venerable institution (known as "Mother of Parliaments") which has, for centuries, been the aegis of British liberty. No other human institution has had such an interesting career, for none can lay claim to such remote origin. Its history goes back to the time when the ancestry of the English people gathered together at the "moots" of Schleswig and Friesland, in the heart of the peninsula which separates the Baltic from the Northern Sea. Here, mid pleasant pastures girt by woodlands which crept down to the sea, the tiny knots of fisher-farmers from whom the English race has sprung learned the worth of discussion and public opinion; and in the assemblies of "town-moot," "village-moot," and "folk-moot," we find the first principles of representation. The "folk-moot" was in reality the general law-court and the parliament of the tribe, at whose meetings, held under the shade of a spreading oak, the clergy proclaimed silence, the eaorldermen spoke, while groups of freemen stood round shaking their spears in assent, clashing them in applause, settling matters finally by loud shouts of "yea" or "nay."

After the fusion of races on British soil those parliaments continued with varying time and place until the reign of the monarch to whom historians accord the title of the "English Justinian" (Edward I., 1272-1307). To his practical sense is due the beginning of Constitutional England; for, in calling together the states of the realm, Edward determined the future course of English history; and Parliament became the center of English affairs. In the hundred years that followed its assembly at Westminster, Parliament rose into a power which checked and overawed the crown; and it laid the basis of the financial fabric of Empire. We are disposed to consider "customs' revenue" a modern function of government; but its legal foundation is found in an Ordinance of Parliament (1225) whereby the King obtained a grant of six-and-eight-pence on each sack of wool exported to Flanders. The origin of "import duties" is found the "New Custom" (an Ordinance of the Parliament of 1303).

It is interesting to note that the chief exporters of wool in those days were the much-abused Cistercian monks of the Midlands.

"Those Parliaments," says Greene (History of England) "are not merely illustrative of the present parliamentary system; they

are absolutely identical with those which still sit at St. Stephen's."
In an Ordinance of the Parliament of 1311 (under Edward II.) we
recognize the prerogative of the present House of Commons, —
the power to make grants for the affairs of the realm; and by an
Ordinance of 1332 the Commons acquired full right to share in all
legislation. At this date there was really no such division of the
Houses as we have at the present time; but the four orders,—Clergy,
Barons, Knights and Burgesses deliberated together, though they
made grants independently of one another. Parliament was divided
into two Houses in the reign of Edward III. (1327-1368) — one
consisting of the Clergy and the Barons, the other of the Knights
with the Burgesses, or Third Estate. Thenceforth we find the Commons taking a growing part in public affairs, though they long
shrank from meddling with purely administrative business. Their
primary business was with matters financial. This is evident from
the following historic incident:—The King, in his anxiety to shift
from himself the responsibility of the war with France, went to
them for advice. "Most dreaded Lord," they replied, "as to the
war and the equipment necessary for it, we are so ignorant and
simple that we do not know what to devise. Wherefore, we pray
your Grace to excuse us in this matter, and may it please you to
ordain with the advice of your council what seemeth best for you
to do for the honor and profit of yourself and the realm; and whatsoever shall be thus ordained we readily assent to, and will hold
it firmly established."

The Commons seem to have lost their timidity and outgrown
their bashfulness by the time of the reign of Richard II (1377-1399),
and they then not only gave advice on matters of State, but they
even dared to investigate royal accounts, impeach the king's ad-
visers, and even set at nought the commands of the sovereign.
During the next two centuries the history of the British Parliament is the record of a continuous struggle with royalty; and in
later times it was not an unusual occurrence for factious members
to approach the House with a small army behind them to enforce
their demands. This was an ordinary *modus operandi* in the reign
of the Stuarts.

One of the many difficulties incident to legislation in former
times was non-attendance of members during the parliamentary
sessions; and delinquent members were mulcted in heavy fines for
failure to be present. Earls were fined one hundred marks, Abbots
and Barons were fined forty pounds for absence during an entire
session. Another difficulty was representation by *proxies*; and it
is recorded that during a session of 1534 a whole day of the time

of the Parliament was taken up in reading *proxies* of absentees. Evidently the law-makers of ancient times were just as remiss in the discharge of public duties as they are to-day; but then, it was sometimes desirable to absent oneself from the parliamentary bench, for on one occasion Henry VIII. threatened to behead any member who offered opposition to his demand for a grant of eight hundred thousand pounds. This grant involved a tax of twenty per cent. on lands and goods.

Numerous instances of bitter antagonism between the Lords and Commons are set down in history, notably in 1671, 1678, 1832; and we must not forget the recent struggle over the Budget, one of the most formidable of all. This struggle began many months ago; and the end is not yet. The House of Lords is now face to face with the most serious problem in its history; and the new Sovereign of the British Empire begins his career with a question of serious moment. How will he solve it? Time alone can tell. The House of Lords has ceased to be a popular institution; and it no longer dazzles the public with its supposed pomp and power. The following extracts (hundreds of a similar nature may be reproduced) show how the wind of public opinion blows:

"The House of Lords has become the refuge of the panic-stricken classes holding titles to lands or breweries or financial and industrial concerns. 'Peerage' should now be spelled 'Beerage,' for the House of Lords is simply an amalgamation of interests bound together by no other tie but fear of financial reform. In the historic sense there is but a feeble trickling of any liquid that can be called blue blood in its veins. Many of the titles are 'faked' like a picture-dealer's 'ancient master.' Many titles record a low amour, a political job, or sheer bribery. But together they have power, and they herd together like wild and domestic animals in a prairie fire — the thin remnant of the old feudal barons — interesting survivals after all the slaughter of the 'Roses,' civil wars, Whig oligarchies, aldermanic ancestries, and American inheritances — money-changers who have never yet been driven out of our temples — and adventurers who know 'a real good thing' on the political turf. All of these are shouting to the bewildered chiefs of the old governing class to risk a revolutionary throw, and chance whatever may come to our rickety old constitution."—(The Positivist Review).

"The House of Lords is a standing business-committee of the very rich to insure, first, that the wildest schemes shall go through quickly and quietly; second, that anything opposed to such schemes shall go through slowly, doubtfully, amid deafening clamors. It is not a place for avoiding revolutions; it is a place for expoiting some revolutions — and for concealing others. The House of Lords has really much the same function as the more vulgar part of the press. It exists to turn on the limelight. It decides what violent changes shall be printed in small letters, what much milder changes in gigantic characters. A bill is introduced to cut off the left leg of every non-conformist minister; the Lords pass it as an unimportant measure. A bill is introduced to charge every millionaire peer a *half-penny* more on his marriage license; the Lords reject it, and it becomes at once monstrously important, filling the land with cries of spoilation and despair. This is the real function of the modern Lords; they have charge of the vulgar department; and they manage the headlines and the loud advertisements in the great modern conspiracy of wealth. They must be destroyed because no nation can have manly control of its destiny so long as a small ring of its rich (often, its basest rich) can decide what things are important. An Englishman must be free, not only as to how he votes, but as to what he votes for. This can never be, as long as the richest class can force a general election by sudden and vulgar exaggeration.''—(G. K. Chesterton).

Arnold White dubs the House of Lords: "A fragment of the wreck of feudalism which has floated into the twentieth century." He says further: "Many peerages are granted as the result of bargains between party managers and aspirants to hereditary honors. In the majority of cases there is some ostensible reason which an easy-going public accepts as sufficient to justify the appointment. If a man brews an ocean of arsenical beer (thereby amassing a great fortune) and gives a small contribution to charity and a large donation to party funds, he is qualified to occupy a red bench in the Upper House. Occasionally, the creation of a peer is accompanied by mystery; and a case in point is a barony recently created. The recipient was a rich man, but there was no reason known to the public for conferring on him the dignity of knighthood. This peerage is still the subject of angry comment, and may some day see the light as a *chronique scandaleuse*."

Discussing the Spiritual Lords, the same writer says: "All bishops of the Established Church are members of the House of Lords, to which they add no strength. They were originally created peers because they were territorial magnates, not because of their ecclesiastical rank; and since they parted with their landed possessions, their presence in Parliament is an anachronism."

Gibson Bowles is responsible for the statement (which has never been contradicted): "that many contributors to Balfour's election fund have been made the recipients of titles, some of them paying $150,000 for a knighthood, others $1,000,000 for a peerage."

A recently-published volume, "The Memoirs" of. Lady Cardigan, sheds very luminous rays on the personnel of the House of Lords; and a reviewer says: "Lady Cardigan shows the English nobility to be morally incapacitated for taking part in the government of a free people, and proves incontestably that the aristocratic order which is now attempting to usurp supreme power over the nation is, from a moral standpoint, very much like the aristocratic order which came to an end by the guillotine in France during the Revolution."

In seeking the causes of the unpopularity of the House of Lords, one—the land question—stands out very prominently. This it is which has given the socialist and radical propaganda such strength. To realize all that this means it will suffice to note that eighty per cent. of the land in Great Britain is held by three per cent. of the people (chiefly members of the House of Lords); and one-quarter of the land in Scotland (lowlands and highlands) is owned by twelve magnates, whose holdings vary from two hundred thousand to one million acres. Little wonder then that:

> "Along the lawn, where scattered hamlets rose,
> Unwieldly wealth and cumbrous pomp repose."

The present agitation in England must necessarily eventuate in the remodelling of the House of Lords. That it will disappear entirely nobody believes, except it be, perhaps, the ultra-radical or the socialist; for every student of politics must see the force of such an opinion as that expressed by the great American (Hamilton) who says: "A second branch of the legislative assembly must, in all cases, be a salutary check on the Government. It doubles the security to the people... Its necessity is not less indicated by the propensity of all single and numerous assemblies to yield to the impulses of sudden and violent passions, and to be seduced by factious leaders and pernicious resolutions."

Efforts have been made within recent times to bring about a reform of the House of Lords that would render it more effective, notably in 1907, by the late Campbell-Bannerman. But Campbell-Bannerman's action was frustrated by the socialist faction in the House of Commons, that demanded the total abolition of the Upper Chamber. The Lords themselves have even made a step towards the reconstitution of their political perch: at the beginning of the year 1909 a committee, under the presidency of the Earl of Cawdor, submitted a proposal to reduce the membership from 618 to 348.

The re-constructed House would be constituted as follows:—3 Peers of the blood royal; 10 Spiritual Peers; 5 Lords of Appeal; 130 duly qualified hereditary Peers (to be chosen from those who had rendered signal service to the Empire); and 200 Peers, to be elected by the hereditary Peers for a limited period. This programme, however, proved abortive, as the House of Commons refused to recognize the findings of the committee which had drawn it up.

Attempts to abolish the House of Lords are not the innovations of the New Liberalism. In 1606 an attempt was made to *remove* the Upper Chamber by violent means; but the attempt was frustrated by the timely discovery of sundry barrels of gunpowder which had been provided for the purpose. Guido Fawkes, the originator of this diabolical plot, was hanged. Some historians (written with a small "h") set down this nefarious plot as a "Jesuitical scheme." Truly, the disciples of the saintly soldier of Manresa have a number of eventful doings set down to their discredit! When will bleareyed scribes learn to abandon their villany?

The House of Lords was actually abolished in 1649 when Pride — the eponymous hero of the historic "Purge" — expelled the members *vi et armis* from their benches, and inaugurated the celebrated "Rump Parliament." The "Rump," however, had but brief existence; for the House of Lords revived again at the "Restoration."

We are disposed to think that raids on the House of Commons by what we now term Suffragettes (women-folk of raucous voice and unlovely manner) is a modern performance. This is not so, as more than two centuries ago (in 1643) "'certain venerable ladies" (less demonstrative perhaps than Mrs. Pankhurst) ventured to invade the legislative precincts and present a petition for peace. The delegation, we are informed, "numbered about 5,000 ladies from London, Westminster, and elsewhere, but they were dispersed without bloodshed."

P. W. B.

Industrial Organization

The terms, industrial organization, concerted labour, and co-operation, can all be used to express the notion of men acting together in the progress of production. Now this co-operation or concert of men may vary in its nature from the simplest to the most complex forms. When we see a gang of men working in a lumber mill we know that their concert is very simple. Each man has his part of the work to do, and all work harmoniously. The more complex is that form of work by which we are able to grow wheat in Manitoba, and sell it in Liverpool. For this purpose many persons, unknown to each other, have worked in concert, each taking his part in the producing and forwarding the grain to Liverpool. There are, indeed, many other examples of concerted labour, both simple and complex, but the above two will suffice to illustrate the meaning. We must now consider whether there are advantages accruing from co-operation.

It appears but reasonable that there should be advantages following concerted labour. One man would indeed find it very awkward to lift a weight of one thousand pounds, while six or seven could do this without over-exertion. There are works which if not done simultaneously are of no avail. While a diver is searching for pearls, there must be men supplying him with air. Another advantage of concerted labour is that of extension in space. It would take one man many months to repair a storm-wrecked telephone line from Ottawa to Montreal, while many men would accomplish this work in a short time. If the arts of production were better organized, more money could be saved. It costs a carpenter or blacksmith quite a sum for tools. The expenditure would be greatly decreased if a concert of men would get together and purchase one set of such tools which they might lend and borrow.

Great as the advantages of industrial organisation may be, still they cannot extend to infinity. We cannot apply these advantages to all concerted labour indiscriminately. Particular attention to one employment is unprofitable where that employment is not continuous, as building or navigation impeded by the cold of our Canadian winters. There is also a limit to production It would not be profiting a man much to grow ten carloads of fruit if he could sell but one.

We see from what has been said that the results and advantages of concerted labour are very great. It would not do to put forth any serious complaints against our system of joint action in production; but if we follow the law that the denser the population up to a certain degree the better organized can be the industry, we may find some inefficency. Some follow the belief of Malthus,— that the cup of general happiness is being snatched from our lips by over-population. This is an error. The restraint to population is not the way to an easy life, but to a miserable toil and the impoverishment of families. We have just to compare the state of affairs to-day with that existing even fifty years ago. It is much easier for a man to get a living to-day than it was in those times. You may say that if the people had the same facilities of transportation in former years they could have lived easier than we to-day. But no matter what facilities the people of other days might have had, if they had not neighbours they would find it very difficult and miserable to work alone. The greatest Economists tell us that the denser the population up to a certain degree the easier it is for them to get a living. Thus the better organized should be the industry.

Great as the advantages of concerted labour may be, still we have to put some further shadows into the picture that seemed at first so brilliant. Man's nature is so vitiated that joint production when it is no longer simple is accompanied by evils of which if it is not the cause is the opportunity.

These disadvantages of concert are many. We see as a result of invention and industrial revolution a man often learns a trade which is afterwards of little use to him. He may also grow the wrong crop or buy the wrong goods. At present the vast majority of the people are buying goods which are known as cheap. The enormous quantities of bad bread, clothing compounded of shoddy, machine-sewn boots of bad leather, houses in which the work has been 'scamped'—such goods are not cheap but wasteful. Another disadvantage is the spread of dishonesty. This is caused by people dealing with those whom they do not know. Firms will sometimes transfer their business to a smart crafty from a simple and conscientious man. In this they lose money; for it takes more money to deceive the people in this way. Those disadvantages are but secondary when compared with this which follows.

The Industrial Revolution has succeeded in so modifying concerted labour that a number of men and women are kept at the same work day by day. This work is often so simple that it requires no effort on the part of the intelligence, and gradually the worker becomes a mental, moral, and physical wreck. When such a labourer is thrown out of work he becomes a tramp in the true sense of the word. He is deprived of his independence because he cannot turn his hand to any other kind of work than the simple work which he had to perform while in the factory. This and other similar problems remain stumbling blocks for our greatest thinkers. Thus I shall go no farther lest I should become entangled in error.

F. CORKERY.

The National Music of Ireland.

"Music!—oh! how faint, how weak,
Language fades before thy spell!
Why should feeling ever speak,
When thou canst breathe her soul so well?
Friendship's balmy words may feign.
Love's are ev'n more false than they;
Oh! 'tis only Music's strain,
Can sweetly soothe, and not betray."

HE subject of this essay is the National music of Ireland, and the Bards of Ireland, as recorded in the history of the nation. Among the grandest and most ancient titles that history gives to Ireland, there was the singular title of "The Island of Song." Ireland alone among the nations of the earth, has for her national emblem a musical instrument. It was in the bygone days, when Ireland had a national standard, it was then that Ireland unfolded that national standard, which floating on the breezes, displayed the golden Harp of Erin.

But, first of all, let us analyze the nature of man. We find that he is a being made up of a body and a soul. Among the senses of the body, although the eye be the master, yet the sensations which the soul receives through the ear, the sense of hearing, are the highest and the most spiritual of all. The evidence of the eye stirs up the mind to consider and think. The ear, on the other hand, seems to bring home its testimony more directly to the spirit. So the sense of hearing appeals more to the heart than to the mind. Men, from the very beginning, have always been wont to express their emotions of joy or of sorrow to the sound of song. The natural melody of music has a powerful influence upon the soul of man. There is no one who has not experienced at some time or other the sensation either of joy increased or sorrow soothed in his soul. Thus, the sense of hearing, through music, is that which seems most directly to touch the heart and the spirit of man.

The effect of music upon the soul is simply magical. There is nothing in this world that so acts upon our memory as the sound of some old familiar song, which we may have almost forgotten. Great, indeed, is the power of music in stirring up all the nobler emotions of man. The soldier, worn out and exhausted after many weary hours of marching, is spurred on at the sound of the national anthem. Every noble emotion of patriotism and heroism is aroused and to the inspiration of the national song he puts forth every effort. Thus, when we consider the nature of music, we find that it is of all other appeals to the senses the most spiritual and the most powerful, causing the spirit of the affections of men to rise to nobler efforts. And so music, of all the other sciences, is the most noble and God-like and the grandest that man can cultivate.

As it is with individuals, so it is with nations. As the individual expresses the joy of his soul by the clear voice of national music, so, too, every nation has its own tradition of music and its own national melody and song. Wherever we discover a nation with a distinct and emphatic tradition of national music, from the earliest times, there we have proof of a most ancient civilization. And Ireland, that ancient isle in the Western Sea, rightly claims the first and grandest pre-eminence among all nations. I do not ignore the high musical standard of the other nations. For depth of expression and purity of style, Germany far surpasses all others. In the lighter and more pleasant style, Italy is the leader; while in her own style of music England is considered by many to be equal, if not superior, to Italy or Germany. Yet, not one of these nations can point to a national music such as the Irish. I do not refer to the compositions of great masters, to the composers of celebrated masses, such as Gounod or Lizt, or to the composers of oratorios as Handel or Mendelssohn,—works that appeal to refined ears; works that delight the critic. But I speak of the song that lives in·the heart of all the people. This is the true song of a nation. Great as the Italians are as masters, they have no commonly accepted tradition of music. Nor can the peasants of Tuscany claim a national music. Not so with the Irish.

Let us go back to the most remote periods of history. It is an historical fact that the sea-coast people of the north and west of Europe were fond of song. We learn that when the sons of Milesius came and settled in Ireland, they brought with them a tradition of civilization, of law and of music. The bards were always given the very first places next to the King. They were the historians and the poets of the country. Long before the dawn of Christianity in Ireland, the bards were the greatest men in the land. And after the fire of faith was kindled in Irish hearts, there began three centuries of undimmed glory. We read from the English historian, Sylvester Giraldus, that the Irish so excelled in music that the Kings of Scotland and Wales came over to bring home minstrels and harpers. At one time there were over twelve thousand musicians in Ireland, and the King became so jealous of their influence that he was ready to slaughter them wholesale, had not St. Columba, leader of the bards, intervened.

But the picture unfortunately has not always been a fair one. Danish invasion came in the eighth century. Yet during the three hundred years of Danish war, Ireland preserved her music. Then followed the sacred war which lasted four hundred years. During these long periods of national struggle, the bards never failed to rouse the national heart and courage. The learned and accomplished Geminiani declared that "There is no original music in the west of Europe, save the Irish." But Queen Elizabeth thought that she could never conquer Ireland as long as the bards were there; so she passed a law that they were all to be hung. Yet they lived on, even in spite of Henry VIII. to the time of Carolan. In the history of Scotland we find that the Scotch, Welsh and English used to cross over to Ireland to study music. Handel, the great composer, was so warmly received in Dublin that, inspired by the Irish welcome, he wrote his immortal Messiah. The star of Ireland's song, Tom Moore, greatest of Ireland's modern poets, immortalized himself as well as his songs in his famous Irish melodies. The great Mozart once said that he would rather have been the author of one of those simple but beautiful melodies than be the composer of his own best efforts.

From Scripture we know that music is the native language of Heaven. And it is a very old and beautiful theory that the spheres move to a grand harmony of their own. But we should regard as a reality the harmony of the divine sphere of Heaven. Even as Moore made every honest heart and every honest and noble mind in the world melt into sorrow at the contemplation of Ireland's wrongs and the injustice that she has suffered, so may we not hope in vain that the dream of the poet and the inspiration of the true Irish heart be soon fulfilled.

J. J. B., '10.

THE FRENCH DEBATING SOCIETY.

On the first of May, at the Monument National, the French Debating Society held with great success their annual public debate.

The subject of the debate was one of actuality and interest: "Resolved that it is both the duty and interest of Canada to build a navy which will be in cooperation with that of the Empire."

The solemnity of the event was increased by the presence of His Grace Archbishop Dontenwill, Superior General of the Oblates of Mary Immaculate, who followed the progress of the debate with fatherly interest.

The Glee Club, composed of about seventy-five voices, and seconded by the orchestra under the able direction of the Reverend Father Lalonde ,was a great factor in procuring the success of the event.

Mr. Arthur Courtois, '11, president of the society, after having addressed a few well-chosen words of welcome to the audience, proceeded to introduce the orators: Messrs. L. Côté and O. Sauvé for the affirmative, and Messrs. O. Julien and L. Lafond for the negative.

Mr. Côté opened the discussion with a volley of well-directed arguments. His speech was the fruit of a methodical and judicious mind, and every auditor was convinced that the building of a navy is an urgent need.

If Mr. Côté compares with Demosthenes by his stern reasoning we might also compare Mr. Julien, the leader of the negative, to Cicero, for he could blend wit and reason, and season the whole by ingeniously exposing his arguments in a way that made many envious.

Mr. Sauvé, seconder of the affirmative, did not surprise his fellow students, for they all knew of what he was capable. But he surprised all those who did not know him, by the perfection of his speech, by his gestures, and by his intonation. Many said that they had never dreamed of hearing such eloquence outside of the House of Commons,—politicians, of course.

Mr. Lafond interrupted the applause raised by Mr. Sauvé to make a last appeal in favor of his cause, and although he did so splendidly, the judges, Hon. Senator Belcourt and the Revs. Frs. David and Roy awarded the victory to the affirmative, and the gold medal, graciously donated by His Grace the Superior General, to Mr. Osias Sauvé.

After having given several selections during the intermissions, the Glee Club closed the evening by the rendition of the chorus, "O Canada."

Much of the success of the French Annual Prize Debate is due to the untiring efforts of the Moderator, Rev. Fr. Normandin, O.M.I.

PRIZE DEBATE

The Medallist's Speech

"Labour Unions are more detrimental than beneficial to society."

HE question which we are about to discuss this evening is one which has hitherto frequently engrossed the minds of many great men both political and ecclesiastical, and one which even at the present day must still command the attention of any one at all alive to the interests of modern civilization.   Now we may ask ourselves the reason of this; why is it that eminent statesmen have spent their lives over the labour question, that socialists have raved and fought over the rights and inequalities of man, and still that nothing satisfactory has ever been reached?   The reason is very simple,—the question has not yet been solved, nor will it ever be solved as long as man remains man and the different grades of society exist.   Poverty and wretchedness will never be entirely wiped out, no matter what the nature of the remedies applied.

Among the remedies suggested at different periods of time we notice one in particular — namely, Labour Unions.   Some say that these unions have taken their origin in the ancient guilds so well known to students of history.   I admit that they may have succeeded them, but by no means have they replaced them.   The ancient guilds were a blessing to the labouring classes, but with the changing of the times they have dropped into disuse; they were abolished in the last century, and as Pope Leo XIII says: "No other organization has since taken their place."

Now let us see what labour unions are; they are societies of working men instituted for the purpose of securing coveted advancements.   Each union has a leader, or at best a few leaders who practically control the whole concern.   As a rule these leaders are men of very extreme opinions, men who have become fanatics over the social questions of the day, and who have secured their places by appealing to the stronger passions of the working classes.   Half of the time they are adventurers, men who are only looking for the betterment of their own condition, for person aggrandisement, and caring nothing whatever about the troubles of the societies to which they belong; and even if they have the interests of the masses at heart, they are often men who can do nothing but excite to fury an already half-crazed mob.

So much for the leaders; now let us look at the organization itself. Here we have a number of men, usually of meagre education, confiding their interests to a union which any one must necessarily admit is far from being perfect. At once the ambitious ones will appear, will try to secure the highest positions or offices, and from that moment on—discord. Our opponents may say that such is true in any society, but how much more would this be apparent in an assembly of uneducated men, suspicious of every move on the part of a fellow member and denouncing any one who fails to meet their wishes? "Ubi Concordia ibi Victoria," says the old proverb. Does any one for a moment think that in an association of this kind there can be peace and concord? It is impossible for such to be the case, and I have the words of Mr. Blackmar, Professor of Economics in the University of Kansas, to prove my statements. It is certain that there will be discord and that it will be of no light nature; quarrels will necessarily spring up about the distribution of work; some will claim that favoritism has been shown, and in the end, although such a thing may take years to develop, this creature of a few individual ambitions is certainly going to fall, thus leaving the working man in a far worse position than he formerly was. Gentlemen, I say this is a society which cannot possibly do any good for the working class, and as such must be detrimental to society.

We admit that the condition of the workingman has of late been somewhat improved, but that this is the result of labour unions we absolutely deny. Working men have not been helped by labour unions, but have progressed in spite of them. The principle of labour unions is fundamentally wrong; their purpose, as our opponents will readily admit, should be to provide work and provisions to the labourer when needed. Do they live up to this principle? I say they do not! As institutions which have been organized for the benefit of humanity, labour unions are not doing rightly by the workingmen in that they will help none except those who are members. It is a well established fact that labour unions do their utmost to monopolize labour and utterly ignore those who are not of their opinions. Every working man is not a unionist, but every working man is a human being, and as such must be considered as well as the members themselves. The illustrious Leo XIII. in one of his encyclical letters says: "There is a good deal of evidence which goes to prove that many of these societies are in the hands of secret leaders and are managed on principles ill-according with Christianity and the public well-being, and that they do their utmost to get within their grasp the whole field of labor, and force working men either to join them or starve. "Is this the philanthropy of which labour unions boast? Is it within the sphere of a philanthropist to cast aside another human being, to brand him with the slanderous term of "Scab," and then reject him with the bitter option, "starve or join our society"? I do not think so, and will leave it to your better opinions to judge whether or not I am right.

Ostensibly, the purpose of labour unions, as stated above, is to improve the condition of the working man, but their greatest purpose if anything is to wring a maximum of wages out of a minimum of work; and even after reasonable terms have been secured, still a dissatisfaction seems to remain. The fact that they have secured their wishes, that they have overcome their employers, tends to encourage them to breed further trouble. I will leave the discussion of the unionists' weapon, the strike, to my worthy colleague, but I may say this much about it, that it is surely a destructive weapon. The immediate outcome of a strike is a shortage in labour, and hence a depression and destruction of industries. Men may talk about trusts and the havoc which they produce, but at last we have found their equal, and that equal is the labour union. Organizations that will deliberately plot to bring about the downfall of industries, without which any country cannot prosper, ought certainly to be abolished. Reverend Charles S. Devas, sometime professor of political economy in the Royal University of Ireland, says: "The strike is a great injury to national wealth, a cruel hardship to many innocent third parties, a grave occasion of this order, and a source of bitter enmities which may become highly dangerous."

(To be Continued.)

University of Ottawa Review

PUBLISHED BY THE STUDENTS.

THE OTTAWA UNIVERSITY REVIEW is the organ of the students. Its object is to aid the students in their literary development, to chronicle their doings in and out of class, and to unite more closely to their Alma Mater the students of the past and the present.

TERMS :

One dollar a year in advance.   Single copies, 15 cents.   Advertising rates on application
Address all communications to the "UNIVERSITY OF OTTAWA REVIEW", OTTAWA, ONT

EDITORIAL STAFF :

J. BRENNAN, '10 ;   A. FLEMING, '11 ;   M. O'GARA, '10 ;
J. BURKE, '10 ;   PH. HARRIS, '11 ;   C. D. O'GORMAN, '10 ;
          M. SMITH, '10·
Business Managers : C. GAUTHIER '10, ;   D. BREEN, '11·
          G. GALLOPIN, Staff Artist.

Our Students are requested to patronize our Advertisers.

Vol. XII.   OTTAWA, ONT., MAY, 1910.   No. 8

EDWARD THE PEACEMAKER.

By the sudden and unexpected death of His Majesty King Edward the Seventh, the British Empire has been plunged in mourning. Catholics can well share the sorrow of their fellow-subjects in the loss of a great and good King, who more than any of his predecessors since the Reformation has been animated by a spirit of fair-play and respect for their most cherished religious convictions. Irishmen the world over will gratefully remember him as a sincere well-wisher of the dear homeland, and their sentiments have found eloquent expression in the resolutions of the representative bodies throughout the length and breadth of the Emerald Isle. The whole civilized world will honor him for his constant and devoted efforts in the cause of international amity, which have given him the glorious title of "Edward the Peacemaker." The widowed Queen and mourning family have our respectful sympathy and our prayers that they be comforted in their sorrow, while for George the Fifth we beseech the Ruler of the World to grant His grace and benediction for the happy fulfilment of the kingly office, during a long and prosperous reign.

CLASSICAL STUDIES.

Signs are not wanting that a decided reaction is taking place on this continent in favor of classical education. Princeton took the lead and the other great colleges are following that great conservative institution. Very significant was the selection in 1907 of Benjamin Wheeler, of the University of California, as President of the Massachusetts Institute of Technology. It was an open secret that the Institute wanted the best man available in America, and was prepared to offer every inducement to get him. That President Wheeler, a former Professor of Greek, and one of the staunchest advocates of classical training, should have been chosen, must have given food for thought to those who are wont to scoff at the Classics. It is a recognition by one of the chief sanctuaries of practical training, of the fact that classical studies develop the highest potentialities of the human mind; not that they furnish practical information to be turned directly into dollars and cents, but because the broadening of intellect which they produce enables the mental faculties to face any problem with satisfactory results. Thus, though the benefits of the classics are mainly esoteric, yet the fully educated man with his all-round information has a better chance to choose his vocation in life than if he has specialized for one thing and then finds himself disqualified.

This reaction towards the classics is a healthy sign in the life of our growing young nations, and gives our Catholic colleges and universities an excellent opportunity of demonstrating their true worth.

Books and Reviews.

"*Brownie and I*," by Richard Aumerle. Benziger Bros. (12mo. 85 cts.).

This is a story of college boys and the favorite dog. The author is a faithful painter of boys as they are at their sports, pranks and studies. As we read we are ourselves transformed into boys, with their joys and sorrows, and indefinable impulses. "Brownie," the college dog, is the faithful friend who takes his share in the college sports and escapades, and succeeds in winning the decisive baseball game of the year. We heartily recommend to our young readers this real boys' book.

"*Clare Loraine*," by "Lee." Benziger Bros., (12mo., 85 cts.).

A charming story of a tomboy gi l who "cuts up" so much at home that she is sent to undergo the refining process at the hands of the gentle nuns of St. Mary's Convent. There she associates Jo, Dumpty and Ladd in the formation of the "Clover," and succeeds in making things decidedly interesting for her teachers. But gradually the surroundings make their influence felt, and when at Christmas her parents visit her they find her quite a little lady. It is decidedly a good story for one who wants a long and hearty laugh.

Among the Magazines.

The current number of the America, under the head of Canadian news, remarks upon the visit of Generals French and Henderson to Canada. It was thought that the King's death would have interfered with their plans, but that such was not the case the Generals themselves p. oved by their arrival in Quebec on May 20. The object of this visit is the inspection of the Canadian forces. This inspection will be conducted by the new famous soldier, General French, at all points in Canada where mobilization usually takes place. It is to be noted in connection with the coming review of the militia that Gen. French is a man who possesses a very full krowledge of the art of war which he professes, and distinguished himself greatly during the progress of the Boer War in South Africa. It is no doubt fresh in the memory of the great majority that he it was who made the sensational dash from Ladysmith on the eve of its investment by the Boers. It is therefore but prudent to say that the General is just the person capable of fulfilling his present mission; and it is greatly to be hoped that the Canadian militia will derive from his experience and advice the lessons which are so sadly needed.

The America also contains an article on the death of King Edward VII. Having succeeded his mother, Queen Victoria, whose reign was a long and prosperous one, he brought the Boer war to a close, and inaugurated a "peace regime," which was so far remarkable in that it was to all appearances preserved throughout the world by the tact and diplomacy of one man. Edward also endeared himself to the Irish race by the practical demonstrations of sympathy which he showed to them. But, unfortunately, his last days were embittered by the rising struggle between the Lords and the Commons. Thus it remains to be seen whether George V. will be able to cope with the situation or not. Time alone will tell whether the new sovereign will fulfill his high office as well as did

Edward VII, who was "the Peace-maker."

Under the title of "The Physical Versus The Intellectual," Honoré Brenot speaks in the latest number of The "Civilian." The style of Honoré Brenot for some reason or other seems very familiar to us, and we should like to become further acquainted with the author. In his article, Honoré Brenot compares the two divergent spirits, the spirit of which prompted the toleration of sports mainly, and the spirit of the intellectual life, and he compares them as they relate to each other here in Ottawa. Throughout the article the writer is evidently decided upon flaying athletics inasmuch as they are carried to extremes, and are indulged in to the detriment of the higher life. Ordinary people are severely criticized for the way in which they follow their instincts only at the games, the theatre, and in music. On the whole, the article above-mentioned, which is without doubt an excellent piece of literary composition, deserves consideration from everybody, and is of especial interest to the students of this University.

Personals.

Among recent visitors we are pleased to mention the following who honored us with a friendly call :—

Rev. A. Gray, of Carleton Place.

Dr. McNally, Chelsea.

Very Rev. T. W. Smith, O.M.I., Provincial, Northern Province, U.S.A.

Rev. J. J. Quilty, P.P., Douglas.

Rev. I. A. French, Brudenel.

Rev. M. J. Whelan, St. Patrick's, Ottawa.

Rev. G. O'Toole, Ottawa.

Rev. Fr. O'Toole has been appointed curate at St. Mary's, Bayswater.

Rev. Fr. Filiatreault has been appointed curate at Aylmer.

Rev. Fr. Keaney, of Lanark, paid us a call last week.

We record with pleasure a visit from His Grace Archbishop MacNeill, formerly of Newfoundland, recently promoted to the Archdiocese of Vancouver.

Rev. Fr. Campbell, of Nova Scotia, was a recent visitor to our halls.

Rev. Dr. O'Leary, of Bathurst, N.S., pleased us with a call.

Baseball.

After getting away to a very poor start by losing two easy games, the "O.U." ball nine has struck its winning stride, and has won three games in succession by very decisive scores. The fourth game ended two all, with the "O.U." nine coming up strong. The bases were filled with two out, but the needed hit was nipped off by fast infielding, and the contest ended seven innings' draw. The team now has a firm hold on second place with very bright prospects of winning back the championship pennant of the City Baseball League, which is held by the O.A.A.C. Rev. Father Stanton nad Bert Gilligan are working hard for the team, and from the present outlook their labors will be crowned with great success.

Ottawa Univ. (11) — Y.M.C.A. (4). Varsity Oval, May 5th, 1910.

GAME NO. 1.

The baseball nine registered its first victory by walloping the "Y" boys to the fast tune of 11 to 4. College just had to win this game to be in the running, and they did it "en masse." Right off the bat of the first man up started the fireworks, and they continued for seven innings, during which stated time the "O.U." team annexed seven hits, ten runs, and nine pilfered bases. The team played snappy ball in the out field, and the infield work was good to look at. The players just couldn't be satisfied with getting safe on first, but kept on all afternoon stealing the bags whenever they felt so inclined. Our pitcher, one "Rene" Lamoureux, he of the massive main, was in fine fettle and held the "Y" players right where he wanted them. Catcher Morriseau has made good with a vengeance, and a great deal of praise is due our husky backstop for the classy brand of ball he is putting up. Charlie O'Neil, Kinsella, Ki lian, Curry, Moriseau, "Mac" O'Neil and Lamoureux secured hits during the game. The attendance was very gratifying and is a clear indication that baseball has "caught on" in Ottawa.

Ottawa Univ. (13) — St. Patrick's (0). Varsity Oval, May 7th, 1910.

GAME NO. 2.

Our second break into the "wins" column was initiated on the above date and place by an overwhelming administration of the kalsomine brush to the baseball nine representing the St. Pat. L. & S. Assn. The final announcements read "O.U." 13, St. Pat's 0, and the crowd filed out. It was a weird exhibition of ball-playing on the part of the "green stockings," while the Varsity nine played an errorless game, hitting the horsehide for ten safe ones, and purloining seven bags, with thirteen runs thrown in. Pitcher Lamoureux was in fine form, and fanned four. Capt. "Mac" O'Neill, l.f.; Curry, 2b.; Killian, s.s.; Muzanti, 3b.; C. O'Neill, 1b.; Lamoureux, p.; Morriseau, c.; Smith, r.f.; Kinsella, c.f., completed the line-up

SCORE BY INNINGS.

	R.	H.	E.
O.U. ... ... 1103062—13		10	0
St. Pat's... ... ... 0000000— 0		4	8

Ottawa Univ. (5) — O.A.A.C. (1). Varsity Oval, May 14, 1910.

GAME NO. 3.

Win number three was marked up for the "O.U." ball team when in a clean-cut victory the ball-tossers from the O.A.A.C., present pennant holders, were outplayed at every stage of the game, and defeated by the decisive tally of 5 to 1. "O.U." won the game by its daring base-running, earning only one of the five runs scored. Three runs were scored on nervy stealing home by Ch. O'Neil, Mac O'Neil and Mike Smith. Rene Lamoureux occupied the pitcher's mound and burned them over, allowing but four hits to the O.A. A. C. team, which possesses a quartette of fence breakers. This loss relegates the champions to an uncertain second place. The brand of ball served up by the Varsity nine was fautless, only one excusable mistake marring the nothingness of the error column. The team showed the results of brainy coaching, and played "inside" baseball all the time. Signals from the bench were executed with swift precision by the players, and as a consequence few misplays were noticed. The team was the same as in the previous game, with Sheehy replacing Curry in the 7th inning.

Pastimes (2) — Ottawa University (2). May 21, 1910.
GAME NO. 4.

Owing to a peculiar rule in the Ottawa City Ball League, the game between O.U. and Pastimes, played on above date, had to be called off at 4 o'clock when both teams secured 2 runs, and College had the Ashburnham Hill aggregation in a tight corner, and were coming all the time. While the game lasted it was a hummer, and easily the best game of the season from every point of view. It was a battle royal between, Lamoureux the "O.U." heaver, and Peterson, the heavy big leaguer of the Pastimes. Our box artist had the better of the fight and fanned eight batters in six innings, allowing only three hits. Morriseau was excellent as a backstop, and got two of the five bungles for College. C. O'Neill, Muzanti, Kinsella, each got hits. The line-up was the regular one, Sheehy replacing Currie after a bad break had been made, letting in two runs for the Pastimes. The game will be re-played at some future date, and the College squad promises to put the first crimp in the Pastimes' winning streak.

Inter-Course Field Sports. May 17, 1910.

The Annual Inter-Course meet of the O.U.A.A. was held at Varsity Oval on Tuesday afternoon, May 17, 1910. About 1,500 spectators were present, and all thoroughly enjoyed the track and field events put on by the athletes of the various courses of the Varsity. Most Reverend Archbishop Dontenwill, O.M.I., D.D., Superior General of the Order of Mary Immaculate, and His Grace Bishop M. F. Fallon, D.D., O.M.I., of London, honored us with their distinguished presence, and expressed themselves pleased with the splendid performances of the student athletes.

The idea of Inter-Course athletics was proposed by the Rev. Father Stanton, O.M.I., and as per usual the proposition was most successful in every detail.

S. Quilty, of the "Arts" Course, succeeded in capturing the prize for the all-round individual championship, with the good total of 14 points. Capt. Charlie Kinsella and Jerry Harrington tied for second with 7 points.

Arts won the Inter-Course championship with 33 points, Collegiate 30 points, Commercial 15, Philosophers 10.

Capt. Charlie Kinsella, as was expected, proved the sensation of the day, winning his heat in the 100 yds. with comparative ease, and tearing off the final in 10⅔ seconds, and even at that was not pressed. S. Quilty excelled in the jumps, taking first in the high and broad jumps.

The following shows the events, the winners, time and distances made:—

100 yard dash—Heat 1 : 1st D. Batterton, 2nd F. Corkery; time, 10 4/5 secs. Heat 2: 1st J. Muzanti, 2nd J. Coupal; time, 10 4/5 secs. Heat 3: 1st C. Kinsella, 2nd S. St. Amour; time, 11 2/5 secs.

Hop, step and jump—1 S. Quilty, 2 J. Harrington, 3 C. Kinsella. Distance 38 ft. 5½ in.

Broad jump—1 S. Quilty, 2 J. Harrington, 3 J. Sammon. Distance, 18 ft.

880 yards run—1 O. Kennedy, 2 L. Chantal, 3 R. Sheehy. Time, 2.24.

Throwing lacrosse ball—1 C. Gauthier, 2 C. O'Halloran, 3 E. Letang. Distance, 224 yards.

Throwing base ball—1 C. Kinsella, 2 J. Routhier, 3 J. Muzanti. Distance, 306 ft. 9 in.

One mile run—1 A. Murtagh, 2 E. Faulkner, 3 Armstrong. Time, 5.31.

High jump—1 S. Quilty, 2 Bonhomme, 3 Lacey. Height, 5 ft. 4 in.

440 yard run—1 D. Batterton, 2 J. Coupal, 3 O. Kennedy. Time, .57.

Potato race— 1 Gauthier, 2 Laroche, 3 Rice.

Relay race—1 Collegiate team, 2 Varsity, 3 Varsity.

100 yards final—1 Kinsella, 2 J. Coupal, 3 D. Batterton. Time, 10 2/5.

Kicking football—1 Quilty, 2 Chartrand, 3 Contway. Distance, 164 ft. 9 in.

Pole vault—1 Lacey, 2 R. Guindon, 3 Sammon. Height, 8 ft. 5 in.

Shot put—1 J. Harrington, 2 S. Quilty, 3 R. Guindon. Distance, 40 ft. 8 in.

The officials were:—Referee, W. J. Stanton, O.M.I.; judges, E. Tassé, Father Sherry and Dr. Chabot; marshal, S. Coupal; announcer, Phil Harris; scorers, Messrs. Kearns, Creighton and Kennedy; offcial timers, Dr. Baird and Dr. Nagle; measurers, Messrs. Fleming, Washington and J. O'Gorman.

The executive of the O.U.A.A., on behalf of the students, desire to express their hearty thanks and appreciation to the following who so generously donated valuable prizes for the field sports: His Grace Archbishop Dontenwill, O.M.I., D.D., Superior General of the Oblates; Very Rev. W. J. Murphy, O.M.I., D.D., Rector; Rev. Fr. Jeannotte, O.M.I., Rev. Fr. McGowan, O.M.I., Bursar; Ketchum & Co., Hurd & Co., J. H. Cowan, The 2 Macs, A. G. Pittaway, Côté & Co., Capital Pharmacy, H. J. Sims & Co., Robt. Masson, R. J. Devlin, McDonald Clothing Co., L. N. Poulin, Provost & Allard, S. Bilsky, Henry Birks & Son, Bedard Bros., J. A. Lapointe, E. B. Fisher, J. Lajoie, A. McMillan, B. Slattery, Moyneur & Co., and O.U.A.A.

Joint Athletic Meet.   Victoria Day, Varsity Oval, 1910.

Everything was in perfect shape for the grand International Track and Field Sports, held on Varsity Oval, May 24, 1910, under the joint auspices of the O.A.A.C. and the O.U.A.A. The committee in charge worked hard for the success of the meet and secured America's best athletes for the afternoon's select offering. Such crack men as Bobbie Cloughan of the Irish-Americans, N.Y.C.; Jack Near of Central "Y.," Toronto; Alex. Cameron of Tecumsehs, Toronto; Bobbie Kerr, world's champion; Frank Lukeman, and Halpenny, of the M.A.A.A., Montreal; Pelletier, Fabre, Lauzon, of the National A.A.A., Montreal; Charlie Kinsella of O.U. A.A.; Ellard White, Brockville Harriers; H. Hebert, Tressiders, and many local athletes were seen in action. Three thousand people were present and enjoyed the thrilling performances very much. The Duke of Cornwall's Own Band, 43rd Regt., played popular airs during the afternoon. A neat programme of events, with the club's colors invested, was compiled by Mr. Nick Bawlf, chairman of Advertising, and many hundreds were sold. Rev. W. J. Stanton, O. M.I., Bert Gilligan and Phil Harris worked in conjunction with Mr. Weldy Bate, H. Washington, R. Gaisford, D. J. O'Donohue, H. Nutting, Dr. D. H. Baird, and J. Marsden, of the O.A.A.C., and made the meet the greatest ever held in Ottawa. Handsome cups and medals were awarded the winners.

The following athletes from Ottawa University took part in the meet, but considering the class of entries they made a most favorable showing, Kinsella getting third in the hundred, while Burroughs and "Joe" Moore each received bronze medals for pluckily finishing out the hard ten mile grind in the Marathon race: Capt. Charlie Kinsella, Sylvester Quilty, Joe Moore, F. Burroughs, R. Guindon, J. Muzanti, G. Guindon, J. Chantal, R. Sheehy, H. Murtagh, P. Lacey, J. Perron, Gustave Gallopin, O. Kennedy and others.

The list of events and winners with time and distance follows:—
SUMMARY OF EVENTS.

100 yards dash, first heat: 1, Kerr (Hamilton); 2, Kinsella (Ottawa College); 3, Pelletier (National A.A.). Time, 10 secs.

Second heat: 1, Lukeman (Montreal A.A.); 2, Cloughan (Irish-American); 3, McPhail. Time, 10 1/5 secs.

Final: 1, Kerr; *Cloughan; *Lukeman; 4, Kinsella. Time, 9 4/5 secs. (*Dead heat).

440 yards dash: 1, Tressider (Montreal); 2, Herbert (National A.A.); 3, Garveck (O.A.A.C.). Time, 54 secs.

Running broad jump: 1, Lukeman (22 ft.); 2, Corbett (19 ft: 9½ ins.); 3, Pritchard (19 ft. 9 ins.).

City School one mile Relay: 1, Ottawa College Small Yard; 2, Glashan School No. 1; 3, Glashan School No. 2.

One mile run: 1, Near (Toronto); 2, Tubman (O.A.A.C.); 3, Vickers. Time, 4.51.

Pole vault: 1, Halpenny (M.A.A.A.); 2, Cameron (Tecumseh A.A.). Height, 11 ft. 6 ins.

220 yards dash: 1, Cloughan; 2, Kerr; 3, Pelletier. Time, 22 2-5.

Running high jump: 1, Lukeman; 2, Cameron. Height, 6 ft. 1 in.

880 yards run: 1, Near; 2, Hebert; 3, Tressider. Time, 2.03.

High School one mile Relay: 1, Renfrew Collegiate; 2, Ottawa College A.A.A.

10 mile Marathon: 1st, Ed. Fabre, National A.A.A., Montreal; 2nd, Ellard White, Brockville Harriers; 3rd, Theriault, St. Patrick's A.A.A.; 4th, Bert George, Gordon Harriers, Montreal; 5th, F. Lauzon, National A.A.A., Montreal; 6th, E. Lefebvre, unattached; 7th, Jack Darragh, O.A.A.C.; 8th, C. Johnson, unattached; 9th, J. E. Langlois, N.A.A.A., Montreal; 10th, Fred Atley, Central Y.M.C.A., Toronto; 11th, F. Burroughs, O.U.A.A.; 12th, J. Moore, O.U.A.A. Time, 58 mins.

Ottawa City Amateur Baseball League, 1910.

OFFICIAL STANDING TO DATE.

	Won.	Lost.	Tie.	Percent.
Pastimes	2	0	1	1000
Ottawa Univ.	3	2	1	600
O.A.A.C.	3	2	0	600
Y. M. C. A.	2	2	0	500
Maple Leafs...	1	2	0	333
St. Patrick's	0	2	0	000

BATTING AVERAGES OF "O.U." PLAYERS.

	Games.	A.B.	Hits.	Percent.
M. O'Neill	6	21	10	.476
C. Kinsella...	4	12	5	.416
Morriseau	6	14	4	.285
C. O'Neill...	6	21	5	.238
J. Muzanti	6	19	4	.219
Lamoureux...	6	19	3	.157
Killean...	6	22	3	.136
F. Curry...	4	10	1	.100
Smith...	5	16	'	.062
Contway...	1	2		.500

Notes and Hits.

Some system to our "Rene" Lamoureux with eight strike-outs in six innings.

* * *

Bert McGraw Gilligan says there's nothing to it but a repetition of 1908.

* * *

Ch. O'Neill has it on Hal. Chase as a first sacker. He can slide for home plate, too. Yes? Not?

* * *

Nothing to it with Kinsella on first but a sure steal of second, third and home.

* * *

Have you seen Johnnie Evers Curry on the second sack? We will have a hard time to hold him for the season with offers being turned down by him every day.

* * *

Father Stanton's Cardinals look like the one best bet for the 1910 pennant.

* * *

Muzanti plays third base like a big leaguer, and Killian has the O.K. sign tacked on him as a short-stop.

* * *

Capt. "Mac" O'Neil looks like a winner with his present batting average. Mac will have the Baird Trophy put in a glass case.

* * *

Mike Smith has made good as an outfielder.

* * *

Oh, you pinch-hitter, Dick Sheehy; and making first base on a dropped third strike!

Of Local Interest.

The Following Addresses were Presented to Reverend Fathers
Filiatreault and O'Toole on the Occasion of their
Sacerdotal Ordination:

To Rev. Father Geo. W. O'Toole, '06.

Rev. and Dear Father,—

As sons of Catholic parents we have, f.om our earliest childhood, been taught to look with awe and reverence upon the holy
office of the priesthood, and to regard it as the loftiest calling to
which man can hope to aspire. We become more and more conscious of the truth of this teaching as years advance, for we find
written in the pages of history of all civilized nations the spirit of
sacrifice, and the persevering zeal, and courage of those men, who
hearkening to their Master's call, cut the bond of earthly ties to
follow in the footsteps of the Saviour. We to-day are witnesses to
the fact that this divinely kindled fire burns as strongly as ever in
the hearts of the Catholic clergy as at any other period of Christianity. It is but natural then, that on an occasion such as this, when
one whom we have been wont to daily greet as friend has been elevated to a place among Christ's chosen band, that we should express to him the depth of the pleasure we experience that a former
companion should be so singularly favored.

You have to-day completed a long and arduous course of academic studies. While a student in Arts in Ottawa University, your
assiduous application to every branch of study, your gentlemanly
deportment, and the active interest you took in all social phases of
college life, gained for you an enviable position among your fellows.
During the past four years you have applied yourself to the study
of the noblest of the sciences, and in fitting yourself to take an
active part in the struggle which the church is ever waging against
the combined forces of untruth and irreligion. You are about to
leave our midst and to enter the world where, no doubt, your many
years of serious study and your careful religious training will bear
their fruit.

We feel, that as friends, we are not asking too great a favor
when we put forth the request that when you are officiating at the
Holy Sacrifice of the Mass you will sometimes remember your friends
of college days.

Be assured, Rev. Father, that in leaving us you carry away
with you our heartfelt wishes for every future success. It is our
hope and prayer that yours may be a long and happy career in the
Lord's vineyard.

THE STUDENTS OF THE UNIVERSITY OF OTTAWA.

May 21st, 1910.

To the Reverend Father,

R. O. Filiatreault.

Reverend and Dear Father,—

We the students of Ottawa University assemble here to-day to give expression to the feeling of gratification which they experience at your elevation to the sublime dignity of Christ's ministry. You have always looked forward with fond hope to the time when you would be raised to the sacred office of the holy priesthood, but to-day your cup of happiness is filled to overflowing, when the cherished goal has been reached.

As students of the University from which you graduated just four short years ago, many of us still remember your familiar face, and recall with delight the many occasions on which you did yeoman service in upholding the honor of old Varsity in the department of athletics. Emblems of the many battles in which you participated upon the gridiron, and in which the colors of the garnet and grey were victorious, still hang upon our walls. Your studious application to duty, and the uniform excellence of your conduct during your college course, won for you the confidence of your professors and the esteem of your fellow students.

As Catholic students of a Catholic University, we naturally entertain profound respect for the priest, whoever he may be. Much more is this veneration felt when we behold one of those whose student life has been passed in our intimate companionship, or who has drunk from the same fountain of knowledge as that from which we are now obtaining the science that will fit us for our future careers. We wish to extend to you to-day our hearty congratulations and our best wishes. In turn we ask you not to forget us when officiating at the altar. Implore God to bless and guide us, that we also may be crowned with success in attaining to whatever vocation God may have called us.

Rest assured, Reverend and dear Father, that you go forth to fulfill the sacred duties of your high calling, accompanied by the earnest prayers and sincere good wishes of

THE STUDENTS OF OTTAWA UNIVERSITY.

The agent: "I would like to call your attention to a little work which I have here."

Gau-t-er: "Well, let me call your attention to a whole lot of work which I have here. Good-bye."

Bu-ke: "What prompts your jokes—inspiration?"

Br-n-n: "No, desperation."

Prof.: "What are bacteria?"

Levi: "Them little anymiles you see in cheese before they're out of their teens. They call 'em parisites in France, germs in Germany, and mikerobes in Ireland."

They say that a certain 7th Form man is threatened with tobaculosis.

O'G.: "Hello, Jack, where are you going?"

B-k-e: "'I have nothing for publication."

We always knew that the comet was a fake.

Prof. in Phy.: Pay attention, this is important.

Tracy: For the exam.?

Subdistinguists may come and subdistinguists may go, but we go on forever.

Prof. in Physics: B is the answer.

Stud.: Is it in light?

Prof.: No, in inches.

We saw many a *tale* about the comet before the 18th, but not a *tail* afterwards.

But this could be understood.

How we shall miss L-cy!

"Naves et pueri"—what's the rest, Ch-rl-e?

Junior Department

Small Yard Lost to Strathconas.

In the first league game of Section B of the Intermediate City League, Strathconas defeated Small Yard by a score of 4 to 3. It looked as if the umpire gave the game to Strathconas; anyway he gave some poor decisions. The second game Strathconas again won, 12 to 8. Strathconas were playing Schultz and Jordan of St.

Pats. these two games. But for the next game, Small Yard took a great brace and won, 7 to 6.

The following was the line-up:—

STRATHCONAS.		COLLEGE.
McCann...	catcher	Milot (Capt.)
Dunne...	pitcher	Deschamps
McCarthy	1st	Renaud
Harris...	2nd	Brady
W. Pasch	3rd	J. Chartrand
Tobin...	s.s.	McCabe
A. Pasch	l.f.	Poulin
Schroeder	c.f.	Martin
Lamb	r.f.	Batterton

Umpire—Rev. Fr. Collins.

And then on Sunday, May 22nd, Small Yard again defeated Strathconas, 17 to 8, thus making the teams even in the race for the championship. The teams were:—

COLLEGE.		STRATHCONAS
Milot	c.	W. Pranschke
Deschamps	p.	W. Pasch
Renaud	1b.	V. McCarthy
Brady	2b.	F. Harris
McCabe	s.s.	J. Tobin
J. Chartrand	3b.	T. Pranschke
F. Poulin	l.f.	A. Pasch
Martin	c.f.	F. Woggan
Batterton	r.f.	J. Nolan

Mr. J. Casey acted as umpire to the entire satisfaction of both teams.

Small Yard also beat Diamonds in baseball by a score of 14 to 2. They were supposed to play Hull seconds, but Hull backed out and wouldn't play.

The League standing at present is:—

	Won.	Lost.	To Play.
Strathconas...	2	2	2
Small Yard...	2	2	2

The remaining games are as follows:—Sat., May 26, Small Yard at Strathconas (Park); Sun., June 3, Strathconas at College (Oval).

The standing of the Intermural League is :—

	Won.	Lost.	To Play.
Sullivan's team...	5	2	1
Madden's team	4	2	2
Renaud's team	3	3	2
Milot's team	2	4	2
Batterton's team...	2	5	1

Small Yard had two teams in the Relay races on Victoria Day, the first and third. The first team ran against the Renfrew Collegiate, Big Yard and Ottawa Collegiate. They were too small for such big men as Renfrews, and Collegiates, and Big Yard. Batterton was the last man to run for Small Yard, but he had too much of a lead to overcome, so he did not win. The third team won the City School Relay race against Glashan No. 1 and 2 and Percy St. School in 3.18. Côté was the first man, and gained a big lead. Then Guertin, Desrosiers and Braithwaite came next and held and increased this lead.

Congratulations, Juniors, on your win in the Relay race.

Reggie D. beware of McDougal Ave.

M-phy, J. D., and S-l-oan, don't you think it would be wise to wait until "the good old summer time" for those little walks.

Remember, boys, you are on the last lap. Get in some good work and make the coming exams. a grand success.

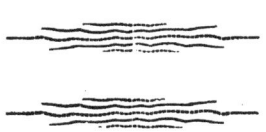

Vol. XII.   OTTAWA, ONT., JUNE, 1910.   No. 9

Entered at the Post Office at Ottawa, Ont., as Second-Class Matter.

PRIZE DEBATE

The Medallist's Speech

"Labour Unions are more detrimental than beneficial to society."

While beforehand friendly relations may exist between masters and men, the introduction of labour unions is sure to breed trouble. They uphold the doctrine that employers and employed are merely two contracting parties, and that the one should show no deference to or admit the superiority of the other.   Gentlemen, I say in this they are wrong; no matter who our masters may be, or what their characters, the fact still remains that they are superior to us, and as such ought to be treated with certain distinction.   Thus antagonism spreads opposition where concord should exist, and then the result of this trouble — the havoc-laden strike comes and spreads strife and confusion where before was all serenity.   As an institution which stirs up discord and trouble, anarchy and socialism, which makes the people discontented and greedy, I say labour unions ought to be entirely abolished.   Labour unions, in many cases unconsciously, arouse among the lower classes a feeling of resentment against the rich, a hatred of the man who controls their income, and little by little the smouldering flame grows greater, and finally bursts forth into a blaze of fury.   I here speak of Socialism, one of the greatest evils with which a country could be attacked.   I do not say that unions directly produce Socialism, but I do say that so great is their tendency towards such, so great is the influence wielded by the speeches clamoring against the wealthy, that nothing short of a miracle can restrain the members from entertaining intense animosity towards their so-called oppressors, and of ultimately joining the Socialistic ranks. Here are a few words from Bishop Spalding, an authority on social questions: "When workingmen have learned to confide their dearest interests to a labor union it will not be difficult to persuade them to surrender themselves both body and soul to a Socialistic state." No one can deny that these unions, however good their intention, contain the first seeds of Socialism — enmity towards the rich.

It seems to be the settled policy of every union that the labourers must not work over-fast, in fact that they should do their utmost to delay the work in order the labour may become better distributed. One of their methods is the short hour day system by which less work will be done, and by which men may have to leave a task the completion of which might be of the greatest importance. But what do the unions care about the conveniences of others? It makes no difference to them who suffers by their regulations; the men are forced to discontinue their work, willingly or unwillingly, at the appointed hour, or they are subject to a heavy fine. Such are the methods employed by labor unions. By the very fact that the unions themselves cause the restriction of work, we must see that they are detrimental to society. By thus teaching the labourer to do the least possible amount of work for his employer, they are installing into him some of the worst principles of dishonesty, and, what is greatly to be regretted, are making direct attacks on his morals. Mr. George Balen, a prominent student of Sociology, says that there is a tendency among ardent unions to disapprove a workman's effort to do the most and best work he can, and that this disapproval comes from motives often very questionable. He says that this is most evident among the "ardent union men," showing that it is the unions themselves, not the individual men, which try to promote this dishonesty. If this is the result of labour unions to breed dishonesty among the men who constitute the bulwark of a nation, how can can anyone assert that they are beneficial?

There is a certain selfishness and jealousy apparent among unionists. There is a feeling of jealousy among the members, which has the effect of discouraging anyone from attempting to rise above his fellows, and hence of killing commendable individual ambition and suppressing all progress. The whole organized labour society seems to be imbued with a selfishness hard to be equalled. In seeking the exclusive advantages of their class, they lose all interest in the reforms which are instituted for the benefit of humanity. They fight the introduction of new methods that tend to facilitate economic production, and which ultimately will do good to the people at large. Thus I say they are holding back prosperity with their one-sidedness and hatred of innovations.

Let us consider lastly the bad influence which labour unions have on the individual man. The fact that a man is bound down to a union, is forced to do absolutely as he is told on matters over which he himself should have the right of exercising control, cannot but have a degenerating influence on those who have all their lives been used to freedom, to doing as they wish, not being forced to live up to certain rules but to work for whom and how long they please. When out of work, a unionist is a mere dependent, relying on a society for sustenance. This idea of surrendering one's interests to a society tends to destroy that individuality and responsibility which constitute two of the most valuable characteristics that a nation can cultivate in its citizens, and especially do we need this spirit of responsibility among the working classes, as on them, after all, depends the material success or advancement of the commonwealth.

There is another fact about labour unions which tends to make them an evil influence. As practically secret societies, with rules and regulations of their own, they have a tendency to turn men against all religion, and even if they do not absolutely do so, they produce in thier members a kind of indifference and give them loose opinions on matters of morals and religion. It is certain that they are frequently so engrossed with the interests of their unions that they begin to disregard all others. Any allegiance that they may hitherto have owed to their religion, they now cast off. If man cannot serve two masters, some of them say that they cannot be ardent unionists and still attend to their religious duties. Here is the declaration of one unionist, a declaration which has been frequently reiterated by various members of the same class:

"My fidelity to the union shall in no sense be interfered with by any allegiance that I may now or hereafter owe to any other organization, social, political, or religious."

What does this say? It says that before the society of the state, before the government of this country, and, worst of all, before the church in whose doctrine he was reared, he places the interests of his union. Does this bespeak a law-abiding society which is doing its utmost for the poor people of the country, and helping them on to better life? I do not think so. Labour unions oppose not only the government and all society, but most of all that mistress of all civilization — the church. When the influence of a labour union is so strong, so pernicious, that it not only prevents a man from performing the sacred duties imposed on him by his religion, but even causes him to regard it as a secondary consideration, then I say it is certainly time for us to awake to the awful menace that the labour union is to society.

MICHAEL J. O'GORMAN, '10.

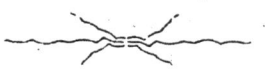

SHAKESPEARE'S AS YOU LIKE IT.

HAKESPEARE laughed out the title one day after reading what he had written. "Take it as you like it, in whatever way it pleases you. Take its mirth or seriousness, its matter of thought or fancy; its grave or lively characters; its youthful love or, self-conscious melancholy— Take anything you like out of it. There is plenty to please all kinds of men. It is written for your pleasure, take it for your pleasure." "I do not mind," he would have said, "how you use my play, if only you let the lover and his maiden, the Duke and his hunters, the fool and the shepherdess, Jaques and Silines and Phoebe, aye and the forest and the deer, do with it also what they like and as they like it. I have made a new thing; let every one enjoy it."

This "Pastoral Drama" is a combination of exquisite poetry, both descriptive and moral, forceful, playful and passionate. For variety and amiability of character, for gravity, wit, and broad humor, so perfect a piece of homage to happy state of a rural, inartificial life, that every scene in it, untainted with bad passions, occurs amid the pomp and garniture of God's creation, the green fields and the forest glades. In nature there is nothing melancholy.

We are in the forest of Arden, and under the green trees will we crack nuts and jokes with that pretty squirrel, the pranksome Rosalind, or descant upon her blithe wisdom with that sedate and most loving, devoted, cordial, confiding Celia. To make the world one "perfect Chrysolite of happiness, let every man respect the predilections of his fellows; nothing is worth quarrelling about, not even unkindness, for that is a mistake which always brings its own retri-

bution." Talk of the gallant and gentle bearing and stalwart proportions of her lover with the crystal-hearted Rosalind.

Rosalind is an enchantingly grand-spirited heroine. She is best
described in the following lines :—

"Nature presently distilled"
"Helen's cheek, but not her heart,"
"Cleopatra's majesty,"
"Atalanta's better part,"
"Sad Lucretia's modesty"
"Thus Rosalind of many parts"
"By heavenly synod was devised"
"Of many faces, eyes and hearts,"
"To have the touches dearest prized,"
"Heaven would that she these gifts should have"
"And I to live and die her slave."

Orlando's love is full of ga'ety and dashed with a shade of natural
melancholy. He is witty and is no mournful, depressing companion.
His love shows no fading in its rose, no false sen'iment, none of the
marks of a dying lover; no lean cheek, no sunken blue eyes, no unquestionable spirit, no beard neglected, no hose ungartered, no
bonnet unbanded, no sleeve unbuttoned, no shoe untied, no careless
dissolution.

Jaques is a solemn pretender to a quality not natural in him, a
grave coxcomb, pompous, and patronizing, ostensibly melancholy
and a cynical philosopher. Some remarkable passages came from
the lips of "Mr. Melancholy."

"I have neither the scholar's melancholy, which is emulation,
nor the musician's, which is fanatical : nor the courtier's, which is
proud, nor the soldier's, which is ambitious, nor the lawyer's, which
is politic; nor the lady's, which is nice; nor the lover's, which is all
these : but it is a melancholy of mind, cross, compounded of many
simples, extracted from many objects and indeed the sundry contemplation of my travels in which my after rumination wraps me
in a most humorous address."

The banished Duke is a noble gentleman worldly wise, gallant
in misfortune, changing stubborness of ill-luck into so quiet and
sweet a style, that every one is happy in his company. The Duke
"finds tongues in trees, books in running brooks, sermons in stones
and good in everything."

In reading "As You Like It" we dwell in a world of moral
beauty. Its characters soothe and heal the troubles of the world.
We see the beautiful forest of Arden, with its broad oaks and quiet
moving streams, new sandy banks, green swards, brawling brooks,
merry-throated birds, herds of deer, thickets of brambles and green
holly, and meadows with sheep. A lovely place for beautiful people
to dwell in and there we will leave them.

PHIL. C. HARRIS, '11.

Fidelity to Principles in Politics

HE sphere of politics is connected most intimately with the government of any country; and the government of a country usually is established by the people. They are living in one great community; they have common interests; and they have given powers to certain bodies of men to look after those interests for the common good of all. Hence, it becomes anyone desiring to enter politics to show that he hás the interest of the people at heart, and that he is ready to do what is fair and honest under all circumstances. And, when he has attained to a seat in Parliament, he should steadily aim to advance the good of those who have placed him there, and not only that, but the welfare of the nation in general. He is there in trust, and must answer to his constituents, as well as to his country.

Now, above all, and before all things else, a politician, especially if he be a Catholic, should adhere firmly to the principles of his faith. He ought never to sacrifice the interests of the Church to the interests of the State. Why so? Because the Church is superior to the State. The Church is universal; at least the Catholic Church is, and, moreover, this institution is the one government established directly by God. And it is doing His work on earth. While, on the other hand, a purely human government is merely the creation and servant of the people of its own particular state. It is for this reason, therefore, that a conscientious politician must not make the State superior to the Church. If a Catholic does so, he is no Catholic at all; and he can never be one until he rectifies his mistake. Moreover, one who is not guided by the principles of religion is seldom restrained by any principles whatever. In politics he is likely to become corrupt, and even dangerous to the country. This has often been exemplified in the French Parliament, where unprincipled scoundrels have repeatedly looted and burned the property and destroyed the lives of the very citizens whom they ought to have protected. Another example, exhibiting the direct opposite of the evils just mentioned, was the action of Mr. Devlin in 1896, if I remember rightly, when that most honorable gentleman stood firm for his religion, and withdrew himself from his party over the Manitoba School Bill. He is famous now, if only for that one act alone. So, there only remains for a gentleman, and a man of noble character, to espouse true religious principles in politics, and to follow them unswervingly. He will then always be found on the side of right and justice, and the people will surely, and with the best of reason, place all confidence in him.

Next, the politician should be honest, and, in his profession, even scrupulous in this respect. For, there is no place where a man gains either greater fame, or greater notoriety, than in the political world. Either he will leave politics with honor attached to his name, or he will be branded as a rascal. He is constantly before the eyes of the public, and they will not fail to scrutinize his actions, especially where it directly concerns their own pockets. Here again, then, let us say that sound principles have the greatest advantage. History, in fact, over and over again, proves it to be true that a man who clings to the policy of honesty is the man who will eventually find his way to success. In ninety-nine cases out of a hundred, the world's great men have been persons of principle. They needed it in order to persevere. Rarely does the dishonest grafter rise to any great degree of public confidence. And why should he ever reach a prominent position when his character, as a public man, is disgraceful? The people will soon find out if their money is being wasted. And then what happens? Notoriety first, and then political oblivion comes as the just punishment of the political sinner. Indeed, there is no other virtue which has so great an effect in politics as that of strict honesty. The government has the control and expenditure of public money. This public money amounts to no inconsiderable sum, and the people know it, as why should they not? And hence the administration that is pure and honest will be like the rotten one, responsible to the people, but, unlike it, honored and sustained by them. Therefore, let the politician look to his public morals. They may need correcting now and then. Let him follow the one straight course of justice and equity if he would become another Gladstone, or another Washington.

So, gentlemen, I would repeat that loyalty to one's trust, and uprightness on all occasions, is the only true and safe road in the maze of politics; that in this rising country of ours nothing is so needful, at present, as good, clean politics; that, if Canada is ever to be the great nation which she promises to become, great and noble men must be found in the lobbies of our Houses of Parliament; men who, like many other noble and distinguished Canadians that have adorned our history, will subordinate all private interest to the one of their country's good, and, dying will still live on through the centuries in the hearts of their countrymen.

J. B. II.

NEVER MIND.

When the day looks sort o' dusty,
An' your grit is gittin' rusty,
An' your courage somewhat musty—
    NEVER MIND!
Keep a-tuggin' at the tether,
Head an' heart an' heads together,
Through all sorts o' wind an' weather
    Bein' kind!

When your burden nearly bests you,
An' no sum o' smilin' rests you,
An' all sorts o' trouble tests you—
    NEVER MIND!
Chuck some cheer into your talkin',
Put some spring into your walkin',
Leave old Gran'pa Grouch a-stalkin'
    Far behind!

When your spirit feels like sighin',
An' it seems there's no use tryin'
To stave off a spell o' cryin'—
    NEVER MIND!
Men were made to bear some sorrow,
Tho' it's not a thing to borrow—
But you're apt to strike to-morrow
    Some big find!

When your way don't bloom with roses,
An' your way no sun discloses,
When your faith in fear reposes—
    NEVER MIND!
Hold your head a little higher,
Draw your hopes a little nigher,
To a better end aspire,
    Through the grind!

'Course, the road is often muddy,
An' the skies ain't always ruddy,
But if you'll jest stop an' study,
    You'll find
That the fellow who's a-winnin'
An' to sunny slopes a-spinnin'
Has kept sayin' since beginnin',
    NEVER MIND!

—Anon.

Quebec and Champlain.

HE recent celebration held at Quebec in honor of its never-to be-forgotten founder, recalls vividly to our minds the history of that grand old city and the wonderful accomplishments of Samuel de Champlain. Situated high on the right bank of the St. Lawrence, whose waters its bristling cannon overlook, it may well be called the Gibraltar of America.

What more pleasing sight, or what will bring back more distinctly the history of New France, than to stand on its walls and view the surroundings? Across the river is Point Lévis, (now crowned with colleges and churches), the silent onlooker when Wolfe's dauntless Highlanders scaled the steep cliffs opposite and prepared the way for the rest of the army, the night before the battle that made Canada a British possession. Below us are the Plains of Abraham. How vivid is the picture of the English army of four thousand five hundred men drawn up ready for battle at daybreak on that memorable day, watching in silence the soldiers of Montcalm mustering for the contest, and determined to conquer a worthy foe fighting for their dearest possession. Those two deadly volleys and that cry—"Charge!"—, the defeat of the French, and the glorious death of both generals, are here pictured as vividly as though we had been eye-witnesses.

Coming down into the city with its narrow streets and many quaint buildings falling into ruin through the medium of time we are at once struck with its charm. Every nook and corner recalls brave deeds and memories of the early pioneers. From here the Jesuits set out on their missions to the savage Indian tribes, giving themselves over to a life of extreme hardships and finally to a cruel death at the hands of those they were laboring to benefit by bringing them to a knowledge of Christianity. Near here Jacques Cartier spent that terrible winter, suffering untold misery among the uncivilized red men. Here, there, everywhere, are monuments and inscriptions to Champlain, Frontenac, Talon, Bishop Laval, and the many other who labored so unceasingly in the interests of Canada, and who laid the foundation of her present glory.

Undoubtedly the first heroic figure among the heroes of New France was Champlain. He was born in 1567 at Saintonge, on the Bay of Biscay. Love for the salt water was inherited from his ancestors and although he served in the army for some time he finally took to the sea.

His most notable undertaking prior to coming to Canada was a perilous expedition in the interests of his Sovereign to the West Indies and Mexico. For his success in this enterprise he was permitted to make an expedition to Canada in 1603. Landing, he met a large party of Indians who gave him an enthusiastic welcome and with whom he formed a friendship which later proved ruinous to Canada by bringing her into collision with the terrible Iroquois. After exploring the Saint Lawrence River and Gulf he returned to France to report his successes to the French king.

In 1604 we next hear of Champlain coming to Canada in company with De Monts to try and found a colony in Acadia at a favorable spot for trade with the Indians. Champlain preferred the St. Lawrence, and in 1606 obtained permission to found a colony there. This he did at Quebec in 1608 and from that date until his death in 1635 the history of Canada is the history of Champlain.

In 1609 in company with some Hurons and Algonquins to whom he had allied himself he sailed up the Richelieu to the lake which still bears his name and here, near where Fort Ticond roga was afterwards built, he had his first encounter with the Iroquois.

Three years later he returned to France in an endeavor to find some organization which would further the welfare of New France. While there he married Helen Boullé, a young girl of Protestant family who became a Catholic and sailed for America six years later where she remained until her death.

Let us now briefly trace the accomplishmen*s in exploration of this wonderful man in 1815. Starting from Quebec he ascended the Ottawa, crossed Lake Nipissing to Lake Huron and Georgian Bay. Having determined on an expedition against the Iroquois he started for their country by way of Lake Simcoe and the waters of the Trent to Lake Ontario, which he now saw for the first time. Crossing the lake he met the Iroquois at Oswego, but the attack on them was repulsed and Champlain wounded. In the middle of the summer of 1616 he got back to Quebec and subsequently sailed for France.

On his return his efforts were renewed with the same vigor as formerly and New France began to grow rapidly. However, bitter disappointment reached the struggling colony in 1628 when Sir David Kirke captured the supply ships coming from France, and appearing below Quebec demanded its surrender. The plucky inhabitants and their brave leader resisted as long as possible, but, having been reduced to eating roots they surrendered in 1629, and Champlain was sent a prisoner to England, where he remained until the Treaty of St. Germain-en-Laye three years' later restored him to Canada.

But the work of this untiring man was almost over, and on Christmas Day, 1635, he left New France and the world forever. His funeral was as magnificent as the young colony could make it, and no greater tribute could be rendered him than the tears of his soldiers and friends.

B. H., '13·

Reminiscences of Lumbering Days.

T was three o'clock when the train slowed up at the little flag-station in the woods.

"Hustle off now, boys," said the conductor. "We haven't long to stop here."

Quickly we bundled out, with our turkeys on our backs, thirty-five rugged lumbermen, bound for the tall timbers of Northern Quebec. The walking-boss was at the train to meet us and smiled approvingly as he ran his eagle-eye over the stalwart forms of this fresh contingent of pine-eaters.

"If you're as good as you look, you'll do me," he remarked with a knowing grin. "We'll try you out by asking you to walk to camp this afternoon; it's a mere step, not over fifteen miles.

"This way! follow me."

With whoops and yells the men started down the steep hill, at the foot of which the mighty Ottawa rolls on its never-changing way, whispering hoarsely to its rocky shores; while here and there the towering pines lean far out over the waters as though they fain would hear what the dark old river is sighing about.

We crossed by means of a heavy old float, which required the united efforts of six of the men to propel it. Then we turned and took a last long look at the Ontario shore and the railway track winding away eastward in the direction of R; but, turning resolutely about again, set our faces northward and entered the grim solitudes of the lumbering wilds, out of which we were not to emerge for seven long months.

It was a beautiful clear day in the latter part of October, and for a time the brisk walk through the pleasant woods proved agreeable and refreshing; but when the dusk began to thicken and the camp was not yet in sight, the songs and laughter suddenly changed to low murmurs and complaints against the boss, who had told us we had only fifteen miles before us. At last, about 8 o'clock, on ascending a steep hill, we beheld far down in the valley below, the light of a camp-fire glimmering on the placid surface of a broad sheet of water, and immediately a shout of gladness went up, which was answered by some twenty voices in camp below.

Here we were treated to a surprise, for now we learned from "the boss" that winter camps had not yet been built and that we should be obliged to sleep in tents for a week or ten days.

This piece of information did not tend to put the crew in any better humour, but in a short time we reached the tents where the jolly old cook received us cordially, and put up so appetizing a supper that the fatigues of the journey were soon forgotten.

That night was my first experience with sleeping in a tent. I did not find it particularly pleasant, as five of us were crowded into a three-man tent, and my feet were forced out under the edge of the canvas. To make matters worse, it snowed during the night, so when I awoke about 3 a.m. I found I had received a cold foot bath, which, however, was rather necessary after the tramp of the previous day. The cook was already astir, so I arose and stood by the big fire until breakfast at 5 a.m., having made up my mind to take the trail eastward as soon as daylight broke. But when the glorious orb of day came up, clear and red, lighting up hill and valley, lake and river; when all the living things of the forest came forth to welcome the grateful warmth of the declining October sun, my feelings on the subject of leaving the premises disappeared as suddenly as they arose, so I joined heartily with the crew in the work of erecting the rude log camps which were to protect us from the cold and tempest of the oncoming winter.

The following two weeks passed merrily. The weather continued warm and bright, so that no difficulty was found in collecting large quantities of moss to fill the chinks between the logs, which formed the walls of cook and sleep camps. When the buildings were all complete, and I had a comfortable little corner set aside as an office. I began to enjoy the life thoroughly, and to-day I look back upon those days spent in the lumberwoods as some of the most profitable and pleasant of my life.

On the morning of Nov. 7th we arose to find that Winter had visited us during the night, and had covered the bare dun-colored earth in a perfectly new garb of shimmering white, and from that day forward until the long, bright March days changed mother earth's covering into little rivulets and freshets, all was stir and bustle around our rude log buildings on the shores of the "Fils du Grand."

Sometimes, it is true, it was quite lonely in the immediate vicinity of camp; particularly about mid-winter, when the men no longer came in at dinner-time. Then the cook, cookees, and clerk, were alone from five until five again, but they enjoyed all the better the presence of the men, when at dusk they came rushing in, singing and shouting; for no class of workmen are happier and more good-natured so long as they have a good boss and a skillful cook. There is a great deal of imposition practiced by designing individuals, who, looking with longing eyes at the neat wages paid for experienced cooks, hire with lumber companies during July and August, relying upon the patience and good nature of the crew to tolerate them until they will really have learned to cook.

This particular winter it was our misfortune to have a very bad cook sent up from Ottawa, with a pocketful of recommendations from the company. After the first day it was apparent that he could not cook at all; one of the crew aptly putting it when he said, "that fellow couldn't boil water without burning it." So the crew began to make it hot for him, and the poetically inclined set to work to compose rhymes by which they could the better express their disgust for the new "chef." Then one of the violinists, who nightly rasped out music for the assembled company, took up the words and set them to jaunty airs which the men yelled at the top of their voices, hoping the cook would hear them in the kitchen. I recall one of those verses which ran somewhat thus:

We go out in the morning to skid the billots,
The pork it is raw and the bread it is dough,
The biscuits are harder than bricks in the wall,
We'd be better by far had we no cook at all,—
Now don't you think so?

This state of affairs lasted about a week, the foreman making no effort to quiet the men, for he felt that if the fellow did not take the hint and go it would be his duty to get rid of him anyway, in spite of company recommendations. However, one morning, becoming thoroughly alarmed at the threats of forcible expulsion, he picked up his belongings and decamped, much to the relief of everybody, the cookee taking his place until a real live cook could be got. In some localities the cookee gets the name of "devil"; this because he is usually so begrimed with black off the pots that it is supposed he resembles His Satanic Majesty.

The evenings are spent in singing, story-telling, and grinding axes for the morrow, while Saturday night is given up to dancing, the foreman showing his approval by giving an extra half-hour before shouting "lights out." Sundays the men have to wash and mend, for no other day is given them on which to do this work. Reading matter is scarce, and at times what is to be found lying around is far from being edifying. There is a

chance here for those who have means to found little libraries
for these poor fellows, shut off from civilization during six or
seven months out of the twelve. Of course irresponsible persons
should not be allowed to scatter literature among lumbermen,
but a few good elevating books and periodicals would do a
great deal, and would be sure to be read by everybody who can
read at all.

One of the most important events of the winter is the visit
of the priest to the camp. It is impossible to estimate the amount
of good that is accomplished by the hardy missionaries who
spend the winter months among these scattered but not forgotten
sheep, dear to the heart of the good shepherd. In the camp the
priest finds many a poor soul who has been away from the sacra-
ments for years. His winters are spent in the lumbering wilds,
his summers perhaps in the city, but while in the city he never
thinks of the more important and spiritual side of life, but returns once more to the old life of the woods, thus remaining
until the priest seeks him out in his own haunts, and in Holy
Confession relieves him of the weight that has bowed him down
for years. It is elevating to behold the bent and penitent forms
of the men as they silently pass to and from Confession. And
oh! with what joy they assist at the Holy Sacrifice on the following morning, offered up on that rude altar, and amidst such rude
surroundings, while overhead the whispering pines sing a new
song of love and peace and pardon. Henceforth the men look
upon their rough old log camp in a new and holy light, for has
not Christ the Prince of Peace deigned to come and dwell therein? Has He not, moreover, shown them that though they be far
away, and forgotten perhaps by the gay world of wealth and
fashion, they are not forgotten by Him, but are still dear, very
dear, to His Sacred Heart. And so they go about their duties
with glad and joyful hearts, and the foreman remarks that it is
a good thing to have the priest come; the men, he says, are
afterwards more reasonable and patient.

An amusing incident occurred the day the priest visited us.
He arrived about noon, and seeing nobody around, was about to
enter the cook-camp when he met the black and grimy cook's
assistant in the doorway.

"Are you the cook?" said the priest.

"No, I'm the devil," replied the boy.

"Well," said Father F., "I have seen a great deal of your
work, but this is my first encounter with the workman."

Our bran new cook was quite skillful in his art. He was a

French-Canadian who spoke little English. The boss was English, and had difficulty in making himself understood to the cook. One day he told the chef that he expected some of the head men of the company that day, and, Fred, said he, "try to have a good meal for them." The cook replied that it was hard to get up specialties on so short notice. "Oh, well then," said the boss, "what you have is good enough. You can make a little apology."

"Look here, now, boss," said Fred, "how you t'ink I go to make dat; I got no heggs."

Often in the dead silence of winter, at the lone hour of one in the morning, while you lie awake in your bunk unable to sleep for some unknown reason, a dread sound shivers through the forests and over the plains. Then the horses tremble and stamp excitedly in their stalls, and a shudder runs through your own frame, for even here, safe in your snug log camp, this cry of the timber wolf—this fierce wail of hunger—is terrifying to listen to.

Then the screech owl flutters into a pine tree overhead and sets up its unearthly croaking. The silence of night no longer oppresses you; on the contrary in order to have silence enough to enable you to again enter the land of dreams, you must arise and shy a few snowballs.

Spring comes at last, and the stern old King Frost is forced to loose his icy grip upon nature. Now the echoing woods ring all day long with the call of the crow and the hollow sound of the wood-cock, drumming on the dry trunks of dead trees. The little squirrels come forth and chirp and twitter around the camp doors; the wild hares frisk and run, chasing each other over logs and snow-heaps.

The music of the waterfalls, faint at first, grows louder and deeper each day, and soon the well-known boom, boom of the logs breaking loose from their ice fetters announce the joyful tidings that the old life of log-cutting and log-hauling is at an end. Now must we say farewell to the dear old camp, and not without feelings of sadness do we depart; the old familiar spot has become engraven on our hearts and memories, but the duties of our calling bid us go forth. In the lumberman's phraseology: "The drive is on."

A. R., '10.

Happiness Little Increased by Wealth

IRST of all, let us determine what we are to understand by the term *wealth*. Wealth, as we see it, is generally recognized as the possession of considerably more property than is necessary for the maintenance of life in comfort. In this sense let us view it; only, I would say, if at all, let it be regarded as meaning more than this. For, the standard by which a man's opulence is estimated depends greatly on external conditions; as now, in our prosperous times, immense numbers of people are in easy circumstances, though not rich, who would surely have been called wealthy in days less fortunate. Therefore, there is a distinction to be made between competency and affluence, or wealth. At any rate, the greater the explanation of the one, the more clear will the other be. When we speak of a competencq, to-day, we mean a state of a man's financial affairs, which preserves him from worry about the future. It releases him from anxiety about his next meal, and removes all fear about his coal bill, or the family needs; while, at the same time, he feels that he can afford to let his wife and children dress well, or go to the theatre when they wish, or even to take long journeys and pleasure-trips. It is this happy condition of affairs that enables a man to leave his work for several days, if necessary, and accompany his family on such occasions. He is not poor; neither is he very rich. He has enough to do to keep him busy. He is happy. Now, there is that other state to be considered — the state of the really wealthy man. But no, not exactly this,—to say that he is really wealthy involves a contradiction. True, he is wealthy in one sense, in that he possesses a superabundance, but he is lacking in what money can never buy, true wealth-happiness. It becomes our business now to consider that money brings little of true happiness.

In accordance with the wording of the main theme of these paragraphs, it is admitted that the money of the middle-class man brings him some happiness; but it does so inasmuch as it saves him from the miseries of poverty. A little more than a sufficiency seems to me to be best and most natural; but, poverty, and likewise great wealth, are two extremes, and abnormal. Why is excess of wealth abnormal? It is so for several reasons. But I shall not speak of them all here. First, however, I may say, the one who is owner of much surplus money is most usually annoyed about it. He has troubles: How will he invest it in order to make more

-money out of it; will the banks break, or the factory burn; have the stocks gone up, and will his money be doubled, or have they gone and left him poor; or,—all the endless complications attendant on great wealth,—will they ever give him rest? I was going to say, yes they will give him rest when he dies,—but no, he may not be sure about this either. Perhaps he has used dishonest methods to amass his fortune; and the image of certain poor, wretched, miserable, starving faces, possibly cold in death, may add to his cares, or form the substance of his troubled dreams.

Many are the anxieties and causes for worry that torment the very rich man. Among them are the manifold dangers of wealth. It is not necessary to mention more than a few of these. Human nature is weak at best, but especially so when surrounded by unhealthy conditions. Hence, when the children of millionaires find themselves in a position in which they can have almost all the money they want, for the mere asking, they are very liable to fall into every sort of excess; because, they have the means wherewith to procure all things that they desire. They are well-versed in the work of evil, and especially the scandals of modern times. They learn how to break the ties of domestic peace and harmony by watching the conduct of their superiors. They receive the training at home which is fitting them to commit afterwards their share of the Sins of Society.

Here we come to the great bane of this age, the so-called High Society, an institution distinctly peculiar to the wealthier class. The things done by members of this class have been so scandalous, in the past, that already a bad meaning is beginning to be attached to the word Society. One of the worst effects of this reign of the Smart Set is the divorce evil. It is the cause of untold misery, and well-night threatens the extinction of good society. Surely, happiness cannot reign where the family ties are broken, and where mutual distrust prevails. Can home be called home, where the husband, or the wife is not welcome? Will children bring happiness to parents, who are themselves divided? Not likely. Are those children not imitative by nature, and will they not follow the example set before them? You have only to consult experience to see. Oh, no! there cannot be peace at home. And where, then, if not at home? Certainly not in the club-room, nor in the gambling-den, nor at the race-track; for, all these mean trouble and anxiety, since they involve money losses, or gains. And, besides, they do not offer the consolation which the righteous man feels, when overtaken by cares and misfortunes. Many rich men live lives which are opposed to their consciences. Rarely do they make the best use of their money. They are annoyed, because they have heard somewhere about Dives who is in Hell for not making proper use of his money. So the wealthy man tries to shun the idea of death, because he knows that after dissolution, wherever he goes, he must leave behind his money. He will no longer possess those earthly goods on which he has set his heart. But, in the face of all this, the deadly love of lucre holds him transfixed, and he returns again to his former practices. Forsooth, there are many, very many people, who wish that they had now the happiness which was theirs when money was more scarce with them.

Is it not justifiable, therefore, to hold the belief that riches are a very precarious source of happiness to anyone? They may bring him some pleasure of a transitory nature, but it is more the satisfaction of human pride than real happiness. Is not the man of moderate means much more to be envied, who can have what he needs, without the troubles of poverty, and who is able to procure some of the things of wealth, without the cares belonging to that state? Assuredly, we must admit this fact. We cannot regard the question in any other light. The middle-class man of to-day has plenty to do to keep him out of mischief, and much good to accomplish in the world, while the millionaire hardly knows how to pass his days. Consequently, the position of the former is more fortunate than that of the latter. The man who sees that his daily work increases the happiness of mankind must be glad in his own heart. But, wealthy, indolent people are not workers. Their time hangs heavily on their hands. They remain undeveloped, and their minds are stagnant. Consequently, they cannot be happy. Of course, this does not apply to all members of the moneyed class; but, it is the general rule. Therefore, in conclusion, I would say that the happy medium is happy, indeed; and that, as truth never exists wholly on one side of an argument, neither does it do so here. Hence, wealth brings a little pleasure, and much unhappiness.

J. S., '11.

The Language of Baseball

O-MINGLED with those luring sounds that now rise from baseball parks throughout America where the home team is doing the entertaining is a discordant note. It emanates from various purists of the press who would eliminate slang from baseball stories and substitute plain English so that the casual reader as well as the faithful fan may comprehend its meaning.

Ever since baseball began it has had a language of its own. The slang that a baseball writer is accused of using profusely has become inseparably a part of the game. It is brief and graphic. It tells the story tersely and to the point. There is a picturesqueness in the accounts of ball games that is nowhere else encountered in the papers. The English which is used may not be errorless, and some of it may be unintelligible to the average reader, but it is vivid, concise, and usually coherent.

Is not the word "fan" picturesque? Imagine us going out to the grounds, sitting on a hard board seat, without any back, for two hours or longer, and acting as dignified as a crowd of old maids. Think of us clapping our hands vigorously when one of the boys stabs a hot grounder. Fancy us waving our handkerchiefs when our pet team has batted the opposing pitcher out of the box. Wouldn't it look sweet if we were to sit there and permit the umpire to give us the wrong end of a decision?

Your fan is no striking likeness of a mummy. He is thoroughly alive and awake. He goes to the game to forget his troubles, and to release the suppressed emotions he has been carrying since the last game. He is out for pleasure and he gets it,—if the home team wins, or the man behind him does not betray peevishness when he feels a pair of feet planted in the middle of his back. He gives convention the glad hand and he rejoices that he is a carefree, exuberant youngster.

Since he is picturesque and active, he demands that the stories about the game have similar qualities. He finds no pleasure in a style such as is used in describing a banquet or a convention. He cares little for the English so long as there is life and vigor in the details. To accomplish this effect the hard and fast rules of college are laid aside, and a new set is evolved which suits his purpose as nicely as a three-bagger, with two on, and two runs needed to tie the score.

The English that the college professor would call perfect was never intended for a sporting page. As a novelty it would be delightful to the fans, but as a continuous diet it would be no more wholesome than breakfast food three times daily. Imagine yourself picking up a favorite paper and finding the game of the previous day described as follows:

The baseball game yesterday between teams representing Pastimes and College respectively was one of the most exciting affairs ever seen at Varsity Oval. The young men of both teams played marvellously well and proved themselves adept in every department. As College made four runs and Pastimes three, the former won the game. Thanks to the ability of Mr. ——, the College catcher, in hitting the baseball, the men representing the College were able to obtain their four runs. Mr. —— distinguished himself by hitting the ball hard in the fifth inning, sending it so far that he was enabled to reach third base before it was retrieved. Needless to say the runners scored. His skill in this respect was the subject of much favorable comment on the bleachers and in the grand stand.

In another paper you might find the same game reported as follows:

Pastimes and College hammered the ball all over the lot on the opening fixture at Varsity Oval, the students running off with the candy, 4-3. Both teams uncorked the ginger bottle in the get-away. The big College back-stop was the star with the willow. He toed the plate with two on, in the fifth, bumped a bender on the trade-mark, and rapped it to the fence for a triple. He encored in the ninth for a smashing double, and the bleachers aeroplaned their emotions as two more runs tickled the score-board.

In this latter account no words are wasted, and no attempt is made to give details in the round-about way declared by the college professor to be correct English.

The nick-names lend additional color to baseball stories, and fans would never think of discarding them. What would we do, were it not for some of the words coined by baseball writers? Even the most exacting college professor does not hesitate to use these expressions. What professor would not use the word "fan" in preference to "a baseball spectator affected with enthusiasm"? "Fan" has become a part of our language. It is closely interwoven in our speech and will remain as long as baseball is America's national game.

There is no doubt but that occasionally some writers make a strained effort in the application of something new, but the critics should attack only these exaggerated instances.

If the language is comprehensible it will satisfy the fans who do not bother about has-beens, who are unable to distinguish between a well-known squeeze-play and a lemon attempt.

J. A. COUGHLAN, '13.

WEEKLY DEBATES, 1909-10.

On December 6, Mr. J. J. Contway, '11' and Mr. A. A. Unger, '14' contended that "The benefits derived from Labor Unions do not counterbalance the evils resulting from them." Mr. S. P. Quilty, '11' and Mr. G. F. Whibbs, '14' opposed this opinion. The judges, Messrs. M. J. O'Gara, '10' M. J. O'Gorman, '11, I. J. Rice, '12' L. A. Landriau, '13' and M. A. Gilligan, '14, decided in favor of the latter. Mr. D. J. Breen, '11' presided.

Mr. D. J. Breen, '11' and Mr. J. B. Muzzanté, '14' were successful in a debate held on December 13, against Messrs. P. C. Harris, '11' and J. D. O'Brien, '14' who were the negative on the subject: "For the common good it is better that public utilities should be owned and operated by governments and municipalities than by private individuals and corporations." The above decision was reached by Messrs. C. D. O'Gorman, '10' C. M. O'Halloran, '12' J. J. Sammon, '11' F. A. Landriau, '14' and L. W. Guillet, '14. Mr. J. J. Contway, '11' occupied the chair.

January 10 saw a very interesting debate as to whether the sufferings of Ireland under England have been greater than those of Poland under Russia. Messrs. C. F. O'Neil, '12' F. W. Hackett, '14' L. W. Guillet, '14' were the affirmative; Messrs. C. M. O'Halloran, '12, T. F. Poulin, '14' J. A. Shanahan, '14' the negative. Mr. M. J. O'Gara, '10' a chairman. The judges were Messrs. W. F. McDougal, '13' A. G. McHugh, '13' R. A. Lahaie, '14' M. J. Hogan, '14'

It was decided on January 17, the Students being allowed to enter upon the course of studies for any of the learned professions should be obliged to take the full Arts Course. The victors were Messrs. J Harrington, '12' F. V. Murtagh, '14' and J. M. Chartrand, '14. The negative was supported by Messrs. A. G. McHugh, '13' A. V. Freeland, '14' and J. S. Cross, '14' The following acted as judges: Messrs. M. J. Smith, '10, J. J. Sammon, '11' C. M. O'Halloran, '12' D. J. Dolan, '13; F. W. Hackett, '14. Mr. F. X. Corkery, '11, was in the chair.

January 24 saw a debate on a very live issue, "The Canadian

naval policy as laid down by the present Government is not that which is best suited to the demands of the Empire." Mr. P. P. Griffin, '11' made an efficient chairman. The debate was declared a draw, the chairman not desiring to give a casting vote. The judges were Messrs. C. D. O'Gorman, '10, P. C. Harris, '11' F. L. Mac-Evoy, '13' and J. J. Hogan, '14. Messrs. I. J. Rice, '12' M. J. Hogan, '14' and R. A. Lahaie, '14' as the affirmative, opposed Messrs. E. B. Letang, '12' P. J. Leacy, '14' and A. J. Martin, '14· At this meeting a vote of thanks and congratulation, moved by Mr. P. C. Harris, '11' and seconded by Mr. M. A. Gilligan, '14' on behalf of the Executive and members of the University Debating Society, was tendered to the victors of the Intercollegiate Debate against Queen's.

On February 7, Messrs. L. W. Kelley, '13' J. J. McNally, '14' and C. A. Mulvihill, '14' proved that a system of proportional representation should not be adopted in Canada. The losers were Messrs. D. J. Dolan, '13' Ellwood McNally, '14' and J. G. Minnock, '14· Mr. P. C. Harris, '11' was a very acceptable chairman. The judges were Messrs. M. J. O'Gara, '10' T. J. N'Neil, '11' I. J. Rice, '12' T. Ham. O'Reilly, '13' and P. J. Leacy, '14·

On February 14 it was decided that the Canadian Senate should not be abolished. Messrs. G. F. Coupal, '13' and R. Carter, '14' were the victors over Messrs. R. Leahy, '14' and F. Ainsborough, '14· Mr. T. J. O'Neil, '11' occupied the chair. Messrs. P. P. Griffin, '10, C. F. Gauthier, '10' S. P. Quilty, '11' T. J. Daley, '13' ard J. M. Martin, '14' were very able judges.

On February 21 a very live issue was debated: "Should the British House of Lords be maintained in its present constitution." The negative, Messrs. W. J. Cross, '13' J. Pelissier, '14' and T. Shanahan, '14' were successful over Messrs. O. E. Kennedy, '13' H. J. Robillard, '14' and S. St. Amand, '14· Mr. L. H. Tracy, '11' proved a very efficient chairman. The judges were F. Higgerty, '10' L. Boyle, '12' J. Harrington, '13' A. V. Murtagh, '14' J. Minnock, '14·

February 28 saw a most interesting debate as to whether "Free Public Libraries are productive of greater evil than greater good." The affirmative, Messrs. W. F. McDougal, '13' F. A. Landriau, '14' and F. X. J. Bourke, '14' were easily the victors over Messrs. T. Ham. O'Reilly, '13, L. A. Landriau, '13' and T. J. Daley, '13. Mr. F. E. Higgerty, '10' was a most able chairman. Messrs. E. A. Letang, '12' J. Q. Coughlan, '13' J. M. Minnock, '14' and J. J. McNally, '14' acted as judges.

March 10 saw one of the most successful debates held this season. The subject under discussion was: 'Resolved, that Labor Unions are more detrimental than beneficial to society." The affirmative, Messrs. F. E. Higgerty, '10' T. J. O'Neil, '11' and B. F. Hayes, '13' won over Messrs. J. J. Contway, '11, S. P. Quilty, '12, and J. Q. Coughlan, '13. Messrs. E. C. Boyle made a very good chairman. The judges were Messrs. J. J. Burke, '10' D. J. Breen, '11' J. J. Kennedy, '12' G. F. Coupal, '13' and C. A. Mulvihill, '14'

On March 14 was held one of the best debates of the season. The question under discussion was: "Resolved, that Great Britain and her colonies should adopt a system of conscription. " The negative, Messrs. I. J. Rice, '12' J. J. Harrington, '13' T. F. Curry, '13' won over Messrs. J. J. Kennedy, '12' E. B. Letang, '12' and A. G. McHugh, '13' Mr. C. F. O'Neill, '12' made a very acceptable chairman. Messrs. B. G. Dubois, '10' J. J. Contway, '11' L. W. Kelley, '13' W. J. Cross, '13' and F. V. Murtagh, '14' reached the above decision.

The last debate of the season of 1909_10 was held on March 21. The question under discussion was whether Free Trade between Canada and the United States would be benficial to Canada. By a very narrow margin the negative won. The victors were Messrs. J. J. Burke, '10' P. P. Griffin, '10' and C. F. O'Neill, '12; their opponents Messrs. B. G. Dubois, '10' F. Corkery, '11' and E. C. Boyle, '12' Mr. J. J. Kennedy acted as chairman. The decision was reached by Messrs. J. T. Brennan, '10, L. H. Tracey, '11' T. L. MacEvoy, '13' O. E. Kennedy, '13' and J. B. Muzante, '14' This debate ended what had proved to be a most successful season.

T. L. M., '13'

RESOLUTION OF SYMPATHY AND CONDOLENCE.

Ottawa University,
Ottawa, June 2, 1910.

WHEREAS, God in His infinite wisdom has seen fit to remove from this world Mr. Michael Mulvihill, the brother of our esteemed fellow-student, Cornelius Mulvihill;

THEREFORE BE IT RESOLVED, that we, the members of the Junior Department of Ottawa University, have learned with profound sorrow of the this untimely event, and respectfully tender to the members of the bereaved family our heartfelt sympathy and earnest condolence in this their hour of sorrow and affliction;

FURTHER RESOLVED, that copies of this resolution be sent to the bereaved family, and to The Review for. publication.

THE STUDENTS OF THE JUNIOR DEPARTMENT,
OTTAWA UNIVERSITY.

University of Ottawa Review

PUBLISHED BY THE STUDENTS.

THE OTTAWA UNIVERSITY REVIEW is the organ of the students. Its object is to aid the students in their literary development, to chronicle their doings in and out of class, and to unite more closely to their Alma Mater the students of the past and the present.

TERMS:

One dollar a year in advance. Single copies, 15 cents. Advertising rates on application Address all communications to the "UNIVERSITY OF OTTAWA REVIEW", OTTAWA, ONT

EDITORIAL STAFF :

J. BRENNAN, '10 ;   A. FLEMING, '11 ;   M. O'GARA, '10 ;
J. BURKE, '10 ;   PH. HARRIS, '11 ;   C. D. O'GORMAN, '10 ;
                  M. SMITH, '10.

Business Managers : C. GAUTHIER '10, ; D. BREEN, '11.
            G. GALLOPIN, Staff Artist.

Our Students are requested to patronize our Advertisers.

Vol. XII.   OTTAWA, ONT., JUNE, 1910.   No. 9

VALEDICTORY.

With this issue the Editorial Board of 1909-1910 brings its labors to a close. We have endeavored to follow the path traced by former editorial staffs, "to aid the students in their literary development, to chronicle their doings in and out of class, and to unite more closely the students of the past and present to their Alma Mater." We take a certain amount of pride in the fact that this year even more than formerly, the "Review" has been largely the work of under-graduates, and a faithful reflection of student life and activity. It is to be regretted that our extra-mural students (with a few honorable exceptions) have not displayed that lively interest in their College magazine which it has a right to expect. Let us hope that the year 1910-11 will see this unfortunate state of affairs remedied, both from the literary and financial point of view. To our subscribers and advertisers we tender sincere thanks for their practical encouragement, which has enabled us to produce a volume not altogether unworthy of its predecessors. In bidding farewell to the students we extend to them our best wishes for a happy vacation.

D. BREEN, '11.   A. FLEMING, '11.   M. O'GARA '10.   I. BURKE, '10.   M SMITH '10.   PH. HARRIS, '11.

LAW-ABIDING CANADA.

During the past year nearly 100,000 farmers have migrated from the United States to Canada. Towns have grown up and prosperity smiles upon them. Why this exodus? The cheapness and richness of our western land is one cause. In the early days of the Northern States the virgin land produced from 40 to 60 bushels of wheat per acre, and hardly ever cost more than $5 per acre. By repeated cropping the yield has dwindled to as low as 10 bushels per acre. The Canadian Northwest is to-day what the United States Northwest was 25 years ago. But another reason is furnished by a farmer who has settled in Saskatchewan, which we reproduce from the "Northwest Review"

"I'll tell you what it boils down to," he says. "Ever since the settlement of this country began, it has been understood and recognized that the man who breaks the law is going to be jailed. It don't matter if he is as spry as a gopher nor as husky as a buffalo. It don't make any odds if he can crawl into a prairie dog's hole. If he breaks the law he is going to be jailed, good and sure! He can have fifty guns and $50,000, he can have any sort of blame pull you like— but he is going to be jailed. It may take a day, a week, or a year; but he'll be jailed, sure. Maybe he'll kill a Northwest policeman— maybe he will Well, then, he'll hang, for a dead sure thing! He'll never buy a Northwest policeman, nor he'll never escape jail if he breaks the law. All Canada knows it, and that's why this country is a good country to live in."

Certainly this crude letter is as strong an indictment of the lax criminal law enforcement in the United States as any learned lawyer or judge could write. Between the lines it tells of the condoning of lawlessness, or misplaced sympathy for murderers, or political chicanery in the granting of pardons and commutations of sentence, which have become so important a part in American criminal jurisprudence. Statistics show that in the United States less than 2 per cent. of homicides arraigned are convicted, while in Germany the figures show 95 per cent., the other European countries showing a gradual decrease in the number of convictions until Scotland is reached, with 34 per cent. Two murderers in a hundred in America are convicted; in Canada, the murderer, according to this letter from a Saskatchewan farmer, will "hang, for a dead sure thing."

This may not furnish the reason for the immigration of the 100,000 farmers into Canada, but there can not be a surer way of attracting good citizens than by a fearless enforcement of the laws; and there can not be a better way of inviting the criminal element than a lax enforcement of those laws. The honest and upright man has no fear of strict enforcement of penal statutes, but the thug will give such a state or country a wide berth.

The "Agnetian Quarterly" is a finely illustrated paper. Articles deserving of appreciation are those on Edward McDowell, Frederic Ozanam, the poem "St. Catherine," and the critical essay on Gilbert K. Chesterton. The high tone of these quarterlies is a strong argument for those who favor less frequent appearance of College papers.

> The night has a thousand eyes,
>   And the day but one,
> Yet the light of the whole day dies
>   With the setting sun.
>
> The mind has a thousand eyes,
>   And the heart but one,
> But the light of a whole life dies
>   When love is done.
>
> —Collegian.

A quarterly exchange of rare merit is "The College Spokesman, from St. Joseph College. The March number just teems with good reading, particularly stories. An article on "Music and Life" shows the influence music has on the lives of men, in a clear and interesting way. Another author shows us in the Empire of Brute a day-dream of a future epoch, how man will have to concede the first place to the animal at some future time.

The appearance of Halley's comet in our end of the Solar system has inspired much poetry among our budding college poets. The following is a sample:

> A solitary wand'rer of the sky,
> Before thy vast immensity I bow
> In dread and awful wonder; knowing how
> Petty, weak, and insignificant I,
> Who looking on thy flaming mass, would cry—

Behold thy feebleness, O mortal man!
Thy puniness! Thy nothingness!
  Who can
But live a little, look about, and die.
But deed within my heart of hearts, I hear
A voice which speaks a language full of cheer,
And says, when in the realms of darkness vast,
Thou comet lost in nothingness hast past,
I shall live on and on, for God, the Just,
Didst give to me a soul, to thee but dust.

Besides the above mentioned, we beg to acknowledge receipt of the following: Vox Colegii, St. Mary's Angelos, The Argosy, Georgetown College Journal, Collegian, D'Youville Magazine, Columbiad, Solanian, Echoes from St. Anne's, Manitoba College Journal, Queen's University Journal, Pharos, St. John's U. Record, Xavier, Niagara Rainbow, St. Mary's Chimes, Trinity U. Review, Victorian, Allisonia, Patrician, St. Mary's Sentinel, Schoolman, The Laurel, Viatorian, University Monthly, The Xaverian, Acta Victoriana, O.A. C. Review.

Books and Reviews.

PHILEAS FOX, ATTORNEY. By Anna T. Sadlier. The Ave Maria, Notre Dame, Indiana. ($1.50).

The Ave Maria press can be relied upon to turn out only the best and choicest literature. The latest book from the busy pen of Miss Sadlier is a good sample of its wares. It is a book that anyone can read with profit and pleasure. It should be a great help to young men about to begin a chosen calling in the world. The hero shows himself to be not only an acute lawyer but a practical, devout Catholic. The story relates how at the outset of his legal career he meets with an opportunity to win fortune at the expense of honesty but he remains true to the high ideals of religion and justice and soon finds a suitable opening for his talents and attainments. There is not a dull page in the whole book, several of the incidents being "quite lively affairs." The love story, skillfully worked out, is not the least interesting part of this really valuable work.

BEST STORIES BY FOREMOST CATHOLIC AUTHORS.

During the past ten years there has been a marked change in Catholic publishing. Catholic newspapers and magazines have created a reading public. Catholic publishers have not been slow to realize this and to offer inducements to make this reading public still larger. Beside the increasing number of new books appearing from year to year, complete libraries are now offered at low prices on the easy payment plan, which enables almost any one to get a fine collection of good Catholic books. In this, as in many other ways, Benziger Bros. have taken the lead, and have recently issued a collection of 10 volumes entitled "THE BEST STORIES BY THE FORE-MOST CATHOLIC AUTHORS," with a splendid introduction by Dr. M. F. Egan. The books are well printed and attractively bound, and contain complete stories by no less than sixty-four Catholic writers, including such literary stars as Dr. Egan himself, Benson, Katharine Tynan, John Talbot Smith and Christian Reid. This splendid collection, published at a moderate price, should be in every Catholic home.

The political situation in England still continues to be featured in many of the leading reviews. *The Nineteenth Century* alone has four well written articles on this much-discussed question. Almost everyone admits that a reasonable reform of the House of Lords is desirable and necessary.

The May issue of the *Century Magazine* contains a very interesting article on Aerial Navigation. It clearly demonstrates the surprising progress of German plan for transatlantic service. The writer says, "It is believed that within five years an air liner will be capable of travelling seventy-five miles an hour ordinarily, and often one hundred miles in the upper levels. It is expected that airships will be able to make 3,000 miles per day." Ten years ago a prophecy of the present achievements of Germany's air navy would have been received with incredulity.

The Nineteenth Century for May has a splendid contribution entitled, "From Art to Social Reform." It is a most entertaining study of John Ruskin's art criticisms and his political economy, or rather his art of living. "Devotion to truth, then, thoroughness and carefullest observation of actual facts, earnest purpose in life, these are the salient points in the plan of Ruskin's training. Taken with the material surroundings, and the conversational and social atmosphere of a home whose head was a qualified lover and no mean supporter of art, they explain alike Ruskin's own excellent art work, the force of his criticisms, the truth as the superlative beauty of many of his descriptive passages, the ultimate trend of his teaching, the peculiarly didactic prophet like method of much of his argument, and above all the overpowering intensity of his appeals to the conscience and heart of humanity. It was the sincere, thorough pursuit of art, that turned the connoisseur of pictures into the most soulstirring optre not widely influential of prophets, perhaps of our time."

Priorum Temporum Flores.

During the past month we had the pleasure of a visit from the following alumni :—

Rev. Father MacCaulay, P.P., Osgoode, Ont.

Rev. Father Raymond, P.P., The Brook, Ont.

Rev. Father O'Toole, Bayswater.

Rev. Father Filiatreault, Aylmer, Que.

Rev. A. Reynolds, College Ste. Therese, Que.

Rev. Dr. O'Boyle, O.M.I., paid us a flying visit the other day. He passed through Ottawa with a party of forty-five French-Canadian families, who are going to settle in New Westminster and work in the great Fraser Valley Lumber Mills there. He says that all of last year's party are delighted with their new home.

An interesting event will take place on Sunday, June 26th, when Rev. John Burke, C.S.P., will celebrate his first mass. Father Burke has just completed a very successful Theological course at the Catholic University, Washington, and will, after a short vacation in Ottawa, begin missionary work with his brethren of the Paulist Order.

We are pleased to hear of the success of the following Ottawa men :—

W. H. Derham, E.E., Toronto 'Varsity.

P. Kirwan, 3rd year Science, Toronto 'Varsity.

G. Kirwan, 3rd year Science, Toronto 'Varsity.

J. B. Macdonald, 3rd year Science, Toronto 'Varsity.

I. Desrosiers, 3rd year Science, McGill.

A. Desrosiers, 2nd year Science, McGill.

E. Beroard, M.D., Queen's.

Dr. Beroard succeeds Dr. Brunet at the Ottawa General Hospital.

—Rev. Father Ross, Professor at Oscott Seminary, England, has been our guest during the last few days. The Rev. gentleman is much impressed with Canada and particularly with the beauty of the Capital.

—Rev. P. M. Cornellier, O.M.I., ex-Bursar at 'Varsity, paid us a call the other day, while en route for the celebration at Joliet, in connection with the fiftieth anniversary of the foundation of that institution. The genial Father is at present stationed in Edmonton, and says there is no place like the West.

—Rev. J. A. Lajeunesse, O.M.I., sailed for Europe with His Grace Archbishop Dontenwill, O.M.I. Father Lajeunesse will spend a year in the University of Cambridge.

—Rev. Father Gavary, O.M.I., sailed on June 12th for Europe, to assume the direction of the new Oblate Scho'as⁺icate in Turin, Italy. He was presented with a purse of gold by the s⁺udents of the Ottawa Seminary, as a token of esteem and affection. We trust that Father Gavary's health will soon be completely re-established. Bon voyage!

—Rev. Father Binet, O.M.I., succeeds Fr. Lajeunesse as Secretary of the University. Prosit!

Ottawa Univ. (7), Maple Leafs (9), May 28, 1910.

The baseball nine met defeat on the above date by the close score of (9) runs to (7). The team had won two games and tied the last with Pastimes, and naturally expected something better than a loss with the Hull aggregation of ball-tossers. "Rene" Lamoureux had his "off" day, while the "M. L." swatters were very much "on" with the willow, getting among several hits, two "fishy" home runs, which with any kind of fielding would not have been good for doubles. The batting of the College Cardinals was very weak, only two safe hits being corralled off "Red" Gendron, but through nervy base-running seven runs were squeezed, just two short of the tieing number. Several miscues around third and second with an over-throw to first donated several runs to the M. L.'s. The following players took part :—

M. O'Neil (Capt.), l.f.; R. Sheahey, 2b.; F. Curry, 2b.; M. Killian, s.s.; T. Muzante, 3b.; C. O'Neill, 1b.; Rene Lamoureux, p.; J. Morriseau, c.; M. Smith, r.f.; C. Kinsella, c.f.; Rochefort, c.f.; Contway. batted for Smith in the seventh inning.

Stolen bases—M. O'Neil, Killian, Muzante, C. O'Neill (2). Sacrifice hit—M. O'Neil.

Ottawa Univ. (2), St. Pats. (5), June 4, 1910.

The much-maglined outfit of ball-players from St. Patrick's L. and S. Association, by steady and errorless ball, inflicted defeat number four to the ball team of "O. U." 'Tis true St. Pat's played a good game, but not sufficiently good to defeat the College, if they were in form. With five errors behind him, Lamoureux couldn't win the game himself. No pitcher can and the support he got was most disheartening. Only five hits, one a three-bagger, were made off his delivery, while he made four "Saints" hammer the liquified ozone. For the "O. U." first baseman, Charles F. O'Neil, played a "star" game, getting two safe biffs in three times up, and annex-ing two bases. Daley, St. Pat's. pitcher, fanned seven batters.

Score by innings :—

		R.	H.	E.
St. Patrick's	0 0 3 0 2 0 *— 5	5	1
College	2 0 0 0 0 0 0— 2	4	5

Some weird and erratic decisions were given by the "Umps," and were justly questioned by the Rev. coach of O. U., who won both points under discussion. The "O. U." ball team can take its medi- cine with any one in the league, but when they complain, you may be assured "there's a reason." (With apologies to Postum!)

Pastimes (7), Ottawa Univ. (11), 1st Game,   Pastimes (13), Ottawa Univ. (12), 2nd Game. June 11, 1910.

Ottawa "U.'s" and Pastimes divided their double-decker base- ball attraction with the above results. The consensus of opinion was that both games would have been won by the Cardinals had not a torrent of rain compelled Mr. "Billy" McEwan to call the game off.

Rene Lamoureux and Big League Peterson went the full four- teen innings for their respective teams, with the exception of the final inning of the first game, when Ch. O'Neill went in the box to give "Rene" Lamoureux a little lay-up for the next game.

The batting of the team was all that could be desired, no less than 23 hits being made in the two contests. Hats off to Catcher Morriseau, who had a grand time at the plate, hitting out six safe bingles in nine times up. Five of the thirteen runs were sent over the pan by his mighty clouting. All the players had their eyes on the ball, and as a result the Batting Averages for the "Dr. D. H. Baird" Trophy were greatly increased.

Base-stealing was a feature with a total of twelve pilfers. One more game against Maple Leafs closes the schedule and will find O. U. well up in the first division of the Ottawa City Am. Ball League.

Hits and Strike-Outs.

STANDING OF THE OTTAWA AMATEUR BALL LEAGUE.

	Won.	Lost.	P.C.
Y. M. C. A.	5	1	.833
Maple Leafs	3	2	.600
O. A. A. C.	3	3	.500
Ottawa Univ.	4	5	.444
St. Patrick's	1	4	.200

BATTING AVERAGES.

	P.C.
M. O'Neill (Capt.)	.412
C. Morriseau	.385
C. O'Neill	.375
C. Kinsella	.333

J. Muzante .... .188
R. Sheehy .... .148
M. Killian .... .125
M. Smith .... .120
F. Curry .... .072

Pastimes played a non-resident pitcher named McIlwaine, and forfeited the game in which he participated. If the game is to be kept clean such tactics will have to be eliminated, or else drop out of the league.

Mr. "Lon" Payne has resigned his position as official umpire.

Mr. "Billy" McEwan is the "new umps" and is a good one, too.

Manager Bert Gilligan will look after the Watertown nine in the New York State League, during vacation.

"Our Exit."

With this issue the sporting editor lays down his pen, after a pleasant year's task of reporting the events in the athletic world of Ottawa University. Many interesting struggles were waged on the gridiron, the ice, and the diamond, and all tended to keep the development of the body abreast with the development of the brain.

The innovation of a series of Inter-Course games created a keen and healthy spirit of rivalry, and bore good fruit, in the discovery of many young players of exceptional ability, and in the improvement of "near-stars," in all branches of sport.

All classes of students were satisfied in the lines of athletics, from the strenuous football game to the nerve-soothing croquet; or from the scientific games of pool and billiards to the great roaring game of bowling; others again chose the favorite pastime of "hand-ball" or the scientific "King of all sports," baseball, and don't forget the rough game of tennis; we have that, too.

To each and all the students we wish a pleasant and prosperous vacation!

To the graduating editors, we say, good-bye, and good luck to you!

PHIL. C. HARRIS, '11·

Of Local Interest.

One of the speakers from the floor in a recent debate is responsible for this: "I find my time is already gone; therefore, I will keep within it."

As a proof of the harm done by the "yellow" press, D—b—s

burst out with : "Why you can see little boys and girls running about the streets with the comic supplement in their hands, cursing and swearing before they can either walk or talk."

Several wins in the local baseball schedule had worked up noisy enthusiasm among the College fans. After a double-header the third baseman made for a barber shop and flopped into the chair.

"Shave, sir?"

"No. Throat cut. College lost."

In Physics—"If a vehicle with two wheels is a bicycle, and one with three wheels a tricycle, what is one with one wheel?"

Student—"A wheelbarrow."

A gentleman was seeking information from a barrister who is also a prominent politician:

"Do lawyers tell the truth?" he queried.

"Yes," answered the legal light. "Lawyers will do anything to win a case."

A parent visiting his boy asked :—

"Well, my son, how are you getting on at college?"

Boy—"Just splendidly. I've only made one error in the last three games we played."

DOMINION DAY EPITAPH.

Here lies I,
James Blye,
Killed by a sky
Rocket,
Shot into my eye
Socket.

For fishermen: If you can't coax a fish to bite, try your persuasive powers on a cross dog, and you will be sure to succeed.

D.—— had tumbled by the stairway from the top deck of the *Empress* to the lower deck plump upon a prefect. "Say, where do you come from?"

"From the North of Ireland, Father."

The men from up-the-creek claim the following is a good quip: Why is a mosquito like a railroad? Because 't fastens upon sleepers and takes many drafts over them.

Said a Professor in one of the Grades:
"Thomas, spell weather."
"W-e-i-a-t-h-i-o-r, weather."
"Well, Tom, you may sit down I think that is the worst spell of weather we have had since Christmas."

Teacher of History: "Can you tell of what nationality Napoleon was?"
Student: "Of course I can." (Corsican).
                    The Ides of June!
                    What, so soon?

Br-n-au: "Who will have jurisdiction over the airships?"
Hig-ty: "Why, the highway commissioner."

Jul'en: Not all who *auto, ought to.*

Are you a good picker?
Why is June a feathery month?

Ancient History Class: The goose that saved Rome just quacked.
Prof. to Tom-y: "Tell us one of the principal events in Roman history and give the date?"
Tom-y: "Marc Anthony went to Egypt because he had a date with Cleopatra."

Junior Department

The Small Yards defeated Strathconas 23 to 6 in the protested game. The Small Yard players were: l.f. Poulin, p. Deschamps, c. Milot, 1b. Renaud, 2b. Brady, 3b. Chartrand, s.s. Lazure, c.f. Martin, r.f. Batterton. Then the following Sunday Small Yards defeated them again, thus winning championship with four wins and two losses. Then they played Collegiates for championship saw-off and were defeated 11 to 7, on Saturday, June 12. Collegiates had Catcher Smith, of Y.M.C.A., who has caught four games in the City League. He was protested by Small Yard and Collegiate instead of replaying the game defaulted to Small Yard, thus making them champions. Small Yards defeated Nationals of Hull by a score of 6 to 2 on Little Farm grounds, Hull, on Sunday, June 12. Doran at third added greatly to the strength of Small Yarders. Charley Rochefort played a great game at right field. Small Yards were defeated by Thistles 5 to 3. They had Thistles 2 to 0 until the end of the seventh inning, then they went up in the air and lost.

The annual picnic was held at Britannia on Monday, May 3·, and was a great success, thanks to the untiring work of Rev. Frs. Veronneau, Collins, Voyer and Jasmin; thanks also to Rev. Br. Gervais.

The following were some of the events :—
High jump, Senior—1, Madden; 2, Batterton; 3, Brady.
Junior—1, Braithwaite; 2, Sullivan; 3, Taschereau.
Midget—1, Langlois; 2, Doucette; 3, Champagne.
Broad jump, Senior—1, Fournier; 2, Brady; 3, Richardson.
Junior—1, Braithwaite; 2, Belanger; 3, Guertin.
Midget—1, Langlois; 2, Couture; 3, Doucette.
Baseball throw, Senior—1, Renaud; 2, Batterton; 3, Milot.
Junior—1, Lamonde; 2, Morel; 3, Gagné.
Midget—1, Couture; 2, Doucette; 3, Langlois.
Three-legged race, Senior—1, Renaud and Richardson.
Junior—1, Lamonde and Bourgie.
Midget—1, Duckette and J. Nault. ·
Free-for-all boot race—1, Coté; 2, C. E. Fournier; 3, Mulvihill.
100 yards, Senior—1, Batterton : 2, E. McNally; 3, Fournier.
Junior—1, Braithwaite; 2, Sullivan; 3, Guertin.
Midget—1, R. Jackman; 2, Champagne; 3, O'Brien.
220 yards, Midget—1, O'Brien; 2, R. Jackman; 3, Champagne.
Senior—1, Batterton; 2, McNally; 3, Fournier.
Junior—1, Braithwaite; 2, Sullivan; 3, Guertin.
880 yards, Senior—1, Batterton; 2, Martin; 3, Richardson.
Junior—1, Braithwaite; 2, Guertin; 3, Sullivan.
Midget—1, Champagne; 2, Doucette; 3, S. Nau't.
Hop, step and jump, Senior—1, Brady; 2, McCabe; 3, Renaud.
Junior—1, Taschereau; 2, Sullivan; 3, Braithwaite.
Midget—1, Langlois; 2, Doucette; 3, Champagne.
Shot put, Senior—1, Madden; 2, Renaud; 3, Marier.
Junior—1, Taschereau; 2, Belanger; 3, Poitras.
Midget—1, Langlois; 2, Champagne; 3, Doucette.
Geo. Braithwaite won the all-around championship.
Some class to M-p-y's new hat, eh?

According to Tommy H., the genial secretary, the Gossip Club will adjourn till September.

When in town call on Q. and have a soda.
Look out for W. M. and his camera.
Study there is no for us, eh! Po-ras?
The Junior editor wishes all a happy vacation,

INDEX.

Lightning Source UK Ltd.
Milton Keynes UK
UKHW011614160119
335572UK00012B/1148/P